MW00767927

Planning Effective Instruction

Diversity Responsive Methods and Management

Fourth Edition

Kay M. Price

Karna L. Nelson

WADSWORTH
CENGAGE Learning

Australia • Brazil • Japan • Korea • Mexico • Singapore • Spain • United Kingdom • United States

WADSWORTH
CENGAGE Learning

Planning Effective Instruction: Diversity Responsive Methods and Management, Fourth Edition

Kay M. Price and Karna L. Nelson

Publisher/Executive Editor: Linda Shreiber-Ganster

Assistant Editor: Rebecca Dashiell

Editorial Assistant: Linda Stewart

Media Editor: Ashley Cronin

Marketing Manager: Kara Kindstrom

Marketing Assistant: Dimitri Hagnéré

Marketing Communications Manager: Martha Pfeiffer

Content Project Management: Pre-Press PMG

Creative Director: Rob Hugel

Art Director: Maria Epes

Print Buyer: Karen Hunt

Rights Acquisitions Account Manager, Text: Bob Kauser

Production Service: Pre-Press PMG

Copy Editor: Pre-Press PMG

Cover Designer: Bartay Studio

Compositor: Pre-Press PMG

© 2011, 2007 Wadsworth, Cengage Learning

ALL RIGHTS RESERVED. No part of this work covered by the copyright herein may be reproduced, transmitted, stored, or used in any form or by any means graphic, electronic, or mechanical, including but not limited to photocopying, recording, scanning, digitizing, taping, Web distribution, information networks, or information storage and retrieval systems, except as permitted under Section 107 or 108 of the 1976 United States Copyright Act, without the prior written permission of the publisher.

For product information and technology assistance, contact us at **Cengage Learning Customer & Sales Support, 1-800-354-9706.**.

For permission to use material from this text or product, submit all requests online at **www.cengage.com/permissions.** Further permissions questions can be e-mailed to **permissionrequest@cengage.com.**

International Student Edition:

ISBN-13: 978-0-495-81298-2

ISBN-10: 0-495-81298-6

Wadsworth
20 Davis Drive
Belmont, CA 94002-3098
USA

Cengage Learning is a leading provider of customized learning solutions with office locations around the globe, including Singapore, the United Kingdom, Australia, Mexico, Brazil, and Japan. Locate your local office at **www.cengage.com/global.**

Cengage Learning products are represented in Canada by Nelson Education, Ltd.

To learn more about Wadsworth, visit **www.cengage.com/wadsworth**

Purchase any of our products at your local college store or at our preferred online store **www.CengageBrain.com.**

Printed in the United States of America
1 2 3 4 5 6 7 14 13 12 11 10

To Steve, Leah, and Jerell

Thanks for the support that made this possible.

To Walter, Mom, and Randi

I couldn't have done it without you.

Contents

Preface

To the Instructor

We wrote this book for *general education* and *special education* teachers to use in a variety of ways. Those just learning how to teach can use this book to provide or supplement initial instruction on planning and delivering inclusive lessons and activities. Experienced teachers can use it as a tool for reviewing essential elements of planning for the diverse classroom. With this versatility, this text is appropriate for use in either undergraduate or graduate courses, for both *preservice* and *in-service* teachers.

We have made important changes to our fourth edition. One is the expansion of our discussion of critical teaching and critical management skills as a foundation for making thoughtful decisions about what to include in lesson and activity plans. We have also provided more information and examples to help teachers develop their diversity responsive teaching skills in order to plan for the success of all students.

There are several new features in this edition that make the text both more readable and more practical. One feature is classroom scenarios that show the application of effective teaching methods. These scenarios showcase a teacher's selection of instructional or management strategies and the reasoning behind the decisions. In addition, they invite the reader to apply the information in the chapter to a "real" lesson.

Other features support understanding of the text as well as provide ready-to-use materials for teachers. For example, planning checklists (e.g., *Teacher Checklist for Planning Active Participation Strategies*) both summarize key ideas for readers and give teachers a useful tool for planning. Mini-lessons provide examples for the reader and can be implemented in the classroom as-is.

Something that hasn't changed in this edition is that we take a very practical, applied approach and incorporate many examples, including examples of plans. In this edition, we again include detailed lesson and activity plans with commentary that makes clear the planner's thinking process. Other plans are written with a level of detail that allows the reader to clearly see how information is applied.

Many teachers work with students from cultural backgrounds very different from their own. They also have students who are English language learners. Many general educators, as well as special educators, teach students with disabilities who are included in their classrooms. Novice and experienced teachers recognize the need every day to plan instruction and create an environment to meet the needs of many different students. Students need diversity responsive teachers, and teacher preparation programs as well as professional development programs are trying to fill that need. We believe that developing attitudes and skills in responding to diversity must begin with the first courses that teachers take and continue throughout our professional lives. And we believe that planning for diversity must be part of all of the lessons and activities we write.

In the fourth edition, we continue to place a heavy emphasis on diversity responsive teaching (DRT). The conceptual framework for DRT that was introduced in the third edition will be used throughout this edition as well. It conceptualizes three areas of daily planning for addressing diversity, that is, in deciding *what* to teach, *how* to teach, and the *context* for teaching and learning. This organization is meant to provide teachers with a structure for thinking about and planning for meeting the needs of a diverse student population within their classrooms, but also to help teachers prepare their students to be responsive to diversity in the world. The book concludes with chapters about the specifics of writing lesson and activity plans that incorporate diversity responsive ideas and strategies. We have expanded on many of the ideas that we presented in previous editions, and we have added much new information as well.

The changes we have made in this edition are in response to our continued observations of teachers in classrooms as well as feedback from our reviewers, from teachers and principals in the public schools, university supervisors and other faculty, and our students themselves. These changes target several challenges that teachers experience.

One problem we continue to encounter is that teachers sometimes struggle with developing plans because they have not thoroughly thought through what they want to teach. They have trouble answering questions along the lines of, "What's the key idea you're trying to get across?" or "What exactly do you want your students to know how to do?" The organizational structure of this book explicitly emphasizes the importance of carefully considering the content you will teach *before* planning the methods of teaching to use. Because planning the curriculum is beyond the scope of this book, Part 1 on planning what to teach is relatively brief. Although the focus remains on daily planning rather than long-term planning, we offer suggestions on making decisions about objectives, content analyses, and responding to diversity through content in "Planning What to Teach." We hope this will help teachers make thoughtful and clear choices.

Another problem teachers may have is a difficulty with managing behavior that sabotages great lessons and activities. In this edition, we have expanded and reorganized information on classroom management. We believe that it is almost impossible to discuss (or implement) effective instruction separately from effective management. In the newly expanded third part of the book, "Planning the Context for Teaching and Learning," we focus on using universal interventions for preventing behavior problems and on building thorough management planning into every lesson and activity. Teaching behavioral skills is strongly emphasized. We also stress creating an environment that sets the stage for learning and truly includes and supports all students.

The third challenge that teachers face—and the most important one in our view—is the diversity

in classrooms and the multitude of diversity strategies. We know that preservice and in-service teachers strive to be diversity responsive, to leave no child behind, but so much information is available about how to meet the needs of diverse learners that knowing where to start can be very confusing and overwhelming. We address this problem through the conceptual framework that we present and the organization of the book. We present and apply many specific techniques for responding to diversity. This edition places strong emphasis on planning for cultural and linguistic diversity in addition to skill diversity.

We had many reasons for writing and revising this book. One is that we continue to see the need for a highly readable, practical text on planning effective instruction and managing classrooms. This is a very desirable tool for use with pre-service teachers, in both coursework and practica, in traditional teacher preparation programs. But, we also recognize that a significant number of teachers today are learning to teach on the job rather than on campus. They also need this type of text—one that provides an easy reference, includes many examples, and lends itself to self-instruction. In addition, we find that many experienced teachers are interested in adding expertise in *explicit* instruction to their repertoires. Student diversity in classrooms increases the need for diversity in teaching approaches. This text offers straightforward recommendations for using an explicit teaching model.

Our reasons for writing this book in the first place still hold, as well. We wrote the first three editions because we noticed that many of the hundreds of practicum students and student teachers with whom we worked experienced some common problems. First, just like young students, preservice teachers cannot automatically transfer what they have learned in classes to real-life situations. In the real classroom, their focus is on survival, and beginning teachers seem to forget what they learned from their training. For example, as they try to figure out how to teach division of fractions to a particular group of fifth graders the next day at two o'clock, they may forget much of what they learned about making instructional and management decisions. Beginning teachers can plan more effective lessons and activities when they have forms that prompt the decisions they need to make.

We also noticed that novice teachers sometimes forget to teach. They like to use exciting and creative approaches and are eager to involve their young students in learning. However, they can have trouble distinguishing between those occasions when students need the opportunity to practice and develop what they know and when students need to be directly taught new facts, concepts, and strategies. In their eagerness to be innovative, they plan fun activities but are unable to express what they want students to learn. Frequently, when they plan and teach lessons, they advance to providing student practice before they have taught enough to enable students to be successful with the practice. Novice teachers may select teaching methods based on their own interests or emerging styles rather than on the needs of their students. For these reasons, we distinguish between activities and lessons, based on their purposes, and suggest different types of planning decisions for each. We also focus on clear objectives and evaluation of learning to emphasize the accountability of teaching so that students learn.

Finally, teachers often say they are overwhelmed by the diversity of their students' needs. They routinely find themselves writing plans and then trying to modify and adjust them to meet these diverse needs. Teachers need a more efficient and effective way to design lessons and activities. We stress the inclusion of universal design and differentiated instructional principles, and of critical teaching and management strategies during the initial stage of planning. Building in these strategies can result in the completion of a more effective plan in a shorter amount of time. We feel that we clearly address these three issues in this edition.

The following are some of the highlights provided in this edition:

- new information on teaching key terms and vocabulary

- expanded information about engaging students in instruction

- reorganized information about planning practice and monitoring progress

- expanded coverage of critical management skills used to prevent behavior problems

- new information on managing challenging classes through behavior games

- teacher checklists summarizing best practices for various critical teaching and management skills that can be used as supports during planning

- new mini-lessons that illustrate how to teach learning and behavior skills needed by students

- scenarios describing teachers planning included at the beginning of many chapters that provide the reader with pre-reading focus for the chapter

- follow-up questions that give the reader an opportunity to see suggestions for application of the skills discussed and think of suggestions of their own

- a conceptual framework designed to help readers understand and apply the key components of diversity responsive teaching

- additional resources

Our book has been used in a variety of ways. We know that principals and teacher in-service providers have used our book as a tool for working with and helping practicing teachers in their buildings or district. University instructors have used it at both the undergraduate and graduate levels. University students have used it at both ends of their teacher preparation programs, during their student teaching, and when planning in their own classrooms. Novice teachers in alternative certification programs have used it. We are confident that our revisions make our fourth edition even more flexible and responsive to classroom diversity.

Supplements

Instructor's Manual and Evaluation Resource

The instructor's manual and evaluation resource are new to the 4th edition. The electronic instructor's manual includes outlines, key ideas, questions for discussion and reflection, and activities for each chapter. *Forms for the Field* is another section in the manual and includes observation forms, teacher checklists, and self-evaluation forms, with cross references to the textbook. The evaluation resource includes assignments, projects, and test questions.

Acknowledgments

We would like to thank our many, many students for the inspiration to write and rewrite this book. Thanks also to the cooperating teachers who have so willingly taken our students into their classrooms to practice their skills, and for welcoming us as well.

We would also like to thank the following reviewers: Deborah Ellermeyer, Clarion University of Pennsylvania; Melissa Engleman, East Carolina University; Jackie Ennis, Barton College; Grace A. McDaniel, Otterbein College; Mary Podlesny, Northland College; James B. Tuttle, Shepherd University; and René E. Wroblewski, St. Bonaventure University.

Introduction

This book addresses how to plan lessons and activities that are effective in classrooms made up of highly diverse individuals. Every teacher's goal is to teach so that all students are successful. With the diversity in today's classroom, however, it often seems an unreachable goal. A one-size-fits-all approach to instruction is clearly ineffective.

On the other hand, writing separate lesson plans for each student in a class is definitely not realistic. So, what can teachers do to help all students be successful? They can design lessons and activities that incorporate diversity responsive practices as they plan *what* to teach (the curriculum), *how* to teach (instructional methods), and the *context for teaching and learning* (classroom management). More specifically, they can incorporate universal interventions designed for all students in the class, and selected interventions to meet the needs of an individual or a small group of students. In this book, you will learn how to be a diversity responsive teacher, that is, one who can design lessons and activities that meet the needs of a whole classroom of diverse learners.

Today's Diverse Classroom

Before we talk about how to respond to classroom diversity, we would like to discuss the students for whom you will plan lessons and activities. The diversity in today's classroom includes factors of culture, language, ethnicity, race, ability, gender, socioeconomic background, religion, age, and sexual orientation (Gay 2002; Gollnick and Chinn 1998; Mercer and Mercer 2005; Sobel, Taylor, and Anderson 2003). You can see that the concept of diversity is broadly defined here; this is how we will apply this concept throughout this book.

Several large, steadily growing groups of students are impacting classroom diversity. First, schools have increasingly larger numbers of students from diverse cultural and linguistic backgrounds. The number of English language learners, for example, has increased approximately 52% on average per year between the school years 2000–2001 and 2005–06. This is remarkable in comparison to the average growth of 2.8% per year for total K-12 enrollment for the same period. (NCELA 2006). Making a successful transition to school can be especially challenging for these students who are trying to learn English as well as subject matter content. Many of them experience "culture shock" as well when their preferences for learning and performing do not match the expectations of the school setting. The presence of these students has created wonderful opportunities for teachers and students to learn about languages, beliefs, and traditions that may be outside of their own personal experiences. Note: It is not unusual to find several different languages spoken as primary languages by different students within one classroom.

Next, students with disabilities have significantly contributed to the diversity of the general education classroom. Special education law provides most students with disabilities the opportunity to spend their time in both special education and general education settings. Students with mild learning problems, who are commonly taught in general education at least part of the day, are increasing in number. The number of students in the learning disability category in special education has more than doubled since 1976. Both special and general education teachers typically provide services to students with disabilities with individualized education programs (IEPs) (Hallahan and Kauffman 2003). Although they have presented unique challenges, they have added a rich dynamic to the classroom.

Finally, students who are considered "at risk" for school failure make up another group of students who contribute to classroom diversity. Factors that put students at risk can be found both within our society at large and within our schools. Drug and alcohol use and abuse, poverty, teen pregnancy, physical and emotional abuse, homelessness, and lack of supervision are only some of the societal problems that can lead to students' coming to school unprepared to learn. Failure to recognize and address student learning problems, irrelevant curriculum, and poor teaching can significantly interfere with student progress in school. Mercer and Mercer (2005) write that 15 to 25 percent of the school population experience risk factors that lead to low academic achievement without intervention. Although these students have learning and behavioral problems that can interfere with school success, they often do not qualify for special education services.

Increasing diversity has heavily influenced classroom dynamics. Sobel et al. (2003) suggest that issues of equity and diversity are two of the most critical issues that challenge teachers on a daily basis. We concur with their assessment. The box below shows examples of some of the challenges faced by today's teachers because of the diversity found in today's classrooms. Teaching really is more complex today than it was in years past for teachers in both general and special education. It can be hard to know where to start when trying to meet the needs of so many different students.

Diversity Responsive Teaching

Diversity responsive teaching (DRT) has emerged as an important approach to the challenges of classroom diversity. In this type of teaching, teachers implement a set of practices to increase the probability that all students will learn. By design, DRT also promotes mutual respect among class members and provides valuable lessons for life by empowering students with accurate information about diversity. Teachers deliver this type of teaching by responding to issues of diversity with understanding, opportunity, and equity for all (Sobel et al. 2003). In addition to teaching so all students can learn, they address diversity directly and teach the students the skills they need to respond appropriately to differing perspectives, lifestyles, and ways of being. They also teach their students to celebrate the differences among people and—perhaps even more important—to recognize their similarities. Clearly, diversity responsive teachers teach attitudes and skills that have direct application to life after school, where diversity abounds in society at large.

A Framework for Diversity Responsive Teaching

The literature is filled with specific techniques and strategies that make up diversity responsive teaching. We find, however, that for many teachers (preservice teachers especially), the sheer number of ideas available makes the task of selecting strategies an overwhelming one. We have developed a three-component framework for helping teachers implement DRT in a classroom setting. Following are summaries of the key components of this framework:

- The first component provides a structure for planning curriculum *content* that is relevant and representative of diversity, while providing P–12 students with opportunities to increase their knowledge about diversity. An additional consideration within this component is making sure that

---

EXAMPLES OF CHALLENGES FOR TODAY'S TEACHERS

- the need to develop a cohesive, well-functioning group from a diverse group of students within a supportive, welcoming environment

- the need to present content in multiple ways

- the need to help some students learn English as well as learn subject matter content

- the need to teach students how to get along with others and/or how to learn and study, as well as teaching important academic content skills

- the need to find ways to honor and accommodate individual student needs and preferences in addition to the needs of the group

the content taught includes varying perspectives and is an accurate representation of all groups involved. This section is about *what* to teach.

- The second component helps teachers address diversity when planning *instruction*. Universal interventions such as the principles of universal design for learning, differentiated instruction, and evidence-based teaching strategies are part of this component, as are selected interventions to meet the needs of individuals. This component addresses *how* to teach.

- The final component structures ideas for creating an inclusive *classroom environment*, one in which all students are supported and accepted. We include aspects of the physical environment, the social environment, and the emotional environment. This component helps teachers arrange the *context for teaching and learning* and use proactive classroom management.

This diversity responsive teaching framework offers a way to think about providing for the needs of diverse learners. In other words, it is very important to respond to diversity when you plan the content to teach, the way in which you will teach, and the way you'll manage behavior. This framework can also help you manage the large amount of information available on the topic of teaching diverse learners. The first three parts of this book are designed around this framework.

Goals of Diversity Responsive Teachers

Diversity responsive teachers strive, by implementing diversity responsive teaching, to teach so that all students can learn. Teachers who help all students be successful are most likely those who make the following their personal goals:

- *To know students as individuals* Diversity responsive teachers find the time to learn their students' likes and dislikes, strengths and challenges, and life situations and experiences.

- *To appreciate similarities and differences among students* Although these teachers notice and respect student variation, they find and appreciate the commonalities among students as well.

- *To connect with families and community* Diversity responsive teachers seek out opportunities to get to know their students' families. They also learn about and participate in the community in which their students live.

- *To teach so that all students are challenged and successful* Diversity in classroom activities

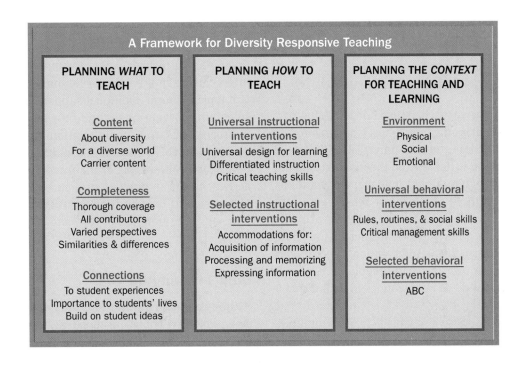

A Framework for Diversity Responsive Teaching

PLANNING *WHAT* TO TEACH	PLANNING *HOW* TO TEACH	PLANNING THE *CONTEXT* FOR TEACHING AND LEARNING
<u>Content</u> About diversity For a diverse world Carrier content	<u>Universal instructional interventions</u> Universal design for learning Differentiated instruction Critical teaching skills	<u>Environment</u> Physical Social Emotional
<u>Completeness</u> Thorough coverage All contributors Varied perspectives Similarities & differences	<u>Selected instructional interventions</u> Accommodations for: Acquisition of information Processing and memorizing Expressing information	<u>Universal behavioral interventions</u> Rules, routines, & social skills Critical management skills
<u>Connections</u> To student experiences Importance to students' lives Build on student ideas		<u>Selected behavioral interventions</u> ABC

and objectives is an idea common to diversity responsive teachers. These teachers take into account what they know about their students as individuals to appropriately challenge them. They maintain high expectations and work hard to help ensure student success.

- *To prepare students for diversity in the world* Diversity responsive teachers look beyond the classroom walls to determine what their students ought to learn. They identify and teach important skills that have broad real-life applications for understanding, tolerance, and social justice.

Diversity responsive teachers examine their own beliefs as well as their students' circumstances and experiences. They learn how their own cultural background affects their beliefs, values, and expectations, and in turn impacts their choices of subject matter, models, methods, management procedures, rules, and so on. Learning about the particular cultures of their students helps teachers understand how the students' cultural backgrounds impact preferences and reactions to the methods and management used in the classroom. Note that it is extremely important to see students first as individuals. The importance of cultural background must be recognized, of course, but it is essential to avoid stereotyping. Culturally aware teachers are more effective decision-makers and problem-solvers, as they are able to generate more ideas or options when planning. These actions will likely result in positive outcomes for students.

Universal and Selected Interventions

Diversity responsive teachers also find it helpful, particularly when planning how to teach and to manage behavior, to think in terms of universal and selected interventions. In other words, they consider using particular instructional and management methods universally (with all students) or selectively (with some students). These general categories of interventions can be broken down further as universal and selected *instructional* interventions, and universal and selected *behavioral* interventions. You will learn more about these interventions in Parts 2 and 3 of this book.

Diversity responsive schools may use a multiple-tiered model (and a response-to-intervention approach) to get at this same idea (National Association of State Directors of Special Education 2005). Tier 1 represents high quality, core instruction and interventions used universally. Tier 2 represents focused instruction/interventions or accommodations used selectively for students experiencing difficulty with universal interventions alone. A third tier could include intensive and long-term interventions in supplemental programs.

Universal Interventions

A *universal intervention* is a strategy, technique, or method that a teacher has decided to use to promote the success of all students and to prevent learning or behavior problems. These techniques and strategies are *built in* as part of your initial planning. This means they are standard procedure, routinely included, something you always do. Many varied universal interventions can be used when planning how to teach and manage student behavior. Examples of instructional interventions to use universally include presenting information in a variety of ways, using visual supports, and keeping students actively involved during instruction. Examples of behavioral interventions that are important to use universally include connecting with each student, establishing classroom rules and routines, and teaching social skills. These universal interventions provide needed support for many students.

Selected Interventions

Even when a teacher includes numerous universal interventions in a particular lesson, some students will typically need additional support. This is where selected interventions come into play. A *selected intervention* is an accommodation or modification designed to solve specific individual learning and behavior problems. It is included in a lesson or activity for an individual student or a small group of students. It is often more costly to implement in terms of time, money, or effort, and it is *added on* to initial planning.

Built-Ins and Add-Ons

Although universal interventions are built in and selected interventions are added on, the line between the two is not always a clear one. Some strategies and techniques should probably always be used universally, such as communicating clear expectations for behavior, putting directions in writing as well as saying them, and monitoring student progress. Also, some interventions would typically be used selectively, such as text in Braille and individual behavior contracts. Many strategies could be used either universally or selectively depending on the makeup of the class.

The Diverse Class

Let's suppose that you are designing a plan for a social studies lesson to be used with your very challenging and diverse group of students. Once you have selected the universal interventions that you think are appropriate, you begin thinking about the selected interventions that could be helpful for your three students who have fairly significant problems with reading. You decide that providing a graphic organizer of key ideas in the textbook chapter would help them. However, you realize that this intervention could benefit many of your students. So, you decide to build it in rather than add it on. What you thought was going to be a selected intervention is now a universal intervention. Remember that, by definition, if an intervention is built in, it is a universal intervention; if it is added on, it is a selected intervention. Planning for a diverse class may result in increased use of universal interventions that in a less diverse class might be considered selected interventions.

We suggest, to make your job easier, that you strive to build in as many interventions as possible up-front. Remember that it often takes more time and effort to incorporate specialized strategies for one or more individuals than it does to build in a strategy that will benefit everyone. Again, build it in if it will benefit many; add it on if it will only benefit certain students and would not be appropriate for the whole class. As the number of built-in strategies increases, the number of needed add-ons decreases.

An Example of Diversity Responsive Teaching

As we mentioned earlier, the most efficient way to meet the needs of all students is to consider those needs up-front—as you design lessons and activities—rather than trying to adjust for individuals after the fact. Start by

A Look at Mrs. Hakim's Planning

Mrs. Hakim has planned an activity in which her students are asked to create an ending to a story. The intention is to provide additional practice on predicting and making inferences after earlier lessons on these topics. After hearing or reading the first half of the story, students are asked to produce their own endings and justify them.

incorporating best practices and building in alternatives that will allow all students access to your instruction. Include other accommodations and modifications based on the makeup of your class. Read the box above and the following to see how one teacher, Mrs. Hakim, built in universal interventions and added on selected interventions to help all of her students be successful. These are Mrs. Hakim's decisions for implementing diversity responsive teaching:

- When Mrs. Hakim selects the story for which the students will create endings, she chooses a story by a Mexican American author. She wants her students to identify with authors, so she chooses stories written by people with ethnic backgrounds similar to those of her students.

- Mrs. Hakim helps students connect their prior knowledge and experience to this activity, an effective teaching strategy that she considers important for the learning of all students. She connects their use of inferences and predictions in everyday situations by asking questions such as, "You see your brother hanging up the phone, putting on his sneakers, picking up his soccer ball, and leaving the house. Where do you think he is going? Why? What is another possibility?"

- She plans to pre-teach key vocabulary using pictures and demonstrations. This is helpful to many of her students and very important for the English language learners.

- At the beginning of the activity, Mrs. Hakim communicates behavior expectations to her students. This is an effective management strategy.

- She plans to review the previously taught skills of predicting, finding clues in the story, and making inferences. Reviewing prerequisite knowledge and skills is an effective teaching strategy.

■ Mrs. Hakim passes out a written copy of the first half of the story. She then reads the story out loud. Presenting information in these two ways (multiple methods of presenting) will allow more of her students to be successful.

■ During her initial planning of this activity, Mrs. Hakim automatically decides to provide both written and oral directions for producing the story endings. She knows that this effective teaching strategy is essential for several of her students and that many of them find it helpful. (She also finds that the process of writing directions results in clearer directions and saves instructional time.)

■ Quite a few of Mrs. Hakim's students have difficulty completing tasks. Therefore, when planning the activity, Mrs. Hakim makes explicit the steps for completing this story-ending assignment. She decides to list these on the blackboard: finish ending, proofread ending, put name on paper, place in box on back table. She has built this conspicuous strategy technique into her initial planning, rather than as a separate accommodation, because the makeup of her class makes this sensible.

■ One student needs more support to complete tasks. Mrs. Hakim plans to give him a personal list of steps, to tell him to check off each step when completed, and to acknowledge his success enthusiastically ("You must be very proud of yourself . . .").

■ Some of the students in Mrs. Hakim's class are more productive when they have the opportunity to work with peers; others prefer to work alone. This may be related to cultural background. Mrs. Hakim decides that the students may consult peers when writing their story endings, if they choose.

■ Two of Mrs. Hakim's students have very serious writing problems. She plans to have them dictate their story endings to a teaching assistant as an accommodation for them. The other students may choose either to handwrite or to type their assignments. She provides sentence patterns to several other students who need more support or scaffolding to be successful in writing (for example, *I think Carlos will _____ at the end because . . .*).

■ She modifies the content of the activity for one student. He is working on a different comprehension objective: recalling factual information. Mrs. Hakim creates questions that a parent volunteer asks him, while recording his responses.

You can see that Mrs. Hakim used both universal and selected interventions. She built in numerous techniques to provide options for all of her students. She then added on selected interventions that she thought would be appropriate for a few of her students. Due to the makeup of her class, Mrs. Hakim decided that at least one of the selected interventions she thought to use would benefit all of her students, so she build it in also, rather than adding it on. Through careful planning, Mrs. Hakim most certainly prevented potential learning problems.

Attitude of the Diversity Responsive Teacher

Your ability to be successful in working with a diverse student population begins with a belief that you have a responsibility to do so. If you believe that your job is to teach *all* students, you will start off much better equipped to meet the challenge. If you believe that your job is to teach only those students who are easy to teach, your ability to be effective is questionable. You will definitely spend a great deal of your time feeling frustrated.

Equally important, you must believe that you can make a difference in teaching a diverse student population. Beliefs about making a difference may have a significant impact on a teacher's success or lack thereof. We encourage you to examine your beliefs in this area. There is no question that the diverse classroom of today requires a special kind of teacher.

Regardless of age and experience level, effective teachers view teaching as an important and exciting profession. They feel a responsibility to teach all students and see student diversity as a fascinating challenge. Effective teachers plan with the needs of all students in mind. These teachers have a strong desire to learn, and stay current in the field by reading professional journals and taking courses and workshops. These teachers develop an ever-growing repertoire of teaching strategies and methods to use with challenging students. These teachers also believe they can be effective and, therefore, are very effective in diverse classrooms. We hope you are or will become one of these teachers.

Summary

Building in the ideas that are suggested in Parts 1, 2, and 3 of this book will result in classrooms that have a new look. This is important, because diversity is the norm in today's classrooms rather than the exception. To be responsive to that diversity, teachers must do things differently. They must provide options and opportunities in what they teach, in how they teach, and in a setting that is safe and inviting.

The Content and Organization of This Book

This book is about diversity responsive teaching. It is designed to help you plan so that your students will learn. We focus heavily on making your lessons and activities relevant and meaningful for a diverse group of students, including those who vary in language, ethnicity, race, socioeconomic circumstances, and learning and behavior needs. This book includes information about the various components of the planning process, and it is organized to provide various levels of planning assistance. This makes it a versatile resource to use in methods courses, practica, and student teaching. It is also a good resource for practicing teachers in both general and special education.

The book is divided into four sections. The first three sections provide the foundational information needed to plan effective lessons and activities in diverse classrooms. In the fourth part of the book, all of the pieces will be put together. You will learn how to write lessons and activities that include thoughtful consideration of content and effective ways of presenting it and of managing behavior. The following box contains a summary of the four sections of our book.

The organizational structure of this text is intended to enable you to select the specific content

CONTENT FOUND IN THE FOUR SECTIONS OF THE BOOK

- *Part 1: Planning What to Teach* This section of the book starts out with a review of types of content and with ideas for addressing diversity through the content being taught. It concludes with how to organize content for teaching. A chapter on writing objectives follows.

- *Part 2: Planning How to Teach* This is the largest section of the book, and it emphasizes universal instructional interventions. We present general approaches as well as specific strategies. The last chapter in this section discusses ideas for selected instructional interventions.

- *Part 3: Planning the Context for Teaching and Learning* Here you will learn about many interventions for classroom management. This section begins with a chapter on universal behavioral interventions for supporting appropriate student behavior and examples of selected interventions. Following it are chapters on critical management skills crucial for successful lessons and activities.

- *Part 4: Writing Your Plan* This section begins by helping you learn how to decide which type of plan to write (lesson or activity). Next, you will learn about specific types of lesson plans, and then how to write effective lesson and activity plans. Finally, you will learn how to put the finishing touches on your plan.

and level of detail in planning, teaching, and management information that you need. The following may guide you in searching for specific material within this text:

1. For information on writing measurable objectives, see Chapter 2.

2. To find information on the differences between lessons and activities, see Chapter 13.

3. To review the basics of lesson planning, read the information in Chapter 14 and Chapters 16 through 18.

4. For specific strategies to support English language learners in lessons and activities, see Chapters 3–12.

5. For information on universal instructional interventions, see Chapters 3 through 8. Universal behavioral interventions are found in Chapters 10, 11, and 12.

6. To locate ideas for selected behavioral interventions or accommodations, see Chapter 10. Selected instructional interventions or accommodations are found in Chapter 9.

7. To focus on identifying or implementing critical teaching skills (planning lesson openings, presenting information effectively, planning for students to work in groups, etc.), you may benefit from the detailed information available in Chapters 4 through 8.

8. To review strategies that are essential for setting up a positive learning environment from the beginning of the year, see Chapters 1 and 10.

9. For behavior management suggestions for a challenging class, see Chapters 10 through 12.

10. To find suggestions for creating a diversity responsive curriculum, see Chapter 1.

11. To learn or review the key ideas that make up various lesson models, see Chapters 16 through 18.

12. For information on teaching behavioral skills, learning and study strategies, and concepts, see Chapter 19.

13. To learn how to analyze the content you will be teaching, see Chapter 1.

14. For practicum students practicing certain models or methods of teaching, you can select the appropriate chapters or sections.

15. For apprentice teachers seeking ideas for building preventive management techniques into lessons and activities, see Chapters 11 and 12.

16. For experienced teachers wishing to add skills for *explicit* teaching, see Chapter 5 and Chapters 16 through 19.

References and Suggested Reading

Bazron, B., D. Osher, and S. Fleischman. 2005. Creating culturally responsive schools. *Educational Leadership* 63 (1): 83–84.

Bowe, F. 2005. *Making inclusion work.* Columbus, OH: Merrill, an imprint of Prentice-Hall.

Brown, M. 2007. Educating all students: Creating culturally responsive teachers, classrooms, and schools. *Intervention in School and Clinic* 43 (1): 57–62.

Cartledge, G., and L. Kourea. 2008. Culturally responsive classrooms for culturally diverse students with and at risk for disabilities. *Exceptional Children* 74 (3): 351–371.

Davis, B. 2006. *How to teach students who don't look like you: Culturally relevant teaching strategies.* Thousand Oaks, CA: Corwin Press.

Gay, G. 2002. Preparing for culturally responsive teaching. *Journal of Teacher Education* 53 (2): 106–116.

Gollnick, D. M., and P. Chinn. 1998. *Multicultural education: Education in a pluralistic society.* 5th ed. Columbus, OH: Merrill.

Guiberson, M. 2009. Hispanic representation in special education: Patterns and implications. *Preventing School Failure* 53 (3): 167–176.

Hallahan, D. P., and J. M. Kauffman. 2003. *Exceptional learners.* 9th ed. San Francisco, CA: Allyn and Bacon.

Harlin, R. 2009. The impact of teachers' expectations on diverse learners' academic outcomes. *Childhood Education* 85 (4): 253–256.

Irvine, J., and B. Armento. 2001. *Culturally responsive teaching: lesson planning for elementary and middle grades.* Boston: McGraw-Hill.

Mercer, C. D., and A. R. Mercer. 2005. *Teaching students with learning problems.* 7th ed. Upper Saddle River, NJ: Pearson/Merrill Prentice Hall.

Moore, R.A. 2008. "Oh yeah, I'm Mexican. What type are you?" Changing the way preservice teachers interpret and respond to the literate identities of children. *Early Childhood Education Journal* 35 (6): 505–514.

National Association of State Directors of Special Education. 2005. *Response to intervention: Policy considerations and implementation.* Alexandria, VA: Author.

National Clearinghouse for English Language Acquisition. 2006. *The growing numbers of limited English proficient students.* http://www/ncela.gwu.edu/files/uploads/4/Growing LEP 0506.pdf

Nichols, W., W. Rupley, and G. Webb-Johnson. 2000. Teachers' role in providing culturally responsive literacy instruction. *Reading Horizons* 41 (1): 1–18.

Obiakor, F. 2007. Multicultural special education: Effective intervention for today's schools. *Intervention in School and Clinic* 42 (3): 148–155.

Richards, H., A. Brown, and T. Forde. 2007. Addressing diversity in schools: Culturally relevant pedagogy. *Teaching Exceptional Children* 39 (3): 64–68.

Salend, S. J. 2008. *Creating inclusive classrooms—Effective and reflective practices for all students.* 6th ed. Columbus, OH: Merrill, an imprint of Prentice Hall.

Shealey, M. and T. Callins. 2007. Creating culturally responsive literacy programs in inclusive classrooms. *Intervention in School and Clinic* 42 (4): 195–197.

Sobel, D. M., S. V. Taylor, and R. E. Anderson. 2003. Shared accountability: Encouraging diversity-responsive teaching in inclusive contexts. *Teaching Exceptional Children* 35 (6): 46–54.

PART

I

Planning What to Teach

A Framework for Diversity Responsive Teaching		
PLANNING *WHAT* TO TEACH	**PLANNING *HOW* TO TEACH**	**PLANNING THE *CONTEXT* FOR TEACHING AND LEARNING**
<u>Content</u> About diversity For a diverse world Carrier content	<u>Universal instructional interventions</u> Universal design for learning Differentiated instruction Critical teaching skills	<u>Environment</u> Physical Social Emotional
<u>Completeness</u> Thorough coverage All contributors Varied perspectives Similarities & differences	<u>Selected instructional interventions</u> Accommodations for: Acquisition of information Processing and memorizing Expressing information	<u>Universal behavioral interventions</u> Rules, routines, & social skills Critical management skills
<u>Connections</u> To student experiences Importance to students' lives Build on student ideas		<u>Selected behavioral interventions</u> ABC

Teachers make important decisions about the content to teach their students. These decisions need to be made before deciding how to teach. In the first part of this book, we will focus on thinking generally about what to teach, how to analyze content, and then how to write specific and measurable objectives. When thinking about content, it's helpful to begin by thinking about what students need to learn—what subjects and what types of knowledge (for example, declarative and procedural knowledge). It is also important to carefully think about diversity so that you teach content about diversity, content that is complete and inclusive, and content that is connected to students' lives.

We will also discuss resources that teachers use when planning what to teach. One of the most important resources is state standards. Teachers must be skilled at using state standards in long-term planning and in developing short-term objectives from those standards. Teachers must also be cognizant of the important generalizations or big ideas in the

1

various subject areas and use those in organizing content in a meaningful way.

An important final step in planning what to teach is deciding the level of understanding you want your students to achieve. It's also essential to know how to conduct content analyses, such as task and concept analyses, and determine key terms and vocabulary and prerequisite knowledge for the content to be taught. These analyses help in selecting important and clear objectives and in beginning to plan the actual lesson or activity plan.

This book is primarily about how to teach. We begin our book by discussing curriculum however, for a variety of reasons.

■ It is not possible to talk about how to teach until you know what to teach. The content itself directly influences how you should teach; for example, certain types of content lend themselves to particular models of instruction.

■ School districts and state offices of public instruction are paying more attention to curriculum because of mandates such as the No Child Left Behind Act and the Individuals with Disabilities Education Act (IDEA). Educators have been prompted to look carefully at the curriculum used in their schools and to attempt to more clearly define learner outcomes in relation to various content areas.

■ Increasing diversity in the schools has resulted in careful evaluation of the effectiveness of curriculum in meeting the needs of diverse learners. Further, schools have struggled with ideas regarding the best ways to create curricula that are inclusive in nature and accessible to all students.

■ A student's ability to learn is affected by how teachers organize and present curriculum content for learning.

In the chapters that follow, you will learn how teachers determine what to teach, and how they describe what their students need to know and do.

Thinking about Content

Introduction

Planning for instruction begins with thinking about content. Before making decisions about how to teach, instructors need to decide what to teach. We'll begin by considering content in terms of the wide variety of subject matter taught in schools, the types of knowledge, and the importance of considering diversity. In addition, we'll focus on standards that guide teachers in selecting what to teach their students. Finally, we'll talk about preparing to teach content, deciding what levels of understanding you want students to achieve, and how to organize content for teaching.

Thinking about What Students Need to Learn

We'll begin by examining the types of subjects that are typically taught in schools.

Subject Matter

Students in our public schools need to learn various subjects. Certainly, everyone agrees that they need to learn reading, writing, and arithmetic. We also teach science and social studies in school. Often, art, music, and health and fitness are taught, although they seem to be cut first during budget crunches. Teachers today also teach a wide assortment of additional subjects including social and emotional skills, cognitive behavioral skills, vocational skills, and technology. Another perspective teachers need to consider is emphasizing critical thinking skills and learning strategies so that students become lifelong learners. You'll make decisions about what your students should learn based on standards, district guidelines, and individual needs.

The following are some examples of skills and knowledge by subject area that are taught routinely in schools today:

- Academics—recognizing letters, knowing the structure of plant cells, finding the circumference of a circle

- Learning strategies—completing an assignment calendar, reading for comprehension

- Social and emotional skills—taking *no* for an answer, joining in activities, dealing with embarrassment

- Arts—appreciating baroque music, drawing faces

- Health and fitness—bandaging a cut, understanding the effects of drugs, exercising aerobically

- Life skills—making a bed, riding the city bus independently, budgeting

- Cognitive behavior skills—interpersonal problem solving, controlling angry outbursts

- Vocational skills—finding a career interest, fixing car engines, using the want ads

- Technology skills—evaluating Web sites for bias, creating spreadsheets, keyboarding

Societal pressures sometimes overwhelm teachers, as they feel compelled to teach everything from responsible credit card use and safe sex to healthy eating and honesty.

Types of Knowledge: Declarative and Procedural

We can think about content in terms of types of knowledge as well as types of subject matter. Knowledge can be categorized as knowing *about* something and knowing *how to do* something. These types of knowledge are called *declarative knowledge* and *procedural knowledge*, respectively. Naming the parts of a lawn mower is an example of declarative knowledge, whereas knowing how to start a lawn mower is an example of procedural knowledge. Knowing the history of the development of the scientific method is declarative knowledge, and knowing how to use the scientific method is procedural knowledge. Understanding the concept of standard units of measurement is declarative, and measuring objects is procedural. Both types of knowledge are important and complement each other. Your students need to learn both.

Declarative Knowledge

Three kinds of information are considered declarative knowledge: facts, concepts, and principles.

The first category of declarative information is **facts**. For example, it is fact that red and yellow make up orange; 10 is a multiple of 5; and 18-year-olds may vote. Other examples of factual information include labels (the parts of a volcano), names (of states and capitals), and words and their definitions (Smith and Ragan 2005).

Concepts is a second category of declarative knowledge. Howell and Nolet (2000) define *concepts* as objects, events, actions, or situations that share a set of defining characteristics. Concepts are categories in which all examples of a concept share certain characteristics. Furniture and democracy are both concepts. Triangle is also a concept. All triangles have three sides and three angles. Examples of triangles include isosceles, equilateral, right, and so on. (See Chapter 19 for more information on concepts.)

The final category of declarative knowledge is **principles**, relational rules that prescribe the relationship between two or more concepts. They are often described in the form of if–then, cause–effect, or "rule of thumb" relationships. Principles can be very simple or highly complex. The following are examples of principles: round up numbers five or

higher; voting is both a right and a responsibility; and thunder is caused as air heats and expands to varying degrees along the path of lightning.

Procedural Knowledge

Whereas declarative knowledge means to know or know *about* something, procedural knowledge refers to knowing *how to do* something. Knowing the steps or methods to follow, processes, strategies, or specific skills to use are all procedural knowledge. Knowing how to change a flat tire, to cut with scissors, to proofread, to multiply fractions, to write a five-paragraph essay, to resist peer pressure, or to register to vote are all examples of procedural knowledge. This type of knowledge involves bringing together various subtasks to complete a whole procedure (Howell and Nolet, 2000).

Obviously, both types of knowledge are extremely important, and they are directly connected. Typically, one must know basic facts before using them. For example, students need to know the steps of the reading comprehension strategy before they use them in their content reading. However, it is possible to memorize and use the steps to divide fractions, for example, without understanding the underlying concepts. It is very important to determine in advance what type of knowledge you are asking the students to learn. This is key in determining how to best organize the content for teaching.

Diversity and Content

When thinking about what students need to learn, you also need to consider content that reflects the diversity of the world and the diversity in your classroom. You may find it helpful to use the content section of the diversity responsive teaching framework (see Part I: Planning What to Teach) as you think about what you want to teach your students. This information is intended to support teachers in creating a diversity responsive curriculum, that is, one that is inclusive and engaging. When working toward creating a diversity responsive curriculum, consider the following three goals to help structure your decisions: (1) teach content about diversity; (2) teach content that is complete and inclusive; and (3) connect the content taught to students' lives (Irvine and Armento 2001). The following teacher checklist is an overview of key elements for responding to diversity in what you teach. You can use it as a guide when you are developing lesson and activity plans.

TEACHER CHECKLIST FOR

Responding to Diversity in What You Teach

❏ Can I teach about diversity directly in my current lesson or activity?

❏ Are there additional objectives I could include that have to do with developing skills for living in a diverse world?

❏ Is there a way I can infuse content about diversity while teaching other knowledge/skills?

❏ What perspectives need to be considered in my lesson or activity?

❏ Have I emphasized similarities among people, rather than focusing only on differences?

❏ Are there ways to connect my lesson to my students' experiences?

❏ Have I made connections between the content and my students' cultural backgrounds?

We'll discuss each of the items in the checklist in turn, with a focus on cultural diversity. Then we'll focus briefly on skill diversity.

Content about Diversity

Teachers can teach directly about individuals, groups, cultures, traditions, beliefs, issues, events, and so on that reflect diversity. These topics can be made the content of lessons, activities, and units. For example, teachers can select diversity responsive content by teaching lessons and activities on any of the following: deaf culture; the art, music, and literature of Mexico; the civil rights movement; female athletes; or different kinds of families.

Teachers can also select objectives that focus on developing skills for a diverse world. For example, when you plan to have students work in small groups or with a partner, you can write objectives for the skills they need to work together effectively. Some examples of important skills for a diverse world are

social action skills, perspective taking, recognizing stereotypes, empathy, cross-cultural communication including sign language, collaboration, conflict resolution, and so on. All of these skills are designed to help students respond to diversity inside and outside of school in a respectful, accepting manner.

Teachers can also consider using *carrier* content related to diversity when teaching any subject matter. Incorporating diversity content while teaching other knowledge or skills helps to engage or inform students. For example, if you are teaching reading comprehension skills, you could choose a story about a family that is homeless. Reading comprehension is your primary objective. The content about homelessness is carrier content. As another example, when fishing is an important aspect of the culture of the community in which you teach, write math problems with content about fishing ("If you caught 300 pounds of cod per day . . ."). This material carries the knowledge or skills you are teaching, informs students about a diversity-related topic, and, potentially, engages students in your class who are from the same background (in these examples, those who are also homeless or those whose families fish).

Content That Is Complete and Inclusive

A second goal to help structure decisions about curriculum is providing completeness (Irvine and Armento 2001). Make sure to include all voices and perspectives when teaching subjects such as history, literature, art, music, math, and science. Include all important, relevant contributors such as historical figures, writers, artists, scientists, mathematicians, and so on from all backgrounds: different genders, races or ethnicities, abilities, classes, and sexual orientations.

Consider these examples. You aren't going to include a Central American author in your literature curriculum just because you have Latino students in your class this year; you'll always want to include the important contributors from all kinds of backgrounds. If you are teaching about environmental issues, logging, fishing, whaling, or hunting, bring in the various and often contentious points of view on these topics. Include Native American and European settler perspectives when teaching U.S. history. When teaching about governing, investigate a variety of ways, such as by the wisdom of elders, by consensus, and by majority vote.

Also, emphasize similarities; avoid focusing only on differences. Look for common themes in folk tales, such as wise animal stories or children who do not obey their parents. Pair folk tales from different cultures. Point out commonalities like caring and sharing among different types of families. Show similarities in the occasions for celebrations (spring, harvest, independence) among cultures.

The most important thing to remember is to be thorough in your coverage of topics. The idea is to teach completely for everyone's benefit, so that all students can be fully educated.

Content That Is Connected to Students' Lives

The third thing to think about when planning topics is how to make connections between the topics and the students. Select examples, images, and metaphors connected to students' experiences and cultural backgrounds (Irvine and Armento 2001). Use examples that show the importance of the content to students' lives. Build on student ideas and examples. For example, when teaching the topic of discrimination, activate the students' background knowledge by having them discuss their own experiences of being discriminated against as young people, people with disabilities, or people of color. If teaching fractions, begin by creating an experience such as dividing a cookie in half to share with a friend. When teaching poetry, connect with nursery rhymes, jump rope chants, song lyrics, or raps.

To find these connections, you will need to learn about your students' cultural backgrounds and about the community in which you teach. You may use books, articles, and Internet sites to gain general information. To learn specifically about your students and community, spend time with student families, read the local newspaper, attend community events, and get to know everyone at school. To summarize, considering these three categories related to curriculum (content, completeness, and connections) will help you be a diversity responsive teacher in *what* you teach.

Considering Skill Diversity

When planning what to teach, you'll also want to consider skill diversity. Your class will include students with disabilities or who simply have fewer academic skills than others. If students have fallen behind in the curriculum, there is no time for fluff and filler, so be sure that you are teaching the most important knowledge and skills. Teach what is most generalizable. Consider the possibility that you need to teach more lessons and fewer activities and reexamine the rationale for your planned activities.

In addition, for students who need to be motivated, engage students by using content based on their interests. Offer choices to students when possible. For example, allow students to read articles from the sports pages to practice reading skills. Teach students to take charge of their learning by setting and monitoring their own learning goals.

Help students learn the skills that will allow them to learn more efficiently. Teach learning strategies along with teaching content areas, such as working on active reading strategies in the social studies textbook. Teach school survival and task-related skills, such as study skills, test-taking skills, problem-solving skills, and organizational skills. Teach students the skills they need to be successful in various teaching models and methods such as discussion, peer interaction skills, and skills for staying focused and for dealing with challenges and frustration.

In summary, when thinking about content, consider what your students need to learn in terms of subject matter, types of knowledge, and diversity. The possibilities of what to teach seem nearly endless. Obviously, you want to teach the most important content to your students. Fortunately, there is help in selecting what to teach.

Guidance in Choosing What to Teach

Teachers aren't expected (or allowed) to make all decisions about what to teach. They receive guidance in selecting content from a variety of sources. These include state standards and standards developed by professional organizations. In addition, teachers are guided by district curricula and, in the case of students with disabilities, individual education programs (IEPs).

State Standards

State standards are a valuable and necessary source for giving direction to teacher planning. States have adopted a set of standards that provide a description of what students across the state will learn as they progress through the K–12 public school system. The standards are meant to guide the general curriculum. They were developed in an attempt to raise student achievement levels and to standardize the learning expectations for all students in the state. The standards appear as sets of goals in content areas such as reading, mathematics, and the arts, and describe what students will accomplish in each area. State tests, given at various grade levels, measure student progress in relation to these standards.

The special education law, Individuals with Disabilities Education Act (IDEA 04), was developed to ensure that special education also connected with state standards. Therefore, students with disabilities also have access to the higher standards of the general curriculum. This allows teachers to plan programs for these students with the state standards in mind.

State standards and goals provide focus in schools in several ways. First, they help describe the general curriculum and provide a guide for planning the content of teaching (King-Sears 2001). These standards ensure that students, including those with disabilities, have opportunities to prepare for the state tests and learn the content considered important enough to appear in state standards. They also serve as tools around which students, teachers, principals, and parents can communicate about learning.

EXAMPLE OF A STATE STANDARD

State Standard Mathematics #1: The student understands and applies the concepts and procedures of mathematics.

Component 1.1: Understand and apply concepts and procedures from number sense.

- Benchmark 1 (Grade 4): Identify, compare, and order whole numbers and simple fractions.

- Benchmark 2 (Grade 7): Compare and order whole numbers, fractions, and decimals.

- Benchmark 3 (Grade 10): Explain the magnitude of numbers by comparing and ordering real numbers.

Note that all examples of state standards in this chapter come from Washington State.

These standards identify accomplishments in a given content area that are considered important for all students in the state. Generally, all lessons and activities taught will be linked to these standards. (See Chapter 2 for how to use state standards when writing objectives.)

Professional Organization Standards and Big Ideas

Other important sources in the development of classroom curricula are professional organizations such as the International Reading Association, National Council of Teachers of Mathematics, National Council of English Teachers, National Council of the Social Studies, and the National Science Teachers Association. Many of these organizations have developed standards and/or have described the important generalizations or "big ideas" in their subject areas. These are meant to help teachers choose the most important content to teach and to connect and organize knowledge and skills with essential understandings for that discipline. Following are some examples of big ideas:

- Economic systems are influenced by supply and demand.

- Patterns are everywhere.

- Geographical features affect where people settle.

- Writers try to persuade their readers to believe or act in certain ways.

- People have created different forms of government to meet their needs.

- All people have a culture that influences how they see the world.

School district curriculum guides can also aid teachers as they plan what to teach. A group of teachers within the district often develops these guides. The guides can include long- and short-term objectives and activities that teachers who helped write the guide have tried. These guides can help teachers plan lessons and activities that are related to the state standards.

Published programs can also be purchased for reading, math, social studies, social skills, study strategies, and so on. These programs usually include long- and short-term objectives and all needed materials. Teachers must be sure that such program objectives meet the needs of their students. If not, they will want to make appropriate adjustments. School district or university curriculum libraries, as well as the Internet, can be good places to start your search for published programs.

It's clear that teachers must make important decisions about what to teach. If you are a practicing teacher, you know that part of your responsibility is to figure out what your students need to learn. If you are a practicum student or student teacher, a classroom teacher who makes these curricular decisions is probably directing you. Important decisions about what to teach must ultimately be based on the learning and behavioral needs of individual students.

When teaching students with disabilities, refer to the IEPs, the most important sources of information to help teachers decide what to teach. The IEP provides teachers with a look at the individualized goals and objectives that the IEP team determined to be most important for particular students to learn. This information can help provide a focus for planning how best to facilitate the learning of students with disabilities.

Once you have consulted the standards and other sources, and have selected the content to teach, you are ready for the next step in planning to teach.

Preparing to Teach

Now that you know what content you need to teach your students, you still have work to complete before you begin actual lesson planning.

Levels of Understanding

As you begin to transition from planning what to teach to planning how to teach it, you'll need to decide the level of understanding that you want your students to obtain at this time. Will you introduce the content, teach it thoroughly, or strengthen previously taught information? Determining this will influence whether you teach in the form of an activity or a lesson, among other things (see Chapter 13).

One level of understanding is introductory knowledge. Teachers introduce content when they want to build background knowledge, to expose students to the content, to build interest or motivation, to prepare students for a series of lessons and activities on a topic, or to introduce a topic or skill that will be taught completely in a future grade. On the other hand, teachers may intend that their students develop a thorough understanding of important knowledge and skills. They want them to remember the information, comprehend it, and be able to apply it.

A third possibility is that teachers want to strengthen their students' understanding of previously learned information. Therefore, they may provide a review, additional practice, or opportunities for generalization. They may integrate content from different subject areas.

Deciding the level of understanding you want your students to gain is essential in planning an appropriate lesson or activity.

Organizing Content for Teaching

Once you know what subject matter and kind of knowledge (declarative or procedural) you will be teaching, you need to determine how to best organize and teach the content. Preparing a thorough content analysis will really pay off in the long run.

Content Analysis

In the beginning stages of planning a lesson or activity, you need to think through the specifics of what you are teaching and how it is best taught by preparing a content analysis. A thorough content analysis could contain one or more of the following: a *subject matter outline*, a *concept analysis*, a *task analysis*, a *principle statement*, definitions of *key terms and vocabulary*, and a list of *prerequisite skills and knowledge*.

ORGANIZING DECLARATIVE KNOWLEDGE
The following are ways to organize declarative knowledge information:

Subject matter outlines are standard outlines of the specific content to be covered in the lesson. They are almost always written for lessons designed to teach specific declarative information (for example, an informal presentation lesson on the causes of the Civil War). The body of the informal presentation lesson consists of a subject matter outline and is used to guide the teacher's delivery of information.

EXAMPLE OF A SUBJECT MATTER OUTLINE

Malignant Melanoma

1. Three Types of Skin Cancer
   a. Basal cell carcinoma
   b. Squamous cell carcinoma
   c. Malignant melanoma—can be fatal

2. Risk Factors of Malignant Melanomas
   a. Sun exposure (repeated sunburns; 80 percent of damage is done during childhood)
   b. Fair complexion (Caucasians, red-heads, and blondes)
   c. Family history (increased risk if parents or siblings have melanoma)

3. Detection: Know the A, B, C, and D of Melanoma
   a. Asymmetrical (a line through the middle would not create equal sides; most moles and freckles are symmetrical)
   b. Borders (uneven: scalloped or notched edges; normal mole: smooth, even border)
   c. Color (begins with varied shades of brown, tan, or black; progresses to red, white, or blue; normal moles are an even shade of brown)
   d. Diameter (larger than normal moles: 6 millimeters or ¼ inch in diameter; normal mole is smaller)

EXAMPLE OF A CONCEPT ANALYSIS

Concept Name: Proper Nouns

- *Definition:* A proper noun is a noun that names a particular person, place, or thing.
- *Critical attributes:* A proper noun, which names a particular person, a particular place, or a particular thing, is capitalized.
- *Noncritical attributes:* The position in the sentence and the number of words are noncritical.
- *Examples:* Seattle Mariners, Golden Gate Bridge, Harriet Tubman, Amsterdam, Curtis Kerce, Orcas Island, Washington State, UW Huskies
- *Nonexamples:* baseball team, bridge, woman, city, man, island, state, football team
- *Related concepts:* common noun

A third type of content analysis is a *principle statement*. Principles are relational rules that show the relationship between two or more concepts. They are often described in the form of if–then, cause–effect, or "rule of thumb" relationships. All content areas have examples of principles.

A *concept analysis* is used for teaching concepts. It is important to do a concept analysis prior to teaching concepts. This type of content analysis helps teachers think through and write down exactly how they will explain the essential elements of the concept. A concept analysis includes: (1) a definition of the concept, (2) a list of the critical attributes that are distinguishing features or characteristics found in all examples, (3) a list of noncritical attributes that are nonessential characteristics not found in all examples, (4) a list of examples, (5) a list of nonexamples, and (6) a list of related concepts, if helpful. Following is an example of a concept analysis:

EXAMPLES OF PRINCIPLES

- When water reaches 32 degrees Fahrenheit, it freezes.
- If your payment arrives late, then you will need to pay a late fee.
- When a wasp's food supply dwindles toward the end of the summer, it is more likely to sting without provocation.
- If a pregnant mother has little or no prenatal care, then the risk of a premature birth increases.
- When effective memorization strategies are used for studying, then retention of information is usually greater.

Be sure that you plan in advance how you will explain the principle to your students. It can be difficult to correctly or accurately explain the principle spontaneously during a lesson or activity. Begin by writing out the complete principle statement; include the condition and the result or the action that needs to be taken. Next, consider carefully which words are best used as part of your explanation. Finally, be sure that you plan many and varied examples to illustrate the principle. It is important for your students to be able to *apply* the principle to unknown examples, not just state it (Smith and Ragan 2005).

A SPECIAL NOTE ABOUT MEMORIZING INFORMATION

Memory tasks need special planning. Generally, you would not use a single lesson when planning for students to memorize significant amounts of information (for example, a long list of steps to follow for a reading strategy or to solve math story problems, a list of states and capitals, chemical symbols, math facts, and so on). This type of information is often initially introduced in a lesson, but needs to be followed by a variety of activities designed to aid memorization. Follow frequent and distributed opportunities to practice with an evaluation.

When you plan your lesson or activity, determine what new information (steps, vocabulary words, content facts) students will need to know to meet the lesson objective. Ask yourself this question: Do my students need to memorize this information? If you answer *yes*, then you may need or want to revise your objective and plan memory devices (mnemonics, for example) as appropriate, with an adequate number of practice opportunities within the lesson. If your answer is *no*, then plan which visual supports are needed to give students access to the information (posters, transparencies, and so on).

ORGANIZING PROCEDURAL KNOWLEDGE

Use a *task analysis* when you plan to teach a how-to lesson, that is, you want your students to do something at the end of the lesson that they cannot presently do. The procedures or strategies you want your students to learn to do are best organized using a task analysis. A procedure is a series of steps that leads to the completion of a task

(Smith and Ragan 2005). Procedures can be academic (how to convert degrees Celsius to degrees Fahrenheit) or social (how to join in a group), or describe a classroom routine (what to do with a late assignment).

Strategies are a subcategory of procedures. Howell and Nolet (2000) define *strategies* as procedures that students follow to combine subtasks into larger tasks. Strategies are techniques that help students learn (how to take notes from a lecture), study (how to memorize lists of items), or organize (how to maintain an assignment calendar).

A task analysis can be written in two ways, depending on the specific content to be taught. It can be written as a list of sequential steps that must be followed in order (how to do long division, for example). It can also be written as a list of various subskills that must be completed but not necessarily in a certain order (how to write out a check, for example). The following box includes examples of both kinds of task analyses.

EXAMPLES OF TASK ANALYSES

How to Alphabetize to the First Letter

1. Underline the first letter of each word in the list.
2. If all letters are different:
   a. Say the letters of the alphabet in order.
   b. As you say each letter, scan the underlined letters.
   c. Stop each time you say the name of an underlined letter.
   d. Write the word that contains the letter you said.
   e. Continue until all words are used.

How to Proofread Sentences

1. Skim the work and check that:
   a. all sentences begin with a capital letter.
   b. all sentences have an appropriate end mark (period, exclamation point, or question mark).
2. Fix any errors.

The most efficient way to conduct a task analysis is to perform the task yourself while writing the steps, including the thinking process you follow. However, you may encounter cases where the process you follow may be different from the process a child or beginner will follow. Preparing a task analysis will help you plan a presentation of information and a demonstration.

KEY TERMS AND VOCABULARY

Identifying and writing out the definitions of key terms or specialized vocabulary words to be used in a lesson is another form of content analysis. The definitions need to be written in words that the students will understand. It is important to do this in advance to avoid incorrect or incomplete definitions. Terms are not as easy to define on the spot as they would seem.

Student dictionaries and textbook glossaries can be good places to start when trying to write a clear definition for a particular term. Generally, though, this is only the first step. Suppose you are preparing a list of vocabulary words as part of a reading lesson, and one of the words is *myth*. You locate a dictionary definition that says that a myth is "a story rooted in the most ancient religious beliefs and institutions of a people, usually dealing with gods, goddesses, or natural phenomena." Suppose that you write this definition into your lesson plan. When you introduce the word *myth* to your second graders the next day, you suddenly realize that not only do they not understand the entire definition, they do not even understand some of the words that make up the definition. All definitions need to be reviewed and stated in words the students will understand.

PREREQUISITE SKILLS AND KNOWLEDGE

One part of a content analysis is determining prerequisite skills and knowledge that students must have to be ready for a particular lesson. Sometimes, these are broad skills: being able to read is a prerequisite skill for using encyclopedias as a resource when writing reports. Sometimes, the prerequisite skills are more specific: for example, long division requires skills in estimating, multiplying, and subtracting; using adjectives is dependent on understanding nouns; and being able to prepare food from recipes is contingent on being able to measure ingredients. It is certainly not necessary, nor desirable, to

list all prerequisites. However, it is important to consider these factors.

Choosing the Analysis

The following guidelines will help you choose the type of analysis to prepare:

- Write a *concept analysis* when you plan to teach a concept.

- Include a *task analysis* when the point of the lesson is to teach a procedure or strategy, that is, a how-to lesson.

- When teaching about a topic (that is, declarative knowledge), a *subject matter outline* will be most beneficial.

- Write a complete *principle statement* (the condition and the result or action to be taken) when the objective of the lesson is to teach a principle.

- *Key terms and vocabulary words* are important to consider in every lesson or activity. Be sure that words are defined in terms that the students will understand.

- It is always important to consider *prerequisite skills and knowledge* as part of a content analysis. This will help you write the objective and determine whether the content is appropriate for the students you are teaching.

Summary

You will find it beneficial to spend time analyzing the subject matter you plan to teach. It is impossible to get a good result from teaching when you are not sure exactly what you want your students to learn. This knowledge links directly to what you will learn in the next chapter on writing objectives. A thorough content analysis helps you organize the content you will teach into a clear framework that benefits both you and your students. Preparing this framework also helps strengthen your understanding of the material. As you communicate the analysis to your students, you provide them with a structured way to consider the content. This can have a very positive impact on student learning and retention.

References and Suggested Reading

Breslyn, W., R. Hirschland, and C. Moffett (eds.). 2003. *Building bridges: A Peace Corps classroom guide to cross-cultural understanding.* Paul D. Coverdell World Wise Schools.

Callins, T. 2006. Culturally responsive literacy instruction. *Teaching Exceptional Children* 39 (2): 62–65.

Green, T., A. Brown, and L. Robinson. 2007. *Making the most of the web in your classroom: A teacher's guide to blogs, podcasts, wikis, pages, and sites.* Corwin Press.

Howell, K., and Nolet, V. 2000. *Curriculum-based evaluation: Teaching and decision making.* 3rd. ed. Belmont, CA: Wadsworth/Thomson Learning.

Irvine, J., and B. Armento. 2001. *Culturally responsive teaching: Lesson planning for elementary and middle grades.* New York: McGraw-Hill.

King-Sears, M. E. 2001. Three steps for gaining access to the general education curriculum for learners with disabilities. *Intervention in School and Clinic* 37 (2): 67–76.

Murrey, D., and Sapp, J. 2008. Making numbers count: How social justice math can help students transform people, politics, and communities. *Teaching Tolerance* 33: 50–55.

Norton, D. 2001. *Multicultural children's literature.* Upper Saddle River, NJ: Merrill Prentice Hall.

Prater, M., and T. Dyches. 2008. Books that portray characters with disabilities: A top 25 list for children and young adults. *Teaching Exceptional Children* 40 (4): 32–38.

Smith, P. L., and T. J. Ragan. 2005. *Instructional design.* 3rd ed. New York: John Wiley & Sons, Inc.

Whittaker, C., S. Salend, and H. Elhoweris. 2009. Religious diversity in schools: Addressing the issues. *Intervention in School and Clinic* 44 (5): 314–319.

Writing Objectives

Introduction

An effective activity or lesson plan begins with a specific objective. We are going to teach you a format for writing objectives in a clear and measurable form. Writing those objectives will enable you to match your activity or lesson with the intended learning outcome, and you will be able to tell if your teaching was effective (i.e., whether your students learned). It is essential, however, to remember that objectives can be well-written in terms of form and yet not be appropriate or important for your students.

Definition and Purpose

Objectives describe where we want students to go and how we'll know if they got there. Objectives pinpoint the destination—not the journey. Well-written objectives help teachers clarify precisely what they want their students to learn, help provide lesson focus and direction, and guide the selection of appropriate practice. Using objectives, teachers can evaluate whether their students have learned and whether their own teaching has worked. Objectives also help focus and motivate students, and are important communication tools to use with other teachers and families.

Objectives are not only written for lessons and activities. They are also written for IEPs and for units of instruction. Objectives may be written for individuals (Ralph will solve . . .) or for groups of any size (Eighth graders will demonstrate . . .). They can be long-term or short-term and can be written for any content area. Teachers write objectives for themselves to help guide the growth of their

teaching skills. Students can be asked to write their own objectives as part of goal-setting and self-management. In all of these cases, writing clear and measurable objectives is important. In this chapter, we will focus on objectives written by teachers for students as part of a lesson or activity, but the form you will learn applies to all kinds of objectives and reasons for writing them.

Process

Backward planning or *backward design*, terms that Wiggins and McTighe (2005) used, are good descriptions of the process that teachers should use in developing lesson or activity objectives. The sequence of planning objectives is very important. First, decide on the learning outcomes. Second, break down general outcomes into more specific goals or objectives. Next, figure out how you'll assess the outcomes or, as Wiggins and McTighe (2005) express it, what evidence you'll accept that students have achieved the understanding. Then, and only then, plan the lessons and activities that will help students achieve those outcomes. For the first step, deciding what you want students to learn, look to state standards.

State Standards: A Source of Objectives

States have developed sets of standards that provide descriptions of learning outcomes for K–12 students across each state. Standards are written as goals in the various content areas: reading, writing, mathematics, science, social studies, and so on. These standards establish priorities in what should be taught to students. They give teachers focus for long-term curriculum planning.

EXAMPLES OF STATE STANDARDS

- Reading 1. The student understands and uses different skills and strategies to read.
- Reading 2. The student understands the meaning of what is read.
- Reading 3. The student reads different materials for a variety of purposes.
- Reading 4. The student sets goals and evaluates progress to improve reading.

Note that all examples of state standards in this chapter come from Washington State.

These standards for reading are very general and long-term. They guide teachers in deciding what their students need to learn. The second step in developing objectives is to make general outcomes more specific.

From General to Specific

In some cases, teachers are provided with state standards that are broken down into more specific components and benchmarks. This is true for the following reading standard:

> **Reading 1.** The student understands and uses different skills and strategies to read (state standard).
> > 1.1. Use word recognition skills and strategies to read and comprehend text (component).
> > > 1.1.1. Understand and apply concepts of print (kindergarten benchmark).

Grade-level expectations (GLE), which are more specific descriptors of components and benchmarks, provide even more specificity. Here is an example:

> **Reading 1.** The student understands and uses different skills and strategies to read.
> > 1.1. Use word recognition skills and strategies to read and comprehend text.

> > > 1.1.1. Understand and apply concepts of print (kindergarten benchmark).
> > > - Use directionality when listening to or following text (GLE).
> > > - Identify front cover, back cover, and title of books (GLE).
> > > - Recognize that print represents spoken language, such as environmental print and own name (GLE).
> > > - Recognize letters and spaces between words (GLE).

In other cases, state standards are kept much more general. For example, for writing:

> **Writing 2.** The student writes in a variety of forms for different audiences and purposes.
> > 2.1. Write for different audiences.
> > > 2.1.2. Show some awareness of audience needs.

Although state standards provide direction, teachers must develop their own very specific objectives for lessons, activities, and units. This is also true in special education, where teachers help develop individual education programs (IEPs) that include goals and objectives intended to enable students to progress in the general curriculum based on the state standards. A teacher's task is to translate the standards into useful, specific objectives that are used to guide instruction. In this way, the learning outcomes included in the objectives will link to the state standards.

Writing specific objectives from standards and goals begins with an understanding of how standards, goals, and objectives differ. The following are some of the main differences:

- *Specificity* Specific learning outcomes are described in objectives, whereas standards include more general outcome statements. Goals may be general (understand the concept of fractions) or specific (write fractions to describe relationships).

- *Long-Term or Short-Term* Objectives are considered short-term because they describe the learning outcome expected in days, weeks, or months. Goals and standards describe learning outcomes expected to occur at the end of a longer period of time—weeks, months, or years; thus, they are long-term outcome statements.

■ *Uses* Objectives are used in lesson and activity plans and sometimes in IEPs. Measurable annual goals are included in IEPs. Goals are also found in units of instruction. Standards are used in state or district curricula, or are set by professional organizations.

Following are two examples of developing a specific objective more suitable for a lesson or activity from a state standard.

Reading 1. The student understands and uses different skills and strategies to read.
    1.1. Use word recognition skills and strategies to read and comprehend text.
        1.1.1. Understand and apply concepts of print.
             ● Recognize letters and spaces between words.

Objective: Student will identify first and last letters of words in context.

Civics 2. The student analyzes the purposes and organization of governments and laws.
    2.1. Understand and explain the organization of federal, state, and local government including the executive, legislative, and judicial branches at, and among, the three levels of government.
        2.1.3. Analyze problems and solutions related to the distribution of authority.

Objective: Students will understand how branches of the government check and balance each other.

Measurable Objectives

The third step in backward planning is to decide how you'll know if students have achieved the learning outcome. This is the process of making objectives measurable.

Objective: Student will identify first and last letters of words in context.

Measurable objective: Student will circle the first and underline the last letters of each word in a given five-word sentence.

Objective: Students will understand how branches of the government check and balance each other.

Measurable objective: Given the power of the legislative branch to enact laws, students will name the other two branches and describe in two sentences how this power is checked and balanced by each.

Notice in the previous measurable objectives that the assessment or evidence of learning is built into the objective. These are what we mean by "measurable" objectives. You begin with the desired learning outcome (apply writing conventions), make the outcome specific (capitalize proper nouns accurately), and define what evidence you will accept that students can do that (correct capitalization errors in a list of nouns and proper nouns). Only then do you plan your lesson or activity. Special educators are very familiar with this process—first come measurable goals, then specially designed instruction.

Multiple Objectives

Teachers sometimes design lessons or activities for the achievement of more than one objective. They do this for a variety of reasons. One such reason is for efficiency, and another is to be responsive to diversity.

Efficiency and Multiple Objectives

Because of the many valuable learning outcomes for students, teachers have tough decisions to make about what to teach and what to leave out. Sometimes, teachers can develop dual-purpose lessons or activities. They might plan class discussions designed to help students develop a deeper understanding of a historical event and to learn to disagree politely. They might plan a math game activity designed to help students achieve a math objective (fluency with multiplication facts) and a social skills objective (showing good sportsman-ship in winning and losing). They might plan a lesson in which they present information to help students learn the planets of the solar system and information on how to use a learning strategy to memorize items in order. It can be more efficient to use one lesson or activity to teach toward multiple objectives.

Diversity and Multiple Objectives

Another purpose for multiple objectives is to be responsive to diversity. Many classrooms today include students who are English language learn-ers. Teachers can respond to linguistic diversity by designing lessons or activities that can be used to help students achieve objectives in subject areas (such as science or social studies) while also meet-ing language objectives for speaking, listening, reading, and writing. For example, you might plan a lesson designed to help students achieve a sci-ence objective such as "describing the life cycle of a butterfly," as well as helping students meet lan-guage objectives such as "using sequence indicator words such as *first, second, next,* and *last* in lists" and "following three-step oral directions for com-pleting tasks."

Teachers can also be responsive to diversity using multiple objectives by creating activities designed to provide instruction or practice for sev-eral students who are working on individual objec-tives. For example, in a special education preschool setting, students may be working on color and shape identification, physical skills, and language skills objectives. Teachers may use one activity, such as snack time, to provide different students with prac-tice on different objectives:

- Rosita will be asked to name the shape and col-ors of plates (objective = producing shape and color names), and

- Wendy will be asked to point to the green plate and the blue plate (identifying colors)

- John will be expected to ask for more by saying, "More juice, please" (using three-word phrases), while

- Bridget signs the word *juice* (increasing sign vocabulary)

- Denzel's objective may be to grasp the handle of an adaptive spoon and take three bites (fine motor skill), whereas

- Desiree's is to sit at the table in a chair without arms (balancing skill)

The same three-step backward planning pro-cess is used to develop objectives regardless of whether multiple objectives will be taught through one lesson or activity. Note that it is our intention to concentrate on specific short- and long-term objectives throughout this book. This means that when we talk about writing objectives for activ-ity plans, for example, we mean writing specific long-term objectives. When we talk about writing lesson objectives, we mean specific, short-term objectives.

The Four Components of Objectives

The easy way to write a measurable objective is to include four components: content, behavior, condi-tion, and criterion (Howell and Nolet 2000). Includ-ing these four components will help ensure that your objectives represent a clear, specific learning outcome and a description of how that learning will be measured. In this section, we provide an exam-ple objective followed by descriptions of each of the four objective components, with examples and nonexamples. Common errors are noted, and sug-gestions for writing each objective component are included.

EXAMPLE OBJECTIVE

Students will write answers to 20 subtraction problems (two-digit numbers from three-digit numbers with regrouping) with no errors, on a worksheet.

Content

This component describes the specific subject matter to be learned. In the example objective, the content is "subtraction problems, two-digit numbers from three-digit numbers with regrouping."

Suggestions When Writing the Content

1. Be specific enough that anyone reading the objective will understand the subject matter.

2. Be sure the description of content can stand alone, that is, be "materials-free." The reader should be able to understand the content of the objective without tracking down specific materials.

3. Be generic enough that the emphasis is on knowledge and skills that are important and applicable in a variety of contexts.

EXAMPLES OF CONTENT

The content component is italicized in the following examples and nonexamples:

■ Add *unlike fractions with common factors between denominators.*

■ Write *two-syllable spelling words with -ing endings (for example, hoping, hopping).*

■ Compare and contrast *fables and fairy tales.*

NONEXAMPLES OF CONTENT

■ Add *fractions* (not specific); answer *fraction problems 1–7 on p. 42* (not materials-free).

■ Write *spelling words* (not specific); complete *Unit 4 in spelling book* (not materials-free).

■ Compare and contrast *"The Lazy Princess" and "Lost in the Woods"* (not generic or materials-free).

Common Errors When Writing Content

A common error teachers make is to include content appropriate for an activity or assignment rather than a learning outcome. The following are examples of errors in writing content:

1. Write *adjectives for 10 animals and plants from the rain forest unit.*

Are you looking for knowledge of the rain forest or knowledge of adjectives? This may be a good integrated practice activity, but it is not a clear objective.

2. Present *five facts about a bird of your choice.*

The content is unclear. We do not know what facts are to be learned. Is the real content using reference books to find facts, making presentations, or summarizing from the unit on birds? Don't confuse an instructional theme with content.

EXAMPLES OF THE CONTENT COMPONENT WITHIN OBJECTIVES

■ Given a chapter in a textbook, students will construct a *concept map* that includes all main headings and subheadings.

■ Students will list the *six steps for treating a burn* as recommended by the American Red Cross, from memory.

Behavior

This component states what students will do to demonstrate their learning. Write the behavior or performance as an observable verb so outcomes can be measured.

In the example objective on p. 16, the behavior is "write." The student will demonstrate knowledge of subtraction by writing the answers to 20 problems.

EXAMPLES OF BEHAVIOR

say	write	list
draw	diagram	paraphrase
operate	throw	volunteer
circle	complete	demonstrate
label	predict	calculate
add	design	select
name	perform	laugh
choose	initiate	put in order
define	compare	contrast

Notice that some of these verbs can be made more specific; for example, one could "define" in writing or orally. You must judge how much specificity is needed, but when in doubt, be more specific rather than less. For example, the commonly used verbs "identify" and "recognize" often need further specifics, such as "identify by underlining."

NONEXAMPLES OF BEHAVIOR

know	realize	comprehend
understand	experience	discover
memorize	believe	appreciate
learn	value	be familiar with

Notice that these verbs may be appropriate when writing general goals, aims, outcomes, or standards. They are not appropriate for measurable objectives because you cannot know that a student "knows" or "comprehends" or has "learned" something unless she does something overt. For example, you may have a goal that your students appreciate poetry. You cannot tell if that objective has been reached unless your students do something (voluntarily check out poetry books from the library or write poetry without being assigned to do so, for example).

Suggestions When Writing the Behavior

1. Decide whether you want students to "identify" or "produce" as you write the behavior component in objectives (Howell and Nolet 2000). A lesson for teaching students to produce or write metaphors will be quite different from a lesson for teaching students to identify or recognize metaphors someone else has written.

2. Include only one or two required behaviors in an objective. Objectives that include many behaviors (for example, students will research, write, draw, and present) make evaluation confusing and often end up being descriptions of activities or assignments rather than learning outcomes.

3. Consider including alternate behaviors (write, type, or say, for example) to provide the flexibility to allow all students, including those with disabilities, to be successful. This is an excellent way to incorporate the principles of universal design for learning.

4. Leave out nonessential or redundant behaviors.
   - "Students will copy the sentences and circle all nouns." Omit "copy the sentences." It has nothing to do with the skill of identifying nouns.
   - Omit "locate" in an example such as, "Students will locate and point to . . ." If the student is pointing to something, then you can assume he has located it.

5. Omit "be able to" as in the example, "The student will be able to make a speech . . ." The phrase adds words but no meaning. Remember that the performance is important, not an assumed ability or inability.

6. Do not use the phrase, "Student will pass a test on . . ." It does not communicate specific information about what the student will do or learn.

7. Write objectives for what the students will do, not what the teacher will do. Objectives may be written for one student or a group of students.

EXAMPLES OF THE BEHAVIOR COMPONENT WITHIN OBJECTIVES

- Given 10 incomplete sentences, students will *rewrite* each as a complete sentence that includes a subject and a predicate.

- Students will *demonstrate* all five steps of the "accepting *no* for an answer" social skill in a role-play.

Conditions

It is important to describe the conditions—circumstances, situation, or setting—in which the student will perform the behavior. These conditions provide additional specificity about what the student will learn. It is the conditions that will apply when the student is being evaluated, rather than the learning condition, which must be described. In the example objective on p. 16, the students must write answers to 20 subtraction problems, with the condition "on a worksheet," not in a real-world context such as "in a check register."

Notice that the *italicized* conditions in the following objectives result in three different learning outcomes. They affect the level of difficulty of the objective, and thus the lesson and practice activities that you need to plan for your students.

- Students will write the capitals of each of the 17 western states *given a list of the states and a list of the capitals.* (They will be asked to recognize state capitals. This is really a matching task.)

- Students will write the capitals of each of the 17 western states *given a list of the states.* (They will be asked to recall the state capitals rather than simply recognize them.)

■ Students will write the capitals of each of the 17 western states *on a blank outline map*. (They must recall the names and locations of the states and the names of the capitals in order to write the capitals in the correct places.)

Types of Conditions

Various types of conditions may be included in objectives.

EXAMPLES OF CONDITIONS

In isolation or in context

■ Compute measurement equivalents *on a worksheet* or *while following a recipe*

■ Respond to teasing *in a role-play* or *on the playground*

■ Correct punctuation errors *in given sentences* or *while proofreading an essay*

■ Pronounce words *when shown flash cards* or *in a story*

Information or materials provided

■ Given an incomplete proof

■ Given population figures for each country

■ With a calculator, ruler, scale

■ From memory, with nothing provided

Setting or situation

■ When given directions

■ In the lunchroom

■ During teacher presentations

■ When teased; when angry; when refused

A combination of conditions

■ Given 10 problems and a calculator

■ Given eight map terms (key) and a dictionary

Independently or with assistance

■ With or without reminders

■ With or without physical assistance

■ With or without verbal cues

A very important condition is whether we are asking students to perform a skill in isolation or in context, or in artificial or real-world circumstances. This is important to think about when sequencing objectives and when planning for generalization or transfer of the skill. The information or materials provided—often called the "givens"—may be important to specify. Visualize the evaluation or testing situation and what the students will have available. A third type of condition—a description of the setting or situation—may help clarify the objective as well, especially social skill and learning strategy objectives. Obviously, all conditions need not be mentioned (for example, the lights will be on in the room). However, be sure to include those that communicate important information about the learning outcome.

You may want to specify whether the student is going to solve mixed math problems or correct mixed grammar errors. Otherwise, you may only be evaluating whether students can figure out the pattern (for example, all problems require regrouping or all sentences are missing a question mark).

In some cases, for example, when writing objectives for students with severe disabilities or for very young students, it may be important to specify whether students will be performing the behavior independently. Note that the "default" condition typically is without assistance. See the boxes on this page and the next for more information on conditions.

Criterion

The criterion specifies the level of acceptable performance, the standard of mastery, or the proficiency level expected. This component describes how well (i.e., how accurately, frequently, or consistently) the students should perform in order to say that they have met the objective. In the example objective on p. 16, students will write answers to 20 subtraction problems (two-digit numbers from three-digit numbers with regrouping) on a worksheet; the criterion is "with no errors."

Common Errors When Writing the Criterion

1. *The criterion is too low.* Keep high performance standards, especially for basic skills in reading, writing, and arithmetic. Do not confuse setting criteria in objectives with assigning grades. It will take some students longer to reach an

NONEXAMPLES OF CONDITIONS

Describing the learning condition rather than the evaluation condition

Avoid using conditions such as:

- As a result of my instruction . . .
- Given a lesson on . . .
- After completing the weather unit . . .
- After studying . . .

It doesn't matter where or when the students learned the knowledge or skill. Remember that objectives focus on outcomes.

Adding unimportant information

Avoid using conditions such as:

- When asked by the teacher . . .
- Given a blank piece of paper . . .

Some conditions are obvious and do not need to be written.

Selecting conditions at random from lists of examples

Incorporate conditions that reflect important decisions about how learning will be measured.

EXAMPLES OF THE CONDITION COMPONENT WITHIN OBJECTIVES

- *Before turning in seatwork assignments*, students will write a heading on their papers that includes name, subject, period, and date, on eight consecutive assignments.
- *Given six topics receiving attention during the congressional campaign* (such as end-of-life issues), students will explain in writing how each candidate would likely vote on the issue (explanation must include a rationale supported by facts).

EXAMPLES OF CRITERION

As a total number or proportion

- Comparing or contrasting four key issues
- With 10 out of 10 correct
- With 90 percent accuracy

In terms of time

- Within 10 minutes; per minute
- The first time
- For five consecutive days

As a variation

- Within plus or minus 1 inch
- Within 1 percent
- To the closest hundredth

As a description or result

- Until consensus is reached
- Story includes a conflict and resolution
- The strategy selected solves the problem in the fewest steps

Using a combination of criteria

- 50 per minute with 100 percent accuracy by March 10
- Backing up opinion with data from three relevant research studies
- Paragraphs include topic sentences and at least three supporting details

NONEXAMPLES OF CRITERION

Does not pass the "stranger test"

- As judged by the teacher
- To teacher's satisfaction

These obviously do not pass the "stranger test" (Kaplan 1995), that is, they are open to interpretation. A stranger may not interpret them the same way as you do. Remember that one of the purposes of writing objectives is to communicate clearly with students, families, and other teachers and professionals.

objective. You may want to set gradually increasing criteria—50 percent accuracy by October 1; 75 percent accuracy by November 1; 100 percent accuracy by December 1. However, be sure that the final outcome is high enough. If a student is only 80 percent accurate on number recognition, she is doomed to failure in arithmetic.

2. *The criterion is set arbitrarily.* Do not make the error of automatically writing 85 percent accuracy for every objective. Set realistic standards and time limits. Establish criteria either by doing the task yourself or by having a successful peer do the task. Do *not* write: ". . . will say the multiples of 10 from 10 to 100 in 3 minutes" or ". . . locate a word in the dictionary in 5 minutes." Try it! If it took you 5 minutes to find a word, you would never choose to use the dictionary.

3. *"Percent accuracy" is misused.*

   ■ When there are many possible divergent or complex responses, percent accuracy as the criterion does not make sense. One cannot write a story with 100 percent accuracy nor manage anger with 80 percent accuracy.

   ■ There needs to be a number of responses for percent accuracy to be sensible—not simply correct or incorrect. For example, choose "name the state you live in" or "correctly name the state you live in," rather than "name the state you live in with 100 percent accuracy." Write "turn off the computer correctly" or "without damaging anything" rather than "turn off the computer with 100 percent accuracy."

   ■ Sometimes "percent accuracy" works, but it would be too much work to compute. To decide if someone reached 85 percent accuracy in punctuating a story, you would first have to count all of the opportunities for punctuation within the story.

4. *There's no end in sight.* If the objective is for the student to spell words correctly in all written work, when would you be able to say that a student had met this objective? At the end of his life?

Suggestions When Writing the Criterion

1. Think about how many times you want the students to demonstrate the skill during evaluation to be confident that they have met the objective. For example, do they need to write their addresses five times to prove they can do it? If Jorge responds to teasing appropriately during one recess, are you sure he has learned that skill?

2. Be specific enough so that any evaluator would reach the same conclusion as to whether the student meets the objective. Avoid vague criteria such as "Student will write *descriptive* sentences." This criterion is not specific enough to determine if the objective of the lesson has been met. The following two sentences cannot be evaluated reliably using this criterion: "The bike is big," and "Perched on the seat of the bike, I felt like Hillary on the peak of Everest."

3. Make sure the criterion addresses the skill you want. For example, if the skill you are looking for is writing descriptively, don't write your criterion as "all words need to be spelled correctly." Do not write a criterion solely because it is easy to think of. In attempting to make the objective specific and measurable, don't end up making it trivial!

EXAMPLES OF THE CRITERION COMPONENT WITHIN OBJECTIVES

■ Given addition problems with sums no greater than 18, students will write *40 correct sums* in no more than *1 minute.*

■ In a debate, the student will argue for one side of a controversial issue (for example, capital punishment) and provide *three reasons supported with facts* for that position.

Help with Including the Four Components in Objectives

When you are learning to write objectives, using a template and scaffold will help ensure that you will include all four components. The template looks like this: The <u>SUBJECT</u> will <u>DO/SAY</u> <u>SOMETHING</u> this <u>WELL</u> in this <u>SITUATION</u>. We have added labels and descriptors for each component to create a scaffold for writing measurable objectives. This is pictured on page 22.

```
┌─────────────────────────────────────────────────────────────────────────────┐
│              TEMPLATE AND SCAFFOLD FOR WRITING OBJECTIVES                      │
│                                                                               │
│  COMPONENTS:        behavior       content        criterion       condition   │
│                        ↑              ↑               ↑               ↑       │
│    The SUBJECT will  DO/SAY       SOMETHING      this WELL      in this SITUATION. │
│  DESCRIPTORS:       observable    specific, but   how accurately,  what setting or │
│                     verb          generic        frequently, or   with what provided │
│                                                   consistently                │
└─────────────────────────────────────────────────────────────────────────────┘
```

Here are examples of filled-in templates:

- The STUDENTS will TELL the TIME with 100% ACCURACY given PICTURES OF 10 CLOCK FACES.

- HAROLD AND MAUD will WALK AWAY from TEASING on 4/4 OCCASIONS at RECESS.

- YUNI will WRITE a SENTENCE that is COMPLETE given a SENTENCE FRAGMENT.

If the objective sounds awkward, rewrite it by changing the order of the components:

- Given a sentence fragment, Yuni will write a complete sentence.

Bloom's Taxonomy of the Cognitive Domain

Benjamin Bloom and colleagues (1956) designed a hierarchy of intellectual skills, called Bloom's Taxonomy of the Cognitive Domain. Bloom developed this hierarchy in response to the observation that teaching in schools focused heavily on having students recall facts (low-level thinking) rather than developing their higher-level thinking skills. The six categories in the taxonomy of the cognitive domain are organized in a hierarchy from basic understanding of information to high-level information processing. The taxonomy was originally developed to help teachers recognize the varying degrees of complexity involved in various classroom activities so they could construct objectives that included higher-level learning outcomes.

Bloom's taxonomy has been used in classrooms in a variety of ways since it was developed, and we will discuss two of those applications. The first application helps teachers plan questions that promote various kinds of thinking. You will read about these questions in Chapter 4. The other application helps teachers write objectives. Heacox (2002)

writes that one of the most important applications of Bloom's taxonomy is in the design of learning activities: "Looking at instruction through the lens of *challenge* means considering the rigor, relevance, and complexity of what you're teaching" (67). By thinking about the instructional challenges of various outcomes included in objectives, teachers can plan for variation that can better meet the needs of a diverse classroom of students.

A group of Bloom's students recently revised the taxonomy that Bloom and colleagues designed. Lorin Anderson and others (Anderson and Krathwohl 2001) updated the taxonomy so it would better mesh with current theories about how children learn. The taxonomy has been renamed "taxonomy for learning, teaching, and assessing" (Arends 2009). When we present each level of Bloom's taxonomy, we will include the label used in the revised version (in parentheses) as well as in the original one. We will also include references and resources about both taxonomies at the end of this chapter.

- *Knowledge* (*Remembering*): This is the lowest level of the cognitive domain. The learning outcome here is the simple recall of facts and information. The information to be recalled can be quite complicated, but nonetheless, all that is required is for one to remember and recall it.

  - General types of outcomes: knows specific facts, concepts, methods, and procedures

  - Behavior stem examples: define, tell, name, label, recite, match

  - *Sample objective*: Teacher education students will recite the names of the levels of Bloom's Taxonomy in order from simple to complex, from memory, without error.

- *Comprehension* (*Understanding*): The learning outcome at the comprehension level of the cognitive domain is understanding. Here students go beyond mere recall and show that they understand.

- General types of outcomes: interprets charts and graphs, estimates future consequences implied in data, understands facts and principles
- Behavior stem examples: restate/rewrite, give an example of, recognize examples, summarize, describe, paraphrase, conclude
- *Sample objective*: When given a list of the levels of the cognitive domain, teacher education students will define the learning task for each, in their own words, with no more than one error.

- *Application (Applying)*: The application level refers to an outcome where students use the new information they have learned. This requires a higher level of understanding than does comprehension.

  - General types of outcomes: constructs charts and graphs, applies concepts and principles to new situations, demonstrates correct usage of a method or procedure
  - Behavior stem examples: predict, solve, demonstrate, operate, illustrate, solve, construct
  - *Sample objective*: When given a list of 12 objectives, teacher education students will select those that are at the application level with 100 percent accuracy.

- *Analysis (Analyzing)*: When students analyze information, they break it down so they can understand the parts as well as the whole. This outcome requires that students understand both the content and the structural form of the material.

  - General types of outcomes: distinguishes between facts and inferences, analyzes the organizational structure of a work (art, music), evaluates the relevancy of data
  - Behavior stem examples: compare, contrast, categorize, diagram, outline, subdivide, distinguish
  - *Sample objective*: When shown a list of objectives from a social studies unit, teacher education students can support their conclusion that the writer did or did not include objectives from all levels of the cognitive domain, citing specific examples of each.

- *Synthesis (Creating)*: This learning outcome of the cognitive domain is where students take the information they know and put it together

into something new. The main idea is the creation of something new to the student.

- General types of outcomes: writes a clearly organized research paper, creates a plan for an experiment to test a hypothesis, designs a new system for organizing information
- Behavior stem examples: produce, design, develop, reorganize, combine, compose, devise
- *Sample objective*: Given a topic, teacher education students will accurately write objectives that represent each level of the cognitive domain.

- *Evaluation (Evaluating)*: The learning outcome for evaluation is the highest level of all, because in order to evaluate, one must use information from the other levels. Evaluation is not random, but rather occurs against a set of criteria.

  - General types of outcomes: judges the adequacy of a rationale, rates how well a written product meets established criteria, selects the most appropriate example
  - Objective stem examples: select, predict, rate, explain, justify, interpret, support
  - *Sample objective*: When given three lesson plans, teacher education students can judge the quality of each and decide which best encourages higher-level thinking skills, giving at least three reasons for this judgment.

EXAMPLES OF OBJECTIVES WRITTEN AT VARIOUS LEVELS OF BLOOM'S TAXONOMY

Knowledge: Students will name two types of graphs (bar graph and line graph), from memory.

Comprehension: Students will explain information displayed on a given line graph.

Application: Students will draw a bar graph given information for five different groups.

Analysis: Students will compare the design of two different graphs of the same information.

Synthesis: Students will design a new type of graph (not a bar or line graph) to effectively display given information.

Evaluation: Students will judge which of two given graphs best displays information and why.

Bloom's taxonomy can be used to help you write effective, relevant objectives. As you plan, make sure that you write objectives that encourage higher-level thinking as well as those that provide students with basic information. This does not mean that your goal should be to include an objective for higher-level thinking in every lesson or activity you teach, as this is probably not reasonable. Rather, strive to emphasize higher-level thinking as often as possible. Objectives written to reflect a variety in outcomes better meet the needs of a diverse group of students. Take a look at the box "Examples of Objectives Written at Various Levels of Bloom's Taxonomy" to see the same content reflected in different levels.

Responding to Diversity When Planning the Objective

Consider the following when writing objectives for the diverse classroom:

- Be sure that your objective represents important learning and is connected to generalizations and big ideas, state standards, or IEP goals.

- Pretest to make sure the objective is necessary for students.

- Examine the criterion. Is it at the right level? Basic skills that are prerequisites for higher-level skills need high criterion levels. For example, 100 percent accuracy is necessary for letter recognition because that is an important basic skill needed for acquiring later skills. On the other hand, 100 percent accuracy in distinguishing reptiles from amphibians may not be necessary.

- Examine the condition. Is it realistic? Students may be more motivated to reach objectives when they can see the real-world applications.

- After analyzing prerequisite skills, the objective for individual students may need to be altered. For example, could students who have poor writing skills demonstrate that they can recognize the key conflict in a short story by saying it rather than writing it? Could students who are inaccurate on multiplication facts demonstrate that they know how to find the area of a rectangle using a calculator? In other words, the purpose of altering the objective is to allow the student to go on learning, not to be held back by those writing or multiplication difficulties.

On the other hand, in most cases, the student continues to need instruction and practice on writing and multiplication.

- Don't rush to make changes in the curriculum for students with learning problems. Changes may affect success in upper grades, options for employment, or further schooling in the long term. Having a student draw a picture or sing a song rather than write a paragraph may provide momentary success, but it is unlikely to be an option offered by future employers.

Summary

The following provides a summary of key ideas to keep in mind when you are writing objectives. The additional examples of measurable objectives on the next page were selected to show the wide range of content for which objectives can be written.

1. Write objectives that describe learning *outcomes*, not activities or assignments (TenBrink 1999).

   NOT: Wally will write spelling words missed on the pretest five times each.

   NOT: Students in pairs will take turns throwing dice, adding the numbers together, and stating the total.

   NOT: Students will play a quiz show game in which they divide into two teams, and ask and answer questions from Chapter 4 in the social studies book.

   NOT: Ben will write letters to the main character in the story.

2. Keep objectives clean and simple. Save creativity for instruction.

   NOT: Students will demonstrate their understanding of the reasons that pandas were endangered by graphing the average number of panda babies born and the number of pandas who died per year for the last 10 years.

   NOT: Students will create a poster that demonstrates their knowledge of modern Mexican culture.

3. Be sure to write objectives that represent *important* learning outcomes!

   NOT: Michelle will write the names of the counties in each state in the United States from memory without error.

EXAMPLES OF MEASURABLE OBJECTIVES

- Given 10 sets of five pictures, four of which are related—belong to the same category, such as vegetables or tools—students will point to the one in each set that does not belong, without error (lesson objective).

- Students will correctly state temperatures, with an accuracy of plus or minus 1 degree, shown on pictures of five thermometers depicting temperatures between 220 degrees Fahrenheit and 95 degrees Fahrenheit (lesson objective).

- Randi will write correct answers to five of five inference questions on a grade-level reading passage (IEP objective).

- Students will return the change from $1.00, using the fewest possible coins, for four purchases, with no errors (unit objective).

- When the fire alarm sounds for a fire drill, Mr. Springsteen's class will form a line within 30 seconds and leave the building following the correct route, without teacher prompting (lesson objective).

- Kathi and Chuck will correctly compute the amount of wallpaper needed to cover a wall of given dimensions (lesson objective).

- When teased by peers, Fadia will respond by ignoring, walking away, or quietly asking the person to stop in eight out of eight observed opportunities by May 1 (IEP objective).

- Richard Michael will complete all of his independent seatwork assignments during class with at least 90 percent accuracy for two consecutive weeks (IEP objective).

A Final Thought

We wish to restate the importance of beginning your lesson or activity planning with a clear idea of what you want your students to learn. Writing a specific, measurable objective will cause you to think this through. It has been our observation that when teachers experience frustration with a particular lesson or activity, it is often the case that they are unable to clearly state what students were to learn.

Using the process of backward planning will prevent this problem. First, decide where you want them to be. Then decide on the steps along the way. Next, decide how you'll know they got there, and last, how to get them there.

Practicing Writing Objectives: Study Suggestions

Once you have mastered the skill of writing measurable objectives, planning useful activities and lessons will be easier and less time-consuming. Following are strategies to help you become accurate and fluent at writing objectives. As with other writing tasks, editing and rewriting will always be important.

1. Study the component names and definitions. Paraphrase them.

2. Review the lists of component examples. Explain why each example fits the definition. Create your own examples.

3. Practice writing your own objectives. You may wish to use the objective scaffold on p. 21.

    a. Think of a general instructional goal, such as the following:

       - Know how to use an index
       - Learn baseball skills
       - Understand cell division
       - Distinguish between fact and fiction
       - Resolve conflicts nonviolently
       - Do homework

    b. Specify the content ("index" becomes "subject index" in textbook, for example).

    c. Specify the behavior ("know how to use" becomes "locate page numbers for topics").

    d. Add necessary conditions (for example, "given a textbook and a list of topics").

    e. Add criteria (no errors, within 30 seconds).

       Notice that there are many possibilities for each component. You may wish to practice writing a variety of objectives on one topic.

    f. Put the components together into a one- or two-sentence objective. For example, "Given a textbook and a list of topics, the student will locate page numbers for topics in the textbook's subject index with no errors, within 30 seconds."

g. Examine for clarity and conciseness, and rewrite as necessary. For example, "Given a textbook, the student will write the correct page number from the index for four out of four listed topics within 2 minutes."

4. After you have written an objective, critique it following these self-evaluation steps:

 a. Are all four components present? (Label them.)

 b. Is each component correct?
  - Content specific? Generic? Materials-free?
  - Behavior observable?
  - Evaluation condition described?
  - Criterion specific? Measurable? Realistic?

 c. Does the objective need editing? Is it wordy? Is it awkward?

 d. Does it pass the stranger test?

 e. Does it represent an important learning outcome?

References and Suggested Reading

Alberto, P., and A. Troutman. 2009. *Applied behavior analysis for teachers.* 8th ed. Upper Saddle River, NJ: Pearson.

Anderson, L. W., and D. R. Krathwohl (eds.). 2001. *A taxonomy for learning, teaching, and assessing: A revision of Bloom's taxonomy of educational objectives.* New York: Longman.

Arends, R. I. 2009. *Learning to teach.* 8th ed. Boston: McGraw-Hill.

Bloom, B. S., M. D. Englehart, E. J. Furst, W. H. Hill, and D. R. Krathwohl. 1956. *Taxonomy of educational objectives, handbook I: The cognitive domain.* New York: David McKay Co. Inc.

Childre, A., J. Sands, and S. Pope. 2009. Backward design: Targeting depth of understanding for all learners. *Teaching Exceptional Children* 41 (5): 6–14.

Gronlund, N. 2004. *Writing instructional objectives for teaching and assessment.* 7th ed. Upper Saddle River, NJ: Pearson.

Heacox, D. 2002. *Differentiating instruction in the regular classroom: How to reach and teach all learners, grades 3–12.* Minneapolis, MN: Free Spirit Publishing.

Howell, K., and V. Nolet. 2000. *Curriculum-based evaluation: Teaching and decision making.* 3rd ed. Belmont, CA: Wadsworth/Thomson Learning.

Kaplan, J. S. 1995. *Beyond behavior modification.* 3rd ed. Austin, TX: Pro-Ed.

Kauchak, D. P., and P. D. Eggen. 2007. *Learning and teaching: Research-based methods.* 5th ed. Boston: Allyn and Bacon.

King-Sears, M. E. 2001. Three steps for gaining access to the general education curriculum for learners with disabilities. *Intervention in School and Clinic* 37 (2): 67–76.

Krumme, G. Major categories in the taxonomy of educational objectives—Bloom 1956. http://faculty.washington.edu/krumme/guides/bloom.html.

Lignugaris/Kraft, B., N. Marchand-Martella, and R. Martella. 2001. Writing better goals and short-term objectives or benchmarks. *Teaching Exceptional Children* 34 (1): 52–58.

Matlock, L., K. Fielder, and D. Walsh. 2001. Building the foundation for standards-based instruction for all students. *Teaching Exceptional Children* 33 (5): 68–73.

Moore, K. D. 2008. *Effective instructional strategies: From theory to practice.* 2nd ed. Thousand Oaks, CA: SAGE Publications.

TenBrink, T. D. 1999. Instructional objectives. In *Classroom teaching skills,* 6th ed., ed. J. M. Cooper. Boston: Houghton Mifflin.

Walsh, J. M. 2001. Getting the "big picture" of IEP goals and state standards. *Teaching Exceptional Children* 33 (5): 18–26.

Wiggins, G., and J. McTighe. 2005. *Understanding by design.* 2nd ed. Alexandria, VA: ASCD.

Planning How to Teach

A Framework for Diversity Responsive Teaching		
PLANNING *WHAT* TO TEACH	**PLANNING *HOW* TO TEACH**	**PLANNING THE *CONTEXT* FOR TEACHING AND LEARNING**
<u>Content</u> About diversity For a diverse world Carrier content	<u>Universal instructional interventions</u> Universal design for learning Differentiated instruction Critical teaching skills	<u>Environment</u> Physical Social Emotional
<u>Completeness</u> Thorough coverage All contributors Varied perspectives Similarities & differences	<u>Selected instructional interventions</u> Accommodations for: Acquisition of information Processing and memorizing Expressing information	<u>Universal behavioral interventions</u> Rules, routines, & social skills Critical management skills
<u>Connections</u> To student experiences Importance to students' lives Build on student ideas		<u>Selected behavioral interventions</u> ABC

Because we are moving on to Part 2, it would be a good time to review the Diversity Responsive Teaching framework that was first shown in the Introduction. It provides the "big picture" of the content and organization of this book. In Part 1, you learned about *what* to teach, that is, the content to be used for lessons and activities. You learned where to go for content ideas, how to decide what to teach, and how to best organize the content for teaching. You also learned about writing instructional objectives, which provide focus for planning what and how you will teach. Once you have made decisions about what you will teach, you are ready to move to the next planning step.

Deciding *how* to teach is what Part 2 of this book is all about. Once teachers know what they will teach, they must determine how to best teach it. Fortunately, teachers today have access to many ideas and strategies that have been proven to be effective through research. This means that even beginning and preservice teachers can develop a repertoire of many effective strategies to use when they teach. Educational journals are just one good source of effective techniques considered to be best practice. Additional sources of specific instructional ideas for use in lessons and activities include teachers' guides that accompany student texts, Internet sites that are designed for teachers, books, and workshops. A teacher's creativity can flourish in designing specific activities to include in instruction.

We will present three general categories of universal instructional interventions in this section of our book: universal design for learning, differentiated instruction, and critical teaching skills. Universal interventions are strategies, techniques, or methods that will benefit most, if not all, of the students in your class. They are built in right from the start—as part of your initial planning. We present many ideas for universal interventions in Chapters 3 through 8. Selected instructional interventions are designed for one or a few students and are accommodations or modifications that are added on. Ideas for selected interventions are presented in Chapter 9. The easiest way to meet the needs of a diverse student group is to build in many options for success in the first place to lessen the need for selected interventions.

General Approaches to Universal Instructional Interventions

Introduction

This chapter includes two approaches to universal instructional interventions. One is *universal design for learning* and the other is *differentiated instruction*. Both approaches are designed to address the diversity found in today's classroom by becoming part of up-front planning. In this chapter, we will also discuss planning for English language learners. These students have specific learning needs, many of which can be addressed through universal instructional interventions, and by strategies that are built in rather than added on later.

Universal Design for Learning

The term *universal design* was first used in the field of architecture. The concept of universal design emerged from the need to construct buildings in a way that provided access to persons with disabilities, for example, individuals who used wheelchairs. As buildings were being retrofitted with options for accessibility, it was noted that many of the modifications benefited people without disabilities. For example, ramps, which are essential for people in wheelchairs, also work well for parents pushing strollers, and are handy for people carrying things. Ron Mace developed the idea of designing buildings from the outset to be accessible to everyone (without the need for adaptation or specialized design) and named it *universal design* (Rose and Meyer 2002).

The principles of universal design were next applied to the field of education. Individuals at the Center for Applied Special Technology (CAST) were instrumental in developing educational curriculum materials that provided access to a wider audience. The idea was to build options into classroom materials so that more students would have access to the information and related activities (Rose and Meyer 2002). Orkwis and McLane explained it well when they said, "In terms of learning, universal design means the design of instructional materials and activities that allows the learning goals to be achievable by individuals with wide differences in their abilities to see, hear, speak, move, read, write, understand English, attend, organize, engage, and remember" (1998). The development of instructional technology (e.g., voice-activated programs), and the design of curricular materials (digital textbooks, for example) are examples of applications that provide built-in options to curriculum and learning activities for all students. The educators at CAST created the term *universal design for learning* to describe these and similar applications. The key idea is that necessary supports are available to provide all students opportunities to learn. Rose and Meyer (2006, xi) point out that "Good teachers make adjustments all the time to accommodate diverse learner needs. The UDL framework helps them do so more effectively."

Applications

You can use the principles of universal design in developing your lessons and activities. When you do so, you build in, rather than add on, alternatives that provide support and choice for all students in your class. For example, building video captions into a lesson may benefit everyone in a noisy classroom—not only individuals with hearing impairments or

English language learners. Using a handout with varying print sizes for a seatwork assignment can both be beneficial to a student with a visual impairment and provide a choice for other students. You can build universal design alternatives into your lesson and activity plans in several ways. Orkwis and McLane (1998) suggest incorporating multiple methods of presenting information and multiple methods of student response and engagement:

1. *Presenting Information* When presenting information in a lesson, plan to say, demonstrate, and write the information. This redundancy allows all students—including those with visual and auditory impairments, those with learning disabilities, and those learning the English language—to access and benefit from the information. When you use visual supports in your lessons or activities, provide verbal descriptions to go with them. Provide written captions for audio materials. Whenever possible, use digital text so that it can be enlarged and changed in other ways to make it more accessible. The following are examples of universal design in presenting information:

   - When teaching the steps for dividing fractions, *state the rule*, "When dividing fractions, invert the divisor and multiply." *Write the steps* on the board. *Show a diagram* of a completed problem. Then *demonstrate* by solving problems on an overhead transparency while *stating the steps again* and *pointing to them* on the diagram.

   - When conducting a lesson about the Vietnam War, the teacher *says* the information, *shows* a written outline on the overhead projector, and passes out a partially filled-out copy of his outline for the students to *write* on as they listen. The teacher also *shows* visual supports (pictures from an Internet site about the war) to illustrate key concepts.

2. *Student Responses* When asking students to express their learning, include every student by providing alternatives, such as saying or recording, writing, typing, drawing, or demonstrating the response. Word-processing programs provide students with many supports, such as grammar and spelling checks. Students who are unable to make oral presentations may create multimedia presentations. Supply computer graphics as an alternative to

hand drawing for students with physical limitations. Decide whether you will select the response type for individuals or allow students to freely choose.

EXAMPLE OF USING UNIVERSAL DESIGN

For Teaching the Identification of the Beginning, Middle, and End of a Story

Presenting Information The teacher will

- act out a simple story holding signs that identify the 3 parts: beginning, middle, and end

- tell a story and verbally label the 3 parts

- draw a story as a cartoon strip with 3 squares

- show a written story with the 3 parts highlighted in different colors

Student Responses After reading or hearing a story, students will

- tell what happened in the beginning, middle, and end

- sort pictures or sentence strips representing the beginning, middle, and end

- write what happened in the beginning, middle, and end

- write what happened in the beginning, middle, and end using a handheld talking dictionary for reading/writing support

- sort pictures or sentences, on the computer, representing the beginning, middle, and end

Student Engagement The teacher will

- use stories about the students in the class and familiar or humorous events

- provide a template/graphic organizer to be used when students are asked to write, tell, or sort

- provide word banks of important words from the stories to be used when students are asked to tell or write

- ask students to set a goal for number of practice tasks completed correctly

---

The following are suggestions for providing alternatives for student responses:

- When responding to a math fact question—"What is 4 times 3?"—allow variety in student response types, for example, writing the answer, saying the answer, or pointing to the answer on a number chart.

- At the conclusion of a series of lessons on Native American history of the 1800s, provide flexibility in how students will demonstrate their knowledge. Taking a written test or putting together a portfolio of assignments that meet unit objectives are examples.

3. *Student Engagement* Keep students engaged in learning by providing variety in supports or scaffolds. This variation will help challenge individuals appropriately. Techniques for maintaining student engagement include planning various student groupings (for example, partner groups, skill groups, peer tutoring), using a variety of lesson models, incorporating students' interests into lessons and activities, and helping students understand the value of what they are learning and how it applies to life outside of school. The following are examples for engaging students:

- Give students opportunities to follow their individual interests by providing choices, such as copying popular music lyrics to practice handwriting.

- Allow flexibility in practice activities (working independently or with peers, for example), as it can be helpful in drawing in some students.

Six Principles for Designing Instruction for Diverse Learners

Coyne et al. (2007) discuss six universal design principles that help students gain cognitive access to the curriculum. These principles were developed to guide the design of curricular materials, but many of the ideas can be applied as you develop lessons and activities. When these principles are built into lessons and activities, they provide support for students with a wide variety of learning needs. The principles are as follows:

1. *Big ideas* are the fundamental concepts and principles in an academic area that help connect or "anchor" the smaller ideas. Big ideas help

teachers decide what to teach, to select and sequence objectives, and to focus on important learning outcomes (see Chapter 1). Big ideas also help students make connections and focus on the most important ideas. Consider big ideas as you design the opening to lessons. When presenting information, summarize and emphasize key points by referring to big ideas. The following are examples of big ideas:

- The interactions of humans with their environments shape the characteristics of both people and the environment.

- People read to be informed and to be entertained.

- Writing is a process.

2. *Conspicuous strategies* are the steps for solving a problem or accomplishing a task. When you teach strategies explicitly, they become clear and usable for students. When preparing a task analysis, list the steps of the strategy. During the lesson, state, list, explain, and model the strategy by using "think-alouds." In extended practice, provide opportunities to use the strategy in varied applications. The following are examples of using conspicuous strategies:

- During a lesson on how to write a capital letter *M*, the teacher says the steps out loud: "I start by putting my pencil on the headline. I draw a line straight down to the foot line," and so on.

- After learning about how to develop and use mnemonics for memorizing information, give students chances to develop mnemonics in geography (the names of the great lakes), science (the steps in the scientific method), and other content areas.

3. *Mediated scaffolding* is the temporary support and assistance provided by the teacher, the materials, or the task during instruction. Provide varying levels of supports, and gradually withdraw them. This allows each student to be successful during instruction and eventually become independent. Mediated scaffolding can include sequencing examples and tasks from easy to more complex; moving from the whole group, to partner, to individual practice; and providing varied materials (such as note-taking guides) to help students learn.

The following are examples of using mediated scaffolding:

- In the math unit where students are learning about adding up to three digits and three digits with regrouping in the ones and tens columns, students are first taught how to regroup in the ones column and then how to regroup in both the ones and tens columns.

- During a lesson where students are learning how to summarize, the teacher provides them with opportunities to practice first as a whole group, then with a partner, and then alone.

4. *Primed background knowledge* is the recalled prerequisite skills and knowledge needed for the new task. Having the necessary background knowledge and applying it to the new task is required for success in learning. List prerequisites in the content analysis. Assess the students' prior knowledge and then remind, review, and develop background knowledge as needed. The following are examples of using recalled background knowledge:

- Suppose that a teacher intends to teach her students how to write a persuasive essay, five paragraphs in length. She plans to concentrate on the persuasive elements of the essay, so she first checks to see that her students remember the main components of a paragraph and the specifics of writing a five-paragraph essay.

- To identify examples of racial stereotyping in their social studies text and chapter books, students are first taught to define racial stereotyping and identify examples in controlled examples.

5. *Strategic integration* involves putting together essential information and skills, which leads to higher-level thinking skills. As part of your long-term planning, be sure to plan lessons and activities in combinations that will lead to integration. The following are examples of such integration:

- As a culminating activity for a unit on nutrition, students designed an informational brochure for teen parents. The brochure included the following information: specific types and amounts of nutrients that infants and toddlers need, foods that are high in particular nutrients, simple recipes that are packed with nutrients, and why nutrients are important (impact on development).

- The civics students put together events and activities designed to ease tensions between different "groups" at school. The planning of these events caused students to draw on a wide variety of concepts that were taught in their class. Some of the key ideas that were incorporated into their planning included learning about and appreciating cultural variation, anti-bullying, and ally-building. These ideas were all woven throughout a series of events that helped students accept each other.

6. *Judicious review* provides opportunities for students to review important learning. Carefully planned review will help students remember and apply what they have learned. Include review in the openings and closings of lessons and activities, and build in extended practice and activities. The following are examples of reviewing:

- After teaching a lesson on how to put a heading on a paper, the teacher follows up by reviewing the essential elements for the heading. Then he instructs his students to write headings on their papers in math, social studies, and science.

TEACHER CHECKLIST FOR

Applying the Six Principles in a Lesson or Activity

❑ Am I referring to the big idea that overlays or anchors the lesson/activity?

❑ Am I making the steps explicit for strategies/procedures I'm teaching?

❑ Am I building in scaffolds and supports for student success in the lesson/activity?

❑ Am I planning to activate or build the background knowledge that will help students learn?

❑ Am I planning for the integration of knowledge and/or skills from various lessons and activities?

❑ Am I planning for the review of important knowledge and/or skills?

- In the opening of a lesson on proper nouns, the teacher reviews what students already know about nouns in general as well as common nouns.

The teacher checklist on page 32 will guide you in applying the six principles for designing instruction for diverse learners as you develop lessons and activities.

In summary, as you design lessons and activities, ask yourself if you are building in multiple methods for presenting, keeping students engaged, and allowing for multiple means for students to respond. Also ask yourself if you are incorporating big ideas, explicit strategies, scaffolding, primed background knowledge, integration, and review in such a way that all students can achieve the objectives.

Differentiated Instruction

Differentiated instruction is another approach or philosophy of teaching with the goal that all students will learn. This type of instruction begins with the assumption that students in a class will vary in their readiness for a particular learning task, and in their personal interests and preferences. "At the most basic level, differentiating instruction means 'shaking up' what goes on in the classroom so that students have multiple options for taking in information, making sense of ideas, and expressing what they learn. In other words, a differentiated classroom provides different avenues to acquiring content, to processing or making sense of ideas, and to developing products so that each student can learn effectively" (Tomlinson 2005, 1). This approach also emphasizes the importance of teaching toward important learning outcomes (that is, crucial concepts and principles, big ideas), assessing each student's prior knowledge and progress, determining student interest, maintaining high standards, and challenging each student.

Providing Options

Differentiated instruction is possible by providing options in content, process, and product:

- *Content* is *what* is taught. Differentiating content means flexibility in choosing curriculum topics,

for example, selecting content that is personally meaningful to students (Heacox 2002) and incorporating big ideas (OSPI 2005). It also means flexibility in providing access to what we want students to learn (Tomlinson 2005). The three guiding themes in differentiating content are student readiness, student interest, and student learning preferences. This means that teachers must routinely assess what students already know and what interests students have, and they must provide multiple ways of presenting information. The following are examples of providing differentiated content:

- As part of a unit on famous non-Caucasian U.S. inventors, students are given an assignment to write a report on an inventor. They are given their choice of which inventor to write about rather than being assigned a particular one.

- When the teacher writes the story problems for math, she includes problems that address occupations of the parents of the students in her classroom. For example, if a teacher has students from dairy farms in her class, she could write problems such as, "If the average milk production of a Guernsey cow is about 5 gallons a day, how many gallons of milk will be produced in a week on a farm where 86 cows are milked each day?" She writes different problems for students who come from logging families. It is hoped these types of problems will grab student interest.

- *Process* means sense-making or, just as it sounds, an opportunity for learners to process the content or ideas and skills to which they have been introduced (Tomlinson 2005, 79). Flexible groupings, cooperative learning activities, and hands-on activities are all examples of techniques that teachers can use to provide options for processing the information that has come to students. The following are specific examples:

- Some students construct models of the heart to increase their understanding of heart anatomy. Others read about and examine diagrams of heart anatomy. Some students orally explain heart anatomy to a peer.

- Students explore the concept of fractions and work with fraction manipulatives individually, in pairs, or in heterogeneous groups.

- *Product* means the end result of learning, that is, what students will do to show you that they know. A key idea here is that students are given options when it comes to demonstrating what they know. Models, presentations, portfolios, tests, and demonstrations are all examples of products. The following are specific examples:
  - When students are learning about the impact of the stock market crash in 1929, they are given the choice to do an oral presentation with charts, a written report, or a PowerPoint presentation.
  - To test students' knowledge of term definitions in science, students are given the choice to say the answers into a tape recorder or write them on the test booklet.

When a teacher uses differentiated instruction, she uses flexibility in her teaching. Teachers can use differentiation in various subject areas, units, or tasks for individuals or small groups by varying materials, pacing, activities, grouping, scaffolding, products, and so on (Tomlinson 1999; Pettig 2000). These choices and options increase the probability that all students will learn.

Similarities between Universal Design and Differentiated Instruction

You have undoubtedly noticed that the concepts of universal design for learning and differentiated instruction have numerous elements in common. The idea behind both philosophies is the same: students in classrooms are all different, and therefore, a single approach to teaching and learning is neither appropriate nor effective. Neither approach is the same as individualized instruction, but both approaches are meant to make learning possible for all students. Their relevance to diversity responsive teaching is obvious.

The concepts of universal design and differentiated instruction have their roots in two different areas of education. Universal design was originally thought of as something specific to special education, because it began as a way to provide access in the physical environment for persons with disabilities. When these principles were applied to curriculum, it was clear that many students could profit from specific universal design strategies. "The

attention of general education has been captured by a compatible philosophy known as differentiated instruction," writes Edyburn (2004, 2). It is apparent that although these philosophies started in different areas of education, there is a great deal of overlap. The Council for Exceptional Children, for example, refers to differentiated instruction as one of a number of effective instructional practices that help make universal design work (CEC 2005). The following, adapted from Hall, Strangman, and Meyer (2003), illustrates how the main elements of one approach line up with the main elements of the other.

Universal Design for Learning	Differentiated Instruction
Flexible Means of Presentation	Content
Flexible Means of Student Engagement	Process
Flexible Methods of Student Responses	Product

Both approaches provide for built-in options and flexibility with the intent that students will be successful. Obviously, as teachers plan how to incorporate these ideas into their classrooms, they are thinking about their specific students and what they know about them. The difference between these general approaches and selected interventions is that these options are almost always built in for all students, whereas selected interventions are often added on for one or a few students. Universal design and differentiated instruction are complementary approaches and both emphasize options. Providing choices for students has a positive impact on student learning (Jolivette, Stichter, and McCormick 2002).

Planning for English Language Learners

We will discuss English language learners in various places throughout this book, but we talk about them here in more detail because of the complexity and importance of this topic. First, we know that these students encounter special challenges in the typical classroom that most other students do not. They are expected to learn content (like other students) but are trying to learn it in a language they do not know well (unlike other students), and they do this with varying amounts of success. They often have difficulty in school when program design, instructional goals, and student needs are mismatched (Echevarria, Vogt, and Short 2008).

Second, many teachers have English language learners in their classrooms, and the numbers of such students are increasing; for example, the number increased 84 percent between 1992 and 2003 (NCELA 2005/06). Traditionally, these students received instruction from specially trained teachers outside of the main classroom. Echevarria, Vogt, and Short (2008) write that increasing numbers of students and a shortage of qualified English as a Second Language (ESL) and bilingual teachers have quickly extended the need to teach content to these students outside of the ESL classroom. This means that general and special education teachers both have an opportunity to greatly impact the success of English language learners. Obviously, the numbers of students and the challenges they have in school makes meeting their needs a high priority for all teachers.

Finally, teachers can impact the success of these students often without much additional planning. You might think that when working with English language learners, you would need to add on numerous selected interventions because of the specialized needs of these students. Interestingly, many strategies and techniques that are used to address general diversity in a classroom are also very effective for students who are learning English. In other words, many of the instructional strategies and techniques that you will learn in Part 2 of this book will apply to English language learners as well. We talk about these students here because we want you to be thinking about them as you peruse the ideas in the chapters that follow.

Stages of Language Acquisition

Although you may not need to become an expert on second language acquisition, it is helpful to have a basic understanding of the stages students go through as they learn English. To begin with, teachers need to understand the distinction between social language proficiency and academic language proficiency. Jim Cummins (1986) called these *basic interpersonal communication skills* (BICS) and

cognitive academic language proficiency (CALP). A student may communicate quite well in social situations, such as chatting with peers at lunch. The same student may need extensive language support during academic instruction. Don't be fooled by oral fluency in conversational English. Cummins (1986) suggests that academic language proficiency may take 5 to 7 years to acquire. A teacher should also understand that the process of acquiring a second language spans predictable and sequential stages. These stages of language development begin with no knowledge of English and end with a command of English much like a native speaker (Reed and Railsback 2003). Planning various types of classroom events, such as questions, is most effective when matched to the students' levels of language development. The following explanations, adapted from Reed and Railsback (2003) and Herrell and Jordan (2008), summarize the stages of language acquisition:

- *Preproduction Stage*   Students in this stage understand more words than they can speak or feel comfortable speaking. Sometimes, students respond through techniques such as gestures, pointing, or nodding. This stage can last anywhere from hours to months, and teachers need to be careful to wait until students are ready to speak, rather than forcing them. These students can understand somewhere around 500 words.

- *Early Production Stage*   During this stage, which can last 6 months or so, the English language learner acquires a receptive vocabulary close to 1,000 words. Answering in one- or two-word phrases is common at this stage, and students can often provide short answers to questions such as those beginning with *who, what,* and *where*.

- *Speech Emergence Stage*   When in the speech emergence stage, students develop a vocabulary of around 3,000 words. They can use short phrases and simple sentences and can also ask simple questions. This stage lasts about a year.

- *Intermediate/Advanced Language Proficiency Stage*   This stage can take up to a year to go through, but it is one of great growth. Those in this stage have vocabularies that grow to about 6,000 words. They are able to speak in much longer sentences and can, for example, make complex statements and express opinions. It may take between 5 and 7 years for students to become academic language proficient. At this time, they know specialized content vocabulary and can actively participate in classroom and school activities. These students may need support at times, but when advanced proficiency is obtained, they are quite independent.

Throughout this section and in other parts of this book, we will focus on providing you with strategies and ideas to include in lessons or activities with the primary objective of content learning rather than learning English. Note, however, that strategies sometimes serve a dual purpose—they help with content knowledge and with learning English. A good place to start when thinking about language acquisition is to recognize whether a student's academic language proficiency may need support, even if the student's social or conversational English is quite fluent.

In the section that follows, two general areas can give direction when planning. The first is what you can do to help students understand what you say or present. The second is what you can do to provide opportunities for language use. (Many of these ideas are adapted from Gersten, Baker, and Marks 1998; Flores 2008.) These two categories of strategies are especially applicable when planning activities and lessons.

Make What You Present Understandable

Many authors call this "comprehensible input." *Comprehensible input* means that students are able to understand the sense or substance of what teachers present, although they may not necessarily understand every word. The following strategies will help make what you present understandable:

1. *Teach vocabulary.*   Selecting and defining key terms and vocabulary is an important part of content analysis (see Chapters 1 and 5). When teaching English language learners, it is absolutely essential to consider the following suggestions:

   - Select a small number of words to introduce at a time. Gersten and Baker (2000) suggest seven or fewer.
   - Select important and useful words.
   - Pre-teach the vocabulary words at the beginning of lessons or activities, or before reading.
   - Present the words in context.

   - Directly teach the words and meanings by saying them, writing them, and using visual supports and active participation strategies.
   - Help the students connect the words with prior knowledge and personal experience through discussions and semantic webs.
   - Provide various practice opportunities, such as acting out meanings, creating word banks, writing journal entries, or defining with partners.

2. *Use visual supports.*   Visual supports are a very important method of scaffolding to help English language learners understand vocabulary, concepts, principles, and procedures. The four types of visual supports described in Chapter 5 are helpful in various ways during instruction. For example, real objects, models, and pictures are very helpful in teaching vocabulary. Demonstrations and role-plays make directions and procedures much more understandable. Writings are helpful for reinforcing verbal information in many parts of activities or lessons. Finally, graphic organizers can improve comprehension, clarify abstractions, organize concepts, or demonstrate connections.

3. *Provide context and activate background knowledge.*   New information is more easily understood when teachers present it in a context rather than as stand-alone material. At the beginning of a lesson, use the following methods to build background knowledge and provide a context:

   - Provide a familiar example (introduce fractions by saying, "Three friends ordered a pizza and they want to share it . . .").
   - Ask questions (introduce a history unit on migrations by asking, "How many of you have moved to a new place? What did you take? How did you get there?").
   - Use group or individual brainstorming for creating webs or maps of what students already know about a topic.
   - Have the class, small groups, or individuals complete "KWL" charts (what I already **K**now about a topic, what I **W**ant to learn, and, later, what I did **L**earn).
   - Connect an introduction of new concepts with the students' native languages.

- Build background knowledge for the students by providing experiences, such as brief activities at the beginning of lessons ("I'm going to give one cookie to each group of three, and you need to share it fairly . . ."); activities that come before lessons (an activity involving experimenting with magnets before a lesson on how magnets work); or field trips, guest speakers, multimedia presentations, or stories that are relevant to the new learning.

- Provide a context as you present by gesturing and demonstrating, showing examples of completed products, using graphic organizers, thinking aloud, or showing objects, pictures, videos, or audio recordings (see Chapter 5).

4. *Use consistent language.* Decide on the important words and phrases to be used in a lesson or activity, teach them, and then use those terms consistently. Avoid using synonyms at random. Name the steps consistently when teaching procedures and strategies. Remember that idioms, metaphors, and other figures of speech can be difficult to understand. Use them carefully and check for understanding frequently.

5. *Give explanations or directions in a variety of ways.* As you speak, use gestures and demonstrations; put information in writing; be explicit and explain step by step; give many examples; use "think-alouds"; show completed products; and check for understanding (see Chapters 5 and 7).

Provide Opportunities for Language Use

In addition to providing comprehensible input, teachers need to help students process that input, and express and practice that learning. Gersten and Baker argue "that both extended discourse about academic topics and briefer responses to specific questions about content are cornerstones of academic growth for English-language learners" (2000, 465). The following are some strategies for providing opportunities for language use in lessons and activities:

1. *Use active participation strategies.* These strategies (discussed extensively in Chapter 6) are designed to keep all students actively engaged in learning. Ask students to actively respond during lessons by talking, writing, or signaling rather than passively listening. As you select

those strategies likely to be most valuable for English language learners, look for strategies that require oral responses from students; provide opportunities for long, complex responses, as well as brief, one- or two-word responses; encourage discussions with peers (Think-Pair-Share, for example); and create nonthreatening opportunities to respond (unison responses).

2. *Use partner and small-group work.* Having students work with partners or in small groups during lessons and activities provides many opportunities for language use. (Formal peer tutoring and cooperative learning programs are highly recommended as well.) Peers act as language models and can provide feedback. Their support can create a safe environment for using language. Chances to discuss new concepts or solve problems with other students, including those who speak the same native language, can be very beneficial. Teachers need to carefully structure and monitor partner and small-group work to be most effective (see Chapter 8 for more on this approach).

You can have a very positive influence on helping English language learners in your classroom learn, even if you are not an expert in second language acquisition. You can begin by carefully analyzing the progress of your English language learners in both content and language acquisition, and planning accordingly. Gersten and Baker point out that "Effective instruction for English-language learners is more than just 'good teaching.' It is teaching that is tempered, tuned, and otherwise adjusted, as a musical score is adjusted, to the correct 'pitch' at which English-language learners will best 'hear' the content (i.e., find it most meaningful)" (2000, 461). This idea implies the importance of trying out techniques and strategies and monitoring their effectiveness (see Chapter 7).

Summary

The students you work with will be successful in varying degrees with a variety of instructional methods and activities. The suggestions presented in this chapter that are designed to help students be successful are only a beginning assortment of ideas.

It is important to continue to add to your repertoire of ideas. When you plan, incorporate the principles of universal design for learning and ideas about differentiated instruction. By applying these principles in your classroom, you will increase the chances that all of your students will learn.

References and Suggested Reading for Universal Design and Differentiated Instruction

Acrey, C., C. Johnstone, and C. Milligan. 2005. Using universal design to unlock the potential for academic achievement of at-risk learners. *Teaching Exceptional Children* 38:22–31.

Baca, L., and H. Cervantes. 2004. *The bilingual special education interface.* 4th ed. Upper Saddle River, NJ: Pearson Education, Inc.

The Center for Universal Design. http://www.design.ncsu.edu/cud/index.html.

Center for Applied Special Technology (CAST). http://lessonbuilder.cast.org.

CAST. 2007. Summary of 2007 national summit on universal design for learning working groups. Wakefield, MA: Author.

Cawley, J., T. Foley, and J. Miller. 2003. Science and students with mild disabilities: Principles of universal design. *Intervention in School and Clinic* 38 (3): 160–171.

Connor, D., and C. Lagares. 2007. Facing high stakes in high school: 25 successful strategies from an inclusive social studies classroom. *Teaching Exceptional Children* 40 (2): 18–27.

Coyne, M. D., E. J. Kame'enui, and D. W. Carnine. 2007. *Effective teaching strategies that accommodate diverse learners.* 3rd ed. Columbus, OH: Merrill.

Council for Exceptional Children (CEC). 2005. *Universal design for learning: A guide for teachers and education professionals,* ed. and rev. J. Castellani. Upper Saddle River, NJ: Merrill Prentice Hall.

Conroy, M. A., K. S. Sutherland, A. L. Snyder, and S. Marsh. 2008. Classwide interventions: Effective instruction makes a difference. *Teaching Exceptional Children* 40 (6): 24–30.

Edyburn, D. 2004. Research & practice associate editor column. *JSET E Journal* 19 (2). http://www.cast.org/teachingeverystudent/ideas/tes/chapter1_4.cfm.

Fahsl, A. 2007. Mathematics accommodations for all students. *Intervention in School and Clinic* 42 (4): 198–203.

Flores, M. M. 2008. Universal design in elementary and middle school: Designing classrooms and instructional practices to ensure access to learning for all students. *Childhood Education* 84 (4): 224–229.

Hall, T., N. Strangman, and A. Meyer. 2003. *Differentiated instruction and implications for UDL implementation.* Wakefield, MA: National Center on Accessing the General Curriculum. http://www/cast.org/publications/ncac/ncac_diffinstructudl.html.

Heacox, D. 2002. *Differentiating instruction in the regular classroom: How to reach and teach all learners, grades 3–12.* Minneapolis, MN: FreeSpirit Publishing.

Hitchcock, C., A. Meyer, D. Rose, and R. Jackson. 2002. Providing new access to the general curriculum: Universal design for learning. *Teaching Exceptional Children* 35 (2): 8–17.

Howard, J. B. 2003. Universal design for learning: An essential concept for teacher education. *Journal of Computing in Teacher Education* 19 (4): 113–118.

Jolivette, K., J. P. Stichter, and K. M. McCormick. 2002. Making choices—improving behavior—engaging in learning. *Teaching Exceptional Children* 34 (3): 24–29.

Kame'enui, E. J., D. W. Carnine, R. C. Dixon, D. C. Simmons, and M. D. Coyne. 2002. *Effective teaching strategies that accommodate diverse learners.* 2nd ed. Upper Saddle River, NJ: Prentice-Hall.

Kingsley, K. 2007. 20 ways to empower diverse learners with educational technology and digital media. *Intervention in School and Clinic* 43 (1): 52–56.

Kortering, L. J. 2008. Universal design for learning: A look at what algebra and biology students with and without high incidence conditions are saying. *Remedial and Special Education* 29 (6): 352–363.

Kurtts, S. 2009. (Dis)Solving the differences: A physical science lesson using universal design. *Intervention in School and Clinic* 44 (3): 151–159.

McGuire, J., S. Scott, and S. Shaw. 2006. Universal design and its applications in educational environments. *Remedial and Special Education* 27: 166–175.

Meo, G. 2008. Curriculum planning for all learners: Applying universal design for learning (UDL) to a high school reading comprehension program. *Preventing School Failure* 52 (1): 21–30.

Mercier-Smith, J. L., H. Fien, D. Basaraba, and P. Travers. 2009. Planning, evaluating and improving tiers of support in beginning reading. *Teaching Exceptional Children* 41 (5): 16–22.

Orkwis, R., and K. McLane. 1998. A curriculum every student can use: Design principles for student access. *ERIC/OSEP Topical Brief.* Reston, VA: Council for Exceptional Children.

Washington Office of Superintendent of Public Instruction (OSPI). 2005. Grade Level Expectations Guidance Task Force. *Connecting systems: A standards-referenced approach to accessing the curriculum for each student.* Olympia, WA: Office of Superintendent of Public Instruction.

Painter, D. D. 2009. Providing differentiated learning experiences through multigenre projects. *Intervention in School and Clinic* 44 (5): 288–293.

Pettig, K. L. 2000. On the road to differentiated practice. *Educational Leadership* 58 (1): 14–18.

Rock, M. L., M. Gregg, E. Ellis, and R. A. Gable. 2008. REACH: A framework for differentiating classroom instruction. *Preventing School Failure* 52 (2): 31–47.

Rose, D. H., and A. Meyer. 2002. Education in the digital age. In *Teaching every student in the digital age: Universal design for learning.* Baltimore, MD: Association for Supervision & Curriculum Development. http://www.cast.org/teachingeverystudent/ideas/tes/chapter1_4.cfm.

Rose, D., and G. Rappolt-Schlichtmann (in press). Applying universal design for learning with children living in poverty. In *Educating the other America: Top experts tackle poverty, literacy and achievement in our schools*, ed. S. B. Newman. Baltimore, MD: Paul H. Brookes Publishing.

Rose, D. H., and A. Meyer (eds.). 2006. *A practical reader in universal design for learning.* Cambridge, MA: Harvard Education Press.

Salend, S. 2009. Using technology to create and administer accessible tests. *Teaching Exceptional Children* 41 (3): 40–51.

Santamaria, L. 2009. Culturally responsive differentiated instruction: Narrowing gaps between best pedagogical practices benefiting all learners. *Teachers College Record* 3 (1): 214–247.

Tomlinson, C. A. 1999. *The differentiated classroom: Responding to the needs of all learners.* Alexandria, VA: ASCD.

Tomlinson, C. A. 2005. *How to differentiate instruction in mixed-ability classrooms.* 2nd ed. Upper Saddle River, NJ: Merrill Prentice Hall.

Tomlinson, C. S., and J. McTighe. 2006. *Integrating differentiated instruction and understanding by design.* Alexandria, VA: ASCD.

Van Garderen, D., and C. Whittaker. 2006. Planning differentiated multicultural instruction for secondary inclusive classrooms. *Teaching Exceptional Children* 38 (3): 12–20.

Watson, S., and L. Houtz. 2002. Teaching science: Meeting the academic needs of culturally and linguistically diverse students. *Intervention in School and Clinic* 37 (5): 267–278.

Zascavage, V., and K. Winterman. 2009. What middle school educators should know about assistive technology and universal design for learning. *Middle School Journal* 40 (4): 46–52.

References and Suggested Reading for Linguistic Diversity

August, D., M. Carlo, C. Dressler, and C. Snow. 2005. Critical role of vocabulary development for English language learners. *Learning Disabilities Research and Practice* 20 (1): 50–57.

Brown, C. L. 2007. Supporting English language learners in content-reading. *Reading Improvement* 44 (1): 32–39.

Brown, J. E. 2008. A cultural, linguistic, and ecological framework for response to intervention with English language learners. *Teaching Exceptional Children* 40 (5): 66–72.

Chamot, A. U., and J. M. O'Malley. 1994. *The CALLA handbook: Implementing the cognitive academic language learning approach.* Reading, MA: Longman.

Cummins, J. 1986. Empowering minority students: A framework for intervention. *Harvard Educational Review* 56 (1): 18–36.

Echevarria, J., M. Vogt, and D. J. Short. 2008. *Making content comprehensible for English learners: The SIOP model.* 3rd ed. Boston: Pearson.

Edmonds, L. M. 2009. Challenges and solutions for ELLs. *The Science Teacher* 76 (3): 30–33.

Fernandez, C. Reexamining the role of explicit information in processing instruction. *Studies in Second Language Acquisition* 30 (3): 277–305.

Gersten, R., and S. Baker. 2000. What we know about effective instructional practices for English language learners. *Exceptional Children* 66 (4): 454–470.

Gersten, R., S. K. Baker, and S. U. Marks. 1998. *Teaching English-language learners with learning difficulties.* Reston, VA: Council for Exceptional Children.

Herrell, A., and M. Jordan. 2008. *Fifty strategies for teaching English-language learners.* 3rd ed. Upper Saddle River, NJ: Prentice-Hall. (See Section IV in particular.)

Herrell, A. L., and M. Jordan. 2005. *Fifty strategies for improving vocabulary, comprehension, and fluency.* 2nd ed. Upper Saddle River, NJ: Prentice-Hall.

Law, B., and Eckes, M. 2000. *The more-than-just-surviving handbook: ESL for every classroom teacher.* 2nd ed. Winnipeg, Manitoba, Canada: Portage & Main Press.

Linan-Thompson, S. 2009. Response to intervention and English-language learners: Instructional and assessment considerations. *Seminars in Speech & Language* 30 (2): 105–120.

National Clearinghouse for English Language Acquisition. 1995/96–2005/06. The growing numbers of limited English proficient students. http://www.ncela.gwu.edu/policy/states/reports/statedata/2005LEP/GrowingLEP_0506.pdf.

Pawan, F. 2008. Content-area teachers and scaffolded instruction for English language learners. *Teaching and Teacher Education* 24 (6): 1450–1462.

Pollard-Durodala, S. D. 2009. The role of explicit instruction and instructional design in promoting phonemic awareness development and transfer from Spanish to English. *Reading & Writing Quarterly* 25 (2/3): 139–161.

Reed, B., and J. Railsback. 2003. *Strategies and resources for teachers of English language learners.* Portland, OR: NW Regional Educational Lab.

Reiss, J. 2008. *102 content strategies for English language learners: Teaching for academic success in grades 3–12.* Boston: Allyn & Bacon.

Swanson, W., and D. Howerton. 2007. 20 ways to influence vocabulary acquisition for English language learners. *Intervention in School and Clinic* 42 (5): 290–294.

Vogt, M. J., and J. Echevarria. 2008. *99 ideas and activities for teaching English learners with the SIOP model.* Boston: Allyn & Bacon.

Critical Teaching Skills for Focusing Attention

Introduction

One of the biggest challenges that teachers encounter is keeping students involved, interested, and learning. Many effective teaching practices can be incorporated into your plans to help you meet this challenge. The critical teaching skills presented in this chapter are designed to help teachers focus the attention of their students on the important elements of any lesson or activity. Effective questioning skills and strong openings and closings are all techniques that teachers can use to help keep students focused and engaged during instruction.

Read about Mrs. Roebuck and see what she is planning for a writing lesson for her class. Then, as you read through this chapter, think about the strategies for openings, questions, and closings that Mrs. Roebuck could select to use in her lesson. You may imagine that Mrs. Roebuck is teaching any grade level.

A Look at Mrs. Roebuck's Planning

Mrs. Roebuck is planning a lesson on how to write a report. Writing for different purposes is an overriding theme of all of Mrs. Roebuck's writing lessons and activities. Report writing fits well into this theme. Students have just completed projects on writing biographies and compare/contrast essays. After the current lesson, they will switch to a unit on fictional narrative (story-writing). She selected report writing at this particular time because it fits nicely with the science unit she is teaching about endangered species. She plans to have students write reports about various endangered animals. Mrs. Roebuck's objective for the current lesson, which she anticipates will take several days, is that "students will write a report that includes a thesis statement, an introduction, a body with main points and detailed subpoints, and a conclusion." She plans to begin by teaching the various parts of the report, followed by having students practice the various parts. Finally, they will put the parts together in an original report on an endangered animal.

Openings

A lesson or activity opening is the component in which the actual lesson or activity begins and is designed to help students focus attention and make connections. The most important function of openings is to help prepare the students for learning. Openings can include specific strategies designed to motivate and focus students, and strategies that help students see the relationship between the new knowledge or skill and other learning. Generally, openings include both kinds of strategies.

Strategies for Openings

You can select ideas for openings from the following two categories.

1. *Strategies to motivate or focus the students*:
   a. Tell and show the objective (write the lesson objective on the board); describe the

evaluation (Mr. DePeralta tells students that they will write two complete sentences in which adverbs are included and used correctly at the end of the lesson).

b. Tell students the purpose, rationale, importance, and application of the lesson or activity objective (for instance, Mrs. Burns explains that the current math lesson will help them double-check the change they receive after a purchase).

c. Use an attention-getting "set" that relates directly to the lesson to capture student interest, such as jokes, stories, riddles, songs, poems, demonstrations, video clips, and so on (Ms. Lobland sings the rounding rap).

d. Preview the sequence of activities in the lesson (Ms. Smit tells students they will read and take notes from their texts and then work in cooperative groups to construct a study guide for their upcoming test).

e. Provide a key idea or generalization as an advance organizer (prior to providing information about specific foods or food groups, Mrs. Whitener explains that all foods fit into five basic food groups and that each group is a primary source of specific nutrients).

f. Preview lesson content through a graphic organizer (Mrs. Metz shows students a concept map of the parts of a paragraph).

g. Provide initial examples that are humorous or personalized (Mrs. Parcher includes the names and interests of students in the classroom in initial story problem examples).

2. *Strategies to help students see relationships between the new knowledge or skill and other learning:*

a. Connect the learning to personal experience and prior knowledge (Mrs. VanSlyke has students brainstorm examples of rhyming words as a way of beginning a lesson on poetry).

b. Build background knowledge (Mrs. Olson shows a video clip of the Grand Canyon before reading a story set there).

c. Activate background knowledge by connecting to earlier lessons or activities (Mrs. Waschke conducts a quick review of regrouping in the ones column prior to teaching regrouping in the tens column).

d. Create a context for learning (Mrs. Petersen provides one set of materials for two students to open a lesson on sharing).

e. Preview upcoming lessons or activities (Ms. Hanna explains that the vocabulary words the students will learn in the current lesson will help them understand the story they will read tomorrow).

f. Show students an outline of the whole unit (for example, Ms. Hendricks shows the table of contents that will be used for the packet of information they will assemble during the respiratory system unit).

g. State the relationship of the objective to a long-term goal (Mrs. Midboe explains how learning conversational skills will help students gain and maintain friendships).

h. Connect to other subject areas (Mr. Kaemingk explains that students will write a letter to a local city council member as part of the social studies lesson, using the same format learned in language arts).

i. Present a graphic organizer (Mr. Taubenheim shows a concept map for the unit on test-taking skills, highlighting multiple choice tests, the topic of the current lesson).

State the Objective and Objective Purpose

One of the most effective strategies to use in the opening of a lesson or activity is to tell students directly what they will learn and why. Generally, students respond more positively when they understand what is expected of them and why the learning is valuable.

When students are told directly what they will be expected to know or to do by the end of the lesson, the teacher is *stating the objective*. For example, "You are going to know the difference between reptiles and amphibians," or "At the end of the lesson, I will ask you to circle the amphibians from a list of animals." One way to illustrate the meaning of the objective is to show the students a target with the objective written on it. Explain that during the lesson, they will learn the information needed to hit the bulls-eye (Parker 2009). Make the statement of objective using words that are appropriate to the age and grade level of the students. It is often appropriate to show the students the objective in writing and have them write it in their notes.

The *objective purpose* is what teachers tell students about the value or rationale of the lesson. State the objective purpose in student terms and let them know why the knowledge or skill they are learning is important to them, that is, how it will help them in their daily lives or in school. Be sure to give specific,

---

Mrs. Roebuck Plans Her Opening

Strategies Selected:
State Objective—Say, "Today, you are going to learn how to write a report." (Objective is written on a poster that Mrs. Roebuck will display.)

Objective Purpose—Say, "One reason that it is important to know how to write reports is because they provide a way to educate others. You have all read reports in order to gather facts about various topics that we have studied. For instance, during our nutrition unit, you read reports about various nutrients and how they provide nourishment for our bodies. The reports that we will write will be used to inform others about endangered species, a topic that we have been studying in science. One way that we can help these animals is by teaching others about them and the kind of habitat they need in order to survive. Your reports will be compiled into a book that will be put into our school library for others to read. Once you know how to write a report, you can write about any topic as a way of informing others."

Reasoning—Mrs. Roebuck has included strategies meant to clearly tell her students about what they will learn and why it is important to learn it. She uses specific examples of the objective purpose because she knows that her students are more likely to engage willingly if they know why they are learning something.

Mrs. Roebuck could have included other strategies to motivate and focus her students or to help them make connections with what they already know. What strategies would you recommend to help make her lesson opening effective?

---

relevant examples when explaining the objective purpose. For example, saying, "It'll help you when you are taking math in high school" isn't as helpful to a group of third graders as saying, "When you know how to count change, you can easily check and make sure that the change you get back from a store clerk is correct" or "Today's lesson will give you the information you need to know about what to do if ever you receive an e-mail that contains inappropriate content." Remember Mrs. Roebuck's lesson on how to write a report? See the box called "Mrs. Roebuck Plans Her Opening" for some of her ideas for opening that lesson.

Responding to Diversity When Planning the Opening

Openings may be simple or highly elaborate. When deciding what to include or exclude in the opening, consider (1) variables such as student background, experience, and prior knowledge of the content; (2) prerequisite skills or knowledge; (3) the abstractness or concreteness of the content; (4) whether this is the first lesson or activity in a series; (5) probable student interest and motivation; and (6) the amount of time available for teaching.

The following suggestions will help you plan an opening intended to engage *all* students:

- Add drama, humor, novelty, or excitement to gain attention (for example, use skits, puppets, music, video clips, jokes, riddles, or demonstrations).

- Personalize by using the students' names and experiences. For example, open a writing lesson with a sentence, or a math lesson with a word problem, about the students ("If Mrs. Donahue's champion third graders win 16 games of four square . . .").

- Involve those students who are the most difficult to motivate or focus (for example, use these students as helpers in the opening demonstration).

- Increase time spent on the review of earlier lessons or prerequisite skills and knowledge. Carefully plan ongoing daily, weekly, and monthly reviews of important content.

- Involve everyone in active responses (for example, have all students write the definition of a term from yesterday's lesson rather than asking, "Who remembers what *ratio* means?").

- Invite students to write or say everything they already know about a topic in 3 minutes (for example, "I'm going to give you 3 minutes to write everything you remember about cyber-bullying. Ready, go.")

- Carefully consider each student's background knowledge. Don't make assumptions. Students from cultural backgrounds different from yours will bring different knowledge and experience to a topic.

- Computer software is available that can help develop graphic organizers to show students connections in learning or to preview lessons.

The opening of a lesson or activity serves a very important role. It can be used to help students make connections between what they already know and what is to come. You can also use openings to develop knowledge and experience or to pique interest in the information that you will present. Openings don't always need to be elaborate, but they should be designed with the needs of your students in mind. A well-planned opening sets the stage for the learning that follows.

Questions

The hundreds of questions the typical American teacher asks on a typical day (Gall 1984), and the various reasons for asking them, speaks to their value. Carefully planned questions focus students' attention on the key ideas of the content that is being presented. Questions play an important role in all lessons and activities.

Sometimes, questions play a major role in lessons. In this case, they are the key instructional component of a lesson or activity. Orlich et al. suggest that "next to lecturing and small-group work, the single most common teaching method employed in American schools (and, for that matter, around the world) may well be the asking of questions" (2004, 240). Inquiry lessons, for example, depend heavily on asking questions to facilitate learning, as do discussion lessons.

Sometimes, questions play a supporting role. None of the models we present in this book, for example, use questions as the major teaching

strategy. Instead, questions support instruction in two ways. First, teachers use questions to provide review, rehearsal, and enrichment of the information being presented (for example, "What might have been another way to solve this problem?"). Second, teachers use questions to monitor students' understanding of the information being presented (for example, "What is the second step of the editing process?"). The questions used in the sample lesson and activity plans included in this book are all questions that play a supporting role.

The following teacher checklist includes a summary of key planning elements for teachers to consider when they plan questions to be included in lessons or activities. More detail about each key idea will be presented throughout this section.

TEACHER CHECKLIST FOR

Asking Questions

❑ Am I planning questions that are clear and specific?

❑ Am I planning prompts, probes, and redirects to facilitate correct student responses?

❑ Am I planning for adequate wait-time?

❑ Am I planning a variety of question types, e.g., convergent, divergent, high-level, low-level?

❑ Am I planning questions to check for understanding of student content learning?

❑ Am I planning to tailor question wording and difficulty to meet individual needs of my students?

❑ Am I planning different types of question response strategies (written, oral, physical)?

❑ Am I planning response strategies to address individual student needs?

Types of Questions

We can think of questions according to their purposes and also according to the type of response they require. The following four types of questions each elicit a specific type of response from students. Each type of question requires a different type of information-processing to answer it. Knowing when and why to use each of the question types will help you construct questions that fit your purpose.

Convergent and Divergent Questions

Teachers use *convergent questions* when looking for one correct answer ("What color is the circle?"). Convergent questions, for the most part, elicit short responses from students and focus on the lower levels of thinking, that is, basic knowing and understanding (Orlich et al. 2010).

EXAMPLES OF CONVERGENT QUESTIONS

- What is the name of the NFL team head-quartered in Seattle?

- Where is the Amazon River located?

- Who is the hero in this story?

Questions that prompt convergent responses often begin with the following types of stems: *who, what, when, where, list as many as you can think of,* and *how many.* Convergent questions can be especially effective during recitations commonly used in teacher-led lessons. They promote active participation by providing students with an opportunity to rehearse and review information, and provide teachers a way to check for student understanding.

Teachers use *divergent questions* when they wish to evoke a wide range of student responses. See the box "Examples of Divergent Questions." This

---

EXAMPLES OF DIVERGENT QUESTIONS

- How would the world be different if the only color was gray?

- What would be another logical ending for this story?

- You have been given the power to stop racism. What would you do first? Why?

- Which political leader would likely be most successful in equalizing job opportunities for all U.S. citizens?

---

type of question also typically elicits longer student responses (Mastropieri and Scruggs 2007). Divergent questions can help promote higher-level thinking and problem-solving skills. They can be especially useful when you want students to consider issues in depth, such as during an extended practice discussion activity used to enrich informal presentations. Because this question type elicits numerous correct answers, its use can be appealing.

Question stems that will likely encourage divergent responses include the following: *What could happen if . . . ?, How many ways . . . ?,* or *How else might this have happened?* Note that the divergent question has no single right answer, but it can have wrong answers. Borich states that "this is perhaps the most misunderstood aspect of a divergent question. Not just any answer will be correct, even in the case of divergent questions raised for the purpose of allowing students to express their feelings. If Johnny is asked what he liked about *Of Mice and Men* and says 'Nothing,' or 'The happy ending,' then either Johnny has not read the book or he needs help in better understanding the events that took place. A passive or accepting response on the teacher's part to answers like these is inappropriate, regardless of the intent to allow an open response" (2004, 240).

High-Level and Low-Level Questions—Bloom's Taxonomy Revisited

Bloom's taxonomy was discussed in the chapter on objectives (Chapter 2) because teachers can use it to help vary the degree of complexity of learning tasks as they plan their objectives. We discuss it again in this chapter because it can also be a useful guide when writing questions. The taxonomy provides a way for teachers to write questions that prompt students to think about content in various ways. Providing a variety of questions to use in any given lesson or activity is one way to address various learning needs of a diverse group of students. This section shows how Bloom's taxonomy applies to planning questions. We present and define each level of the taxonomy with examples of question stems and questions (as adapted from Sadker, Sadker, and Zittleman 2010; Kauchak and Eggen 2007). As in the chapter on objectives, the original level labels and the revised labels (in parentheses) will be used.

A *low-level question* is one that is usually convergent in form and involves repetition or restatement of previously covered information. It is often used in basic skills instruction, or in early stages of learning (Mastropieri and Scruggs 2007). These questions are important building blocks leading to higher-level or divergent questions. It is unlikely that a student can analyze or evaluate information without an understanding of basic facts and information. The first two (or three) levels of Bloom's taxonomy provide a good resource for developing lower-level questions. The following are examples of question stems and sample questions that use Bloom's taxonomy to help design low-level questions and learning tasks:

Knowledge (*Remembering*): Questions at the knowledge level prompt factual recall of information.

Question stem examples: who, what, when, where, name, list, define, identify

Sample questions and tasks:

- Define *punctuation*.

- What is a mutual fund?

- When was the *Brown v. the Board of Education of Topeka* case tried in court?

Comprehension (*Understanding*): Questions at the comprehension level go beyond factual recall and are designed to help determine whether students understand the meaning of the content presented.

Question stems examples: explain in your own words, restate, describe, interpret

Sample questions and tasks:

- Give additional examples of punctuation.

- What are the key features of a traditional individual retirement account (IRA)?

- Explain the ruling of the *Brown* case—"separate is not equal."

Application (*Applying*): Application-level questions prompt students to solve problems or situations stated in the question by using the information they have learned.

Question stem examples: explain how, explain why, demonstrate, operate, illustrate

Sample questions and tasks:

- Explain how to punctuate this sentence.

- What type of an investor typically buys a Roth IRA?

- Explain why the lawyers who brought forth the *Brown* case were unsatisfied with the "separate but equal" ruling in *Plessy* v. *Ferguson*.

High-level questions ask students to make inferences, to analyze, or to evaluate, and are often divergent in form. They require more in-depth thinking to answer than do low-level questions. In order to answer a high-level question, however, a student must know the basic facts. The upper three (or four) levels of Bloom's taxonomy provide a good resource for developing higher-level questions.

Analysis (*Analyzing*): Analysis questions prompt students to look carefully at the organizational structure of the information presented to formulate ideas.

Question stem examples: compare, contrast, how, why, diagram, distinguish, differentiate

Sample questions and tasks:

- Compare the use of colons and semicolons.

- What are three main differences between a Roth IRA and a traditional IRA?

- How would you describe the impact of the *Brown* case ruling in its attempt to equalize educational opportunities for all students in the United States?

Synthesis (*Creating*): Synthesis questions give students an opportunity to come up with something new with the information they have learned.

Question stem examples: design, construct, create, propose, formulate, catalog, plan

Sample questions and tasks:

- Create marks to punctuate sad, quiet, hesitant, anxious, bored, and quiet statements (as exclamation points are used to punctuate forceful statements), and argue for their use.

- Design a portfolio of mutual funds for an individual who is 10 years from retirement.

- Make a plan that a state could implement that would help decrease the achievement gap between non-white and white students.

Evaluation (Evaluating): Students are asked to make a judgment about two ideas or concepts using a predetermined set of criteria.

Question stem examples: evaluate, appraise, judge, choose, predict, rate, estimate

Sample questions and tasks:

- Select the sentence that is best punctuated for clarity of meaning.

- Which of these stock and mutual fund options is best for a 401K plan for a 25-year-old?

- Which court case (*Plessy* v. *Ferguson* or *Brown* v. *the Board of Education*) had the most positive impact on equalizing resource allocation between African American and European American children in the public schools?

High- and low-level questions have different purposes, and both play an important role in lessons and activities. A student's ability to answer a high-level question about a topic is dependent on having an understanding of the basic facts about that topic; the basic fact knowledge is assessed through the use of low-level questions. In this way, the question types at various levels of Bloom's taxonomy are interconnected, and questions at one level of the taxonomy may serve as a foundation for the next. This taxonomy provides a structured way to plan both high- and low-level questions.

You have undoubtedly noticed the overlap among question types. For example, a convergent question is often also a low-level question, whereas a divergent question response may require higher-level thinking skills. It is important to understand that one question type is not necessarily superior to another; that is, high-level questions are not "better" than low-level

---

> ### Mrs. Roebuck Plans Questions to Ask
>
> *Questions Planned—*
>
> - What is included in an introductory paragraph? (knowledge/convergent)
>
> - Write another example of a conclusion for this topic. (comprehension/divergent)
>
> - Of these two examples, which body is the best? Why? (evaluation/divergent)
>
> - How is the structure of a report similar to the structure of an essay? Different? (analysis/convergent)
>
> *Reasoning—*Mrs. Roebuck wants to make sure that her students know the basic parts of a report but also wants her students to think beyond the basics. She designs some low-level factual recall questions to get at the basics, as well as high-level questions that require students to apply the basic information.
>
> *What other questions could Mrs. Roebuck ask that would help ensure that her students are challenged in their thinking, but also know the basic parts of a report?*

questions. Kauchak and Eggen point out the importance of having clear goals for questions: "Goals that are appropriate for the topic, the age of the students, and their backgrounds should determine the level of question" (2003, 176). This means that the important thing to remember is that questions should be planned to fit the purpose for which they are designed. Now think about Mrs. Roebuck and her lesson on report writing. She wants to challenge her students' thinking as she works through the lesson, but she also wants to know they understand the basic parts that make up a report. Look at the box above for ideas of some of the questions she has planned.

Guidelines for Planning and Delivering Questions

It is always best to plan questions in advance. It can be difficult to come up with questions that meet your goals when you are in front of a group of students. This is especially true for beginners or for experienced teachers who are planning to teach new or difficult content. Think about the following guidelines as you plan your questions (Borich 2007):

- Be clear and concise. For example, "How do the cones of volcanoes vary?" is a clear question, as opposed to "We've studied three kind of volcanoes. They all have different kinds of cones and their cones vary in a number of ways; for example, some are larger than others—what would be the things we would study in the cone of a volcano that would tell us about the volcano type, and why?"

- Use vocabulary that is appropriate for the age and ability of the students. For example, ask first graders, "What do you think Harry Potter meant when he said . . . ?" rather than, "What is your interpretation of the verbalizations of Harry Potter when he said . . . ?"

- Plan questions that are short enough for students to remember. Don't ask, "What are some of the ways we can preserve energy, water, and timber resources; why do we need to preserve these resources; and what techniques can we use to communicate the need for resource preservation to others in the community?"

- Follow questions with time for students to think (see wait-time 1 and 2 below). Provide adequate wait-time for more meaningful, thoughtful student responses.

- Follow questions with redirections, prompting, and probing as necessary. These cues can help students recall information and formulate more complete, complex answers.

- Follow questions with honest feedback. Correct responses can be acknowledged or praised. Incorrect responses need to be corrected so students do not learn or practice incorrect information (see Chapter 7 for information on feedback).

- When you ask questions of your students, your goal should be to involve as many of them as possible. See ideas for specific response strategies in the chapter on active participation (see Chapter 6).

- Avoid ridiculous questions, like asking a group of schoolchildren from Seattle, "Have any of you ever seen a cloud?"

Wait-Time

No discussion about questions would be complete without also talking about the importance of wait-time. Wait-time 1 and wait-time 2 are both variations of the idea that students need time to formulate answers to questions.

Wait-time 1 refers to the time between when a question is asked and when a student answers (Rowe 1986; Orlich et al. 2010). When teachers provide students with 3 to 5 seconds after asking a question, more students usually respond, more responses are correct, and the responses are generally more complex (Rosenberg, O'Shea, and O'Shea 2006).

Wait-time 2 is the time between when a student apparently finishes a response and when the teacher redirects, prompts, or moves on. Adequate think-time at this point in the questioning sequence generally results in more elaborate answers because students are given a chance to add to or modify their initial responses (Rosenberg, O'Shea, and O'Shea 2006).

Consider some special points when planning wait-time. First, low-level, convergent questions usually do not require much wait-time. The purpose of these questions is factual recall, so the student generally either knows or does not know the answer (an exception may be students with learning disabilities or English language learners needing more processing time). Second, higher-level or divergent questions need more time. Also, some individuals seem to need additional thinking time to respond to higher-level questions (Mastropieri and Scruggs 2007). Finally, during fluency-building drills and practice activities when speed and accuracy are being developed, wait-time is not desirable (Rosenberg, O'Shea, and O'Shea 2006).

Engaging All Students through Questioning

Asking questions serves a variety of benefits. As mentioned earlier, questions can provide review, rehearsal, and enrichment of the information being presented, and they can also be used to monitor students' understanding of the content being taught. Yet another benefit is that all students can be kept involved in the lesson or activity when the teacher plans for the use of response strategies that require participation by everyone. For example, all students can write down an answer, all students can share an answer with a partner, or all students can point to the correct answer. In summary, giving all student opportunities to respond to the questions you ask benefit students in a number of ways—everyone gets to practice, everyone has their understanding checked, and everyone is engaged. See Chapter 6 for more ideas of how to keep students involved through the use of questioning.

Teachers sometimes choose to call on individual students rather than have all students respond at once. They may use a repetitive question-and-response pattern that works something like this: The teacher asks a question and calls on a student to answer, then the teacher asks another question and calls on another student to answer, and so on. This "calling on individuals" technique deserves special attention when thinking about using questions to monitor students' understanding of content or to keep students involved. Since only one student answers at a time, only one student is involved, and only one student's understanding is being monitored.

If you are trying to assess the understanding of the group, calling on an individual won't work. You'll need to use other strategies. When active participation response strategies (asking students to signal a response or hold up a written response, for example) don't fit, you can sample the group's understanding by calling on several selected students. Don't call on volunteers. Instead, call on students who represent a range of knowledge and skill in the topic you are teaching.

While it is common practice for teachers to call on individuals to answer questions, it is not appropriate to use this method extensively or exclusively, given all of the reasons discussed previously. When using the calling-on-individuals technique, however, there are some things that can be done to make its use more effective. These ideas are summarized in the following box, then discussed in detail.

The following are specific strategies for the purpose of involving all students when calling on individuals:

1. Ask a question, pause, then call on a student by name, rather than saying, "Ben, what is the definition of . . .?" This encourages all students to think of the definition, not just Ben.

2. Call on non-volunteers rather than calling on students who raise their hands to answer. Tell the class in advance that you will be calling on

---

EXAMPLES OF INVOLVING ALL STUDENTS WHEN CALLING ON INDIVIDUALS

When only one student will be called on to answer a question, an important goal is to keep the rest of the class engaged and accountable. These ideas will help you achieve this goal:

- Ask the question before calling on anyone.
- Call on non-volunteers.
- Develop a system to keep track of who has been called on.

---

non-volunteers and allow them to pass if they choose. The purpose is to keep all students attentive and to send the message that you want to hear from everyone—even those in the back row. If a student knows he could be called on at any time, he is more likely to be attentive. In addition, selecting non-volunteers at random ensures that you include everyone. Here are some ideas to make your selection random:

- Draw cards or sticks (tongue depressors or ice-cream bar sticks) with student names on them.

- Use a seating chart or class list that includes all students' names.

- Assign each student a number and draw numbers.

- Using a spinner board, call on the student whose name the spinner lands on.

Don't hesitate to intersperse calling on volunteers with calling on non-volunteers. Sometimes, a student is very excited about a topic and bursting to respond. By all means, call on him (Delpit and White-Bradley 2003). Just remember that when you call on volunteers, it is important to avoid calling only on the same few students who raise their hands quickly. Increasing the wait-time between when you ask the question and when you call on someone to answer may help produce more volunteers.

3. Develop a system that allows you to keep track of students who have been called on so you

don't inadvertently leave students out. Here are some suggestions:

- If you use a class list or seating chart, put a check by students' names as they answer.

- Imagine the class divided into quadrants and call on a student from the first quadrant, then the second, and so on.

- Develop a system to replace name sticks in the can or name cards in the deck so you remember who you've called on (replace them upside down, for example). Don't lay drawn name sticks or cards aside after you have called on a student. It does not take long for students to realize that once they have been called on, they are off the hook until everyone has been called on to answer.

Remember that the purpose of calling on students at random is to keep everyone involved and on their toes. Keeping track of who has answered is a way that you can help students be accountable. It also keeps *you* accountable for equitable participation of all students. If students are permitted to call out answers rather than required to raise hands, keep track of (or ask someone else to keep track of) who is responding. If some students are consistently left out, rethink the use of this method.

A final consideration when calling on individuals is that it is never appropriate to call on non-attending students with the intent of embarrassing them. If you call on a non-attending student as a management technique, prompt the student by repeating the question.

A variety of strategies will help keep the rest of the class engaged and attentive when you choose to call on individuals rather than use active participation strategies. Asking the question before calling on a student, calling on non-volunteers, and keeping track of who has responded are all techniques that will make calling on individuals more effective.

Responding to Skill Diversity When Planning Questions

There are a variety of ways that you can plan questions in response to the varying skill levels of your students.

- Don't make the mistake of only asking low-level and convergent questions of students who are low achievers. For example, in math, if you only ask some students specific computation questions (e.g., "What is the next step in solving this problem?"), they will have difficulty learning higher-level skills (e.g., "When could you use this type of computation skill?")

- Vary wait-time. Some students will take longer than others to construct answers to questions. Adjust the amount of wait-time as needed.

- Provide additional prompting ("Yes, we do import more oil today than we did 20 years ago. What has happened in terms of our lifestyles that may help explain that?") and probing ("What did you do this weekend that made it fun?" or "We've been studying three ways to make our writing more interesting. What is one of those ways?") as necessary.

- Ask questions that help students connect new learning with prior knowledge or personal experience. For example, "Think of a time when you noticed one of your classmates standing up for another classmate when she was being teased. What did he say or do?"

- Ask a sequence of questions that build and lead students to correct or higher-level responses. For example, "What was the port of Seattle best known for during the late nineteenth century and early twentieth century?" (timber and fish exports). "Why was Seattle such an important port for these exports?" (proximity to major logging and fishing industries and a terminus for major transportation modes). "What other cities might have become (and didn't) important Washington state ports for the same commodities?" (Port Townsend, Port Angeles, Bellingham).

- Present important questions in writing as well as asking them orally. For example, questions can be written on the board, on a transparency, on cards to be passed out, or on a worksheet. The important thing to remember is that it can be easier for some students to see the question as well as hear it.

Responding to English Language Learners When Planning Questions

When planning questions for English language learners, it is important to consider several factors. First, where students are in relation to the stages of English language acquisition will help a teacher determine the kinds of questions that are appropriate to ask. Second, the stage of English learning influences the type of response that a student is able to produce (see Chapter 3 for more information about language acquisition stages). This means that diversity responsive teachers must match their questioning strategies to the language levels of their English language learners. Following are the language stages (adapted from Herrell and Jordan 2008) and examples of questions and expected responses that match each language stage:

Preproduction Stage

- *Sample questions*: Is this a man? Point to the girl. Show me "quickly."

- *Typical question responses*: pointing, nodding, physically demonstrating

Early Production Stage

- *Sample questions*: What did Jack do? Is it red or blue?

- *Typical question responses*: providing one- or two-word responses, making choices

Speech Emergence Stage

- *Sample questions*: Why did Jerell laugh? What will happen next?

- *Typical question responses*: providing short phrases or sentences (grammatical errors are not unusual)

Intermediate/Advanced Fluency Stage

- *Sample questions*: What is your opinion on this issue? How are these two stories similar?

- *Typical question responses*: providing longer sentences, with fewer grammatical errors

The following are additional suggestions for designing questions for English language learners:

- Use consistent language in questions. Be sure the language in the question matches the vocabulary used in the lesson or activity.

- Use simple vocabulary and shorter sentences, and limit the use of idiomatic expressions, slang, and pronouns (Salend and Salinas 2003).

- Provide opportunities for students to work with peer language models when answering questions.

- Encourage students to answer questions by providing visual supports and clues such as pictures, gestures, and words (Salend 2008).

Questions can encourage students to think about and act on the material the teacher has presented (Borich 2007). They can be used to enrich content learning and help students review and rehearse information. Questions can also be crafted to help teachers monitor the learning of their students. Arends states that "beginning teachers should keep in mind one important truth, that is, that different questions require different types of thinking and that a good lesson should include both lower and higher-level questions" (1997, 214). Questions can play varied and valuable roles in all lessons and activities. (See the resources listed at the end of this chapter for more information about questions.)

Closings

The closing is an ending to a lesson or activity. All lessons and activities should include a closing that gives students one more opportunity to consider the learned material. The closing can help create a smooth transition from one lesson or activity to the next.

Strategies for Closings

Closings can help tie things together for students. They may include one or more of the following:

1. *A review of the key points* of the lesson or activity (for example, after reading a biographical sketch to her students, Mrs. Affolter reviews major accomplishments in the life of Langston Hughes).

2. *Opportunities for students to draw conclusions* (Mrs. Harrigan helps students examine the relationship between lack of supervision and juvenile crime).

3. *A preview of future learning* (for example, following an activity designed to create interest in an upcoming unit on the solar system, Mr. Sanderson gives a brief explanation of unit lessons and activities that will occur in the next few days).

4. *A description of where or when students should use their new skills or knowledge* (for example, Mrs. Sanderson reminds students to try out their new social skill of "joining in" at recess).

5. *A time for students to show their work* (Mr. Craig has students share the three-dimensional shapes they constructed during the math lesson).

6. *A reference to the lesson opening* (Mrs. Begay restates the lesson objective as she prepares to begin the evaluation portion of her lesson).

Mrs. Roebuck plans to include a variety of strategies in her closing. Below is one of her ideas.

Mrs. Roebuck Plans the Closing

Closing Strategy Selected: Review
Mrs. Roebuck plans to bring her students back together to review what they have learned in this lesson. She will begin by showing the poster that lists the steps for writing a report. She asks students to discuss in their small groups a definition and example of each part of the report. Mrs. Roebuck calls on a few students to share with the whole group.

Reasoning: She knows that the content she is teaching in this lesson is complex in nature. In order to write an effective report, students need to know how to do all of the various parts of the report. Mrs. Roebuck decides that one final review of the parts will help bring the lesson together. She also wants to provide every student with one last opportunity to process the information that she has presented, so she uses small group discussions to involve everyone.

Besides this review, what else could Mrs. Roebuck do to in her closing to provide an effective wrap-up for her lesson?

Responding to Diversity When Planning the Closing

Consider the following when planning the closing:

■ Do not assume that students will automatically apply or generalize the new skill or knowledge.

TEACHER CHECKLIST FOR

Openings and Closings

Openings:

❑ Am I planning a strategy to grab my students' attention?

❑ Am I planning a way to clearly state the objective of the lesson/activity in terms my students understand?

❑ Am I planning specific examples to explain the value of the lesson/activity?

❑ Am I planning to build or activate necessary background knowledge?

❑ Am I planning a way to get my students involved right from the start?

Closings:

❑ Am I planning a way for students to review the key information/main ideas of the lesson/activity?

❑ Am I planning how to directly state the importance of the content that was developed or practiced?

❑ Am I planning to give students an opportunity to practice the content one more time?

❑ Am I planning to give my students an opportunity to show their work?

❑ Am I planning to refer back to the lesson opening and the lesson or activity objective?

❑ Am I planning a way to have all students involved?

Be very direct about where and when to use it. For example, "When you go to the cafeteria at noon, look around for someone who is sitting alone. Use the steps for 'introducing myself' and ask him/her if you can sit down and visit."

- Actively involve students in summarizing at the end of the activity or lesson. For example, "Write down three ways that recycling saves energy."

- Use the closing as one more practice opportunity. For example, "On your whiteboard, write 368 minus 147. Work the first step. Now the second step," and so on.

A closing is an important component of lessons and activities. You can wrap up your lesson or activity in many different ways. You will want to select strategies that are appropriate to the content being taught and the students you are teaching. Although a closing doesn't need to be long and complex, every lesson and activity should have one.

The checklist on page 52 includes considerations for planning lesson or activity openings and closings. It can be used as a guide when planning either or both.

Summary

This chapter has provided numerous ideas for helping students focus their attention on the important parts of lessons and activities. Planning meaningful openings and closings can help set students up to learn, and then help them review their learning. Important questioning strategies and an overview of question types have been included to provide structure for planning questions that help students process important information. The ideas presented in this chapter can guide you in involving your students and keeping them involved in your instruction.

References and Suggested Reading

Arends, R. I. 1997. *Classroom instruction and management*. New York: McGraw-Hill.

Arends, R. I. 2009. *Learning to teach*. 8th ed. Boston: McGraw-Hill.

Blanton, P. 2009. Develop your questioning techniques. *The Physics Teacher* 47 (1): 56–57.

Bond, N. 2007. 12 questioning strategies that minimize classroom management problems. *Kappa Delta Pi Record* 44 (1): 18–21.

Bond, N. 2008. Questioning strategies that minimize behavior problems. *Education Digest: Essential Readings Condensed for Quick Review* 73 (6): 41–45.

Borich, G. D. 2004. *Effective teaching methods: Research-based practice*. 5th ed. Columbus, OH: Pearson Prentice Hall. (See Chapter 7 in particular.)

Borich, G. D. 2007. *Effective teaching methods: Research-based practice*. 6th ed. Columbus, OH: Pearson Prentice Hall. (See Chapter 7 in particular.)

Cohen, L., L. Manion, and K. Morrison. 2004. *A Guide to Teaching Practice*. 5th ed. New York: Routledge. (See Chapter 13 in particular.)

Delpit, L., and P. White-Bradley. 2003. Educating or imprisoning the spirit: Lessons from ancient Egypt. *Theory into Practice* 42 (4): 283–288.

Echevarria, J., M. Vogt, and D. J. Short. 2008. *Making content comprehensible for English learners: The SIOP model*. 3rd ed. Boston: Pearson.

Freiberg, J. H., and A. Driscoll. 2005. *Universal teaching strategies*. 4th ed. Boston: Allyn & Bacon.

Gall, M. 1984. Synthesis of research on teachers' questioning. *Educational Leadership* 42:40–47.

Guillaume, A. M. 2008. *K–12 classroom teaching: A primer for new professionals*. 3rd ed. Columbus, OH: Merrill.

Herrell, A., and M. Jordan. 2008. *Fifty strategies for teaching English-language learners*. 3rd ed. Upper Saddle River, NJ: Prentice-Hall.

Jacobsen, D. A., P. Eggen, and D. Kauchak. 2009. *Methods for teaching: Promoting student learning*. 7th ed. Columbus, OH: Allyn and Bacon/Merrill. (See Chapter 7 in particular.)

Kauchak, D. P., and P. D. Eggen. 2007. *Learning and teaching: Research-based methods*. 5th ed. Boston: Allyn and Bacon.

Kellough, R. D. 2000. *A resource guide for teaching: K–12*. 3rd ed. Columbus, OH: Merrill/Prentice Hall. (See Chapter 10 in particular.)

Kinniburgh, L. H., and E. L. Shaw. 2009. Using question-answer relationships to build reading comprehension in science. *Science Activities* 45 (4): 19–28.

Krumme, G. Major categories in the taxonomy of educational objectives—Bloom 1956. http://faculty.washington.edu/krumme/guides/bloom.html.

Mastropieri, M. S., and T. E. Scruggs. 2007. *The inclusive classroom: Strategies for effective instruction.* 3rd ed. Upper Saddle River, NJ: Prentice Hall.

Moore, K. D. 2005. *Effective instructional strategies: From theory to practice.* Thousand Oaks, CA: SAGE Publications.

Orlich, D. C., R. J. Harder, R. C. Callahan, and H. W. Gibson. 2004. *Teaching strategies: A guide to better instruction.* 6th ed. Boston: Houghton Mifflin.

Orlich, D. C., R. J. Harder, R. C. Callahan, M. S. Trevisan, and A. H. Brown. 2010. *Teaching strategies: A guide to effective instruction.* 9th ed. Florence, KY: Cengage.

Parker, J. 2009. Personal communication.

Rosenberg, M. S., L. O'Shea, and D. J. O'Shea. 2006. *Student teacher to master teacher: A practical guide for educating students with special needs.* 4th ed. Columbus, OH: Merrill/Prentice Hall.

Rowe, M. B. 1986. Wait time: Slowing down may be a way of speeding up. *Journal of Teacher Education* 23 (January–February): 43–49.

Sadker, D., M. Sadker, and K. R. Zittleman. 2010. Questioning skills. In *Classroom Teaching Skills,* 9th ed., ed. J. Cooper. Florence, KY: Cengage.

Salend, S. J. 2008. *Creating inclusive classrooms: Effective and reflective practices for all students.* 6th ed. Upper Saddle River, NJ: Pearson.

Salend, S. J., and A. Salinas. 2003. Language differences or learning difficulties: The work of the multidisciplinary team. *Teaching Exceptional Children* 35 (4): 36–43.

Tincani, M. 2008. Comparing brief and extended wait-time during small group instruction for children with challenging behavior. *Journal of Behavioral Education* 17 (1): 79–92.

Vallecorsa, A. L., L. U. de Bettencourt, and N. Zigmond. 2000. *Students with mild disabilities in general education settings: A guide for special educators.* Columbus, OH: Merrill/Prentice Hall.

Walsh, J. A., and B. D. Sattes. 2005. *Quality questioning: Research-based practice to engage every learner.* Thousand Oaks, CA: Corwin Press.

CHAPTER 5

Critical Teaching Skills for Presenting Information

Introduction

This chapter is about critical teaching skills that are needed in order to present information clearly. Most of the skills presented have to do with what the teacher actually says and/or does with the content being taught, that is, explaining, demonstrating, using visual supports, and clarifying key terms and vocabulary. Giving clear directions is also included here because the techniques used to make directions clear are very similar to those that make content presentations clear. Clarity of directions impacts overall lesson or activity clarity, and because so many directions are given throughout a day, it is important to know how to give them

effectively. Following the information about each critical teaching skill are suggestions for how to respond to diversity. When the skills presented in this chapter are implemented correctly, they can greatly increase the probability that students will learn the information being presented. They are all easily built in during the initial stages of planning, making them useful for implementing principles of universal design for learning.

Read about Ms. Vandermay and the lesson she is planning for teaching her students about the scientific method. Then, as you read this chapter, think about which critical teaching skills for making clear presentations would be effective at various parts of the lesson.

A Look at Ms. Vandermay's Planning

Ms. Vandermay is planning a series of lessons and activities for teaching students about the scientific method. The longer-term objective for this series is for students to apply the scientific method, that is, to test various original hypotheses. Ms. Vandermay has already taught a lesson that explained what the scientific method was and why it is important, which served as an overall introduction to the lesson and activity series. The lesson she is currently planning begins a study of the individual steps in the scientific method (question, research, hypothesize, experiment, analyze data, communicate results). The short-term objective is that students will *identify*

good examples of each step so that they can learn in future lessons to *produce* such examples. She recognizes that if students are to apply the steps to a variety of questions or problems later on, they will need to have a very thorough understanding of each one. This means that she must teach clearly and completely. In order to do so, Ms. Vandermay plans to explain each step and demonstrate each one as well, using products and processes as appropriate. She will then have students practice identifying examples of each step as she presents new examples and nonexamples of each one. During this lesson, she will also provide some initial opportunities for students to practice memorizing the steps so that naming them will eventually become automatic.

Explanations

One of the hallmarks of an effective teacher is being skilled at giving clear explanations. Explanations are what the teacher says about the information to be learned. A thorough and easy to follow explanation has a strong positive effect on learning. As a teacher, you will be explaining facts, ideas, rules, strategies, processes, concepts, principles, and so on. You will also be explaining what, where, when, how, and why. In addition, you will use explanations as part of all lesson models and activities.

Components

There are many possible components of good explanations. Choose which ones to use depending on what you're explaining—whether it's a concept, fact, or strategy; how complex the information is; how concrete or abstract it is; and/or how familiar students are with the information. Supplement verbal explanations with the use of visual supports such as written steps and key ideas, study guides, and graphic organizers, as their use can help make explanations easier to understand. Demonstrations are very helpful as well. (See more information about visual supports and demonstrations in other sections of this chapter.) A clear and complete explanation itself, however, might include some of the following:

- *Paraphrases* Use different words in phrases and sentences—("*i before e except after c means i is usually written in front of e unless there is a c in front of the two vowels*")

- *Definitions* Tell what a word or term means—(*setting means where and when the story takes place*)

- *Descriptions* Tell about something, such as what it looks like or sounds like—(a desert is hot, dry, and sandy)

- *Elaborations* Give more details, more information—(settings can be big or small, general or specific, real or imaginary)

- *Synonyms or antonyms* Tell another word that means the same or opposite—(*setting = location and time*)

- *Characteristics or Attributes* Tell the special qualities, features, or properties that make it

what it is—(a characteristic or attribute of a triangle is that it has three sides)

- *Examples and Nonexamples* Presenting instances of what something is and/or what it is not—("Treasure Island" is a proper noun because it is a specific island, whereas "island" is not a proper noun because it is not specific)

- *Connections to Prior Knowledge/Personal Experience* Tell how it's related to something they already know—(rounding: If you are halfway or more across the street when the light changes,

---

Ms. Vandermay Plans Explanations

Strategies Planned:

Definition—Explain that "ask a question" is the first step in the scientific method; it comes as a result of observing something and formulating a question about what you observe; it is something you wonder about; questions are about the physical world or facts and have answers that can be discovered.

Elaboration—Explain that the question may begin with *how, what, when, who, which, why,* or *where*; after doing some research on the topic, the question may be used to construct a hypothesis; it's something that can be measured; it's something that can be tested.

Examples—Explain that the following are examples of appropriate questions: What makes a daisy change the position it faces throughout the day? Why don't mosquitoes lay eggs in water with a current?

Reasoning: Ms. Vandermay chose several strategies in order to be very thorough in her explanations because students need to know details about each step of the scientific method. Application of the steps is only possible with a thorough understanding. By supplementing her definition through elaboration and examples, Ms. Vandermay considers her explanation complete enough to communicate the full meaning of each step.

What else could Ms. Vandermay do to make sure that her explanations are clear?

does it make sense to keep going, or turn around and go back?)

- *Comparisons* Tell what it is like or not like. Use similes and metaphors—(a setting is like a scene in a movie or play)

- *Categories* Tell what it is an example of; tell about the big picture—(Cinco de Mayo is an example of a national celebration of a historical event)

Giving clear explanations can be accomplished by carefully selecting specific strategies to use, and the ideas just stated can be used in any combination. Their selection and use can be adjusted as dictated by student need. Remember Ms. Vandermay's lesson on the scientific method? She planned to teach the steps of the scientific method so that later on students can set up effective experiments to test their hypotheses. See the box "Ms. Vandermay plans Explanations," for some of her ideas for helping to explain the "ask a question" step. She will use a similar procedure for presenting each step, making adjustments as appropriate.

Responding to Skill Diversity When Providing Explanations

The following suggestions will provide support for students in learning the information you present:

- Explain the whole idea, rule, strategy, concept, or principle as well as the component parts.

- Present information in smaller portions and provide practice after each portion.

- Increase opportunities for all students to be involved with the explanations being presented by using active participation strategies, responding to questions, encouraging discussion, and so forth.

- Use frequent checks for understanding.

- Use analogies, metaphors, or vivid language.

- Stop more often to summarize, review, and clarify how this information fits into the larger picture.

- Pair all explanations with visual supports.

- Use classroom amplification (for example, wireless microphone and speakers) when you explain orally.

- Provide partially filled-in note-taking guides or graphic organizers that students can complete (outlines, concept maps, or webs, for example).

- Provide mnemonic devices and other memory supports to help students remember explanations.

- Adjust pacing; a brisker pace typically helps students attend and allows for more teaching.

- Provide a note-taker for a student who has difficulty taking notes while listening.

Responding to English Language Learners When Providing Explanations

Some of the strategies previously mentioned are also helpful for English language learners. For example, using visual supports, stopping frequently to check for understanding, and using culturally relevant examples can also benefit English language learners. Following are more ideas:

- Communicate meanings of new terms and concepts by using gestures, facial expressions, voice changes, pantomimes, demonstrations, rephrasing, visuals, props, manipulatives, and other cues (Salend and Salinas 2003).

- When you present, enunciate clearly, but don't raise your voice (Reed and Railsback 2003).

- Repetition can help students acquire the rhythm, pitch, volume, and tone of the new language (Salend and Salinas 2003).

- Don't speak too quickly, and use brief pauses at natural points to allow learners to process what they are hearing.

- It is important to write clearly and legibly. Print rather than use cursive until you are sure your English language learners can read cursive (Reed and Railsback 2003).

- Avoid idioms (*backseat driver, cute as a bug's ear*) and slang (*hangout, deep pockets*), as they can be confusing for English language learners (Reed and Railsback 2003).

- Summarize the important points of the presentation frequently (Reed and Railsback 2003).

Responding to Cultural Diversity When Providing Explanations

■ Use culturally relevant examples. (Urban students may not identify goats or rabbits as pets, for example.)

■ Students from various backgrounds may prefer listening quietly or call-and-response approaches.

■ Allow for active physical responses to the presentation when students are used to that style.

■ Emphasize the big picture; create a context for new information.

You can use many techniques to help you explain information in a way that engages students and increases their understanding. Providing options in your explanations, such as saying the information and putting it in writing, will help make your presentations clear and focused. Over time, many of the available options become second nature.

Demonstration or Modeling

In addition to explaining information, you will often also demonstrate or model information before, during, or after explanations. This is especially important when teaching how to do something. Demonstration or modeling means showing the students what it is they are expected to do. When a teacher shows students how to do a computation skill by first doing it herself, she is offering a demonstration. When a teacher role-plays for his students how to respond to teasing, he is providing a model of how the expected skill should look. Effective demonstrations play a key role in helping students better understand what you are teaching.

Types of Demonstrations

Teachers can use two types of demonstrations. The first is a *demonstration of a product*. This means that the teacher shows the students a finished product or pieces of a finished product. For example, Mrs. Wines plans an activity where students make origami birds. Mrs. Wines prepares a model (product) of the bird at each step of completion (after each new fold). This allows her students to see what

the bird should look like as it is being created as well as when it is finished.

The second type of demonstration is the *demonstration of a process*. This is when the teacher shows the students how to do the steps of the task. Here, Mrs. Wines completes each step of creating the origami bird while her students watch. She carefully explains what she is doing as she does it, for example, "Now I fold the paper across the diagonal and line up the edges of the paper so that they match exactly." Role-plays and skits can also be used as demonstrations of a process. For example, Mrs. VanBerkum acts out how students are to get under their desks during an earthquake drill. Often, teachers will use both a demonstration of process and a demonstration of product. This of course, will depend on the content of the lesson.

EXAMPLES OF DEMONSTRATIONS

Product
■ a completed concept web
■ a paragraph that already includes descriptive language
■ a finished note-taking guide for a science investigation

Process
■ working through the steps for solving for x as I say them
■ modeling "how to start a conversation"
■ thinking aloud the steps for "finding the main idea" as I do them

---

It is very important that the teacher or other expert do the demonstration in the initial phases of learning. This will help ensure that students get an accurate picture of the learning task. Demonstrations can be made even more effective by adding clear oral explanations as you do the demonstration. The following ideas may help when planning demonstrations:

■ Actually act out the skill you are teaching, rather than just explaining and asking students to imagine what you want them to do. For example, when demonstrating the routine for entering class, you should walk to the coat hooks and hang up a real coat rather than saying, "Next, I would put my coat away" and pantomiming hanging up a coat.

- Use a "think-aloud" to explain what you are doing as you do it. For example, when teaching the steps of a proofreading strategy, say, "I'm looking at the sentences in my paragraph one sentence at a time to see if each has an end mark. Oh—my third sentence is missing an end mark!" Be explicit.

- Supplement the demonstration with visual supports. For example, when demonstrating how to preview a chapter in a content area textbook, post the steps to follow and refer to them.

- Demonstrating the new skill or knowledge only once is generally not enough. For example, if you are teaching students to find the common denominator of fractions, let them watch you find the common denominator of several different pairs of fractions.

- Actively involve students in the demonstration as appropriate, being careful about not asking them to do the demonstration for you. For example, when teaching how to add two-digit numbers to two-digit numbers without regrouping, ask students to say the answers together.

- When teaching a complicated skill, demonstrate each individual step of the skill, but also demonstrate all steps together. For example, when teaching the routine for doing their daily math timings, show students how to do each part, then show students how to do the whole routine together.

Responding to Diversity When Planning Demonstrations

- Increase the number of demonstrations.

- Emphasize or highlight important parts or steps in demonstrations with words ("Look carefully at what I do next. . .") or with visual supports (highlighting key words in the list of steps written on the poster).

- Be sure to use consistent terms and phrasing when demonstrating with think-alouds.

- Point to the steps on a written list as they are demonstrated.

- Show videotaped demonstrations of real applications.

A demonstration is an integral part of teaching information clearly and effectively. Teachers can use demonstrations before, during, or after explaining the information they teach. Remember that it is important to actually do the demonstration rather than to simply tell how to do it. You can increase student understanding about the information being taught by giving effective demonstrations, along with clear explanations. Remember Ms. Vandermay's lesson on the scientific method? Below are some of her ideas for planning the demonstration parts of that lesson.

Ms. Vandermay Plans The Demonstration

Strategies Planned: (for data analysis step): *Demonstration of a product*—Show examples of data collections and related conclusions (displayed on charts and graphs) that have been collected and analyzed on previous experiments that students have done in science (e.g., *how the slant of an incline place is related to its mechanical advantage; results from the "hours of sleep students get each night" survey.*) Explain the data displayed on the charts and graphs, that is, what data is displayed, why the display works for the type of data, and so forth. Emphasize how the raw data was analyzed, summarized in a visual display, and how the conclusions were supported by the data.

Reasoning: The demonstration of product strategy was selected because it provided a concrete way to show clearly to students the various components of the data analysis step (raw data, summarized data, and conclusions). Not only did this approach provide clarity, it provided a display of what the students' final products for this step will look like. Finally, using data displays that students have worked with before provided valuable scaffolding between what they have done before and what they will do now; therefore, relevance in the information being taught was established.

How else could Ms. Vandermay use demonstrations (product, process) to help students learn each step?

Visual Supports

Using visual supports effectively is another critical teaching skill. Visual supports can increase the effectiveness of instruction by making information, explanations, and directions more comprehensible to learners. They are very helpful in teaching vocabulary, giving directions, building background knowledge, clarifying difficult concepts and strategies, and providing scaffolds for new learning. Although visual supports are important in all lessons and are helpful to everyone, they are absolutely essential for students who have difficulty learning or for English language learners.

Categories of Visual Supports

The following four categories provide some idea of the broad range of visual supports from which to choose:

1. *Realia or Pictures: real objects, animals, people, working models, models, multimedia presentations, video recordings (including YouTube), computer graphics, photographs, drawings, or maps.* Incorporating these as props in your instruction will help make new information more real and clear to students, especially when they can see, hear, and touch what they are learning about.

   ■ *Example:* Mr. Zegers wants his activity on making change to be interesting and relevant. He brings in food boxes and cans, as well as toy boxes. Each item is marked with a price. Students are given play money and count back change for the item.

2. *Actions: gestures, demonstrations, or role-plays.* These are especially helpful in teaching procedures and behavioral skills.

   ■ *Example:* Mrs. Boyd shows students how to use a proofreading strategy, "First, I underline the first letter in each of my sentences. I'm looking to see that each sentence starts with a capital letter. Ms. Boyd actually circles, underlines, crosses out, and writes changes directly into written work along with saying out loud the steps of the proofreading strategy.

3. *Writings: on posters, a whiteboard, overhead transparencies, PowerPoint slides, handouts, labels, books, magazines, sketches, newspapers, and computer text.* Providing information in

writing so students can read it as well as hear the teacher speak it is very helpful to many learners.

   ■ *Example*: Mr. Norman prepares a PowerPoint slide that shows the directions needed in order to complete the writing assignment.

4. *Graphic organizers: outlines, concept maps, diagrams, webs, T-charts, story maps, word banks, Venn diagrams, compare and contrast charts, problem–solution–effect charts, note-taking guides, and so on.* These are used to depict connections and relationships among ideas. Show graphics during instruction, or ask students to fill them in as part of brainstorming, during presentations, while reading, with peer partners or in groups, and as practice or evaluation activities.

   ■ *Example*: When teaching about different forms of government, Ms. Branham uses a compare/contrast map to illustrate the ways in which a democracy and a dictatorship are the same and different.

Various visual supports can be combined during instruction. For example, when teaching students how to put together a completed circuit, the teacher can demonstrate using real objects and provide written directions with diagrams, as well as giving directions orally. The important idea is that seeing something, in addition to hearing about it, can greatly enhance learning.

Responding to Diversity When Planning Visual Supports

■ Increase the number of visual supports used.

■ When using writings as visual supports, help students (including English language learners) read and comprehend.

■ Use visual prompts (for example, color-code) to highlight essential information.

■ Provide individual copies of the visual support (such as checklists of steps to follow for getting help) for students to have at their desks.

■ Use pictures to supplement written words on a visual support. For example, include picture cues for behavior expectations written on a poster so that students can read and see what is expected.

Many sources for visual supports are available. They can be ordered from catalogs or borrowed from libraries, museums, and universities. Teachers can make files of photographs and drawings, and collect objects from garage sales. They can bookmark Internet sites and put photos, drawings, and diagrams on transparencies and slides. Computer software and the Internet have greatly expanded what is available to teachers. A visual support library can be a very valuable asset for teachers in any content area.

The importance of visual supports cannot be stressed enough. Visual supports can help teachers increase interest in the content they are teaching, and can help students "see the big picture" and organize information for learning. They can also make the difference between a lesson or activity that is understood and one that is not. Think carefully about appropriate visual supports as you plan lessons and activities. Think again about Ms. Vandermay's lesson on the scientific method. Look at

the box "Ms. Vandermay's plan for visual supports" to see some of the visual supports she plans to use to help promote student learning.

Teaching Key Terms and Vocabulary

When presenting information about any topic, it is important that students understand the terms and vocabulary that are to be part of your presentation. This is true of the words that you will use as part of your explanations and demonstrations, as well as key terms and vocabulary words that are specific to the content being taught. You might have a great presentation planned, but if students are confused by words or meanings that are unfamiliar to them, it will be hard for them to follow along. We will focus on words that are important to know for a specific lesson or activity—not for vocabulary development in general.

There are four decision points or steps through which a teacher works as he plans for teaching key terms and vocabulary. These decisions are much like the decisions made for planning to teach any content. Begin by selecting important words, then decide on an objective, then determine student understanding, and then choose how to teach the words.

Decision Steps

Step 1—Select Important Words Review the materials for your lesson or activity, and look for the words that your students may not know at all or may not know well. These could be words used in readings and words used in your explanations or directions. Next, decide which of those words are essential to being successful in participating in and/or learning the current lesson or activity content. Those are the words you would consider to be "key" and will want to address with your students. Select only a few important words to focus on, words that are essential to understanding. Some of the words you select may be vocabulary words and some may be terms. You'll determine that from the context of the word.

Step 2—Decide on an Objective Once you have identified the words that are important to address, you will need to decide on your objective for the word, that is, how well you want your students to know the word. The following questions will assist you in determining the objective.

Ms. Vandermay's Plan for Visual Supports

Visual Supports Planned:

PowerPoint slide presentation—Each slide will include the name of the step, and a few important words to help students remember what it means will flash across the screen.

Poster of lesson objective—The poster will be left up during the whole lesson.

Photographs—She will use photos of examples (such as time-lapse photography of a flower face changing position throughout the day).

Reasoning: Ms. Vandermay thinks that the slides will create interest, and important words for each step will help with memorization. Keeping the poster on display gives ongoing opportunities to refer to the poster while emphasizing each step. Photographs will create interest and ensure clarity of examples.

What other visual supports could Ms. Vandermay use to strengthen her lesson presentation?

■ Do I want the students to recognize and understand the meaning of the word when they hear it? When they read it?

■ Do I want the students to use the word (and pronounce it) correctly when speaking? To use the word (and spell it) correctly when writing?

■ Do I want the students to be able to define, state synonyms/antonyms, give examples/nonexamples, or to apply the meaning of the word to new examples or situations?

Step 3—Determine Student Understanding   Once you have decided which words are critical for understanding the lesson or activity content, and you know how well your students need to know them, you can determine the present level of student understanding by conducting assessments. These assessments do not need to be time-consuming or complicated. An assessment can be as simple as having students say/write definitions of terms, show/explain examples of the term, or explain the context from which their familiarity with the word comes. Suppose that you want to know if students understand the term *denominator* when they hear it. You could write a couple of fractions on the board, point to numbers in the fractions, and have students signal "thumbs up" if the number is the denominator. Results of assessments are valuable in helping you decide how to approach the presentation of important vocabulary words or terms with students.

Step 4—Decide How to Teach the Word   After you have determined how familiar students are with the important words that will be a part of your lesson/ activity, you are ready to decide how to teach them. Of course, your objective will have the largest impact on how you teach. If the objective is only that they understand the word when they hear it or read it, then a "quick-teach" may be appropriate. In a quick-teach, you typically define or give synonyms of the word and/or demonstrate it (if possible) followed by asking the students to repeat the term and its meaning.

For example, a quick-teach for teaching the vocabulary word *startled* might look like this:

■ Write *startled* on the board.

■ Say that it means surprised or shocked; it's when something unexpected makes you jump.

EXAMPLES OF WORD TYPES DETERMINED BY CONTEXT

Term

■ *Definition*: a word that is specific to a particular content topic/subject. It is considered "technical language," it has no substitute, and its definition is one that is generally agreed upon by experts in the content area.

■ *Example*: Mrs. Arnold is planning to teach her students about plants and what they need in order to grow. She will teach the word *photosynthesis* as a key term because it is routinely used to describe the impact of the sun on plant growth.

■ *Other Possible Examples of Terms*: meter, linear measurement, beaker, quotient, fossil, topography, Congress, latitude/longitude, sum, syllable, hyperbolist, force, chronological order, persuasive, compass rose, evaporation

Vocabulary Word

■ *Definition*: a word that is found in a story or reading for a particular lesson or activity. It is not a "technical" term and could, in many cases, be replaced by another, but an understanding of it is needed so that students can be successful in the current lesson or activity.

■ *Example*: Mrs. Cornelsen is going to read her class a story in which a boy acts out of character because he was *startled*. Mrs. Cornelsen considers this a vocabulary word rather than a key term because it could be replaced by words such as *shocked* or *scared*. The students need to know the word to understand the story being read.

■ *Other Possible Examples of Vocabulary Words*: meandering, naughty, circulate, apologize, cheer, obey, dedication, tripped, coach, vast, curious, faithful

- Act it out briefly by pretending to be busy; a helper comes up from behind and grabs your shoulders; you jump and say, "Oh, you startled me."

- Ask, "When something unexpected makes you jump, you are—what, everyone?"

If the objective is that students will be able to use the word correctly in speech and written work, you'll probably need to use a mini-lesson. You'd also typically use a mini-lesson when the objective is that students produce new examples of the term. A mini-lesson is longer and more thorough than a quick-teach. You explain more completely, show more examples or demonstrations, *and* include student practice. Mini-lessons are often used to teach key terms. For example, a mini-lesson for teaching the key term *landform* might look like the one in the box below.

You'll also need to decide *when* to teach key terms and vocabulary. If it is necessary to do in-depth teaching of a term, teachers often choose to teach it prior to the main lesson or activity. Another option is to teach words as part of the lesson or activity opening. Sometimes, words can be quickly taught during a lesson or activity. Choose the approach that will lead to student understanding and decrease the chances of having to stop in the middle of the lesson for a significant amount of time.

Strategies for Defining Words

The strategies that you can use to teach key terms and vocabulary are varied and many, but you will almost always define the word for the students. The following are some considerations in selecting strategies that will help ensure that your students, including English language learners, understand the definitions you provide.

1. Let students know if the word has multiple meanings and/or is used as different parts of speech (e.g., noun and verb). Example: One meaning of the word *bridge* is "a structure carrying a road or railway over a river" (noun); another meaning is "to close a gap, pause" (verb).

2. Evaluate carefully the use of a definition. Sometimes, definitions are not helpful, as they may be too abstract. It can be better to use synonyms and antonyms. Example: A dictionary definition of the word *replenish* is "to make full or complete again by supplying what has been used up." Using the words, *fill, stock, supply, restock* may be easier to understand.

3. Provide students with both oral and written definitions. The word(s) can be written on the whiteboard or a poster. Another possibility is to provide students with a list of terms and definitions to be used throughout a lesson or unit. Or, students could write terms and definitions in their notes and/or locate them in their text. Posting word banks and semantic webs in the classroom could also be used to provide written definitions for students. Example: As each new word is introduced in the science unit, it is added to the word bank on one of the classroom walls.

4. It can be helpful to talk about examples and nonexamples of the word meaning, that is, what it's *like* or *not like*. Showing words used in various sentences can be very helpful in getting across

---

MINI-LESSON

For Teaching the Key Term Landform

Objective: Students will list at least 10 important landforms as part of the environmental report they are writing on their home county.

Explain: A landform is any naturally occurring physical feature of the earth's surface. They come in all sizes. Some are above the earth's landscape, some are below. None are created by man—instead, they occur naturally, generally over millions of years.

Show: pictures of examples (valley, plateau, mountain, plain, hill, glacier, cliff, continent, delta, butte, cave, bay, island, mesa, plateau) and nonexamples (manmade tunnels, canals, levees, bridges, pyramids, Mount Rushmore, etc.)

Check for Understanding: Show pictures and have students signal *yes* if the picture is of a landform, *no* if it's a manmade structure.

Practice: Students are given large picture books on different countries and asked to list landforms.

the meaning as well as showing it in context rather than in isolation. Example: When teaching the word *polite*, the teacher shows examples and nonexamples of polite statements.

5. Activating background knowledge/experience and building background knowledge are important in helping students make connections to or expand what they know. Example: Ask students to think about a time when they saw someone getting hurt physically or being teased as a segue into teaching about the word *bystander*.

6. Provide pictures, models, and other visual supports to help illustrate important terms. Remember that visual supports can sometimes be realia, photos, sketches, diagrams, or demonstrations, and some types work better for different kinds of words. Example: The word *respect* is best shown by demonstrating examples and nonexamples, whereas a diagram may best illustrate the cone of a volcano.

7. Incorporate appropriate checks for understanding to ensure that students understand the words. Example: Have students circle more examples of *direct speech* in a new paragraph of text.

8. Use repetitive call-and-response if the objective is for them to know and use the word. Example: While working through a quick-teach on the meaning of the word *sum*, the teacher repeats in a number of ways, ". . . and what's the answer to an addition problem called, everyone?"

9. Memorization of terms can be facilitated by providing memorization strategies along with time to practice. Flashcards, computer games, and mnemonic devices can all be used for practice. Example: The key terms from the writing unit are put on 3 × 5 cards, which students take out and practice several times during the day.

10. Be consistent in the terms you use with students. Example: If you decide to use the term *subtract*, don't randomly alternate with *minus* or *take away*.

11. Make sure that definitions are in words the students understand. Example: Say *impressive* rather than *bodacious*; say *stream* or *river* instead of *watercourse*.

Ms. Vandermay is planning for teaching key terms and vocabulary in her lesson on the scientific method. Below are some of her ideas.

Ms. Vandermay Plans for Teaching Key Terms and Vocabulary

Word Selected: Ms. Vandermay decides to teach the word "data" because it is a key term.

Objective: Students will recognize examples that match the definition of "data."

Strategy for Teaching: Ms. Vandermay decides to use a mini-lesson. She will begin by explaining what the word means, and showing examples and nonexamples of data. Students will practice identifying data by explaining why it matches or doesn't match the definition.

Reasoning: The term will be used throughout the research unit and in a number of ways. Students will learn to gather data and analyze it and in order to do this, they need to know what data is and what is considered a reliable data source. The mini-lesson was selected for teaching the word because of the depth of understanding needed.

What other words might Ms. Vandermay select, and how could she teach them?

Giving Directions

Teachers use directions to communicate to students the details regarding the assignment, or task they are to complete, or procedures they are to follow. Teachers give many directions to students throughout the school day and school year. They may need to give directions for how to complete seatwork assignments, projects, games, homework, and so on. They may give directions for routine tasks such as cleaning up or putting away the microscopes, or for procedures regarding earthquake drills. How directions are given impacts clarity.

Making Directions Clear

- Make wording clear and concise. For example, do not use more words than necessary, and be sure to use words your students will understand.

- Make directions as short as possible. Avoid long, drawn-out explanations that students cannot follow.

- Present directions orally and in writing, use picture directions, and provide demonstrations of what students are to do.

- Emphasize key words in oral directions ("Notice . . ." or "This is *very* important . . .") and highlight them in written directions.

- Use numbers to emphasize the sequence of directions.

- Follow the directions with questions to check for understanding. Plan responses that require students to explain or demonstrate the directions. Do not simply ask, "Does everyone understand?"

Ms. Vandermay Plans for Giving Directions

Strategies:
Written directions—Write directions on a homework assignment sheet, using concise, numbered directions.

Oral directions—Using a transparency of the assignment sheet on the overhead, go through each direction and show an example of each.

Reasoning: Ms. Vandermay gives directions orally and in writing because these strategies together make it more likely that all students will understand what is expected of them. The assignment sheet that is to be sent home with each student will serve as a reminder of what needs to be done.

What else can Ms. Vandermay do to help ensure that her directions are easy to understand and follow?

Think back to Ms. Vandermay's lesson on the steps of the scientific method. After the initial teaching in class, she wants students to practice identifying the steps of the scientific method at home. The assignment is to match the steps with descriptions of step examples. For this task, students will be given a handout of descriptions (minus the step label), and they will take home the note-taking guides that they filled in during her lesson. The guide has all the information needed to do this task. Ms. Vandermay has carefully thought through how to give directions for this assignment. Read some of her ideas in the box "Ms. Vandermay plans for Giving Directions."

Responding to Diversity When Giving Directions

The following suggestions may help English language learners or students with learning problems understand directions:

- Shorten and simplify directions.

- Give fewer directions at a time and have students repeat or paraphrase what they are to do (check for understanding).

- Cue directions with numbers (for example, "first" or "second") and gestures (showing one finger, then two).

- Emphasize key words with intonations in your voice and with gestures.

- Make the directions into a list of steps that students can check off as they complete each step.

- Check for understanding by asking specific questions to prevent cultural misunderstandings. Some students will say they understand the teacher's directions (even when they don't) to be respectful. Avoid asking, "Do you understand the directions?" Instead, ask a question like, "What is the first thing you should do?" (Zirpoli 2005).

Clear directions make an important contribution to the smooth running of a classroom. When students understand the directions they are given, teachers can avoid the confusion that leads to wasted time as students try to figure out what they are to do next. Careful advance planning of directions for lessons and activities will help ensure that they are clear and effective.

General Tips for Planning Effective Presentations

Teachers strive to be clear and interesting whenever they teach. The following summary of ideas can help accomplish those goals:

- Provide complete explanations and many examples. Teach, teach, teach!

- Teach the content in a step-by-step, piece-by-piece manner. Teach some information, check for understanding, and then reteach or move on.

- Break up the information. Teach a couple of steps and have the students practice; teach a couple more steps, and so on. Keep reminding the students of the whole task or big picture through demonstrations or by using graphic and advance organizers.

- Use visual supports (diagrams, photographs, concept maps, and so on) to supplement explanations.

- Vary voice tones and inflections to create interest. Sound enthusiastic.

- Be sure to use examples that are familiar to the students.

- Repeat key ideas often, using the same wording.

- Tell students which information is important to remember.

- Write important information down, for example, on a transparency, poster, or PowerPoint slide(s).

- Increase interest by using sound effects and animation in PowerPoint slides.

- Use pauses to allow students time to think and write.

- Ask for frequent, active responses. For example, ask all students to process, orally or in writing, the information just presented. Decrease the use of strategies that involve calling on a few students who raise their hands or asking several students to come up to the board and do a problem.

Instead, ask all students to solve a problem on their individual whiteboards.

- Cue note-taking (for example, "first," "second," or "this is important") to help students recognize key ideas to add to notes.

The teacher checklist below includes key ideas about making clear presentations. It can be used as a guide to help you plan your lessons or activities.

TEACHER CHECKLIST FOR

Making Clear Presentations

❑ Am I planning complete, thorough *explanations* of the content analysis using student-friendly wording?

❑ Am I planning to show a *demonstration* of a product or to use a "think-aloud" to demonstrate a process as described in the content analysis?

❑ Am I planning ways to teach important *key terms* and *vocabulary*?

❑ Am I planning to use multiple *visual supports* to illustrate key concepts, steps, relationships among concepts, and so forth?

❑ Am I planning to put my *directions* in writing, say them, and demonstrate them?

Summary

This chapter has been about critical teaching skills that impact the effectiveness of presenting information to students. These skills will have a major effect on how well students understand what is being presented. Complete, thorough explanations, along with demonstrations when appropriate, provide an effective foundation for learning. Visual supports can be used to help students "picture" the information presented. Making good decisions about teaching key terms and vocabulary can have a positive impact on student understanding. Finally, giving effective directions to students so they know how to complete tasks they are assigned influences their opportunities for success. Part of being an effective presenter is knowing when to use which combination of the strategies presented in this chapter.

References and Suggested Reading

Baumann, J. F., and E. J. Kame'enui. 2004. *Vocabulary instruction: Research to practice (Solving problems in the teaching of literacy)*. New York: Guilford Press.

Boudah, D. J., B. K. Lenz, J. A. Bulgren, J. B. Schumaker, and D. D. Deshler. 2000. Don't water down! Enhance content learning through the unit organizer routine. *Teaching Exceptional Children* 32 (3): 48–56.

Boyle, J. R., and N. Yeager. 1997. Blueprints for learning: Using cognitive frameworks for understanding. *Teaching Exceptional Children* 29: 26–31.

Bromley, K., L. Irwin-DeVitis, and M. Modio. 1995. *Graphic organizers: Visual strategies for active learning*. New York: Scholastic Professional Books.

Colvin, G., and M. Lazar. 1997. *The effective elementary classroom*. Longmont, CO: Sopris West.

Coyne, M. D., E. J. Kame'enui, and D. W. Carnine. 2007. *Effective teaching strategies that accommodate diverse learners*. 3rd ed. Columbus, OH: Merrill.

Cruickshank, D. R., D. B. Jenkins, and K. K. Metcalf. 2009. *The act of teaching*. 5th ed. Boston: McGraw-Hill.

DiSarno, N. J., M. Schowalter, and P. Grassa. 2002. Classroom amplification to enhance student performance. *Teaching Exceptional Children* 34 (6): 20–26.

Dye, G. A. 2000. Graphic organizers to the rescue! Help students link—and remember—information. *Teaching Exceptional Children* 32 (2): 72–76.

Echevarria, J., M. Vogt, and D. J. Short. 2008. *Making content comprehensible for English learners: The SIOP model*. 3rd ed. Boston: Pearson/Allyn and Bacon.

Forte, I., and S. Schurr. 1996. *Graphic organizers & planning outlines for authentic instruction and assessment*. Nashville, TN: Incentive Publications.

Gallavan, N. P., and E. Kottler. 2007. Eight types of graphic organizers for empowering social studies students and teacher. *Social Studies* 98 (3): 117–128.

Guillaume, A. M. 2008. *K–12 classroom teaching: A primer for new professionals*. 3rd ed. Columbus, OH: Merrill.

Hall, T., and N. Strangman. 2002. Graphic organizers. Wakefield, MA: National Center on Accessing the General Curriculum. http://www.cast.org/publications/ncac/ncac_go.html.

Helman, L. A., and M. K. Burns. 2008. What does oral language have to do with it? Helping young English-language learners acquire a sight word vocabulary. *Reading Teacher* 62 (1): 14–19.

Herrell, A. L., and M. Jordan. 2005. *Fifty strategies for improving vocabulary, comprehension, and fluency*. 2nd ed. Upper Saddle River, NJ: Prentice-Hall.

Jaime, K., E. Knowlton. 2007. Visual supports for students with behavior and cognitive challenges. *Intervention in School & Clinic* 42 (5): 259–270.

Lee, H., and L. Herner-Patnode. 2007. Teaching mathematics vocabulary to diverse groups. *Intervention in School and Clinic* 43 (2): 121–126.

Lenz, K., G. L. Adams, J. A. Bulgren, N. Pouliot, and M. Laraux. 2007. Effects of curriculum maps and guiding questions on the test performance of adolescents with learning disabilities. *Learning Disability Quarterly* 30 (4): 235–244.

Lewis, R. B., and D. H. Doorlag. 2009. *Teaching special students in general education classrooms*. 8th ed. Upper Saddle River, NJ: Pearson.

Lorenz, B., T. Green, and A. Brown. Using multimedia graphic organizer software in the prewriting activities of primary school students: What are the benefits? *Computers in the Schools* 26 (2): 115–129.

Luckner, J., S. Bowen, and K. Carter. 2001. Visual teaching strategies for students who are deaf or hard of hearing. *Teaching Exceptional Children* 33 (3): 38–44.

Mastropieri, M. S., and T. E. Scruggs. 2007. *The inclusive classroom: Strategies for effective instruction*. 3rd ed. Upper Saddle River, NJ: Prentice Hall.

Morgan, M., and K. B. Moni. 2007. 20 ways to motivate students with disabilities using sight-vocabulary activities. *Intervention in School and Clinic* 42 (4): 229–233.

Pilulski, J. J., and S. Templeton. 2004. *Teaching and developing vocabulary: Key to long-term reading success*. Boston, MA: Houghton Mifflin.

Reed, B., and J. Railsback. 2003. *Strategies and resources for teachers of English language learners.* Portland, OR: NW Regional Educational Lab.

Robinson, D. H., A. D. Katayama, A. Beth, S. Odom, H. Ya-Ping, and A. Vanderveen. 2006. Increasing text comprehension and graphic note-taking using a partial graphic organizer. *Journal of Educational Research* 100 (2): 103–111.

Salend, S. J., and A. Salinas. 2003. Language differences or learning difficulties: The work of the multidisciplinary team. *Teaching Exceptional Children* 35 (4): 36–43.

Spencer, B. H., and A. M. Guillaume. 2006. Integrating curriculum through the learning cycle: content-based reading and vocabulary instruction. *The Reading Teacher* 60 (3): 206–219.

Taylor, D. B. 2009. Using explicit instruction to promote vocabulary learning for struggling readers. *Reading & Writing Quarterly* 25 (2/3): 205–220.

Vesely, P. J. 2009. Word of the day improves and redirects student attention while supporting vocabulary development. *Intervention in School and Clinic* 44 (5): 282–287.

Wallace, C. 2007. Vocabulary: The key to teaching English language learners to read. *Reading Improvement* 44 (4): 189–193.

Zirpoli, T. J. 2005. *Behavior management: Applications for teachers.* 4th ed. Upper Saddle River, NJ: Pearson.

CHAPTER
6

Critical Teaching Skills for Promoting Active Participation

Introduction

Active participation, also called *active student responding* (Salend 2008) or *active student engagement* (Cohen and Spenciner 2009), is a way of involving students in lessons or activities. Active participation strategies, planned by the teacher, are directly related to the content of the lesson or activity, ask for overt responses made by all students at once, and are requested frequently during presentations. As you will see, we define *active participation* very specifically. Each characteristic is defined below.

- Active participation responses are *overt* student responses such as speaking, writing, and signaling. Students are asked to respond actively, rather than only responding passively or covertly (listening, watching, or thinking about the content).

- Active participation responses occur *during* teacher presentations rather than after or instead of presentations. Students can make active responses during teacher explanations, demonstrations, directions, reviews, openings, closings, readings, videos, and so on. These are different from the practice tasks that may *follow* a presentation, for example, the teacher presents information on how to make change from a dollar and then the students complete practice problems. Active participation responses are also different from the hands-on activities that *follow or replace* presentations. Having students paint a picture of a story's main character, create a video play of Lewis and Clark's expedition, or make boats from cardboard and duct tape that will carry students across the lake are examples of hands-on activities.

- Active participation responses are made by *all of the students at once*. For example, *everyone* says the definition in unison; *everyone* writes an example; *everyone* explains to a partner. Calling on individuals to answer a question or selecting one or a few students to demonstrate something or to do a problem on the board are *not* examples of active participation.

- Active participation responses are *frequent*. They allow students many brief opportunities to practice and process information as it is being presented and to build understanding. They keep students steadily engaged rather than waiting until the end of a presentation to give them something to do. Some active participation strategies are very quick. Notice the back-and-forth, call-and-response quality to the following example of a teacher using active participation as she introduces a new term to her students.

EXAMPLE OF QUICK, FREQUENT ACTIVE PARTICIPATION RESPONSES

Teacher: says new term
Students: repeat it in unison
Teacher: defines term
Students: paraphrase definition to partner
Teacher: shows an example
Students: write another example
Teacher: shows several examples and nonexamples
Students: identify correct examples by signaling thumbs up

Techniques that a teacher uses to bring about the involvement of all students at once during a presentation are active participation strategies. Most lessons and activities eventually involve all students in active practice or processing of some sort. However, it is very important that teachers provide students with opportunities to actively respond right from the start.

Importance of Active Participation

Strategies for active participation provide students with opportunities to respond, and are valuable for several reasons. First, using these strategies keeps students engaged, making them more likely to learn, retain, and process the information presented. Next, various active participation strategies allow the teacher to check for understanding early and often during instruction. When students are involved in lessons or activities made interactive through the use of active participation strategies, they are also more likely to be attentive, less likely to be off-task, and more likely to feel good about their competence (Lewis and Doorlag 2009). Finally, the use of these strategies is likely to make lessons and activities more fun and interesting for students and teachers.

Read about Mr. Reyna and the lesson he is planning for his class in the box called "A Look at Mr. Reyna's Planning." Then, as you read this chapter, think about how Mr. Reyna could use active participation to help his students learn, retain, and use the lesson information. You may imagine that Mr. Reyna is teaching any grade level.

Types of Active Participation Strategies

Many kinds of active participation strategies can be incorporated into lessons or activities. Recognizing the variation of strategies in terms of their response type and purpose can help teachers select which strategies to use at various points throughout lessons and activities.

One way to think about active participation strategies is by the type of response they require:

- written responses
- oral responses
- signaled responses

A Look at Mr. Reyna's Planning

Mr. Reyna is preparing to teach a series of lessons and activities about stereotyping; this is part of a school-wide anti-bullying and anti-bias curriculum. During this series, students will learn skills such as how to debunk stereotypes, how to avoid perpetuating stereotypes, and so forth. His objective for the current lesson is that his students will locate instances of stereotypes in segments of popular videos and books. The lesson will begin with Mr. Reyna providing a context for this lesson. He'd like for students to clearly understand his expectations for their learning and also wants to determine what they already know about this topic. After this introduction, Mr. Reyna will briefly present background information about stereotyping: a definition, explanations of types of stereotypes, and how stereotypes develop. He will then spend the majority of his time showing how to recognize stereotypes in films and books. He'll show a variety of examples and nonexamples and point out the signal words and images that help us recognize stereotyping. Following the presentation, the students will be given practice opportunities for finding stereotypes in other book excerpts and video clips.

Written responses involve having students write answers, on a chalkboard or "paper think pad," for example. Calling out answers or discussing ideas with partners are examples of *oral responses*. Finally, *signaled responses* include actions such as pointing or holding up cards.

Another way to think about active participation strategies is by their purpose. Most strategies can be loosely organized into three main categories:

- involvement strategies
- rehearsal strategies
- processing strategies

Involvement strategies are designed to keep students alert and attentive. *Rehearsal strategies* are used to provide students with opportunities to practice or rehearse the information presented. A third category, *processing strategies*, help increase comprehension by providing opportunities to think about, mull over, or discuss content to develop a deeper understanding of the material.

Many strategies serve several purposes. As you read through the specific strategies described on the next pages, notice how various strategies easily fit into more than one category. For example, unison response can be both an involvement strategy and a rehearsal strategy. Notice also that some active participation strategies allow the teacher to check each student's understanding. (You will learn more about checking for understanding in Chapter 7.) The organization of strategies by response type and purpose providesa general guideline to consider when selecting strategies. It is far more important to select an appropriate variety of strategies that fit your purposes than it is to spend time trying to correctly label a particular strategy.

Note that teachers can use numerous strategies designed to elicit responses to teacher questions. Considering that teachers ask many questions each day, it is very important to decide carefully how students will participate during question-asking situations. Be sure to select response strategies that will involve as many students as possible during these sessions. An important point must be made here: The act of asking a question is not an active participation strategy, whereas the strategy used for getting a response from students can be.

The box "Teacher Checklist for Planning Active Participation Strategies" provides an overview of key elements to think about when planning the use of active participation strategies. You can use it as a guide when you are writing lesson and activity plans.

Consult the following lists of involvement, rehearsal, and processing strategies for specific ways to elicit active participation responses from your students. Notice that written, oral, and signaled responses are included.

Involvement Strategies

An important purpose of this type of active participation strategy is to keep students alert and attentive during instruction. The following are some examples of how to achieve this goal.

TEACHER CHECKLIST FOR

Planning Active Participation Strategies

❑   Am I planning *frequent* opportunities for all students to actively respond while I present (i.e., explain, demonstrate, review, give directions)?

❑   Am I planning strategies for *various purposes*, such as helping students process information, rehearse information, and stay involved?

❑   Am I planning strategies that require *different types of responses*, such as, written, oral, signaled?

❑   Am I planning strategies to be used in *every part of my lesson or activity*, such as the opening, body/middle, closing?

❑   Am I planning strategies to *meet the diverse needs* of my students, such as oral responses to include students who have difficulty writing?

1.   Ask for *unison responses* from the whole class or from rows or groups. Say, "The name of this river is . . . Everyone?" Make sure that everyone is, in fact, responding.

2.   Ask students to use *response cards*. Say, "When you hear one of the new words in the story, hold up that card."

3.   Ask students to *write a response*. Say, "On your list, check off the steps for resolving conflicts as I model them."

Strategies 1, 2, and 3 work well as response strategies when questions or requests require brief responses.

4.   Have students *stand to share answers* (Kagan 1992). When students have an answer, have them stand up. Call on one student to share the answer. Have everyone with the same or similar answer sit down. Students continue to answer until everyone is sitting down.

5. Have students do *choral reading* of content text as an alternative to "round-robin" reading. Students can read sentences or paragraphs as a group. As a teacher reads aloud, she can stop at various places and have the class fill in words or phrases.

6. Have students *take notes* during teacher presentations, speeches, films, or readings. Skilled note-takers can write their own notes; provide others with partially completed notes.

7. Use a *"think-to-write preview"* to get students thinking about today's topic. Give students 3 minutes to write down everything they know about the topic.

8. Active participation responses are meant to be overt, but covert strategies such as a *"think-about"* or *visual imagery* can also increase student involvement. For example, say to the students, "Imagine for a minute what it would feel like to be teased about the color of your skin," or "Think about a time when you helped a friend." Use visual imagery by asking students to "picture" something in their minds (for example, "Try to imagine how the ferocious lion looked.").

9. *Brainstorming*, followed by the teacher calling on individuals randomly, gives students an opportunity to participate. This isn't technically an active participation strategy since not *every* student is expected to respond at once, but it certainly can help get more students involved.

Rehearsal Strategies

One goal of active participation strategies is to give students a chance to practice or rehearse new information. The following are some examples of how to achieve this goal.

10. Ask a question, and then ask students to *say the answer to a neighbor.*

11. Ask partners to *take turns* summarizing, defining terms, or giving examples.

Strategies 10 and 11 work well when you ask questions that require somewhat longer answers. They are also effective when many students are eager to speak but there is not enough time to call on each student individually.

12. Ask everyone to *write down an answer* on paper, on a small blackboard, or on a dry-erase board. Then have them hold it up so you can see it. For example, tell everyone to write an adjective that describes your chair.

13. Ask students to respond using student *response cards* or other objects. Say, "Hold up the green card if the word is a noun," or "Hold up the isosceles triangle" (Heward et al. 1996; Lambert et al. 2006).

14. Ask for *finger signals* from everyone. Guillaume suggests, for instance, that "students hold up numbers of fingers to respond to mastery questions (e.g., 'How many sides on a triangle?'). Other gestures can also be used. For instance, 'I will watch while you draw a triangle in the air'" (2004, 51). Or you could say, "As I point to each number, put thumbs up if you would round upward."

Strategies 12 through 14 work well when questions require brief answers. Notice that in addition to promoting active participation, they allow you to check the understanding of all students.

15. Use the *pausing technique* (Guerin and Male 1988; Salend 1998). Stop for 2 minutes after every 5 to 7 minutes of lecturing. Have students discuss and review their notes and the content presented (they can rehearse important points or discuss how the information relates to their own experiences, for example).

16. Use *drill partners* to work on facts students need to know until they are certain both partners know and remember them all (Johnson, Johnson, and Holubec 1991).

17. Have *board workers* work together to answer questions. Have each student play a role: one student is the Answer Suggester; one acts as Checker to see if everyone agrees; and one is the Writer (Johnson, Johnson, and Holubec 1991).

Processing Strategies

Another goal of active participation strategies is to allow students the opportunity to process new information. The following are some examples of how to achieve this goal.

18. Ask students to think about the answer to a question. Have them then discuss the answer with their neighbor. Call on pairs to share their answers, such as in Think-Pair-Share (Lyman 1992).

19. Two students become Worksheet Checkers and complete a worksheet together. One student is the reader (reads the question and suggests an answer) and the other is the writer (agrees with the answer or comes up with a new one). When both students agree, the answer is written on the worksheet (Johnson, Johnson, and Holubec 1991).

20. Ask a question, and then ask students to share and discuss their answers in small groups, such as in Buzz Groups (Arends 2009).

21. Ask a question, and then call on individual team members to answer, such as in Numbered Heads Together. After you ask a question, the students in each team (who have numbered off) put their heads together and make sure everyone knows the answer. Then, call out a number and students with that number provide answers to the whole group (Kagan 1992).

Strategies 18 through 21 are especially effective when the content you are teaching is complicated or difficult. They also work well when you want long and varied responses. Keep groups accountable for involving all members by asking the students to record all answers or to defend their method of reaching consensus, or tell them that you may pick one student at random to speak for the group or pair.

22. "*Bookends* is a cooperative learning strategy whereby students meet in small groups before listening to an oral presentation to share their existing knowledge about the topic to be presented. The groups also generate questions related to the topic, and these questions are discussed during or after the oral presentations" (Salend 1998, 231). This technique could also be used with a group discussion or a video presentation.

23. Have students complete a *think-to-write review* in which they write what they learned. Give students 3 to 5 minutes to write down everything they remember from the lesson or activity just taught.

As you can see, there are many, varied strategies that can be used to keep students involved and learning while a teacher is delivering instruction. Let's look at how to incorporate strategies into a specific lesson. Remember Mr. Reyna's lesson on stereotyping? He planned to present basic information about stereotyping and then show students examples of stereotyping in movies and books. Below are some of Mr. Reyna's ideas for including active participation in various parts of his lesson.

Mr. Reyna's Plan for Active Participation

Strategy: Ask students to hold up yes/no *response cards* to designate examples and nonexamples of stereotyping.

Reasoning: Having the opportunity to immediately rehearse the information on stereotyping will help his students remember it; this strategy will also allow Mr. Reyna to check for understanding.

Strategy: Have students *choral read* the objective that he has put in writing on a poster in front of the room.

Reasoning: This strategy will involve and focus students from the very start of the lesson.

Strategy: Pose questions throughout his presentation and have students discuss answers in Buzz Groups to help them process new information.

Reasoning: Having opportunities to think in depth about the information presented is very important for setting the foundation for higher-level thinking.

How else could Mr. Reyna use active participation to keep his students engaged in learning?

Responding to Diversity When Planning for Active Participation

As with all teaching and management practices, you need to consider the diversity in your classroom as you design active participation strategies. Think about skill diversity, cultural diversity, and linguistic diversity.

Responding to Skill Diversity When Planning for Active Participation

A group of students will vary in their behavioral, learning, and academic skills. Consider the following ideas addressing classroom diversity when planning opportunities to respond.

- Increase the number of involvement strategies for students who have difficulty sitting and listening. For example, use frequent choral responses during fast-paced instruction.

- Look around to make sure everyone really is participating during unison and signaled responses. Use proximity or prompts with students who aren't responding.

- Use a variety of response strategies to increase interest and motivation. For example, students can answer questions using choral responses, writing on a whiteboard, or telling a partner.

- Allow students to help plan various physical gestures or signals to be used in lessons or activities. This can be motivating (Salend 2008).

- Provide opportunities to respond in nonverbal ways for students who may be uncomfortable or unable to respond verbally.

- When using strategies that require written responses, match the length of the responses to students' writing skills.

- Use preprinted response cards for students who have difficulty writing.

- Vary the amount of wait-time given. Don't mistake a hesitation to respond as a sign that a student does not know that answer. Students may need extended wait-time, particularly for questions with complicated answers.

- Plan how to regain attention, or how to have students show they are ready to go on (for example, they will look at you or put their pencils down after writing a response).

Responding to Cultural Diversity When Planning for Active Participation

As you plan active participation strategies (and discussions, brainstorming sessions, and questioning techniques) consider the following student variables.

- students' comfort levels with stating opinions, stating opinions passionately, and disagreeing with others, including the teacher

- students' comfort level with volunteering to answer questions or initiating their own questions or comments

- experience with divergent (open-ended) and convergent questions

- beliefs as to what constitutes polite responses to questions or statements, and methods of interrupting

- beliefs about how much talking is polite

- students' comfort with same-gender partners, such as in Think-Pair-Share

Responding to English Language Learners When Planning for Active Participation

The following strategies can benefit your students as they learn English.

- Encourage the participation of English language learners with very limited English proficiency by asking *yes* and *no* questions at first. As language acquisition increases, intersperse more difficult questions such as *who, what, when, why, where,* and *how* (Gersten, Baker, and Marks 1998).

- Provide English language learners with opportunities to practice their English skills as they answer questions. When appropriate, ask questions that require long, complex sentences rather than one or two words. Remember that English language learners can use complex thinking skills even when they are not fluent in English (Gersten, Baker, and Marks 1998).

- Pair English language learners with peer language models. Both English speakers and students who speak the same native language can be excellent models. This support can provide a safe environment for discussing new learning. Students who are uncomfortable speaking to the entire class may more readily speak to a neighbor or small group.

Number of Strategies to Include

When planning lessons and activities, strive to use active participation strategies frequently. While there isn't a rule about how frequently they should be used, the following are guidelines. Cegelka and Berdine (1995) suggest that teachers plan for students to respond in some way several times during each minute of a lesson. The three-statement rule—the teacher will make no more than three statements without having students make a response—is another guideline that points out the importance given to frequent student participation during lecture presentations (Christenson, Ysseldyke, and Thurlow 1989).

It may be impossible, impractical, or unnecessary to try to specify an exact number of response opportunities to include in any lesson or activity. Instead, consider (1) using strategies during all parts of the lesson or activity (the opening, closing, and all parts in between); (2) using numerous strategies that focus on the key ideas you are trying to emphasize (have students say the main points to a partner, for example); and (3) adjusting the number of strategies based on student learning and behavior (if you notice that many students are confused, increase their opportunities to rehearse or process information). Remember that having students actively rehearse information will help ensure the transfer of that information into long-term memory.

Teaching Active Participation Response Strategies

It is important that students know exactly how to perform the active participation responses to be used, for several reasons. It's important because if the students are confused (as to whether signaling thumbs up means *yes* or *no*, for example) the teacher won't get accurate information about student understanding. It is also important when using partner and small-group active participation strategies. If students don't know how to correctly use strategies such as Think-Pair-Share or Buzz Groups, it may result in some students not having the opportunity to be involved. It's also important for students to know how to use active participation materials, such as signal cards and whiteboards, correctly in order to prevent distractions and behavior problems. Taking the time to teach students active participation responses is time well spent.

Some active participation strategies are relatively easy to implement. Others require more detailed directions and opportunities for practice with feedback. It is important to recognize that active participation strategies need to be taught to students, and a direct approach is generally the most effective technique to use for teaching them. For example, when using a strategy such as unison response, students need to have the signal explained ("When I say *everyone*, answer out loud"), be shown how they are expected to respond, and have the chance to practice ("Let's try again to say it all at once"). When having students write answers on a whiteboard, it is important to develop and teach a procedure that will make it less likely that students will copy a neighbor's board and that will make it easier for the teacher to read all boards.

Look at the box "Mini-Lesson: Teaching an Active Participation Response" on the next page for an example of how a response strategy can be taught to students. Lessons for teaching such strategies do not need to be long or elaborate. Often, it will take just a few minutes to teach students what is expected of them. Practice time will vary, of course, depending on the students and the response strategy being taught.

Notice in the mini-lesson that the teacher is presenting information orally, in writing, and through modeling. She is also using repetition of key information and asking for quick and frequent responses from the students. Notice that she uses a simple math problem during the rehearsal so that the focus is on practicing the procedure for using whiteboards rather than practicing math skills.

You may need to provide a review of how to do a strategy that has been taught if a lot of time goes by between uses. Generally, however, it would not be necessary to spend a great deal of time reteaching. If the initial teaching was solid and successful, an occasional review may be all that is needed until the strategy becomes a well-engrained habit.

Summary

Active participation strategies are designed to get all students in the class to respond at once, to have *everyone* actively participating throughout the lesson or activity. You may ask students to say, write, or signal their responses. These active participation strategies encourage attentiveness, provide immediate

MINI-LESSON

*Teaching An Active Participation
Response Strategy*

Objective: Class will correctly follow the steps of the whiteboard procedure (write, face down, up on signal) five times in a row.

Explain:

■ While I'm teaching, I'll ask you to write responses on your whiteboards. (*Hold up whiteboard.*) This will help you practice the information you are learning and will give me a chance to see how well I'm teaching.

■ I'm going to teach you a procedure for using whiteboards that will let me check everyone's answers. (*Point to poster of the steps.*) Read the steps with me: write, face down, up on signal.

■ (*Explain each step:*)
  1. You'll *write* your answer on your board big enough so I can see it from here.
  2. Turn the board *face down* on your desk as soon as you're finished writing.
  3. When I say the signal "Boards up!" you'll raise your board *up on signal* as high as you can and turn it so that I can see it. (*Use a whiteboard as a visual support—an answer is already written on it.*)

■ Remember: write, face down, up on signal. What's the signal, everyone? (*Students should respond by saying* Boards up!) Say the three steps together. (*Students should respond by repeating the three steps.*) Again. (*Students should repeat the three steps again.*)

Show:

■ Watch me while I show you how to use the whiteboard procedure. (*Demonstrate the steps with the instructional assistant.*) She'll be the teacher and I'll be the student. Say the steps with me as I do them.

Rehearse:

■ Let's practice. Write 2 + 4 on your whiteboard. Now:
  1. Write answer. What do you do next?
  2. Face down. Wait for signal. . . . Boards up!
  3. Up on signal.

Look carefully to make sure that students are doing the procedure accurately. Give feedback about how they followed the procedure. Practice with several more problems.

Follow-up: Once the procedure has been taught, carefully monitor and give feedback regarding its use during lessons. Reteach if needed.

---

practice, and encourage students to think about new ideas. Some of these strategies also help you monitor progress by checking the understanding of each student. Set a goal to use a variety of active participation strategies and to use them frequently in all lessons and activities.

References and Suggested Reading

Arends, R. I. 2009. *Learning to teach*. 8th ed. San Francisco: McGraw-Hill.

Blackwell, A., and T. McLaughlin. 2005. Using guided notes, choral responding, and response cards to increase students' performance. *International Journal of Special Education* 20: 1–5.

Berrong, A. M., J. W. Schuster, T. E. Morse, B. C. Collins. 2007. The effects of response cards on active participation and social behavior of students with moderate and severe disabilities. *Journal of Developmental and Physical Disabilities* 19 (3): 187–199.

Boyle, J. R. 2007. The process of note taking: implications for students with mild disabilities. *Clearing House* 80 (5): 227–232.

Cegelka, P. T., and W. H. Berdine. 1995. *Effective instruction for students with learning difficulties*. Boston: Allyn and Bacon.

Christenson, S. L., J. E. Ysseldyke, and M. L. Thurlow. 1989. Critical instructional factors for students with mild handicaps: An integrative review. *Remedial and Special Education* 10 (5): 21–29.

Cohen, L., and L. J. Spenciner. 2009. *Teaching students with mild and moderate disabilities: Research-based practices.* 2nd ed. Upper Saddle River, NJ: Pearson/Merrill Prentice Hall.

Conroy, M. A., K. S. Sutherland, A. L. Snyder, and S. Marsh. 2008. Classwide interventions: Effective instruction makes a difference. *Teaching Exceptional Children* 40 (6): 24–30.

Delpit, L., and P. White-Bradley. 2003. Educating or imprisoning the spirit: Lessons from ancient Egypt. *Theory into Practice* 42 (4): 283–288.

Feldman, K., and L. Denti. 2004. High-access instruction: Practical strategies to increase active learning in diverse classrooms. *Focus on Exceptional Children* 36 (7): 1–11.

Gersten, R., S. K. Baker, and S. U. Marks. 1998. *Teaching English-language learners with learning difficulties: Guiding principles and examples from research-based practice.* U.S. Department of Education: ERIC/OSEP Special Project.

Godfrey, S. A., J. Grisham-Brown, J. W. Schuster, M. L. Hemmeter. 2003. The effects of three techniques on student participation with preschool children with attending problems. *Education & Treatment of Children* 26 (3): 255–273.

Guerin, G. R., and M. Male. 1988. *Models of best teaching practices.* Paper presented at the meeting of the Council for Exceptional Children, Washington, D.C.

Guillaume, A. M. 2004. *Classroom teaching: A primer for new professionals.* 2nd ed. Upper Saddle River, NJ: Merrill.

Guillaume, A. M. 2004. *Classroom teaching: A primer for new professionals.* 3rd ed. Upper Saddle River, NJ: Merrill.

Gunter, P., J. M. Reffel, C. A. Barnett, J. M. Les, J. Patrick. 2004. Academic response rates in elementary-school classrooms. *Education and Treatment of Children* 27 (2): 105–113.

Harper, G. F., and L. Maheady. 2007. Peer-mediated teaching and students with learning disabilities. *Intervention in School and Clinic* 43 (2): 101–107.

Haydon, T., C. Borders, D. Embury, and L. Clarke. 2009. Using effective instructional delivery as a classwide management tool. *Beyond Behavior* 18 (2): 12–17.

Haydon, T., G. R. Mancil, and C. VanLoan. 2009. Using opportunities to respond in a general education classroom: A case study. *Education & Treatment of Children* 32 (2): 267–278.

Heward, W. L., R. Gardner, R. A. Cavanaugh, F. H. Courson, T. A. Grossi, and P. M. Barbetta. 1996. Everyone participates in this class. *Teaching Exceptional Children* 28 (2): 4–10.

Johnson, D. W., R. T. Johnson, and E. J. Holubec. 1991. *Cooperation in the classroom.* Edina, MN: Interaction Book.

Kagan, S. 1992. *Cooperative learning.* San Juan Capistrano, CA: Kagan Cooperative Learning.

Kagan, S., and M. Kagan. 2009. *Cooperative learning.* San Clemente, CA: Kagan Publishing & Professional Development.

Kern, L., and G. Sacks. 2003. *How to deal effectively with inappropriate talking and noisemaking.* Austin, TX: Pro-Ed.

Lambert, M. C., G. Cartledge, W. Heward, and Y. Lo. 2006. Effects of response cards on disruptive behavior and academic responding during math lessons by fourth-grade urban students. *Journal of Positive Behavior Interventions* 8 (2): 88–89.

Lewis, R. B., and D. H. Doorlag. 2009. *Teaching special students in general education classrooms.* 8th ed. Upper Saddle River, NJ: Pearson/Merrill Prentice Hall.

Lewis, T. J., S. I. Hudson, M. Richter, and N. Johnson. 2004. Scientifically supported practices in emotional and behavioral disorders: A proposed approach and brief review of current practices. *Behavioral Disorders* 29 (3): 247–259.

Lyman, F. T. 1992. Think-pair-share, thinktrix, thinklinks, and weird facts: An interactive system for cooperative thinking. In *Enhancing thinking through cooperative learning*, eds. N. Davidson and T. Worsham, 169–181. New York: Teachers College Press.

Maheady, L, J., G. F. Michielli-Pandl, B. Harper, and B. Mallette. 2006. The effects of numbered heads together with and without an incentive package on the science test performance of a diverse group of sixth graders. *Journal of Behavioral Education*, 15 (1): 24–38.

Mastropieri, M. S., and T. E. Scruggs. 2007. *The inclusive classroom: Strategies for effective instruction.* 3rd ed. Columbus, OH: Prentice Hall/Merrill.

Randolph, J. J. 2007. Meta-analysis of the research on response cards: effects on test achievement, quiz achievement, participation, and off-task behavior. *Journal of Positive Behavior Interventions* 9 (2): 113–128.

Salend, S. J. 1998. *Effective mainstreaming: Creating inclusive classrooms.* Columbus, OH: Merrill.

Salend, S. J. 2008. *Creating inclusive classrooms: Effective and reflective practices for all students.* 6th ed. Upper Saddle River, NJ: Pearson/Merrill Prentice Hall.

Simonsen, B., S. Fairbanks, A. Briesch, D. Myers, and G. Sugai. 2008. Evidence-based practices in classroom management: Considerations for research to practice. *Education and Treatment of Children* 31 (3): 351–380.

Critical Teaching Skills for Planning Practice and Monitoring Student Progress

Introduction

This chapter is about planning student practice and monitoring student progress. We are presenting these topics together because their uses are intertwined. Student practice events provide opportunities for teachers to monitor learning progress. In this way, practice with monitoring provides teachers with necessary information to determine what to do next. For example, if a teacher notices that many students are making mistakes when he monitors student practice, he will most likely go back and teach some more. Or, he could decide that more practice is needed. On the other hand, if he notices that nearly all students are successful with the practice, he will likely decide to go on to the next lesson and provide some additional assistance to any students who need it. Student practice and teacher monitoring are presented together in this chapter because they each play an integral role in instructional decision-making.

In this chapter, you will learn about different types of practice, their purposes, and how to set them up so they are effective. You will also learn about various types of monitoring activities, some of which occur during and some of which occur at the end of lessons or activities. Read about Ms. Kelley and the lesson she is planning for her class. As you read the rest of the chapter, think about how Ms. Kelley could implement practice and evaluation strategies effectively.

A Look at Ms. Kelley's Planning

Ms. Kelley is planning a lesson to teach her students a strategy for finding missing addends (e.g., $4 + \_\_\_ = 10$). Her objective is: Given eight addition sentences with one missing addend and a sum not greater than 10, students will write the missing addend correctly for all of them. She plans to open her lesson by telling little scenarios, such as "Imagine that you are sitting on your couch watching television. You put your hand under one of the cushions and you find 4 pennies. You're very excited, because you have been wanting a gumball from the machine at the grocery store. The gumball costs 10 pennies. How many more pennies will you need to have enough for the gumball?" Next, she will show a poster of the strategy steps and have students read the steps with her. Then, she'll explain and demonstrate the strategy steps (*Say the number you know. Count on to 10. Write the missing addend.*) with several more scenarios. Ms. Kelley plans to have her students practice using the strategy following her instruction.

Planning Practice

One key to student success in learning new information and skills is having the opportunity for adequate practice with feedback. There are a couple of factors to consider when planning practice. When teaching something new, the teacher first looks for students to be accurate with the new information. They need to be monitored carefully to check progress to make sure they are not practicing errors. This type of practice, therefore, generally takes place in the classroom as seatwork or performance practice. Once students are accurate, additional practice helps develop the fluency that is necessary for generalization to new settings and situations. Practice for fluency can take place without close supervision, such as homework. Some practice opportunities help students become accurate; others help students become fluent; still others are designed to promote application of the knowledge or skill. In this way, practice serves different purposes. Student progress is used to determine whether they need more instruction, or more or less practice. Teacher monitoring and feedback are instrumental in making practice sessions effective.

Students participate in many practice activities throughout the course of the day or week. Two key planning considerations for teachers are how much support will students need and where the practice is to be done. In-class practice (or *classwork*) occurs in the classroom within close proximity of the teacher, so that close monitoring by the teacher is possible. Some examples of in-class practice activities are listed below.

- If students are practicing a computation skill such as how to multiply fractions, they will most likely practice solving problems on a worksheet.

- If students are learning how to interrupt politely, then role-plays are appropriate.

- A presentation in front of the class would be an authentic practice activity for students who are learning group presentation skills.

- Working with a partner on some kind of a project would be appropriate for students who are practicing how to work together.

All of these in-class practice opportunities allow for close teacher monitoring.

When students have become accurate, but not yet fluent, with the new skill or knowledge, practice often occurs out of class as *homework*. For example, a student may play the first 25 measures of the newly learned musical piece on her flute or conduct a diet survey with members of her family. When students practice out of class, they don't have immediate teacher monitoring and support. Feedback will be delayed—that is, the teacher will check the homework assignment and give feedback later. The lack of close supervision is appropriate when practice for fluency is the desired learning outcome.

In summary, teachers provide many different opportunities for student practice. Practice can occur inside or outside of the classroom and with varying degrees of teacher support. In the section that follows, you will learn about several major types of practice opportunities.

Two Types of Practice

Two specific types of practice that teachers typically provide for students as they learn new information are *supervised practice* and *extended practice*. These types of practice are similar in *what* is practiced, but vary in terms of *how* the practice occurs. In general, the amount of teacher support available to students and the setting in which the practice occurs are the major differences between these two types of practice.

Supervised Practice

Supervised practice is an essential type of in-class practice in many lessons and activities. It provides the first opportunity for students to practice all parts/pieces of the new skill/information together. For example, students learning the formula for converting degrees Celsius to degrees Fahrenheit will practice all of the steps of the algorithm in sequence during supervised practice. During this type of practice, students practice with fairly continuous supervision from the teacher after he has presented necessary information about the skill or knowledge to be learned. Supervised practice is extremely important when students are first learning new information so teachers can check for accuracy. While the specific activities that are used for this practice are varied, all involve direct supervision and immediate feedback. For example, the teacher checks the problems students are completing on a worksheet and gives feedback. Effective supervised practice activities allow the teacher to see directly if the students are learning.

There are various levels of supervised practice that teachers can use, and each has a different purpose. The following are three levels.

1. *Whole-Group Supervised Practice* After the teacher has demonstrated the new skill numerous times and has checked to see that students understand the various parts of the new skill, she now involves the class in practicing the whole skill, that is, all parts together. For example, she may say, "Let's all do a problem together. What should I do first? Second?" or "Say the whole formula. . . . Everyone?" Notice that the teacher is checking student knowledge of the learning as it is described in the objective. This helps her determine if the students are learning the whole skill. Note: Whole-group supervised practice looks much like a whole-group check for understanding (CFU). The main difference is that a CFU checks parts of the skill while supervised practice involves putting all parts of the skill together.

Whole-group practice offers support for the rehearsal of new learning when students are not yet accurate or confident alone. Note that whole-group supervised practice may not always be possible. For example, let's say that you are teaching a social skill lesson where the objective is to perform a social skill. The performance would need to occur in a role-play or authentic situation, and it would not be feasible for the teacher to monitor and provide feedback to everyone at once.

2. *Small-Group or Partner Supervised Practice* The second level of supervised practice involves asking students to practice with the support of peers while the teacher monitors and provides feedback. Students must be told exactly how to work together (for example, "Partner 1 will circle the errors, and Partner 2 will correct the errors; then switch roles for the second sentence").

The first two levels of supervised practice provide a bridge between teacher presentations and individual practice. This means that initial attempts to perform or express the learned information have peer, as well as teacher, support. This is a form of scaffolding.

3. *Individual Supervised Practice* The final and essential level involves asking each student to practice alone while the teacher checks and corrects. The key here is that the teacher monitors and provides feedback. He does not wait until a student raises a hand, but rather checks everyone. Note: If the skill being learned is something like "how to share," then individual supervised practice will involve working with a partner. This is, of course, because one cannot share alone—this type of skill has to occur in interaction with others. The third level provides the teacher with an opportunity to see what students can do individually (alone, without peer help). This is the only required type of supervised practice, and it is an extremely important one. It provides the teacher with information needed to determine what to do next. If students perform accurately during the individual practice phase, the teacher knows that she may move ahead. If students have difficulty at this stage, the teacher knows to go back and reteach. The following shows examples of using supervised practice, each of which take place under the close supervision of the teacher.

EXAMPLE OF USING ALL LEVELS OF SUPERVISED PRACTICE

- *Whole-Group Practice*: Students "talk the teacher through" one more addition computation problem. They call out what to do next as the teacher works the problem on the overhead and asks questions such as "What is the first step?"

- *Partner or Small-Group Practice*: Students work with a partner to sort more examples of proper and common nouns. Each student is assigned a role, and each student has practice sorting both kinds of nouns. The teacher monitors and gives feedback.

- *Individual Practice*: Students circle examples of mammals on a worksheet that includes both examples and nonexamples of mammals. The teacher monitors and gives feedback.

The three levels of supervised practice allow for flexibility in planning the rehearsal of new information. The essential individual supervised practice portion gives all students an opportunity to receive feedback on their own progress. When the new knowledge or skill is especially difficult or complex, or if prior checks for understanding show that students are struggling, the teacher will probably want to use whole-class, small-group, or partner practice prior to individual practice.

Note that individual supervised practice is *not* the formal evaluation, although it is like the formal evaluation in that the skill practiced is congruent with the objective (and the instruction). This practice is designed as an opportunity for each student to receive performance feedback from the teacher and is a step toward the objective. It is also an opportunity to build high levels of accuracy and fluency before moving to extended practice. During the evaluation portion of the lesson, however, students must perform the objective individually and independently, without the help of peers or the teacher. The evaluation follows the instruction and all practice opportunities.

RESPONDING TO SKILL DIVERSITY WHEN PLANNING SUPERVISED PRACTICE

- Provide more structure and cues at first (such as an outline of a letter showing where to write the date, the greeting, and the other parts).

- Use similar examples for initial practice. Gradually change to more difficult or less similar examples.

- Provide error drills. When you notice that students are making a specific error repeatedly, provide feedback and then additional practice on the correct way.

- Increase the amount of initial practice with teacher support (for example, "Say it with me," or "Do it with me."). Some students will need more practice than others.

- Check on students you think might have difficulty, but do not spend too much time with any one student.

- Increase the amount of initial practice with peer support by using more partner or small-group situations. Remember that although individual supervised practice is the only required type of supervised practice, partner and small-group practice can provide very necessary scaffolding for some students.

- Structure small-group and partner practice by teaching students how to work together (see Chapter 8 for more information).

- Increase the amount of immediate feedback.

RESPONDING TO ENGLISH LANGUAGE LEARNERS WHEN PLANNING SUPERVISED PRACTICE

- Decide if it would be advantageous or possible to partner same-language speakers for practice.

- Consider providing longer periods of group- and partner-supported practice.

- Let students practice without being corrected for speaking errors that do not impact the new learning.

- Try to build in as much listening, speaking, reading, and writing practice as possible.

Supervised practice is one of the most important steps in helping students learn. It mirrors the instruction it follows, and provides students with an excellent way to gain accuracy. The individual supervised practice piece allows each student a way to receive feedback from the teacher. The teacher is able to see which students are accurate and which students are not. It also provides the teacher with the information needed about whether to move ahead or to go back and reteach. Supervised practice is an essential step toward evaluation.

Extended Practice

Extended practice is another part of the lesson where the teacher plans opportunities for students to practice what they are learning. The purpose of this practice is to help students deepen their understanding, develop high levels of accuracy and fluency, and/or help students generalize the new information. Extended practice provides less continuous and less direct support for students than does supervised practice, and often takes place outside of the classroom as homework. It is important that it be used only when students have shown that they are accurate with the new information. This is one reason why careful monitoring during supervised practice is important. Generally, the teacher moves to extended practice only when it is obvious that the students will be successful with less support.

Teachers can provide extended practice for students in a variety of ways. First, students may be given an additional in-class practice activity, such as additional paragraphs to read and then summarize, or role-plays to practice "taking no for an answer." Second, students can be given out-of-class activities (homework), such as additional algebra problems to compute. Extended practice activities vary in what students will actually be doing, but they are all designed to provide additional practice on the information presented.

A main outcome of extended practice is student preparation for the evaluation portion of the lesson. Teacher feedback during extended practice is an essential part of this lesson component (see more information about monitoring and feedback later on in this chapter). When students turn in their homework assignments, for example, the teacher must look carefully at the assignment to see whether students were successful. When students do role-plays, the teacher will observe them carefully, make suggestions, and give positive performance compliments. In all cases, teachers should communicate the results of their examinations to students so they know how they are progressing. This careful examination of student performance helps teachers decide whether the students need more extended practice or more instruction. Once a teacher is satisfied that students have been successful in extended practice, she will move the lesson to evaluation.

A SPECIAL NOTE ABOUT IN-CLASS PRACTICE ACTIVITIES

Cegelka and Berdine (1995) state that students spend anywhere from 50 to 70 percent of the school day in independent activities. When you consider the importance of opportunities to respond in student learning, it follows that students need to be provided with opportunities for active engagement in practice. The following suggestions can help you plan effective in-class practice activities:

- Explain the purpose of the seatwork practice so that students will know why they are doing it.

- Be sure directions are clearly stated and written, and carefully check for understanding.

- Move around quickly at the beginning to make sure each student gets started quickly.

- Don't just wander; look carefully at each student's work, not just those who raise their hands.

- It may be best to have students complete just a few items before correcting their work.

- Use peers to help monitor ("Compare your answers to questions 1 and 2 with your partner and let me know if they are different.").

- Once students begin working on seatwork, stop and reteach or reexplain if you notice that many students are asking the same questions. Getting the whole group together again will save you time.

PROVIDING EFFECTIVE PRACTICE USING ROLE-PLAYS

When practicing communication skills, social and emotional skills, or classroom routines and rules, role-plays can provide performance practice. The following suggestions can help you plan effective practice (see Chapter 19 for additional ideas).

- In role-plays, be sure each student has the opportunity to take the lead role. If students are practicing making apologies, then each student must *make* an apology.

- Use a variety of scenarios for role-plays so students see the various applications of the skill.

- Get ideas for scenarios from students to make sure they are relevant to students' lives.

- Provide support for success in role-playing the skill correctly. Coaching, opportunities for rehearsing with peers, and steps written on posters can help.

- If a student makes an error during a role-play, stop him immediately, correct the error, and let him do the role-play again.

A SPECIAL NOTE ABOUT OUT-OF-CLASS PRACTICE ACTIVITIES

Remember that in extended practice, as we are using the term here, students are doing additional practice of the new skill or knowledge rather than acquiring new information, such as reading a chapter of a social studies text. Consider the following when planning out-of-class activities:

- Consider the resources that are available to students at home. Be sure that students are accurate enough with the new information that they can do the homework without help.

- Homework assignments should be work that students can complete successfully. They should be considered practice, not a continuation of instruction (Arends 2009).

- Vary the amount of practice assigned based on student need. Some students need a lot of practice, whereas others need very little.

- Provide incentives for homework completion.

- Go over homework directions and begin the assignment during class. Be sure the task is the same or similar to supervised practice (Salend and Gajria 1995).

- When assigning homework, tell students the purpose of the assignment, directions for completion, due date, required format, needed materials, and source of help (Wood 2006).

- Devise a system to let parents know what their students are to do at home.

- Start a homework club. Regardless of where the club meets (school, library, community agency) or who supervises the students (teacher, social worker, college students), make its main purpose to support a school's efforts to help struggling learners succeed (Sanacore 2002).

- Don't just check off that the homework was turned in. Be sure it was complete and accurate.

RESPONDING TO SKILL DIVERSITY WHEN PLANNING EXTENDED PRACTICE

Some of the most challenging times in the classroom can be when students are expected to work independently. You can help students be successful by building in meaningful adjustments to extended practice activities. The following are some examples:

- Reduce the length of each practice session, but provide more sessions.

- Provide varying amounts of homework based on a realistic idea of what each student can finish. Some students can complete more than others (Wood 2006).

- Change the task without changing the content to avoid boredom during a practice session. For example, have students select an answer versus writing an answer; have them write the answer on paper, the blackboard, or a transparency; or have them use computerized practice programs.

- Make the practice interesting and fun (for example, use a game format). This applies to both seatwork and homework.

- Increase the amount of support during practice (study guides, peer tutors, and visual supports such as posters and desktop number lines, for example).

- Set up a homework Web site (Salend et al. 2004). This can be of benefit to both students and their parents. Students can double-check assignments and parents can know what their students are being asked to do.

- When possible, provide authentic practice in context as part of real tasks. For example, when students are practicing lining up, let them practice when they must line up to transition to another room.

- Recruit parents to serve as "homework coaches" to their children. The coach can look over assignments, monitor homework completion, and review finished work for accuracy and neatness (Wright 2004).

- Encourage students to submit assignments online (Salend et al. 2004). This eliminates having to keep track of papers.

- Teach a strategy for homework completion, such as the PROJECT Strategy (Hughes et al. 2002).

- Give directions for homework assignments at a reading level appropriate for your students. Use picture cues when possible. This is especially beneficial for students who are English language learners and students who have difficulty reading.

Teachers can use varying types of activities to help students practice the material they are learning.

Examples of practice activities include setting up an experiment to test the effect of gravitational pull, playing and replaying one section of a piano sonata, role-playing how to ask for help, drawing various types of angles with a protractor, and writing answers to addition problems on a whiteboard. Prepare some practice activities to be completed in class and others out of class. More direct supervision is provided during in-class activities than for homework. All practice activities should help students work toward the learning outcome that is planned in the lesson or activity objective. Remember Ms. Kelley's lesson on missing addends? She taught a strategy for finding missing addends by presenting a variety of scenarios that could be solved using the strategy. She explained the strategy and demonstrated how to use it. Then she provided practice. Read her plan in the box "Ms. Kelley Plans Student Practice."

Monitoring Student Progress

When teachers prepare lessons and activities, they start by selecting important content in a particular content area from state standards, national content standards, IEP objectives, and district curriculum guides (see Chapter 1 for more information). The teachers then try to determine what their students already know about the topic through the use of varying assessment methods. Sometimes, this assessment is informal. For example, teachers could try to get a general idea of what their students may already know about intersecting angles by examining the curriculum that students have moved through. Teachers might also use a more formal test, such as a survey-level test that gives them an overview of students' skills or knowledge (Howell and Nolet 2000). Teachers follow this survey-level test with a specific-level test that gives them very specific information about prior knowledge. The important thing to remember about assessment is that it helps teachers prepare relevant, appropriate objectives and related lessons and activities. This is why assessment is such an important place to start in instructional planning.

Once the objective and the lesson or activity plan has been written, you are ready to teach and monitor student progress. Monitoring allows both you and

Ms. Kelley Plans Student Practice

Supervised Practice Strategy: One idea she has is to have students play a "missing addend game" with a partner. Each pair will be given a set of 10 beans and a paper cup (turned upside down). One student hides some of the 10 beans under the cup while the other student closes his eyes. The student whose eyes were closed guesses the number of beans under the cup based on the number still visible and then works the steps while the other student checks for accuracy. Students will switch roles after each problem.

Reasoning: Ms. Kelley determines that her students need a great deal of practice on this skill because many of her students find it quite challenging. She chooses the partner activity because she thinks it will be a fun way for her students to practice, and games are very motivating for her students. Ms. Kelley will move around the room quickly as students work and give feedback regarding accuracy of their use of the strategy.

What other types of supervised practice (remember that individual supervised practice is a must) could she use, and what would it look like?

Extended Practice Strategy: Students will work missing addend problems on a worksheet at home after they have had individual supervised practice at school.

Reasoning: Ms. Kelley wants to provide more practice for fluency and the worksheet is an effective way to provide that practice. Note that she is confident they are ready for fluency practice because when she monitored individual supervised practice, she saw that students were accurate.

What else could be planned for extended practice?

your students to know how they are progressing. It is imperative that you set up opportunities during lessons and activities to help you determine whether the students are grasping the desired learning. After all, that is the purpose of your planning. You need to know whether your students are progressing toward the objective and when they have met it. It is equally important that you let your students know how they are progressing by giving them useful feedback.

Terminology Used in Monitoring Progress

Various terms and concepts are key to better understanding the monitoring process. Because there is variation in the usage of these terms, we are going to define terms the way they will be used in this book. Also, we list resources at the end of this chapter that provide more in-depth reading on all of these topics.

The first terms are *assessment* and *evaluation*. Sometimes, the term *assessment* is used to describe the process of trying to determine what students already know about a topic before instruction, whereas the term *evaluation* refers to the process of monitoring progress during and after instruction. These two terms are often used interchangeably, and that is how we will use them. For example, one can evaluate or assess progress before and during lessons and activities. Both terms mean that the teacher is trying to determine what students already know, what they are learning, and what they learned.

The terms *formative evaluation* and *summative evaluation* refer to when the evaluation occurs. Teachers conduct formative evaluation (or assessment) once the lesson or activity is started to see if students are learning. A teacher's moving about the room looking at her students' performance on a seatwork assignment is an example of formative evaluation. Teachers conduct summative evaluation after instruction or at the end of the lesson or activity to determine whether the students have learned what was specified in the objective. When teachers observe the final role-plays in a social skill lesson, they are performing summative evaluation, because the role-plays were part of the lesson objective. Both types of evaluation play an important role in helping teachers know if students are learning or have learned.

Alternative assessment or *authentic assessment* are terms used to describe methods that are unlike traditional testing done through paper-and-pencil tests. This type of assessment is one where

a student is asked to demonstrate new learning in a real-life setting. *Performance assessments* are a type of alternative assessment in which a student shows what he knows by carrying out an activity or producing a product (Kauchak and Eggen 2007). Examples of alternative assessment activities include (1) a teacher observing a student's use of the newly learned reading strategy during a content reading time; and (2) students writing short stories to be made into books that will be given to younger students.

Types of Monitoring

Formative and summative evaluations occur at different times when teaching lessons and activities. They have different purposes as well. Each of these types of monitoring is discussed below.

Formative Evaluation

Formative evaluation happens prior to the evaluation of the objective (summative evaluation). This evaluation allows teachers to see whether students are progressing successfully toward the objective. It also allows teachers to determine what to do next, that is, whether to go back and teach more. Students benefit from formative evaluation because they receive important feedback on their performance. When teachers use effective formative evaluation techniques, they preserve valuable instructional time by preventing students from practicing errors.

Teachers can monitor student progress during the lesson or activity in several ways. Monitoring during initial instruction (checking for understanding) and careful monitoring of practice activities where students work with varying amounts of teacher support (supervised and extended practice) can be used to determine whether students are making progress toward the objective.

CHECKS FOR UNDERSTANDING

Checks for understanding are monitoring opportunities that, when done correctly, provide teachers with excellent ways to evaluate whether students are learning. They are times when students are asked to identify or produce correct responses, so that the teacher can use their answers to decide whether to move forward in the lesson or activity or to go back and reteach. For example, imagine that your lesson is on complete paragraphs. You begin by teaching topic sentences and then stop to monitor learning before going on. You might check for understanding by:

- asking students to identify topic sentences ("Signal with thumbs up if it's a good topic sentence for this paragraph, thumbs down if it isn't.")

- asking students to produce topic sentences ("Write a topic sentence for this paragraph on your scratch paper.")

Depending on their responses, you will decide whether to spend more time on topic sentences or go on to supporting detail sentences. Teachers should conduct checks for understanding early in both lessons and activities and continue them at appropriate times throughout (when content needs to be rehearsed or when directions are given, for example). Because of their importance, these strategies should be noted directly in the written plan.

Parts of the whole, rather than the whole itself, are the focus of CFUs. Checking various parts of the skill or knowledge allows the teacher to see clearly whether students are ready to go on to supervised practice, where all parts of the skill or knowledge are put together. For example, a teacher would want to check the understanding that students have of each step of a study skill before having students practice all steps of the skill together.

There are many different strategies that can be used to check for student understanding that allow teachers to actually see or hear whether students are on the right track. The most reliable strategies are those where students respond overtly in some way. Answering questions orally, showing thumbs up or thumbs down in response to questions, writing information on pieces of scratch paper, and holding up response cards are examples of overt responses that can help teachers monitor for student understanding and progress during a lesson or activity. See Chapter 6 for many ideas about how to provide opportunities to respond to many or all of your students at once.

Monitoring the understanding of every student at once, such as having each student write an answer on a whiteboard, is the best type of CFU. When you call on only one student to answer a question, you can only check the understanding of that one student. Strategies that are written, oral,

or signaled can all work to check individual understanding. However, with a large group, you'll need to ask for written or signaled responses because you won't be able to hear individual voices in a unison response, and calling on every individual would take too long. As long as every student has an opportunity to answer questions or do something without the influence of others, an individual check for understanding can be accomplished. Occasionally, it may only be feasible to select a few students who seem to represent the whole class. When you prepare the questions you want to use for your CFUs, also carefully plan the response strategies that will provide you with information about every student's progress. The following are examples of CFUs.

EXAMPLES OF USING CHECKS FOR UNDERSTANDING

- In a lesson where students are learning how to do double-digit addition with regrouping in the ones column, Ms. Luce has all students write one step of the problem at a time on a whiteboard and hold it up for teacher viewing.

- When students follow a series of directions for setting up the science experiment, Mr. Doering moves around the room and looks at the work of each group member after they do each step. (Each group member has a specific task to perform for each step.)

- Ms. Slagle has each student in her small group say a new example of a proper noun.

- After being shown shapes and objects that are/are not symmetrical, Mrs. Heppner has the students hold up yes/no response cards to signal whether a shape is symmetrical.

- A transition from one part of the lesson to another requires that students follow a series of directions. Before students begin the transition, Ms. Herwerden calls on selected students (non-volunteers) to check that students know what to do. She is quite confident the selected students are representative of the entire class.

Note that whole-group supervised practice is much like whole-group checks for understanding but with one main difference. A whole-group check for understanding is used to determine whether students understand the various pieces of the skill being learned (for example, "Work the first step of the problem on your whiteboard, and I'll check it."). Whole-group supervised practice is used when students practice all of the steps together (for example, "Work the first problem on your whiteboard, and I'll check it."). Both monitoring activities serve different purposes, but play an equally important role in monitoring student learning.

SUPERVISED AND EXTENDED PRACTICE

A second way to conduct formative evaluation is through careful monitoring of practice opportunities that teachers provide for students. Specific activities (worksheets, role-plays) within the supervised and extended practice portions of a lesson are examples of these opportunities. Remember that these practice opportunities can occur both in and out of the classroom. The following are some examples of how practice activities can be monitored.

EXAMPLES OF MONITORING PRACTICE ACTIVITIES

- Students complete a five-paragraph essay as an extended practice homework assignment. Mrs. Updike reads each essay and provides written feedback about how each student's work matches up with the essay rubric.

- Following a supervised practice activity where groups of students wrote topic sentences for sets of supporting detail sentences, individual students are given a handout that contains five more sets of supporting detail sentences. Mrs. Slentz moves around the room and checks each student's work, giving corrective feedback as necessary.

- Students work with a partner on a math game for supervised practice writing number sentences. Mrs. St. Julien checks in with students as they work.

- Students demonstrate speaking up when a peer is being bullied. Mrs. Mansfield observes carefully and provides feedback.

Summative Evaluation

Teachers use summative evaluation to compare student performance to the standard of performance outlined in the lesson or activity objective; the evaluation should match the objective exactly. Summative evaluation for a lesson objective occurs at the end of a single lesson; summative evaluation for an activity objective will generally take place after a longer period of time, that is, a week or month, or 6 months. Whereas formative evaluation helps the teacher determine whether students are moving toward the objective, summative evaluation tells the teacher whether the students have mastered the objective. The information gained from summative evaluation procedures provides the teacher with important information with which to make future instructional decisions.

In the evaluation section of a lesson plan, which describes the plan for summative evaluation, the teacher writes a clear description of the method that will accurately determine whether the students have mastered the lesson objective. The importance of this section seems obvious, yet it is frequently overlooked or addressed as an afterthought. The information gathered through evaluation helps to make sensible planning decisions for the future. It allows teachers to determine whether they should build on the current lesson, or whether they need to reteach some or all of the information again.

When teachers write the lesson objective, they also plan the summative evaluation. A well-written objective contains a clear description of what students will do to provide evidence that they have learned. Consider the following objective: "When shown a blank diagram of a volcano, students will label all five parts correctly." It is easy to imagine what will be happening during the evaluation of this objective. At the end of the lesson, the teacher will pass out an unlabeled diagram of a volcano, and students will label the various parts. The students will label without help from anyone (no "hints" from the teacher, no help from a partner). Remember that teachers use evaluation to determine an individual student's independent performance in relation to an objective.

Summative evaluation is often much more complex than that described in the volcano example. The evaluation may occur in steps or at various times or locations. This additional information should be explained in the evaluation section of the plan. For example, imagine that you want to teach students to use a reading comprehension strategy. The lesson objective is "Students will use all steps in the XYZ strategy when reading for information in content area texts." You decide to teach the lesson over two days. The steps of the strategy will be taught on Day 1 and the application of the steps on Day 2. The following are Mr. VanderYacht's thoughts on the evaluation component of his lesson:

- "I won't be able to test the objective at the end of the first day because all of the necessary content will not have been taught. I will, however, test to see that my students have learned the strategy steps because, if there is confusion, I will need to reteach rather than go on to the application step. The evaluation completed after instruction on Day 1 will be the strategy steps written from memory."

- "I can evaluate the objective following Day 2 because students should have the information and practice needed to successfully meet the objective. The evaluation will consist of my observing individual students performing the overt strategy actions during short content area reading assignments throughout the day."

At times, it may also be desirable to include a description of a long-term objective and evaluation that relates to the short-term objective for the day. The long-term objective for the reading comprehension strategy might be, "Students will use all steps in the XYZ strategy whenever reading for information in content area texts." Obviously, students cannot be evaluated on their use of this strategy when the teacher no longer has contact with them on a regular basis. However, teachers should still include plans to provide ample generalization and review opportunities for the remainder of the school year. This will increase the likelihood that students will use the strategy following that year. Plans are needed to monitor the use of the strategy during these times. The teacher may wish to note this plan in the evaluation section of the lesson plan.

Students need to be monitored carefully during the lesson—especially during individual supervised and extended practice—so the teacher can determine when they are ready to be formally evaluated. Teachers should evaluate only when students are ready, which may or may not be when the teacher

had planned for evaluation to occur. This definitely speaks to the importance of having a backup plan for when students progress more or less quickly than expected.

As objectives are planned, it should be remembered that evaluation is not necessarily a paper-and-pencil test. In fact, that type of evaluation would not be appropriate in many instances, such as when teaching social skills or learning strategies. An alternate assessment should be used. This can take many forms: learning may be evaluated by asking students to make oral presentations, answer questions orally, make products, perform, or participate. Strive for relevance and authenticity in evaluation methods, and routinely use a combination of techniques. In all cases, however, be sure that you have taught what you are testing.

As a note of caution, try not to affect the evaluation by incorporating unrelated skills. For example, an evaluation technique—such as asking students to create a bulletin board to show their understanding of the life cycle of the salmon—may actually be an evaluation of their artistic or organizational skills. Keep the form of evaluation as direct and simple as possible so that you are not inadvertently testing skills irrelevant to the objective (testing reading skills in math word problems, for example). Think back to Ms. Kelley's lesson in which she teaches students a strategy for finding missing addends. Read about her ideas in the box "Ms. Kelley Plans for Monitoring Student Progress" on the next page.

Responding to Diversity When Planning an Evaluation

The following suggestions will help you plan your evaluation:

- Keep evaluating for retention and for improvement.
- Adjust the amount of time given to students to complete evaluation tasks.
- Consider options for responding. For example, if a student has difficulty writing, allow him to explain orally. Include alternatives in the objective.

The Role of Performance Feedback

Throughout this chapter, the use of feedback has been mentioned numerous times. Teachers assist students as they learn new information and skills

Ms. Kelley Plans for Monitoring Student Progress

Strategy: Ms. Kelley plans to *check for understanding* by asking questions and having students respond using finger signals. For example, she will ask questions such as "Show me with your fingers the number I start with."

Reasoning: She wants to make sure right from the start that her students are learning the individual steps of the strategy. This will help ensure they will be able to effectively put all of the steps together later on in the lesson. Finger signals allow her to see what each individual can do.

How else could Ms. Kelley check for understanding?

Strategy: When all of the practice has been finished, Ms. Kelley is going to give the students a set of eight new number sentences with missing addends. She'll have the students set up their study screens.

Reasoning: Ms. Kelley wants to make sure that her students are ready for the evaluation, which is why she waits until she has had a chance to monitor each student during the practice portion of her lesson. She has them use study screens because her objective is written such that students will work the problems independently and individually.

Do you have suggestions for other ways that Ms. Kelley could evaluate whether the students have met the objective?

important learning outcomes. Without feedback, students may not have an accurate idea of their progress. Effective performance feedback is one of the most important tools teachers can use as they monitor student practice activities completed in or out of the classroom.

Feedback is sometimes used in combination with praise for correct responses ("That's correct! Great!"). Negative feedback for incorrect responses is most effective when it is combined with a statement, an example, or a demonstration of the correct response. Such feedback is often called *corrective feedback*. Corrective feedback is academic and should be delivered respectfully. It focuses on the lesson content rather than the personality of the student. All feedback should be specific rather than general ("Your definition of photosynthesis includes all key points!," rather than "Nice job!").

Note that sometimes, practicum students and student teachers feel reluctant to give corrective feedback because they are afraid that telling students their answers are wrong will hurt their feelings. Consider this example: Mrs. Baker-Couch is teaching a lesson on nouns. After some initial instruction, she has students brainstorm new examples of nouns. Cindy calls out "sit." Mrs. Baker-Couch says, "Well—yes . . . that could be a noun," and then calls on Jerome. Mrs. Baker-Couch did not want Cindy to feel bad because her answer was wrong, so she gave Cindy and the rest of the students inaccurate information about what she was teaching. Mrs. Baker-Couch could have said, "Cindy, that's a great example of a verb. Remember that a noun names a person, place, or thing. Can you think of an example of a thing that someone would sit on?" This response would have given Cindy, and the other students, an additional reminder of the definition of a noun (and Cindy an easy opportunity to come up with a correct answer).

The Teaching/Learning Cycle

Teacher monitoring plays a key role in the teaching/learning process and informs us about two important instructional outcomes. One of the main pieces of information that teachers learn through monitoring, during and after actual instruction, is whether students have learned. Moore writes, "The ultimate question in the instructional process is whether you have taught what you intended to teach and

by giving *feedback* on their performance; it is a way of communicating progress. *Feedback* refers to statements teachers make to students about the accuracy or inaccuracy (or quality) of their responses. During the initial phases of learning, feedback helps ensure that students do not practice errors. Continued monitoring of student work provides additional opportunities for the teacher to let students know how they are progressing toward

whether students have learned what they were supposed to learn" (2005, 161). This means that when teachers monitor progress during instruction as well as when testing the objective, they are able to determine whether students are learning the information being taught. This information helps teachers decide what to do next. For example, if a teacher notices through formative evaluation that students are making numerous errors, she can decide to stop, regroup, backtrack, and teach some more. If she sees that students know the new information, she may proceed with the next objective.

The second valuable bit of information that teachers can gain through monitoring student progress is whether the instructional methods being used are working. Stanford and Reeves address this issue: "[A] fundamental truth in effective teaching is that assessment strategies, both formal and informal, must help the teacher determine the most appropriate instruction, in addition to assessing progress" (2005, 18). They imply that the information that teachers gather can inform decisions about which methods are effective with which students. Because it is commonly understood that not all methods are equally effective with all students, the data teachers collect through monitoring can help them decide appropriate methods. For example, let's say that you notice that many of your students are having difficulty accomplishing the objective for the inquiry math lesson. Decide whether this particular group of students needs a more direct approach and try a direct instruction lesson on the same material.

Teachers have various sources from which they can and should gather information about student progress. Cruickshank, Jenkins, and Metcalf write that effective classroom assessment is more than just paper-and-pencil tests or projects that are completed at the end of instruction. They state that good classroom assessment "requires teachers to continually gather information about their students from a variety of sources, to synthesize that information, and then to make a judgment or evaluation about how well or how much each student has learned" (2003, 271). Gathering this information allows teachers to make informed decisions about student progress.

The following teacher checklist is a summary of important considerations when planning practice and evaluation. You can use it as a guide when you plan these important parts of your lesson or activity.

TEACHER CHECKLIST FOR PRACTICE AND EVALUATION

Practice

❑ Am I planning practice opportunities for early in the lesson/activity?

❑ Am I planning to determine student learning of parts of the whole skill or knowledge?

❑ Am I planning to determine student learning of the whole skill or knowledge?

❑ Am I planning practice that exactly matches my instruction?

❑ Evaluation

❑ Am I planning to test students on the very same thing I explained, demonstrated, and had them practice?

❑ Am I planning to evaluate each student, individually and independently, in relation to the objective?

❑ Am I planning to evaluate after all students have practiced with feedback?

❑ Am I planning a context for evaluation (described in my objective) that is as authentic as possible?

Summary

This chapter has addressed how to provide students with opportunities to practice what they are learning. It has also discussed how to determine whether they are learning. Both play a very important role in the teaching/learning cycle. When planning monitoring opportunities and activities, consider the following:

■ Projects such as informational posters or brochures and demonstrations are all examples of how students can show what they know (Tomlinson 2005: Castellani 2005), rather than using just paper-and-pencil tests.

- Rubrics, T-charts, rating scales, checklists, systematic observations of student performance, and portfolio assessments are examples of techniques that can be used to score performance (Kleinert et al. 2002; Kauchak and Eggen 2003; Cruickshank, Jenkins, and Metcalf 2009). It is important to remember that in all cases, performance is compared to a preset standard.

- Assessment results are an important communication tool for talking with students and parents about progress (Pemberton 2003).

- Self-charting of progress can be an important motivational strategy (Gunter et al. 2002).

- Learning is facilitated when teachers regularly integrate assessment into instruction and involve students in assessment, such as having a student help assemble her own portfolio of products (Kleinert et al. 2002).

- Assessments differ based on the setting in which they take place. Authentic assessments take place in real-life settings, whereas other performance assessments take place in testing situations (Arends 2009).

References and Suggested Reading

Andrade, H. 2009. Promoting learning and achievement through self-assessment. *Theory into Practice* 48 (1): 12–18.

Arends, R. I. 2009. *Learning to teach*. 8th ed. Boston: McGraw-Hill.

Beatty, I. D., and W. J. Gerace. 2009. Technology-enhanced formative assessment: A research-based pedagogy for teaching science with classroom response technology. *Journal of Science Education and Technology* 18 (2): 146–162.

Castellani, J. (ed.). 2005. *Universal design for learning: A guide for teachers and education professionals*. Arlington, VA: The Council for Exceptional Children.

Cegelka, P. T., and W. H. Berdine. 1995. *Effective instruction for students with learning difficulties*. Boston: Allyn and Bacon.

Conroy, M., K. Sutherland, A. Snyder, M. Al-Hendawi, and A. Vo. 2009. Creating a positive classroom atmosphere: Teachers' use of effective praise and feedback. *Beyond Behavior* 18 (2): 18–26.

Cruickshank, D. R., D. B. Jenkins, and K. K. Metcalf. 2003. *The act of teaching*. 3rd ed. Boston: McGraw-Hill.

Cruickshank, D. R., D. B. Jenkins, and K. K. Metcalf. 2009. *The act of teaching*. 5th ed. Boston: McGraw-Hill.

Cizek, G. J. 2009. Reliability and validity of information about student achievement: Comparing large-scale and classroom teaching contexts. *Theory into Practice* 48 (1): 63–71.

Clarke, S. 2009. Using curriculum-based measurement to improve achievement. *Principal* 88 (3): 30–33.

Cusumano, D. L. 2007. Is it working?: An overview of curriculum based measurement and its uses for assessing instructional, intervention, or program effectiveness. *Behavior Analyst Today* 8 (1): 24–34.

Demmert, W. G. 2005. The influences of culture on learning and assessment among Native American students. *Learning Disabilities Research and Practice* 20 (1): 16–23.

Espin, C. 2008. Curriculum-based measurement in writing: Predicting the success of high-school students on state standards tests. *Exceptional Children* 74 (2): 174–193.

Flowers, C. 2009. Links for academic learning (LAL): A conceptual model for investigating alignment of alternate assessments based on alternate achievement standards. Educational Measurement: Issues and Practice 28 (1): 25–37.

Foegen, A. 2008. Progress monitoring in middle school mathematics. *Remedial & Special Education* 29 (4): 195–207.

Fore, C. 2009. Validating curriculum-based measurement for students with emotional and behavioral disorders in middle school. *Assessment for Effective Intervention* 34 (2): 67–73.

Fuchs, L. S. 2008. Using curriculum-based measurement to identify the 2 [percent] population. *Journal of Disability Policy Studies* 19 (3): 153–161.

Griffiths, A. J. 2009. Progress monitoring in oral reading fluency within the context of RTI. *School Psychology Quarterly* 24 (1): 13–23.

Gunter, P. L., K. A. Miller, M. L. Venn, K. Thomas, and S. House. 2002. Self-graphing to success: Computerized data management. *Teaching Exceptional Children* 35 (2): 30–34.

Haas, K. P. 2008. Questioning homework. *English Journal* 98 (2): 14–15.

Hattie, J., and H. Timperley. 2007. The power of feedback. *Review of Educational Research* 77: 81–112.

Hong, E. 2009. Homework self-regulation: Grade, gender, and achievement-level differences. Learning and Individual Differences 19 (2): 269–276.

Hosp, M. K., J. L. Hosp, and K. W. Howell. 2007. *The ABCs of CBM: An easy guide for implementing curriculum-based measurement.* New York: Guilford.

Howell, K., and V. Nolet. 2000. Curriculum-based evaluation: Teaching and decision making. 3rd ed. Belmont, CA: Wadsworth/Thomson Learning.

Hughes, C. A., K. L. Ruhl, J. B. Schumaker, and D. D. Deshler. 2002. Effects of instruction in an assignment completion strategy on the homework performance of students with learning disabilities in general education classes. *Learning Disabilities Research & Practice* 17 (1): 1–18.

Kauchak, D. P., and P. D. Eggen. 2003. *Learning and teaching: Research-based methods.* 4th ed. Boston: Allyn and Bacon.

Kauchak, D. P., and P. D. Eggen. 2007. *Learning and teaching: Research-based methods.* 5th ed. Boston: Allyn and Bacon.

King-Sears, M. 2007. Designing and delivering learning center instruction. *Intervention in School and Clinic* 42 (3): 137–147.

Kleinert, H., P. Green, M. Hurte, J. Clayton, and C. Oetinger. 2002. Creating and using meaningful alternate assessments. *Teaching Exceptional Children* 34 (4): 40–47.

Konold, K. E., S. P. Miller, and K. B. Konold. 2004. Using teacher feedback to enhance student learning. *Teaching Exceptional Children* 36 (6): 64–69.

Mangione, L. 2008. Is homework working? *Phi Delta Kappan* 89 (8): 614–615.

Marzano, R. J., D. J. Pickering, and J. E. Pollock. 2001. *Alexandria, VA: Association for Supervision and Curriculum Development.* Upper Saddle River, NJ: Pearson/Merrill Prentice Hall.

Mastropieri, M. S., and T. E. Scruggs. 2007. *The inclusive classroom: Strategies for effective instruction.* 3rd ed. Columbus, OH: Prentice Hall/Merrill.

Mendicino, M. 2009. A comparison of traditional homework to computer-supported homework. *Journal of Research on Technology in Education* 41 (3): 331–359.

Merriman, D. E. 2008. The effects of coaching on mathematics homework completion and accuracy of high school students with attention-deficit/hyperactivity disorder. *Journal of Behavioral Education* 17 (4): 339–355.

Moore, K. D. 2005. *Classroom teaching skills.* 5th ed. Thousand Oaks, CA: Sage Publications.

Moore, K. D. 2007. *Classroom teaching skills.* 6th ed. Boston: McGraw-Hill. (See Chapter 12 in particular.)

Moore, K. D. 2008. *Effective instructional strategies: From theory to practice.* 2nd ed. Thousand Oaks, CA: Sage Publications.

Pemberton, J. B. 2003. Communicating academic progress as an integral part of assessment. *Teaching Exceptional Children* 35 (4): 16–20.

Rock, M., and B. Thead. 2009. 20 ways to promote student success during independent seatwork. *Intervention in School and Clinic,* 44 (3): 179–184.

Salend, S. 2008. Determining appropriate testing accommodations. *Teaching Exceptional Children* 40 (4): 14–22.

Salend, S. 2009. Using technology to create and administer accessible tests. *Teaching Exceptional Children* 41 (3): 40–51.

Salend, S. J., D. Duhaney, D. J. Anderson, and C. Gottschalk. 2004. Using the Internet to improve homework communication and completion. *Teaching Exceptional Children* 36 (3): 64–73.

Salend, S. J., and M. Gajria. 1995. Increasing the homework completion rates of students with mild disabilities. *Remedial and Special Education* 16: 271–278.

Sanacore, J. 2002. Needed: Homework clubs for young adolescents who struggle with learning. *The Clearing House* (November/December). Washington, D.C.: The Clearing House.

Stanford, P., and S. Reeves. 2005. Assessment that drives instruction. *Teaching Exceptional Children* 37 (4): 18–22.

Stiggins, R. J. 2008. *An introduction to student-involved assessment for learning.* 5th ed. Upper Saddle River, NJ: Pearson/Merrill Prentice Hall

Tomlinson, C. A. 2005. *How to differentiate instruction in mixed-ability classrooms.* 2nd ed. Upper Saddle River, NJ: Merrill Prentice Hall.

Willner, L. S., C. Rivera, and B. D. Acosta. 2009. Ensuring accommodations used in content assessments are responsive to English-language learners. *Reading Teacher* 62 (8): 696–698.

Wood, J. W. 2006. *Teaching students in inclusive settings—adapting and accommodating instruction.* 5th ed. Upper Saddle River, NJ: Pearson/Merrill Prentice Hall.

Wright, J. 2004. *Classwork and homework: Troubleshooting student problems from start to finish.* Tips for Study and Organization. http://www.interventioncentral.org.

CHAPTER 8

Critical Teaching Skills for Planning Partner and Small-Group Work

Introduction

This chapter is about another important aspect of preparing activities and lessons for a diverse classroom: planning how students will work and learn together. Throughout various chapters of this book, we emphasize the importance of active student participation in the diverse classroom. Teachers must carefully and imaginatively plan to ensure that all students are involved and can obtain success. Because teachers cannot be everywhere at once, an abundant source of help can come from students. Having students work with their peers can increase opportunities for active responses and practice with immediate feedback. Having students work with partners or groups may also be motivating, provide practice in social skills, increase social integration, and offer more variety in methods. All of this helps satisfy individual differences and preferences, and increases engaged time.

Read about Ms. Wakamatsu and what she is planning for her class. Then, as you read this chapter, think about how she could use peers in instruction. You may imagine that Ms. Wakamatsu is teaching any grade level.

Examples of Using Peers in Instruction

Teachers can have peers work together in many ways. Here are some examples.

- *Active Participation Strategies* As teachers present and explain during lessons, students may be encouraged to process new information with

A Look at Ms. Wakamatsu's Planning

Ms. Wakamatsu has been teaching reading comprehension skills. She typically presents information about a comprehension skill to the whole class. Following this, she meets with small groups one at a time, leading them in reading and discussing what they've read. The rest of the class works independently during this time, usually on worksheets meant to provide practice of the comprehension skill. She is not satisfied with the independent work time. She doesn't think her students are learning very much and that the time is largely wasted. A recent conversation with a teacher friend has made her interested in planning for using peers in instruction, particularly during what has been independent work time.

peers through techniques such as "tell your neighbor."

- *Support Strategies* Peer helpers may provide assistance with paying attention, reading directions, homework, and so on to students with learning or behavior problems.

- *Activities* An activity plan may incorporate the use of groups or teams of students for working on projects, solving problems, engaging in discussions, playing games, and so on.

- *Supervised Practice in Lessons* Include partner or small-group practice as a bridge between teacher demonstrations and individual practice.

- *Extended Practice* Plan ongoing partner practice, such as using flashcards for building accuracy and fluency on math facts, for enhancing vocabulary, and so on.

- *Structured Discovery* Pairs or groups of students may work together to discuss examples and non-examples in order to discover a concept or rule.

- *Informal Presentation* Following a presentation, students may form debate teams and prepare arguments based on the information presented.

- *Behavior Management* Teams may earn points for quick transitions with students helping and reminding each other of the rules.

Notice that, in all of these examples, partner or group work builds on teacher instruction but does not replace it.

Carefully planned partner and small-group activities can provide English language learners with many opportunities for language use. Peers can serve as language models and can provide feedback within a safe setting. Opportunities to discuss new information with other students, including those who speak the same native language, can facilitate learning.

Many formal cooperative learning and peer-tutoring programs can also be very effective in a diverse classroom. Individual teachers may implement some of these programs, and some are school-wide programs. See the suggested readings at the end of this chapter for information on cooperative learning and peer-tutoring programs.

Potential Problems

Although there are many benefits to using student pairs or groups in instruction, there are potential hazards as well. Simply telling students to work together is rarely enough. Most people have had experience working with others at school or at work when much time was wasted, when one person did all of the work, or when nothing was accomplished. Using peers, like all other teaching techniques, requires careful planning to avoid time spent chatting, fighting, exchanging misinformation, or chaos as students are forming groups or moving furniture. Students will not necessarily know how to work together, cooperate, share, listen, encourage, or challenge each other. It is important to establish and communicate rules or routines and to assess and teach necessary cooperative social skills (see Chapters 10 and 19 for more information).

Planning for Using Peers in Instruction

Spending time on advance planning goes a long way in helping peer work go more smoothly. You'll need to consider a variety of variables.

When to Plan

There are two times to plan for using peers in instruction. One time is at the beginning of the year and the other is when you are developing a lesson or activity plan. If you will be routinely using a particular type of partner or group work, such as buddy reading or study groups, then plan and teach those procedures early in the year. That time will be well spent because it will help avoid repeated planning and teaching time later. For example, in plans for reading lessons, you may simply write, "Find your reading partner and follow the buddy reading routine." That will be sufficient if students have previously been taught the routine and have established partners. If you have taught a mini-lesson on using the "Numbered Heads Together" procedure (Kagan 1992), such as the one in the box on the next page, you only need to write "Form Heads Together groups" in your activity and lesson plans. See Chapter 10 for more information on planning mini-lessons to teach behavioral skills.

In some cases, teachers will plan for the use of peers as a one-time event. For example, suppose you are planning an inquiry activity in science. For that particular activity, you must plan the membership, the meeting places, and the procedures for the groups to follow. You would write detailed directions into the "activity middle" component of the activity plan.

Planning Decisions

Regardless of when you plan for using peers in instruction, it will be necessary to make decisions about why, how, who, and where. In other words, consider the reason for using peers, the size of the

MINI-LESSON

The "Heads Together" Procedure

Objective: Class will follow the Heads Together Procedure (form group, count off, begin discussion) within 1 minute.

Explain:

- Sometimes, when I ask a question, I'll ask you to get in Heads Together groups to talk over answers.

- You'll follow three steps (*on poster*)

  1. Form groups. This means turn your chairs so two people in one row and the two people across from them in the next row become a group. (*diagram on board*)

  2. Count off. Count off from 1 to 4 so each person in the group has a number.

  3. Begin discussing. Start sharing ideas right away. Everyone must be heard. Make sure everyone understands and can summarize the group's ideas.

- Do this quickly, beginning your discussion within 1 minute.

- When you've finished discussing, I'll draw a number and ask the person with that number to speak for the group.

Show: (*arrange in advance*)

- Everyone watch while we show you what this looks like. Signal the number of the step when you see it.

- *A student (acting the part of the teacher) reads question from board ("What color are the principal's eyes?") and says, "Get in your Heads Together group to answer this question."*

- *I (sitting in student desk) and three students turn chairs, count off, and begin discussing. We agree on an answer.*

- *Acting teacher draws a number and asks that person to share the group answer.*

Rehearse:

- Now everyone will practice.

- The question is: "Were there more days of sunshine than days of rain this week?" Get in your Heads Together groups to discuss it.

- *Give positive and corrective feedback as needed; keep track of time.*

- *Call on different numbers in each group to give answer.*

---

groups, how tasks will be shared, the prerequisites, who will work together, and the context for partner and small-group work. Some of the following suggestions are adapted from various authors (Arends 2004; Johnson, Johnson, and Holubec 1991; Slavin 1995).

Reasons to Use Peers in a Lesson or Activity

Don't assume that using peer collaboration is always superior to individual work. Consider the reason for using partners or small groups. For example, in an activity, the benefits of having students work on group projects rather than on individual projects might be to generate more ideas, provide the opportunity for individuals to study one narrow topic in depth, and provide practice on cooperative social skills. To bring about a higher success rate, you may use peers as part of supervised practice to provide additional support as students are attempting new skills. Be sure that all students involved in peer practice will benefit from it.

Determining the Size of Groups

Decide whether it is preferable to use pairs of students or small groups. Small groups typically range from three to six members. Consider the following factors when trying to determine the most appropriate group size:

1. *More cooperative social skills are needed in larger groups.* It is easier to share materials, take turns, or reach consensus with one other person than it is with five other people. Also, in larger groups, equal participation is more

difficult to achieve. The decision about group size, therefore, should be partly based on the level of cooperative skills the students have.

2. *All groups do not necessarily have to be the same size.* You can accommodate diversity by having some smaller and some larger groups. This may need to be done anyway, depending on the total number of students in the class. For example, if you have 23 students, you can form five groups with three members and two groups with four members.

3. *The type of task may influence the group size.* If students are to take turns reading aloud, they will get more practice in groups of two than in groups of three or more. Larger groups may be appropriate if the task is a project where each student has something different to do, such as researching a different topic, and all tasks can be done at once.

4. *The task may logically divide itself.* Group size may be determined by needed roles, such as a reader and a writer, or according to the content, such as reporting on the three branches of government.

5. *Time is a factor.* Typically, the larger the group, the more time will be needed. For example, if the students are to discuss or solve problems together, more time will be needed for larger groups so that each member gets a chance to contribute.

6. *Sometimes, more mundane elements must be considered.* The number of materials or available equipment, the size of tables, and so on may all affect group size.

Determining How Students Will Share Tasks

It is important to consider what each student will do during the partner or group work and to communicate this to the students. It is usually not enough to simply tell students to work together, cooperate, help each other, teach each other, or discuss. It is essential to be much more specific. For example, for partner practice on vocabulary, you might say, "Partner 1 will define the first word, and Partner 2 will use it in a sentence. Then switch for the second word."

Teachers may think about the typical roles needed in partner or group work, such as reader, recorder, checker, encourager, and timer. Then, they may

decide which roles are needed in a particular task. It's most efficient to directly teach those roles that they will commonly use, so all students know how to carry them out. It is also necessary to decide whether the teacher or the group will assign the roles.

If it is difficult to figure out what each student will do, ask yourself whether this is a task that can be shared or whether the size of the group is appropriate. Remember that not all learning is best done in group situations.

Determining Prerequisite Skills and Knowledge

In addition to analyzing whether students have the necessary content knowledge and skills, it is essential to analyze whether they have the interaction skills required to be successful at the task. The following examples illustrate how you may consider required academic and social skills as you plan:

1. Provide instruction on summarizing paragraphs before partner work. This ensures that all students have the necessary preliminary content knowledge on how to summarize. However, you would also need to decide whether students have the skills to listen to each other, to accept criticism, to take turns, and so on.

2. Before planning to have students discuss a particular topic in small groups, decide whether they have the necessary information or knowledge about the topic to make a discussion productive. You also need to analyze the students' discussion skills, such as making relevant comments, criticizing ideas rather than the person, and asking for clarification.

3. To form groups and pick a subject to investigate, students have to possess not only the necessary research skills, but also skills in offering ideas, reaching consensus, and so on.

Several options are available for teaching students who do not have the prerequisite cooperative social skills to be successful at the task. First, avoid the problem by changing the lesson or activity to eliminate the use of peers, or structure the task carefully to help students be successful—that is, provide clear and specific directions, change the group size, assign specific roles, and so on. Finally, you may wish to pre-teach the necessary social skills (see Chapters 10 and 19 for more information on teaching social skills).

Deciding Who Will Work Together

Teachers may sometimes choose to form groups at random or to allow students to decide. More typically, they will want to plan the membership of pairs and groups carefully. When students will be working together for more than brief periods of time (for a one-hour science experiment or a month-long reading partnership), consider the following factors when planning who will work together:

1. *Skills* Consider the task and purpose when choosing whether to pair or group homogeneously or heterogeneously. For example, if you intend to individualize the content of the tasks, with some students needing to practice addition facts, some working on multiple-digit addition, and some working on multiplication, then choose homogeneous pairs so both students are getting practice on the skills they need. On the other hand, if all students are practicing the same skills, it makes sense to pair a higher achiever with a lower achiever. In that way, students who are skilled at the task can help the lower achievers, while reinforcing their own learning by giving those explanations. When forming pairs and groups, it is important to consider the study and interaction skills of the students, in addition to academic skills.

2. *Compatibility* It is also necessary to consider how students get along together when forming pairs and groups. Students who actively dislike each other or who distract each other should not be put together, unless the purpose is to provide practice on conflict resolution or on ignoring distractions. Also, consider cultural diversity in cooperation and communication skills. For example, discuss with students variations in what is considered acceptable in expressing opinions and disagreements. Some students may be uncomfortable with raised voices and table-pounding. This is a good opportunity to broaden perspectives.

3. *Integration* Another consideration in forming pairs and groups is that of promoting social integration. Mixing boys and girls, individuals with and without disabilities, and students from varied cultural backgrounds can increase tolerance and promote friendships in the classroom. However, the teacher must carefully plan for this outcome.

The following teacher checklist is an overview of key considerations when planning for partner and small group work. You can use it as a guide as you write lesson and activity plans.

TEACHER CHECKLIST FOR

Planning Partner/Group Work

❑ Do I have a rationale for using partner and/or group work in this lesson or activity?

❑ Am I planning appropriate group size(s)?

❑ Am I planning how students will share tasks?

❑ Should I assign roles within pairs/groups?

❑ Do my students have the necessary academic knowledge/skills to do the partner/group work?

❑ Do my students have the necessary cooperative social skills to do the partner/group work?

❑ Am I planning the membership of pairs and groups carefully?

❑ Am I planning for classroom organization and proactive behavior management?

Planning the Context for Partner and Small-Group Work

The teacher needs to support cooperative behaviors by careful planning for management and organization. That is the last element in the teacher checklist and one of the most important. Following are examples of how you can use critical management skills to plan effective partner and small-group work (see Chapters 11 and 12 for a complete discussion of these critical management skills):

1. *Arrange the room to facilitate group or partner work.* When students will be working together

briefly, as in active participation strategies, it makes sense for students who sit near each other to be grouped together. Teach students who their "neighbor" is (for example, the person to their left) and who is included in their small group so these groupings can be set up quickly during instruction. If desks are in rows, plan for odd numbers and for the person at the end of the row when thinking about partnerships. Show students how to turn or move their chairs to form small groups. (Note that you will not want much furniture-moving for brief group work.) If your typical arrangement is to have desks in clusters or if students sit at tables, then you'll need to designate partners. Consider whether peer practice will be used often when making desk arrangements and seating assignments.

Sometimes, you will form pairs and groups based on factors other than seating proximity. In that case, decide where in the room they will meet and plan for moving desks or tables. If students are to work together, they will need to be physically close together. No one should be physically excluded from the group, and everyone should be able to see the materials and each other. Situate the pairs and groups far enough apart so that groups do not distract each other and so they can be easily monitored.

2. *Plan how to gain attention.* When students are focused on each other in pairs and small groups, they may not easily see or hear the teacher. Therefore, plan a strong signal for attention such as ringing a bell or turning off the lights. Also, when students are working and talking together, it can be difficult for them to shift their attention back to the teacher. It may be helpful to provide practice in responding quickly to the signal for attention. It may also be helpful to provide time alerts, such as, "In 3 minutes, I'll ask you to finish your discussions and listen to my directions for the next activity."

3. *Communicate behavior expectations.* Think about the rules and routines that apply and the social skills that students will need for success during the partner or small-group work, and communicate these to the students. Consider the examples of cooperative social behaviors

---

EXAMPLES OF COOPERATIVE BEHAVIORS NEEDED FOR GROUP WORK

- moving into groups
- staying with the group
- talking in quiet voices
- accepting partners politely
- taking turns
- doing your share
- listening to others
- disagreeing politely
- accepting feedback
- reaching consensus
- getting help
- sharing materials
- encouraging participation
- taking others' perspectives

---

in the box above. They demonstrate how complex partner and group work can be and how important it is to teach students relevant rules, routines, and social skills.

In addition, plan how you will communicate the procedures for working together to the students. Be sure that your directions are clear and concise. Be sure that students know the task expectations, that is, individual and group objectives, the time lines, and the evaluation procedures. Put all of these in writing rather than simply saying them.

4. *Acknowledge appropriate behavior.* Plan to acknowledge students for following the behavior expectations you've communicated and for using other important cooperative skills. Think about the behaviors that are challenging for individuals. If some students tend to dominate, acknowledge them for letting others participate. If some students are uncomfortable talking in groups, acknowledge them when they make a contribution. Acknowledge the group as well as acknowledging individuals: "Your group managed to reach consensus even though each of you began with very different goals. Well done."

These kinds of statements provide students with valuable feedback that is directly related to the skills needed to work with others.

5. *Monitor student behavior.* Be sure to move around to monitor each group or pair. Your proximity will encourage students to stay on task. If you are sitting with a group, position yourself to see the other groups. Think about which pairs or groups may need more monitoring and more interactions (encouragement, feedback, reminders) with you.

6. *Plan for logistics.* You may want to designate, or have the groups designate, individuals to gather, distribute, and return needed materials and equipment for the group.

7. *Manage transitions.* The transition to and from group or partner work has the potential to be chaotic. Don't let this keep you from using this effective teaching method; instead, plan carefully to avoid wasted time and behavior problems. Plan how to communicate who will work together, such as listing groups and their members on a transparency for students to read. Plan where groups will meet. You may display a diagram or map, or put signs up to show where groups are to sit. Describe and demonstrate how to move desks and chairs if that's necessary. Communicate behavior expectations for the transition itself. (Proactively teaching the routine of how to move into groups may be time well spent.)

Responding to Skill Diversity When Planning Partner and Small-Group Work

If students are not yet skilled at working with partners or in small groups, don't avoid using these techniques, but do temporarily minimize the cooperative skills needed. You can do this in various ways:

- Use smaller groups; students will find it easier to cooperate with one or two people than with four or five.

- Assign roles and tasks rather than having the group make all decisions.

- Provide enough materials to minimize the necessity for sharing.

- Be careful in assigning group members; good friends or bad enemies may have difficulty working together.

- Focus on one cooperative skill at a time, and review it just before the partner or small-group work. For example, ask students to state what listening to your partner looks like and sounds like.

- Be direct about how to solve problems. For example, say, "If more than one person wants to go first, then use rock-paper-scissors to decide."

Remember Ms. Wakamatsu and her plan for trying to use peers in instruction when teaching reading comprehension skills? Below are some of her ideas.

Ms. Wakamatsu's Plan for Using Peers in Instruction

Strategy: While the teacher is working with a small group, the rest of the class will work in groups of three to complete worksheets intended to provide practice with the comprehension skill she taught to the whole class. The groups will be made up of three students who Ms. Wakamatsu selects based on their reading skills and how well they work together.

Reasoning: Ms. Wakamatsu believes that using small groups in this way will benefit students by providing support in practicing their reading comprehension skills when she isn't available to them. She thinks that three will be a good group size because it is small enough that everyone will get to read and discuss frequently but large enough to make it likely that they will be able to figure out answers.

What else does Ms. Wakamatsu need to consider to ensure that her plan for using groups will be effective? How else could she use peers in instruction?

Summary

Having students work with partners or in small groups during lessons and activities is a strategy with many potential benefits. However, careful planning is needed to ensure that students work together effectively and efficiently. Planning is necessary to determine the size and membership of groups, how students will share tasks, and how to evaluate the knowledge and skills needed by students.

References and Suggested Reading

Arends, R. I. 2004. *Learning to teach.* 6th ed. Boston: McGraw-Hill.

Arreaga-Mayer, C. 1998. Increasing active student responding and improving academic performance through class-wide peer tutoring. *Intervention in School and Clinic* 34 (2): 89–94.

Bowman-Perrott, L. 2009. ClassWide Peer Tutoring: An effective strategy for students with emotional and behavioral disorders. *Intervention in School and Clinic,* 44 (5): 259–267.

Cohen, L., and L. J. Spenciner. 2005. *Teaching students with mild and moderate disabilities: Research-based practices.* Upper Saddle River, NJ: Pearson.

Copeland, S., J. McCall, C. Williams, C. Guth, E. Carter, S. Fowler, J. Presley, and C. Hughes. 2002. High school peer buddies: A win-win situation. *Teaching Exceptional Children* 35 (1): 16–21.

Fuchs, D., and L. Fuchs. 2005. Peer-assisted learning strategies: Promoting word recognition, fluency, and reading comprehension in young children. *Journal of Special Education* 39: 34–44.

Greenwood, C., C. Arreaga-Mayer, C. Utley, K. Gavin, and B. Terry. 2001. Class wide peer tutoring learning management system: Applications with elementary-level English language learners. *Remedial and Special Education* 22 (1): 34–47.

Greenwood, C., J. Delquadri, and J. Carta. 1997. *Together we can! ClassWide Peer Tutoring to improve basic academic skills.* Longmont, CO: Sopris West.

Greenwood, C., L. Maheady, and J. Carta. 2002. Classwide peer tutoring programs. In *Interventions for academic and behavior problems II: Preventive and remedial approaches,* eds. M. Shinn, H. Walker, and G. Stoner. Washington, D.C.: National Association of School Psychologists.

Goodwin, M. 1999. Cooperative learning and social skills: What skills to teach and how to teach them. *Intervention in School and Clinic* 35 (1): 29–33.

Harper, G. F., and L. Maheady. 2007. Peer-mediated teaching and students with learning disabilities. *Intervention in School and Clinic* 43 (2): 101–107.

Heron, T., D. Villareal, M. Yao, R. Christianson, and K. Heron. 2006. Peer tutoring systems: Applications in classrooms and specialized environments. *Reading and Writing Quarterly* 22 (1): 27–45.

Hock, M. F., J. B. Schumaker, and D. D. Deshler. 2001. The case for strategic tutoring. *Educational Leadership* 58 (7): 50–52.

Jenkins, J. R., L. R. Antil, S. K. Wayne, and P. F. Vadasy. 2003. How cooperative learning works for special education and remedial students. *Exceptional Children* 69 (3): 279–292.

Johnson, D. W., R. T. Johnson, and E. J. Holubec. 1991. *Cooperation in the classroom.* Edina, MN: Interaction Book.

Kagan, S. 1992. *Cooperative learning.* San Juan Capistrano, CA: Kagan Cooperative Learning.

Kroeger, S., C. Burton, and C. Preston. 2009. Integrating evidence-based practices in middle science reading. *Teaching Exceptional Children* 41 (3): 6–15.

Lovitt, T. C. 2000. *Preventing school failure: Tactics for teaching adolescents.* 2nd ed. Austin, TX: Pro-Ed.

Maheady, L., B. Mallette, and G. Harper. 2006. Four classwide peer tutoring models: Similarities, differences, and implications for research and practice. *Reading & Writing Quarterly* 22 (1): 27–45.

Marzano, R. J., D. J. Pickering, and J. E. Pollock. 2005. *Classroom instruction that works: Research-based strategies for increasing student achievement.* Upper Saddle River, NJ: Pearson/Merrill Prentice Hall.

Mastropieri, M. A., and T. E. Scruggs. 2004. *The inclusive classroom: Strategies for effective instruction.* Upper Saddle River, NJ: Pearson.

Mastropieri, M. A., T. E. Scruggs, L. J. Mohler, M. L. Beranek, V. Spencer, R. T. Boon, and E. Talbott. 2001. Can middle school students with serious reading difficulties help each other and learn anything? *Learning Disabilities Research and Practice* 16 (1): 18–27.

Mathes, P. G., and A. E. Babyak. 2001. The effects of peer-assisted learning strategies for first-grade readers with and without additional mini-skills lessons. *Learning Disabilities Research and Practice* 16 (1): 28–44.

McMaster, K. N., and D. Fuchs. 2002. Effects of cooperative learning on the academic achievement of students with learning disabilities: An update of Tateyama-Sniezek's review. *Learning Disabilities Research & Practice* 17 (2): 107–117.

Mercer, C. D., and A. R. Mercer. 2005. *Teaching students with learning problems.* 7th ed. Upper Saddle River, NJ: Pearson.

Olson, J. L., and J. M. Platt. 2003. *Teaching children and adolescents with special needs.* 4th ed. Columbus, OH: Merrill/Prentice Hall.

Palincsar, A., and L. Herrenkohl. 2002. Designing collaborative learning contexts. *Theory into Practice* 41 (1): 26–32.

Polloway, E. A., J. R. Patton, and L. Serna. 2004. *Strategies for teaching learners with special needs.* 8th ed. Upper Saddle River, NJ: Pearson.

Rohrbeck, C., M. Ginsburg-Block, J. Fantuzzo, and T. Miller. 2003. Peer-assisted learning interventions with elementary school students: A meta-analytic review. *Journal of Educational Psychology* 95:240–257.

Salend, S. J. 2005. *Creating inclusive classrooms: Effective and reflective practices for all students.* 5th ed. Upper Saddle River, NJ: Pearson.

Simonsen, B., S. Fairbanks, A. Briesch, D. Myers, and G. Sugai. 2008. Evidence-based practices in classroom management: Considerations for research to practice. *Education and Treatment of Children* 31 (3): 351–380.

Slavin, R. E. 1994. *A practical guide to cooperative learning.* Needham Heights, MA: Allyn & Bacon.

Slavin, R. E. 1995. *Cooperative learning: Theory, research, and practice.* 2nd ed. Needham Heights, MA: Allyn & Bacon.

Sonnier-York, C., and P. Stanford. 2002. Learning to cooperate: A teacher's perspective. *Teaching Exceptional Children* 34 (6): 40–44.

Stenhoff, D., and B. Lignugaris/Kraft. 2007. A review of the effects of peer tutoring on students with mild disabilities in secondary settings. *Exceptional Children* 74 (1): 8–30.

Utley, C. A., S. L. Mortweet, and C. R. Greenwood. 1997. Peer-mediated instruction and interventions. *Focus on Exceptional Children* 29:1–23.

Vaughn, S., M. T. Hughes, S. W. Moody, and B. Elbaum. 2001. Instructional grouping for reading for students with L.D.: Implications for practice. *Intervention in School and Clinic* 36 (3): 131–137.

Wolford, P. L., W. L. Heward, and S. R. Alber. 2001. Teaching middle school students with learning disabilities to recruit peer assistance during cooperative learning group activities. *Learning Disabilities Research & Practice* 16 (3): 161–173.

Wood, C., S. Mackiewicz, R. Van Norman, and N. Cooke. 2007. Tutoring with technology. *Intervention in School and Clinic* 43 (2): 108–115.

Selected Instructional Interventions

Introduction

When you are planning lessons and activities, you are not only thinking about the various components of your plans and how to make them most effective, you are also thinking about your students. You may be thinking, "There is a long list of steps to follow in this lesson, and my class has trouble with that. What can I do to help them be successful?" Or you may be thinking, "Tim, Andrew, Bridget, and Anne are going to have a hard time sitting down long enough to finish this assignment. How can I support them?" Depending on the makeup of the class, the suggestions presented in this chapter may be built into initial planning for the whole class or added on as individual accommodations (Cohen and Lynch 1991).

Distinguishing between Universal and Selected Interventions

In the preceding chapters in Part 2 of the book, you learned many methods that are generally considered universal interventions—they are built in to help most of the students in your class. For example, when teachers plan to say, show, and write the key ideas of the lesson, every student will benefit. When they consider cultural diversity, everyone benefits. When they use evidence-based critical teaching skills, everyone benefits. In spite of all of the up-front planning that teachers do to address classroom diversity however, some students will need more support.

Selected instructional interventions come into play here. Selected interventions are accommodations or modifications that are added for some of the students. They may not be appropriate for all students and may even be detrimental to some students. For example, it would not be appropriate for a teacher to provide reading material on a content topic at a reduced reading level when only one or two students need such an accommodation. This strategy could be detrimental to the grade-level readers in the classroom. However, many interventions can be used either universally or selectively, depending on the makeup of the class. For example, a teacher may provide reading material on a content topic with key ideas highlighted and important terms defined when he believes all of his students would benefit from support in comprehending difficult text.

Accommodations and Modifications

Selected interventions can be accommodations or modifications. Accommodations and modifications affect teaching and learning in different ways, so it is important to understand how they are different. An *accommodation* is a change in the *how* of teaching. All students are expected to meet the same objectives, but the path to the objective varies. Take a look at the following examples of accommodations. Notice that none of them change the learning outcome; they simply change the route one takes to reach the outcome.

EXAMPLES OF ACCOMMODATIONS

- more instructional time
- note-taking guides
- more practice opportunities
- peer tutoring
- preferred seating
- templates for written responses

On the other hand, a *modification* is a change a teacher makes to *what* is taught. It may be a change in curriculum or in expectations. For example, a teacher may teach the same subject matter but at a different level of difficulty (she may have one student work on locating named cities on a map while the rest of the class learns to predict the locations of cities based on natural features such as rivers). Other examples include reducing the criterion in an objective (accepting 75 percent rather than 100 percent accuracy on capitalizing), or teaching different content (functional academics or life skills). These strategies change the expected outcome for the students for whom the modification is made. We are going to focus on accommodations, not modifications, throughout this book.

Sometimes, a modification is used temporarily, assuming that students will catch up with their peers. Consider the serious implications if students are learning less than their peers in the long run due to the modifications. Changing what you teach students can impact their future success in school and employment. Make these modifications very thoughtfully and involve families in decision-making. Teachers should always begin with the assumption that students, including students with disabilities, will learn the same content as their peers. However, if instructional accommodations do not allow the student to progress in the general curriculum and meet state standards, then modifying expected learning outcomes may be in the best interest of the student.

Choosing Universal or Selected Interventions

The issue of building in versus adding on (or universal versus selected interventions) comes into play as teachers choose interventions to include in their plans. Remember that the needs of a particular class of students dictate whether to build in or add on. Here are some examples that help explain this issue.

- One teacher finds that he can meet the needs of his students by using techniques that are typically considered effective teaching practices and universal design principles. He builds in these strategies.

- Another teacher decides that, to meet the needs of her two students with significant difficulties with

math, she will need to add on a strategy for them that would not be appropriate for all of her students. In fact, she thinks that the strategy may have a negative effect on the learning of most of her students. So, she adds on a selected intervention.

- A third teacher decides that the add-on intervention that he originally thought he would use to meet the needs of four of his students would really be helpful for all the students. So, he decides to build it in for everyone rather than add it on. The intervention, at first considered a selected intervention, becomes a universal intervention instead.

When you begin planning which interventions to include in a lesson or activity, first think about universal interventions and build them in. Next, decide on selected interventions and add them on. Consider that selected interventions can be more time-consuming or take more effort to add on, and incorporate them only when universal interventions are not enough for each student's success.

Specific Areas of Challenge

In the following sections of this chapter, we are going to present interventions that are categorized by fairly common challenges that some students face. We have loosely organized the strategies into general categories of difficulty (acquiring information, processing information, expressing information). We have further organized them by specific challenge, for example, difficulty maintaining attention or beginning tasks.

Some of the ideas in the following sections come from the literature on instructional recommendations for students with attention deficits, but will be helpful for many students (Bender and Mathes 1995; Council for Exceptional Children 1992; Dowdy et al. 1998; Kemp, Fister, and McLaughlin 1995; Lerner, Lowenthal, and Lerner 1995; Rooney 1995; Yehle and Wambold 1998). The suggestions that are included focus on mild to moderate learning and behavioral problems and do not include accommodations necessary for complex, low-incidence disabilities. Notice that these strategies provide positive behavioral support for students as well as increase academic learning.

We will not be referring to selected interventions that involve remedial or specialized instructional programs in reading, writing, math, and so on. Of course, entire books and programs are available for how to teach reading to students who are not learning to read in the regular classroom program, for example. In this chapter, we refer to less-intrusive selected interventions.

Acquisition of Information

The first general area of student challenges has to do with acquiring information. Students who have difficulty reading, attending, and sitting still can have difficulty learning. The following are some strategies to try.

Difficulty Maintaining Attention

Consider the following suggestions for students who have difficulty staying focused:

- Provide preferential seating. Sit the student near the teacher or another adult, near quiet peers, or at an individual desk rather than at a table with other students, and away from high-traffic areas.

- Teach the student to ignore distractions in the long run. Reduce distractions in the short run through preferential seating, the use of study carrels, screens, or headphones, or by reducing sounds and visual stimuli.

- Provide more frequent breaks or changes in tasks.

- Use more active participation strategies.

- Regain the student's attention frequently through proximity, touch, eye contact, or private signals.

- Teach students to self-monitor their own behavior.

- Have a peer helper prompt the student to pay attention.

Difficulty Keeping Still

When teaching students who have difficulty remaining still, consider the following strategies:

- Let students stand or move when this doesn't disrupt learning. For example, let them stand at their desks to do independent work or walk around while doing oral practice.

- Allow students to use various desks or work areas.

- Let students use worry beads or doodle when this does not interfere with the task.

- Build in movement for students in the daily schedule (hand out papers, run errands, clean up, or do stretching exercises).

- Build in movement in lessons and activities by using active physical responses. For example, tell students to "stand up if you think this is the topic sentence," or "walk to the blackboard and write the definition."

- Teach students to signal when they need a break.

Difficulty Reading

When teaching reading is not the objective, the following suggestions may help students who experience difficulty in reading:

- Have a peer or other volunteer read to the student.

- Have a peer summarize information orally to the student.

- Provide highlighted text.

- Provide study guides, outlines, or graphic organizers to go with the reading to help with comprehension.

- Provide assistive computer technology that supports reading, such as a talking dictionary.

- Provide the necessary information in other forms, such as oral presentations, audiotapes, videotapes, or computer multimedia programs.

Difficulty with Selective Attention

Students who have difficulty with selective attention have trouble attending to the important aspects of a task or information. The following suggestions help with this challenge:

- Use color cues, or highlight or bold important details.

- Provide study guides or advance questions to go with readings or presentations.

- Provide flashcards or cue cards that include key information and examples with no extraneous information.

- Use a consistent format for instruction and on worksheets.

Processing or Memorizing Information

The second general area of challenge for many students involves processing and/or retaining information. Behaviors such as impulsiveness, difficulty starting and finishing tasks, and organizing information can create substantial difficulty.

Difficulty Waiting or Impulsiveness

This may be a problem when students are standing in line, taking turns, responding on assignments or tests, during discussions, and so on. The following suggestions may help students with such difficulties:

- Use a cue that reminds students to remain quiet during the wait-time after questions.

- Tell students to discuss responses with their partners before saying or writing the answers.

- Teach students to highlight important words in test questions or in assignment directions.

- Cue the use of problem-solving steps.

- Teach students to outline essay test answers before writing.

- Teach students to think of the answer on their own before looking at multiple choices on a test.

- Teach students what to do while waiting for help (try another problem or task, ask a partner for help, or reread directions, for example).

- Cue the use of self-talk (for example, "I need to take a deep breath and . . .").

- Provide students with something to do while waiting in line or for a turn (play a game, sing a song, have something in their pockets to play with, for example).

- Teach students how to interrupt politely.

Difficulty Beginning Tasks

When students find it difficult to begin tasks, consider the following suggestions:

- Provide cue cards on their desks, describing how to begin a task. Have students check off steps as completed. For example: (1) write name on paper, (2) read directions, and so on. (This is similar to reminders that appear on billing envelopes, such as "Have you written the account number on your check?")

- Go to the student right at the beginning of seat-work to help her start. Say that you will be back shortly to check.

- Provide a peer helper to prompt or to do the first step or problem with her.

Difficulty Completing Tasks

To ensure that students finish tasks, consider the following methods:

- Assist students in setting goals for task completion within realistic time limits, and help them self-reinforce.

- Clarify what constitutes completion, and write this on the board or on cue cards on the student's desk (for example, "Answer all five questions in complete sentences, put name on paper, and place paper in assignment box on teacher's desk.").

- Establish routines for turning in assignments.

- Provide peer help in reminding students to finish and turn in completed tasks.

- Help students list tasks to do and check them off as completed.

Difficulty Organizing

The following suggestions may help students to organize:

- List assignments and materials needed on the board or a transparency.

- Teach students to use an assignment calendar or a checklist.

- Have students use notebooks with pockets or dividers.

- Provide places to put materials in desks or in the room (in boxes or trays).

- Help students to color-code materials needed for various subjects.

- Provide time to gather materials at the beginning or end of each class or day.

- Teach a consistent routine for turning in or picking up assignments.

- Provide peer help.

- Help students divide assignments into steps or parts.

Difficulty with Tasks That Require Memorization

Help students increase their ability to memorize by incorporating (and teaching) memory strategies, such as mnemonics, visualizing, oral practice or rehearsal, and many repetitions. For example, teach students to make a word or sentence using the first letters of words in a list to be learned, or help students memorize new terms using picture clues and known words (Mastropieri and Scruggs 1998).

Expressing Information

The third main area of challenge refers to students expressing what they know. Sometimes, students are challenged by the actual writing of the information, sometimes, by difficulty with following directions or sticking with the task at hand, and other times, because of inadequate test-taking skills. In all cases, these challenges can make it difficult for a student to show what they know.

Slow or Poor Handwriting

When students exhibit handwriting difficulties, consider the following suggestions:

- Teach handwriting and provide for increased practice to build fluency. Provide practice that uses content of personal interest (for example, have students copy information about skateboarding).

When the objective of the lesson or activity is not to teach or practice handwriting, consider the following:

- Decrease nonessential writing. For example, don't require students to copy questions before writing the answers.

- Give students a copy of your notes or a copy of a peer's notes.

- Allow the use of other methods, such as using a word processor, giving oral presentations, having someone take dictation, or taping answers.

- Don't worry about handwriting as long as it is readable.

Messiness

Use the following techniques to help students maintain neatness:

- Allow students to use a pencil and eraser, graph paper that helps organize writing on a page, or a word processor.

- Provide time and support for cleaning a desk or work area.

- Provide storage places (boxes, shelves, extra desks, or notebooks) and reminders of where to put things.

Difficulty with Taking Tests

When students find it difficult to take tests, consider the following options:

- Allow alternative forms of testing (oral rather than written, for example).

- Provide help with understanding directions for taking tests.

- Teach test-taking skills (for example, cross out incorrect answers on multiple choice tests or outline answers on essay tests).

Difficulty Sticking with Routine Tasks

The following methods may be effective when teaching students who find it difficult to persevere with tasks:

- Divide tasks into smaller segments, with brief breaks or reinforcement between segments, or spread tasks throughout the day or class.

- Remove anything unnecessary from tasks, such as copying sentences before correcting them.

- Analyze the amount of practice needed and remove unnecessary repetitions. Make sure the difficulty level is appropriate, and the objective is important.

- Alternate preferred tasks with less preferred ones.

- Alternate forms of practice and offer choices (for example, students can practice math problems on paper, the board, with a partner, or using a computer).

- Add novelty and interest with games, materials, personal interests, and so on.

- Teach on-task behaviors, including self-monitoring and self-reinforcement.

Difficulty Following Directions

If students find it difficult to follow oral or written directions, consider the following methods:

- Before giving directions, make sure you have the student's attention (for example, gain eye contact, say a name, or touch).

- Give only one or two directions at a time.

- Teach and follow consistent routines so directions do not have to be given too often.

- Simplify the language and vocabulary.

- Emphasize key words with your voice or with gestures.

- Ask the student to repeat the directions, at first to you and eventually to self.

- Give students their own copies of written directions.

- Teach the meaning of "direction" words.

- Underline key words in written directions.

- Teach the students to circle important words in written directions.

- Have a peer read directions to the student.

Summary

Many more selected interventions are described in the professional literature. See the references and suggested readings for more ideas. Remember that when you select strategies that you think will benefit one or a few of your students, be sure to determine whether the strategy would in fact, benefit many students in the class. If it would, build it in rather than adding it on.

References and Suggested Reading

Algozzine, B., J. Ysseldyke, and J. Elliott. 2000. *Strategies and tactics for effective instruction.* 2nd ed. Longmont, CO: Sopris West.

Banikowski, S. K., and T. A. Mehring. 1999. Strategies to enhance memory based on brain research. *Focus on Exceptional Children* 32 (2): 1–16.

Bender, W. N., and M. Y. Mathes. 1995. Students with ADHD in the inclusive classroom: A hierarchical approach to strategy selection. *Intervention in School and Clinic* 30: 226–234.

Bos, C., and S. Vaughn. 2006. *Strategies for teaching students with learning and behavior problems.* 6th ed. Boston: Pearson.

Bowe, F. 2005. *Making inclusion work.* Upper Saddle River, NJ: Pearson.

Bullard, H. 2004. 20 ways to ensure the successful inclusion of a child with Asperger's syndrome in the general education classroom. *Intervention in School and Clinic* 39 (3): 176–180.

Cegelka, P. T., and W. H. Berdine. 1995. *Effective instruction for students with learning difficulties.* Boston: Allyn and Bacon.

Childre, A., J. Sands, and S. Pope. 2009. Backward design: Targeting depth of understanding for all learners. *Teaching Exceptional Children* 41 (5): 6–14.

Cohen, S. B., and D. K. Lynch. 1991. An instructional modification process. *Teaching Exceptional Children* 23:12–18.

Council for Exceptional Children. 1992. *Children with ADD: A shared responsibility.* Reston, VA: Author.

Cox, P., and M. Dykes. 2001. Effective classroom adaptations for students with visual impairments. *Teaching Exceptional Children* 33 (6): 68–74.

Cruickshank, D. R., D. B. Jenkins, and K. K. Metcalf. 2009. *The act of teaching.* 5th ed. Boston: McGraw-Hill.

Cummings, C. 1990. *Teaching makes a difference.* 2nd ed. Edmonds, WA: Teaching, Inc.

Dowdy, C., J. Patton, T. Smith, and E. Polloway. 1998. *Attention-deficit/hyperactivity disorder in the classroom.* Austin, TX: Pro-Ed.

DuPaul, G., and G. Stoner. 2003. *ADHD in the schools: Assessment and practice.* New York: Guilford.

Evertson, C. M., E. T. Emmer, and M. E. Worsham. 2006. *Classroom management for elementary teachers.* 5th ed. Needham Heights, MA: Allyn and Bacon.

Finstein, R., F. Yao Yang, and R. Jones. 2007. Build organizational skills in students with learning disabilities. *Intervention in School and Clinic* 42 (3): 174–178.

Fisher, J. B., J. B. Schumaker, and D. D. Deshler. 1995. Searching for validated inclusive practices: A review of the literature. *Focus on Exceptional Children* 28:1–20.

Goodman, G., and C. Williams. 2007. Interventions for increasing the academic engagement of students with autism spectrum disorders in inclusive classrooms. *Teaching Exceptional Children* 39 (6): 53–61.

Harlacher, J., N. Roberts, and K. Merrell. 2006. Classwide interventions for students with ADHD: A summary of teacher options beneficial for the whole class. *Teaching Exceptional Children* 39 (2): 6–12.

Howell, K. W., J. L. Hosp, and M. K. Hosp. n.d. *Curriculum-based evaluation: Teaching and decision making.* 4th ed. Belmont, CA: Cengage. Forthcoming.

Jaime, K., and E. Knowlton. 2007. Visual supports for students with behavior and cognitive challenges. *Intervention in School and Clinic* 42 (5): 259–270.

Kaplan, J. S. 1995. *Beyond behavior modification.* 3rd ed. Austin, TX: Pro-Ed.

Kemp, K., S. Fister, and P. J. McLaughlin. 1995. Academic strategies for children with ADD. *Intervention in School and Clinic* 30:203–210.

King-Sears, M., and A. Evmenova. 2007. Premises, principles, and processes for integrating TECHnology into instruction. *Teaching Exceptional Children* 40 (1): 6–14.

Larkin, M. 2001. Providing support for student independence through scaffolded instruction. *Teaching Exceptional Children* 34 (1): 30–34.

Lerner, J. W., B. Lowenthal, and S. R. Lerner. 1995. *Attention deficit disorders.* Pacific Grove, CA: Brooks/Cole.

Lovitt, T. C. 1995. *Tactics for teaching.* 2nd ed. Englewood Cliffs, NJ: Prentice Hall.

Mancil, G., and Maynard, K. 2007. Mathematics instruction and behavior problems: Making the connection. *Beyond Behavior* 16 (3): 24–28.

Mastropieri, M. A., and T. E. Scruggs. 1998. Enhancing school success with mnemonic strategies. *Intervention in School and Clinic* 33: 201–208.

Mastropieri, M. A., and T. E. Scruggs. 2007. *The inclusive classroom: Strategies for effective instruction.* 3rd ed. Upper Saddle River, NJ: Pearson.

Mathews, R. 2000. Cultural patterns of South Asian and Southeast Asian Americans. *Intervention in School and Clinic* 36 (2): 101–104.

Meltzer, L. J., B. N. Roditi, D. P. Haynes, K. R. Biddle, M. Paster, and S. E. Taber. 1996. *Strategies for success: Classroom teaching techniques for students with learning problems.* Austin, TX: Pro-Ed.

Mercer, C. D., and A. R. Mercer. 2005. *Teaching students with learning problems.* 7th ed. Upper Saddle River, NJ: Pearson.

Ormsbee, C., and K. Finson. 2000. Modifying science activities and materials to enhance instruction for students with learning and behavioral problems. *Intervention in School and Clinic* 36 (1): 10–21.

Pakulski, L. A., and J. N. Kaderavek. 2002. Children with minimal hearing loss: Interventions in the classroom. *Intervention in School and Clinic* 38 (2): 96–103.

Prater, M. A. 1992. Increasing time on task in the classroom. *Intervention in School and Clinic* 28:22–27.

Prestia, K. 2003. Tourette's syndrome: Characteristics and interventions. *Intervention in School and Clinic* 29 (2): 67–71.

Reid, R. 1999. Attention deficit hyperactivity disorder: Effective methods for the classroom. *Focus on Exceptional Children* 32 (4): 1–20.

Rhode, G., W. Jenson, and H. Reavis. 1993. *The tough kid book*. Longmont, CO: Sopris West.

Rooney, K. J. 1995. Teaching students with attention disorders. *Intervention in School and Clinic* 30:221–225.

Salend, S. J. 2008. *Creating inclusive classrooms: Effective and reflective practices for all students*. 6th ed. Upper Saddle River, NJ: Pearson.

Salend, S. J., and M. Gajria. 1995. Increasing the homework completion rates of students with mild disabilities. *Remedial and Special Education* 16:271–278.

Salend, S. J., H. Elhoweris, and D. VanGarderen. 2003. Educational interventions for students with ADD. *Intervention in School and Clinic* 38 (5): 280–288.

Shaw, S. 2008. An educational programming framework for a subset of students with diverse learning needs: Borderline intellectual functioning. *Intervention in School and Clinic* 43 (5): 291–299.

Sprick, R., M. Sprick, and M. Garrison. 1993. *Interventions: Collaborative planning for students at risk*. Longmont, CO: Sopris West.

Stormont-Spurgin, M. 1997. I lost my homework: Strategies for improving organization in students with ADHD. *Intervention in School and Clinic* 32 (5): 270–274.

Thompson, S., A. Morse, M. Sharpe, and S. Hall. 2005. *Accommodations manual: How to select, administer, and evaluate use of accommodations for instruction and assessment of students with disabilities*. 2nd ed. http://osepideasthatwork.org/toolkit/accommodations.asp.

Uberti, H., M. Mastropieri, and T. Scruggs. 2004. Check it off: Individualizing a math algorithm for students with disabilities via self-monitoring checklists. *Intervention in School and Clinic* 39 (5): 269–275.

Welton, E. N. 1999. How to help inattentive students find success in school: Getting the homework back from the dog. *Teaching Exceptional Children* 31 (6): 12–18.

Williamson, R. D. 1997. Help me organize. *Intervention in School and Clinic* 33 (1): 36–39.

Wood, J. W. 2006. *Teaching students in inclusive settings—adapting and accommodating instruction*. 5th ed. Upper Saddle River, NJ: Pearson/Merrill Prentice Hall.

Yehle, A. K., and C. Wambold. 1998. An ADHD success story: Strategies for teachers and students. *Teaching Exceptional Children* 30:8–13.

Zentall, S. 2006. *ADHD and education: Foundations, characteristics, methods, and collaboration*. Upper Saddle River, NJ: Pearson/Merrill/Prentice Hall.

PART III

The Context for Teaching and Learning

A Framework for Diversity Responsive Teaching		
PLANNING *WHAT* TO TEACH	**PLANNING *HOW* TO TEACH**	**PLANNING THE *CONTEXT* FOR TEACHING AND LEARNING**
<u>Content</u> About diversity For a diverse world Carrier content	<u>Universal instructional interventions</u> Universal design for learning Differentiated instruction Critical teaching skills	<u>Environment</u> Physical Social Emotional
<u>Completeness</u> Thorough coverage All contributors Varied perspectives Similarities & differences	<u>Selected instructional interventions</u> Accommodations for: Acquisition of information Processing and memorizing Expressing information	<u>Universal behavioral interventions</u> Rules, routines, & social skills Critical management skills
<u>Connections</u> To student experiences Importance to students' lives Build on student ideas		<u>Selected behavioral interventions</u> ABC

Teaching and learning don't happen in a vacuum. Rather, they happen in a place that has a climate or atmosphere. We call this place the *context* or the *environment* for teaching and learning. This context is made up of physical, social, and emotional elements.

A positive context for teaching and learning is welcoming, safe, supportive, engaging, challenging, inclusive, and respectful. This context has the appropriate amount of structure, orderliness, and efficiency. It is responsive to diversity. A positive context for teaching and learning supports appropriate student behavior. A positive context doesn't just happen; it results from careful planning. It's just as important for teachers to plan the context for teaching and learning as it is for them to plan curriculum and instruction.

Teachers take action to create a positive context at the very beginning of the year. They create this environment by connecting with each student, by being responsive to diversity, by encouraging compliance, and through the use of universal and selected behavioral interventions. Universal interventions are those that are used proactively for all students. Selected interventions are targeted only to those students who need them. In Chapter 10, we will describe these aspects of planning the context for teaching and learning.

Teachers also take action to create a positive context in each lesson and activity they teach throughout the year. They do this by incorporating critical management skills in their lesson and activity plans. Planning for these management skills helps support appropriate behavior and prevents behavior problems. We'll focus on each critical management skill in Chapters 11 and 12.

Many, many variables impact the context for teaching and learning. Our primary focus is to show how to build in preventive management and to support appropriate behavior in positive ways.

Supporting Student Behavior

Introduction

You create a positive context for teaching and learning when you support appropriate student behavior, which is behavior that promotes, or does not interfere with, the learning of the student or classmates. Supporting appropriate student behavior begins with connecting with each student. Creating a diversity responsive environment that welcomes and includes each student is another fundamental aspect of this support. In addition, teachers must implement proactive universal behavioral interventions such as establishing and teaching classroom rules, routines, and social skills, and encouraging compliance. Finally, teachers must use selected or individualized interventions for those students who need them. Developing a positive context for teaching and learning starts at the beginning of the school year and continues throughout the year. Planning for the support of appropriate student behavior in each lesson and activity can then rest on this foundation. [Note: Student teachers and long-term substitute teachers must also spend time establishing a positive context as they begin their time with a class.]

Read about Mr. Dees and his beginning-of-the-year planning in the box called "A Look at Mr. Dees's Planning." Then, as you read this chapter, think about what he can do to support appropriate student behavior from the start.

Connecting with Students

Connecting with students is fundamental to all else in creating a positive context for teaching and learning. This is easier with some students than others. The key is acting like you like your students. Let

A Look at Mr. Dees's Planning

It's the beginning of the school year, and Mr. Dees is planning for his class. Last year wasn't so good, and this time he wants to start the year off right by creating a positive context for teaching and learning. He wants to encourage and support his students in appropriate behavior from the start rather than waiting for problems to arise and reacting to them. He has big goals for being proactive and positive, minimizing behavior problems, and creating a strong feeling of class community and mutual respect. He knows he needs to plan and implement concrete strategies to reach these goals—it won't happen just by wishing.

us repeat that. Act like you like them! *All* of them. Show that you are thrilled to have each of them in your class. Act like it makes your day when they walk in the door. There are many ways to connect with students. The following is a list of ideas for getting started.

- Greet them—know their names and pronounce them correctly.

- Smile and make eye contact.

- Be available to them and listen—*really* listen.

- Have informal conversations with them and spend time with them outside of class, such as at lunch.

- Get to know their families, ask about them, and invite them to school.

- Attend their school and community activities.

- Remember their interests and concerns, and share yours.

- Joke with them and laugh at their jokes.

- Do favors for them and let them do favors for you.

- Plan surprises for them.

- Notice when they've been absent and welcome them back.

- Deal with their misbehavior calmly and matter-of-factly, and never hold a grudge.

Responding to Diversity When Connecting with Students

You will want to consider diversity as you attempt to connect with students. The following are some key ideas to think about.

- Students will vary in their expectations of relationships with teachers: some will prefer close, warm, informal relationships, and others more distant, formal relationships. They will have preferences about touching and being touched.

- Don't assume your students are just like you. Some may be horrified if you sit on the floor with them or ask them to call you by your first name. On the other hand, others may believe you don't like them if you don't hug them or ask about their families.

- Students' beliefs regarding talking and conversations will vary, such as the amount of talking that's polite, who initiates, sharing personal information, and what is considered private.

Take time to learn about your students' cultural backgrounds so you can reach out to them in ways with which they are comfortable, and recognize their attempts to reach out to you.

Make a special effort to connect with students who have emotional or behavioral difficulties and are typically rejected or ignored by their peers and by adults. They may resist your overtures at first, but stick with it. Connecting with you can make a huge difference in their lives.

Creating a Diversity Responsive Environment

As a diversity responsive teacher, you will attempt to make connections between the classroom environment and the students' experiences—at home, in their communities, and perhaps in other countries. You can develop these connections through instructional methods, curriculum, management, and all aspects of the environment. Mismatches between home and school culture can result in misunderstandings and a less-than-positive context for teaching and learning.

You may find it useful to use the "Planning the Context" component of the Diversity Responsive Teaching framework (in the Introduction to Part 3 of this book) as you develop the context for teaching and learning in your classroom. It is intended to support teachers in creating diversity responsive environments, that is, those that are welcoming, safe, supportive, and respectful to *all* students and families. This doesn't happen by chance; it takes careful planning. Think of the environment as being made up of physical objects, social interactions, and emotional climate.

The Physical Environment

When planning a diversity responsive environment, think about how you can make the physical environment both welcoming and stimulating for all. A *welcoming* classroom environment is one where people feel considered and represented. When students and families walk in the door, you want them to think, "Hey, I can read that sign," "There's a picture of someone who looks like me," "Whew, the aisles are wide enough for my wheelchair," or "There's a poster about a holiday my family celebrates." A diversity responsive environment is also one that *stimulates* interest in diversity. You want your students, when they enter the classroom, to think, "I wonder what language I'm hearing," "There's a book about someone who is deaf, I wonder what that's like," or "I'd like to know more about the people who make that art."

Begin your planning by thinking about all of the things that make up the physical environment in a classroom, and then work at making these objects and materials fully representative of diversity. Think about the books you have available, the photographs

---

EXAMPLES OF OBJECTS IN THE PHYSICAL ENVIRONMENT TO MAKE REPRESENTATIVE OF DIVERSITY

- books
- magazines
- photographs
- drawings
- posters
- videos
- recordings
- music
- signs

- artifacts
- art objects
- dolls
- toys
- games
- technology devices
- school supplies
- furniture
- food

---

you put on bulletin boards, the sizes and types of furniture in your classroom, the kinds of snacks you provide, the accessibility of equipment and materials, and so on.

The desired outcome is a physical environment where all students and families feel welcomed and comfortable, and where students are stimulated to learn about diversity.

The Social Environment

The creation of a diversity responsive social environment in the classroom is something else that must be carefully planned. The social environment is made up of interactions among students and between adults and students. Your goal is to ensure that all students are part of these interactions, that no one is excluded, and that the interactions are positive. Building a community and fostering friendships is essential to creating a diversity responsive social environment. You want all to feel included, including those who look or speak differently from the majority, or who have different skills, different family structures, different economic resources, different sexual orientations, different beliefs, and so on. Again, this doesn't happen by chance—you must take actions that will promote a diversity responsive social environment. Here are some examples.

- Model acceptance by making warm, personal connections with *all* of your students.

- Demonstrate respect in your verbal and nonverbal communication through correct pronunciation of names, culturally correct use of touch and gestures, and greetings in student languages, for example.

- Encourage inclusion and interaction as you form cooperative groups, devise seating arrangements, and develop buddy systems.

- Build community as you teach students how to solve problems together, develop rules about name-calling, help students develop cross-cultural social skills, teach students to be allies, and implement bullying prevention programs.

The desired outcome is a social environment where all students are welcomed and supported, where friendly and respectful interactions are the norm, and where there is full social inclusion and integration.

The Emotional Environment

A third area to think about when planning a positive context for learning is the creation of a diversity responsive emotional environment in the classroom. In this case, you will focus on the activities and assignments used. The goal is to ensure that no one is inadvertently made to feel embarrassed or abnormal. When you are planning holiday activities, writing assignments, and homework, consider individual differences and examine your assumptions about students and their families.

- If you use holiday activities in the classroom, be sure they reflect diversity in religion, ethnicity, and family structure. For example, think about Mother's Day activities and the fact that your students may be mothered by a variety of people or not at all. That doesn't mean that making Mother's Day cards should be eliminated, but make sure that you are inclusive in how you design this activity.

- Another area in which to be respectful of varied family structures is in assignments for writing autobiographies or family trees, or interviewing grandparents.

- Consider diversity in family resources if you assign students to bring treats for the class or to pay for field trips. When you give homework assignments, be careful of assumptions about materials available at home and the availability of help for schoolwork.

Being sensitive and respectful does not mean lowering expectations. It doesn't mean eliminating homework that's necessary for achievement, for example. Everyone should be challenged. The desired outcome is an emotional environment that is sensitive to all students and families, where all are considered and respected, and where feelings are considered as you plan activities and assignments.

Creating a diversity responsive environment and connecting with students are both important parts of establishing a positive context for teaching and learning. Remember Mr. Dees and his beginning-of-the-year planning? See the box on this page for some of his ideas.

Universal Behavioral Interventions

Another important part of developing a positive context for teaching and learning is the use of universal behavioral interventions. Universal behavioral interventions are those interventions that are used proactively for the whole class. They are meant to encourage appropriate behavior by making expectations clear and specific, and by teaching students the important behaviors they will need to be successful in learning and in getting along with others. We will discuss the universal behavioral interventions of establishing and teaching rules, routines, and social skills, and interventions for encouraging compliance.

It is important to establish classroom rules and routines at the beginning of the school year. Students are more likely to behave appropriately when they know what is expected and when they are involved in setting those expectations. Further, this provides you with a solid frame of reference for communicating expectations for behavior throughout the year.

Developing Classroom Rules

Basic to planning the context for teaching and learning is developing classroom rules. The goal is to create a physically and emotionally safe environment

---

Mr. Dees's Planning for Connecting with Students and Creating a Diversity Responsive Environment

Strategies for Connecting: Each day, Mr. Dees will ask several students to have lunch with him in the classroom until all have been invited.

Reasoning: Eating and conversing together in a small group creates a comfortable social atmosphere for getting to know students personally and for them to get to know him.

What else could Mr. Dees do to begin connecting with his students?

Strategies for a Diversity Responsive Environment: Two students with disabilities, who seem to have low social status in the class and few friendships, have fun, interesting assistive technology devices (a scan-and-read pen and a talking calculator). Mr. Dees will arrange for them to share the devices during partner work with other students in the class and to show their partners how to use the technology.

Reasoning: Adding to these students' desirability as partners and putting the students with disabilities in the position of experts may increase their status and help promote social inclusion.

What else could Mr. Dees do to create a diversity responsive physical, social, and emotional environment?

---

with the right amount of structure. Ideally, school-wide general rules will be enacted and then made specific for the classroom (and other settings, such as the lunchroom and playground). Both types of rules are useful as part of a basic plan for classroom management.

- *General Rules* Some examples of general rules include "Respect others," "Be prepared," "Always do your best," and "Be kind." General rules establish standards of behavior. They define "ways to be." They are general enough to apply in a variety of settings and to a variety of situations. General rules by themselves don't tell students what (and what not) to do. They *must* be clarified with specific rules.

■ *Specific Rules* Examples of specific rules include "Be inside the classroom when the bell rings," "Raise your hand and wait to be called on before speaking," "Turn in tasks on time," and "Keep your hands and feet to yourself." Specific rules describe what (or what not) to do; they specify how to behave. Specific rules help students understand what is expected and translate general rules into visible actions. Well-written specific rules are observable, measurable, short, simple, and stated positively—that is, what *to do* (walk) rather than what *not to do* (don't run)—(Rhode, Jenson, and Reavis 1993).

Notice how the following paired examples of general and specific rules differ and how they connect:

General Rule	Specific Rule
Be safe.	Walk inside the building.
Be responsible.	Bring notebook and pencil to class.
Be respectful.	Touch people only with their permission.
Be a learner.	Ask questions when you don't understand.

As guidelines to follow in establishing rules, (1) develop rules with students, (2) keep them few in number so everyone can remember them, (3) post them, (4) refer to them often, (5) support students in following them, (6) teach the students what each rule means, (7) acknowledge students for following them, and (8) enforce them consistently.

Responding to Diversity When Developing Classroom Rules

General rules such as "Be respectful" or "Be responsible" are open to interpretation. People from different cultural backgrounds will have different ideas on how to show respect, responsibility, and so on. For example:

■ Strong teasing and verbal sparring are valued in some cultures but considered disrespectful in others.

■ Some people would see making independent choices (such as leaving class to use the restroom) as responsible behavior, whereas those who value adult permission would see it as irresponsible.

■ Different cultures vary in valuing simultaneous talking, entering conversations at the briefest of openings, or leaving long pauses in discussions.

■ In some cultures, silent listening to a speaker is respectful, whereas in others, calling out responses and affirmations is polite (Weinstein, Curran, and Tomlinson-Clarke 2003).

These differences are one reason it is important to have specific rules for common understanding. They are also a reason why it is so important to involve students in developing rules and to learn what you can about the cultural backgrounds of your students. Don't automatically impose your cultural view when establishing rules; make room for varied perspectives and compromises. For example, some of your students may have a strong sense of private property and may have difficulty sharing their school supplies unless specifically asked permission. Others may come from a more communal background and are comfortable with general sharing. Through discussion, the students may compromise on a rule that says items inside student desks and backpacks may only be borrowed with permission, and that materials may be freely taken from the community resource boxes.

The purpose of rules should be to promote comfortable, predictable, orderly environments where people can teach, learn, and feel safe. The purpose should not be obedience for its own sake. Carefully examine rules about being quiet, sitting still, walking in lines, and so on to make sure they are in the students' best interest and are not over-controlling. Don't automatically require certain behaviors (such as raising hands) in every situation without thinking about whether they will encourage learning for all students.

Establishing Classroom Routines

Routines are ways of getting things done in the classroom. Many events, such as the beginning or ending of class, turning in assignments, or lining up, need to happen efficiently to avoid wasted time and behavior problems. It is important that teachers establish and teach routines to students, just as it is important to establish and teach rules. Once students are familiar with classroom rules and routines, the teacher can state behavior expectations at the beginning of each lesson or activity by telling the students what specific rules and routines apply.

Some examples of events for which you may want to establish classroom routines include the following:

- responding to a signal for attention
- correcting assignments in class
- leaving class to use the restroom
- using the pencil sharpener
- getting assignments when absent
- free time, snack time
- finding a partner, forming groups
- completing an assignment calendar

There are three stages in establishing routines. First, decide what classroom events would benefit from clear procedures to avoid wasted time, prevent behavior problems, and foster student independence. For example, perhaps you want to prevent the problem of students having nothing to do and disturbing others when they finish tasks early. You choose to establish a routine for "Finishing Tasks Early."

Second, you (and perhaps your students) will decide on the steps for students to follow for the routine. This is called a task analysis (see Chapter 1 for more information on task analyses).

Finally, you will decide how to teach the routine to the students. (This is discussed in a following section.)

EXAMPLE OF A TASK ANALYSIS FOR A ROUTINE

What to Do When You Finish a Task Early

1. Check that your work is correct and complete.
2. Turn it in to the teacher or to the assignment box.
3. If there is time left, read a book at your desk.

Responding to Diversity When Establishing Classroom Routines

Established routines are helpful for English language learners because they help these students predict what's expected and to follow what is happening even when they don't understand what is said. They are especially important to students new to this country and unfamiliar with the school system. Routines create stability, reduce anxiety, and allow English language learners to be more fully involved in the classroom. Consider using buddies to teach or model routines (Herrell and Jordan 2004; Law and Eckes 2000; Curran 2003). Established routines are also very helpful to students who have difficulty with change and novelty, such as students with autism spectrum disorders.

Establishing Social Skills

An important aspect of the context for teaching and learning is the social environment, the interactions between people. Students need many social skills to negotiate this environment. They need social skills to be successful in lessons and activities, to follow the class rules and routines, to make friends, to get along with adults in authority, to solve interpersonal and intrapersonal problems, and so on. Think about the social skills you'll want your students to use with you and with each other. (See Chapter 19 for more information about social skills.)

It makes sense to teach these skills proactively to everyone because they are so important for a positive context. Some students will have picked up these skills without formal instruction, but teaching them universally is important as a way of establishing classroom expectations, demonstrating how important they are, getting everyone on the same page, and preventing the development of antisocial behavior patterns (Walker, Ramsey, and Gresham 2004). All students could benefit from more instruction on at least some social skills (such as conflict resolution).

You will need to decide which (of the many) social skills to teach universally in your class. There are a variety of ways to do this.

- Analyze the instructional methods you use often in lessons and activities, such as partner work, group work, or discussions. These methods will require social skills such as giving and receiving feedback, active listening, and disagreeing politely.

- Examine typical events and activities in your class, such as free time, lunch, or show-and-tell. Figure out which social skills they require—perhaps joining in, starting a conversation, inviting others to play, or taking turns.

- Analyze your classroom rules for embedded social skills, such as showing respect or including others.

- Think about typical issues for the age group or setting, such as name-calling, sharing, teasing, peer pressure, accepting *no* for an answer.

Responding to Diversity When Establishing Social Skills

Remember that social competence is culturally defined. For example, children being assertive is valued in some cultures and families and not in others. You will need to know whether the social skills you plan to teach are accepted in your students' families, communities, and peer groups. When there are differences, you will want to teach alternatives and help students decide how to choose the skills to use in a given situation. Talking with families, attending community events, observing students with their peers, and facilitating class discussions on this topic will help you understand diverse perspectives on what is socially skilled behavior.

Think back to Mr. Dees and his beginning-of-the-year planning. He has been considering the rules, routines, and social skills that he needs to establish in his class. Read the box titled "Mr. Dees's Planning for Rules, Routines, and Social Skills" on the next page for some of his ideas.

Teaching Rules, Routines, and Social Skills

Establishing rules, routines, and social skills by telling them to the students, discussing them, putting them in writing, and so on is important—but isn't enough. They must be taught. Deciding how to teach them will depend on your students and on the rule, routine, or social skill itself.

Begin by evaluating your students' present levels of understanding and performance of the rule, routine, or social skill. Perhaps your students know the behavior or skill but are not following it or using it consistently. Perhaps your students know the behavior/skill but don't use it correctly or aren't applying it where needed. Perhaps students don't know the behavior/skill and can't use it. Depending on the

case, you will decide to use a class precorrection, an activity, a mini-lesson, or a full lesson. Each is described below.

Precorrection

Use a class precorrection when the rule, routine, or social skill has been previously taught and the students know it but are inconsistent in using it. You recognize that they would benefit from a brief reminder of how and when to use it. *Precorrection* means you are correcting the behavior in advance rather than waiting for students to make a mistake and then dealing with it.

Precorrections should be used immediately before the situation in which the behavior or skill is needed. Students are much more likely to recall and follow or use a rule, routine, or social skill if they have just been reminded of it. For example, there is an assembly today, and you have noticed that your class hasn't been consistent recently in using the social skill of *polite listening*. Minutes before leaving for the assembly, you deliver a class precorrection. An effective class precorrection includes three parts.

1. *Name* Name the behavior/skill to use. Tell the students the rule, routine, or social skill that they should use in the upcoming situation. "When we are at the assembly, you will need to use the skill of *polite listening*."

2. *Review* Review the behavior/skill. Have the students tell you what the steps or components of the rule, routine, or social skill are. You may point to written steps on a poster. Use active participation and checks for understanding. "Remember what you learned about polite listening. Talk it over with your neighbor. Then I'll ask you to share what polite listening is."

3. *Performance* Have students perform the behavior/skill, not just talk about it. Have them show you what the behavior/skill looks like and sounds like. "Imagine that I'm the assembly speaker and show me polite listening [*begin speaking*]."

Precorrections are very quick—only a few minutes. This is not initial teaching—just a reminder of what they already know. Colvin (2004) suggests that with older students, a reminder of the skill, supervision while they use it, and feedback may be all that is necessary.

See the end of the chapter for more examples of precorrection teaching plans.

Mr. Dees's Planning for Rules, Routines, and Social Skills

One of the teaching methods that Mr. Dees wants to use frequently in his class is having his students do role-plays and skits. He believes that this can be a great way for students to immerse themselves in the study of both fictional characters and important people and events in history. But he also knows that problems can arise with this method, such as wasted time, arguing, and unequal participation. He plans rules, routines, and social skills to prevent these problems.

Rule: Mr. Dees decides on a rule for his class: *Do your fair share during partner and group work.* He will explain that this rule will be followed during role-play/skit preparation when everyone offers ideas, no one dominates, and no one just listens in their groups. At first he'll provide structure to help them follow the rule. He'll give each student three slips of paper. When a student contributes an idea, he'll put a slip back in the cup. Each student must use all of his slips. When a student's slips are gone, he may not make another suggestion until all group members' slips are gone.

Reasoning: Doing role-plays/skits won't be effective in increasing each student's understanding of content if each student isn't actively involved. Students won't necessarily know how to contribute equally in groups. Establishing a rule and supporting students in learning to follow it will help prevent this problem.

Routine: Mr. Dees decides on a routine to establish: *How to decide the order of presentations.* A basket of number tiles is kept on the teacher's desk, and a list of numbers from 1 to 15 is permanently written on the board. Each pair or group selects one person. That person draws a number for her group and writes her name next to that number on the board. The groups present in order from lowest to highest number.

Reasoning: Establishing a routine that the students can take care of themselves will save time and argument about who presents first, last, and so on.

Social Skill: Mr. Dees analyzes the social skills needed with this method and realizes that students will need to be able to *reach consensus in a fair way* in their pairs/groups as they pick topics and develop their role-plays/skits. He decides to establish and teach this skill.

Reasoning: This is an important social skill in many situations. It will be important in the pairs/groups as all students suggest ideas. Students won't continue to contribute if their ideas are never used and they believe decisions aren't made fairly.

Mr. Dees also wants to use whole-class discussions. What rules, routines, and social skills should he establish to make this teaching method effective?

Activity

Use an activity when students are familiar with the rule, routine, or social skill but need a more elaborate review, additional practice opportunities, instruction in applying it to different situations, and/or motivation to use it. There are many ways to use activities to teach, and they are presented in Chapter 15, as is a form/template to use when planning activities. Here are two examples of how you could use activities to teach a social skill and a rule.

1.   You taught your students how to calmly accept *no* for an answer, and they do quite well with

you. However, they have been getting in trouble with other adults in the school for arguing, whining, or having tantrums when told *no*. They know how to use this skill (they use it with you), but need to be taught to apply it with all adults. You decide to develop an activity that will provide additional practice in using this social skill in various situations with various people. After creating a variety of role-play scenarios in which a student asks for permission to do something and is told *no*, you invite various school staff members to come to your class over the next few days to do the role-plays with your students.

2. Your students know that they are not supposed to use name-calling with their peers, but they are doing it anyway. They know what words and names they should and shouldn't use, so they don't need instruction on that particular aspect. What they do need is a better understanding of why they should avoid name-calling. You create an activity where students interview family members and close friends about their feelings when they've been called names and then share the results in a class meeting. Your hope is to develop empathy and motivation to follow the rule.

Lesson

Use a lesson when students don't have the necessary knowledge to follow or perform the rule, routine, or social skill. The behavior/skill may be brand new to them or they may have some familiarity, but they need complete instruction—more than just review or extra practice—to use the behavior/skill correctly. It is even possible that the students have previously been taught the rule, routine, or social skill, but the teacher has discovered that there are major confusions and errors.

FULL LESSONS VS. MINI-LESSONS

You will need to choose whether to use a mini-lesson or a full lesson. In fact, mini-lessons are not *true* lessons because they don't include formal evaluation of individual students' independent use of the behavior/skill. (See Chapter 13.) However, they do include teacher "show-and-tell" and student practice, which are central elements of full lessons, so we consider them "almost lessons" or "mini-lessons." They are a short form of full lessons and only include four parts (objective, explain, show, rehearse).

Go to Chapter 19 for information on planning full lessons for teaching rules, routines, and social skills, and an example plan. There is also an example full lesson plan for teaching a rule in Chapter 21.

MINI-LESSONS

Mini-lessons are used when students don't use a behavior/skill because they don't know how. They need instruction. For example, Mrs. Troxel knows she needs to teach her young students the routine she wants them to follow when they arrive in the classroom in the morning. Just telling them will not be enough; she'll need to show them and have

---

WHEN TO USE MINI-LESSONS

Rather than full lessons

- when you believe formal evaluation will be unnecessary and that checks for understanding, monitoring practice, and corrective feedback will be sufficient

- when the behavior/skill to be taught is important—but perhaps not essential. For example, behaviors and skills such as *coming to class with needed materials* or *apologizing* or *raising a hand before speaking* may be important, but they are not essential in the same way that *resolving conflicts without violence, dealing with bullying,* or *resisting peer pressure to use drugs* are.

- when the rule, routine, or social skill you intend to teach is quite straightforward and when you believe your students will "get it" easily. A more complex skill (one that has many steps or options) or an interactive skill (where behavior depends on others' responses and has to be adapted to the situation) may be best taught through longer, more elaborate, full lessons.

---

them practice. An effective mini-lesson includes the following four components.

1. *Objective* As always when instructing, you will begin with a measurable objective. Write it to guide your planning and also to share with students. "Students will follow the morning classroom routine (hang up coat and pack, put home folder on desk, sit on the carpet) every day."

2. *Explain* Tell students (orally and in writing) what the rule, routine, or social skill is and how to follow/do it. You may explain it using definitions, examples and nonexamples, descriptions, elaborations, and so on. Start with a task analysis or principle statement. Build in active participation and checks for understanding. Say, "When you come into the classroom in the morning, follow the morning routine:

   - *Hang up your pack and coat* Hang up your stuff (pack, coat, scarf, etc.) on your hook in the back of the room. This way, you'll know where they are, and no one will trip over them.

- *Put your folder on your desk* Take your home/school folder out of your pack and put it on your desk so I can check them while you're reading.

- *Sit on the carpet* Sit on the carpet and talk with your friends or look at a book until the bell rings. This will give you some calm time after the bus and the playground, so you'll be ready to learn."

3. *Show* Demonstrate or model the behavior/skill. You show what it looks like and sounds like when the rule or routine is followed or when the social skill is used. "Watch while I show you what following the morning routine looks like." (*Wearing coat and pack, come in the door and follow the steps while thinking aloud.*)

4. *Rehearse* The students practice the behavior/skill as you watch and provide positive and corrective feedback as needed. The practice takes the form of performance of the behavior/skill, not just talking or writing about it. "Now you're going to practice following the morning routine. Everyone put on your coat and pack. I'm going to send one group out the door at a time. The rest of you watch and put your hands on your head when you see them following each step of the morning routine."

See the end of the chapter for more examples of mini-lesson plans.

In summary, an important part of developing a positive context for teaching and learning is establishing and teaching rules, routines, and social skills. Do this with your class from the beginning of the year. This will encourage appropriate behavior by making expectations clear and by teaching students the important skills and behaviors they will need to be successful in learning and in getting along with others.

Encouraging Compliance

Another important part of the context for teaching and learning is an appropriate level of compliance. When students comply with reasonable directives from the teacher, instructional time is preserved and a positive atmosphere is strengthened.

By *compliance*, we mean following a directive or command within a reasonable amount of time; doing what one is told; "minding." A directive may involve telling a student or a group to do something or to stop doing something. Examples of directives are:

- Start working.
- Give that back to George.
- Line up.
- Put that away.
- Stop talking.
- Everyone sit down now.
- Take out your math books.

You probably won't get and shouldn't expect compliance 100 percent of the time; 80 to 90 percent compliance is typical of average students (Rhode, Jenson, and Reavis 1993; Walker, Ramsey, and Gresham 2004) How do you decide when noncompliance is a problem? It's a problem when it's frequent and/or accompanied by inappropriate behaviors such as aggression, tantrums, or whining. A *reasonable* level of compliance is important for long-term adjustment.

Universal Interventions for Gaining Compliance

Connecting with students and creating a diversity responsive environment will make it more likely that students will comply with your requests. Students respond better to teachers they like and respond better in environments where they feel respected. Establishing and teaching rules, routines, and social skills will promote compliance because they ensure that students know exactly what is expected and how to meet those expectations. In addition, there are several other things you can do to set the stage for compliance and prevent noncompliance. These are universal interventions that are used proactively with the whole class: giving directives effectively, following through, making it easy, and sharing the power.

1. *Give directives effectively.*

   The way you tell students what to do affects their compliance. The following strategies will make your directives more effective.

- Communicate an attitude of confidence and calmness through your voice and body language. Act like you assume they'll do as you ask.

- Gain the attention of the group (ring a bell or turn the lights off/on) or individual ("Look at me") before you give a directive. Label it as a directive ("I'm going to give you a direction," or "This is what I need you to do."). Young people sometimes tune out adult talk, so make sure they're listening.

- Give direct, simple, clear directives. Say "Give Walter the pencil" rather than "Why can't you two get along? I need you to cooperate right now! Don't you know that you're disrupting the class?"

- Be reasonable. Give the students enough time to comply. When you tell them to stop doing something, consider whether you need to tell them what to do instead. When they are unhappy with the directive, let them know that you'll listen to their point of view later but that you need compliance now. ("Give Walter the pencil. Get another pencil from the box. We'll discuss ownership of the pencil later.")

2. *Follow through.*

   If you have given a directive to your students, you need to follow through with it.

   - Be sure to appreciate compliance. Say "thank you." Let students know why compliance is important. ("Well done! You did as I asked right away. Because of that, everyone got a turn.")

   - Decide how many times you'll state directives (no more than twice) and stick with it.

   - Plan in advance what you will do if students refuse to comply. Be sure they know what the consequences are. Implement the negative consequences fairly and in a matter-of-fact, rather than angry, way.

   - Be consistent. The worst thing you can do is to nag and insist and then let it go if the student(s) don't comply. If you don't care if students comply, then make a request instead of a directive.

3. *Make it easy.*

   - Pair directives: one they'll want to do with one they won't. "Clean up your area and then we'll use the last few minutes to play Math Survivor."

- Ask for a series of favors that you know the student will be glad to do. Make the final one your directive. "Could you get that off the top shelf for me? Would you turn on the overhead projector? Loan me an eraser, okay? Open your math book, please."

- Pick your battles. Try to avoid giving directives that you know students are unlikely to comply with. For example, if your students are very excited about something, don't demand total silence.

- When giving directives to individuals, try to give them privately. Students may be more likely to comply if they don't have an audience. It's not always cool to do what the teacher says.

- When the situation is tense, give the directive and then turn away and give a little time for the student(s) to comply. You don't want to invite refusal and face-saving.

4. *Share the power.*

   Remember that it's the students' class, too, and they need to feel that they have some control over what happens there.

   - Make fewer commands necessary by establishing class rules and routines. That way, students know what to do and you won't always be telling them what to do.

   - Involve students in developing class rules and routines in the first place.

   - Give students leadership and decision-making responsibilities.

   - Give students choices whenever possible. "Would you rather do math timings or correct papers first?"

Responding to Diversity and Compliance

It's important to recognize that there are varied family and cultural beliefs or expectations regarding the compliance of children with authority.

- Some adults expect immediate and unquestioning obedience.

- Some want their children to question authority.

- Some adults expect to have to give a directive more than once.

- Some expect argument or negotiation.

Students aren't going to automatically know your expectations. How do you decide? Consider the best interest of your students rather than automatically imposing your own beliefs.

Some children and youth are used to directives being phrased differently than others.

- Some are used to directives being stated directly. ("Sit down.")

- Some are used to directives being phrased as questions or requests even when a "no" response is not acceptable. ("Do you want to sit down now?" "Sit down, okay?" "Could you please sit down?")

In the latter case, some students recognize that it's not really a question or an optional request, and others don't. We recommend as least confusing to everyone that you always use a polite statement form ("Sit down, please.") when giving a directive/command.

You'll want to consider individual differences and needs, of course, as you plan how to give directives to your students. Here are some examples.

- Help English language learners comprehend your directives by demonstrating, using gestures, and using simple vocabulary and few words.

- For some students (including those with cognitive disabilities), one clear directive at a time works best.

- For students who have difficulty switching activities (perhaps including those with autism spectrum disorders), try preparing them for the change rather than giving an abrupt directive/command.

- There can be cultural and class differences regarding males responding to directives from women. Find ways to support these students in complying rather than setting up power struggles. See *making it easy* and *sharing the power* above.

In summary, you will strengthen compliance in your classroom when you plan to give directives effectively, follow through with your directives, make it easy for students to comply, and share power and control. It's important that you are com-

fortable with yourself as an adult in charge. A harsh, aggressive approach and a weak, passive approach both promote noncompliance.

Selected Behavioral Interventions

Universal behavioral interventions will likely be sufficient for creating a positive context for teaching and learning, and for preventing behavior problems with the majority of your students. Some students, however, will need additional interventions. These are called *selected* or *targeted interventions*. We will briefly discuss types of selected interventions and describe a few examples. Recognize, however, that many behavior interventions can be used universally and selectively.

When to Use Selected Behavioral Interventions

Use selected interventions as small-group or individual accommodations when one or a few of your students are having a difficult time behaving appropriately. Some students might have trouble with self-control, paying attention, following rules, getting along with others, handling frustration, resolving conflicts, complying with adult requests, dealing with change, or staying on task, to mention a few.

You need to begin by evaluating your own behavior and your use of universal interventions and critical management skills to determine whether you are implementing these strategies consistently and correctly. (Note that it is much easier to refine a strategy you are already using than to implement a selected intervention.) Then observe carefully and interview to gather information about the student behavior (for example, its frequency), what happens before the behavior (its antecedents), and what follows the behavior (its consequences).

If you think the whole class could benefit from an intervention, by all means, build it into the lesson or activity—that is, use it universally rather than selectively. For example, perhaps a few students are having a great deal of difficulty working with peers. You decide to try having them use goal-setting for improving peer interactions during partner practice. You then decide that everyone could benefit from experience with goal-setting and improvement in

A Look at Mr. Dees's Planning

One of Mr. Dees's students has "meltdowns." Mac becomes extremely upset at times and yells, screams, and throws things. Through careful observation, Mr. Dees has discovered that Mac's meltdowns typically occur when he comes to class already upset, usually due to peer teasing, and then gets frustrated with long, independent seatwork tasks. Mr. Dees wants to plan behavior interventions for Mac.

getting along with others, so you build this intervention into the opening of the lesson for everyone.

Remember Mr. Dees and his beginning-of-the-year planning for his class? Read about one student for whom he needs to do additional planning in the box titled "A Look at Mr. Dees's Planning." Then, as you read the rest of the chapter, think about selected interventions he could choose.

Types of Selected Behavioral Interventions

One way to categorize selected interventions is as Antecedent interventions, Behavior replacement interventions, and Consequence interventions—ABC. It can be helpful to use the ABC acronym/organizer to develop a variety of types of selected interventions. Some teachers have a tendency to overuse consequence interventions, particularly punishments. Avoid that. We strongly encourage that you use positive behavior support as much as possible and especially avoid negative interventions that exclude students from instruction.

Many resources on behavior management are available to teachers, and we encourage you to use them. However, you'll find that you can also generate ideas of your own by using ABC, your common sense, and your belief that everyone can learn and change. Following are a few examples to stimulate your thinking.

A (Antecedents)

Antecedent interventions are those that you implement to make it less likely that the inappropriate behavior will occur. Think of them as scaffolding

or support for appropriate behavior. They include advance changes to the setting, the situation, the task, the prompts, and so on. Following are a few examples of antecedent interventions:

- Make adjustments to the curriculum to make content interesting, relevant, and at the correct level of difficulty for individuals. Inappropriate behavior can be a reaction to inappropriate content.

- Instructional accommodations may be needed for the academic success and challenge of individuals. Effective teaching can prevent behavior problems from arising. Chapters 3 through 9 have many suggestions that will help you make accommodations.

- Provide choices, such as allowing students to choose how they do tasks, the carrier content, the order of tasks, materials to use, where to work, and so on. When students are given the opportunity to make even very simple choices, behavior problems decrease significantly (Kern and State 2009).

- Intensify and individualize universal interventions, such as using individualized precorrections of behavior expectations or small-group teaching of social skills.

- Arrange peer support such as modeling, buddying, assistance, or encouragement. An assigned buddy for recess, for example, can prevent behavior problems that arise when a student has no one with whom to play.

So many variables affect behavior that this is an area where careful assessment followed by team brainstorming is particularly useful.

B (Behavior Replacement)

These interventions involve teaching students alternative behaviors to replace the inappropriate behaviors they display. For example,

- teach verbal conflict-resolution skills to replace fighting,

- teach asking for help to replace crying.

Think about the function of the inappropriate behavior and an appropriate behavior that would achieve the same purpose.

You can teach needed replacement behaviors/skills to small groups and individuals through precorrection, activities, mini-lessons, and full lessons, just as you do with whole classes. It's essential to follow up with prompts, corrective feedback, strong reinforcement, and other coaching techniques in the context where the behavior/skill is needed. Look for "teachable moments" to promote generalization. (See Chapter 19 for additional information about teaching behavior/social skills.)

C (Consequences)

Consequences are what happens after a behavior. Consequences can be positive or negative. They can be used to strengthen appropriate behavior and to weaken inappropriate behavior. Consequence interventions are important selected interventions.

When a student who struggles with self-control *does* display appropriate behavior, use strong, immediate, and frequent reinforcement consequences. Verbal acknowledgements alone may not be enough. Rewarding the student with preferred activities and privileges or with tangible items may be needed to strengthen the appropriate behavior.

When the student behaves inappropriately, use systematic warnings and negative consequences carefully. Be sure these are planned, fair, and explained to the student ahead of time. They must not be random punishments by an annoyed adult—that doesn't teach the student self-control. Response cost is a commonly used negative consequence. Misbehaviors cost the students lost privileges, points, or time from desired activities. It's very important to use positive interventions along with these. Positive support is the preferred and most effective approach.

You can use written behavior contracts to spell out an agreement between the student and teacher. They are negotiated as business contracts. You and the student agree upon a goal (such as being on time) and pinpoint a specific behavior (student will be inside the classroom when the first bell rings). Decide upon the positive consequence for fulfilling the contract (extra computer time). Make the terms explicit (on time for four days equals extra computer time during lunch period). It's important that the contract is very clear, written and signed, fair, and likely to result in success.

Another useful selected intervention is a self-management plan. Teach students to self-evaluate, self-monitor/record, set goals, and self-reinforce. This, of course, is very empowering and promotes independence. The teacher and the student develop a self-management plan and the teacher gradually turns more and more of the responsibility over to the student.

Mr. Dees's Plan for Selected Interventions

Antecedent Strategies: When Mac arrives in class looking upset, Mr. Dees will ask sympathetic questions or let him go talk to his mentor. He'll also offer choices for doing independent tasks, such as whether to handwrite or type and who to sit by.

Reasoning: If Mac is allowed to express his feelings in an appropriate way before being asked to do an assignment, he may not blow up later. Having choices on his assignment may prevent feelings of frustration.

Behavior Replacement Strategies: Mr. Dees will teach Mac to ask for breaks when he is getting frustrated with long tasks, and will teach him skills for dealing with teasing.

Reasoning: If Mac learns how to deal effectively with teasing, he will not become so upset by it, and teasing by peers may decrease. Learning to ask for breaks when he begins to feel frustrated can prevent outbursts. (Several other students in the class could benefit from small-group instruction in these skills as well.)

Consequence Strategies: If Mac gets through the day without a meltdown, he may attend the after-school recreation program. If he has a blowup, he must attend after-school detention/study hall.

Reasoning: Earning a privilege will remind Mac of his progress in learning self-control. A negative consequence such as after-school detention/study hall fits the problem, as the meltdowns result in lost learning time.

What other selected interventions can you think of to help Mac?

You can put the three types of interventions (ABC) together in individual behavior plans. These plans should be developed as a team effort that includes families. The purpose is to provide positive behavior support for students who need more help than the universal interventions used in the class provide.

Remember Mr. Dees's student and his meltdowns? In the box on the previous page are some of Mr. Dees ideas for behavior interventions for Mac.

Responding to Diversity

Don't mistake behavior differences for behavior problems. For example, teachers who are from a different cultural background than their students may mistake exuberance, enthusiasm, and liveliness for disrespect, aggression, or hyperactivity. Or they may mistake politeness and respect for lack of interest, lack of motivation, or lack of attention. Consult with families and/or cultural experts for help in interpreting behavior.

Also, don't mistake language learning issues for behavior problems. Curran (2003) points out that when students don't understand the language of instruction, their anxiety may come out as laughter; they may speak to peers in their first language to seek understanding; they may become tired and silent. It can be easy to misinterpret these behaviors.

Summary

The suggestions in this chapter are based on several assumptions or beliefs. One is that teachers need to support appropriate student behavior in positive ways. Another is that it is most helpful to see misbehaviors as behavior errors and to emphasize teaching rather than punishment. A third assumption is that our job is to help students learn self-control and self-management rather than trying to do all the controlling ourselves.

Following the references and suggested readings are sample plans for teaching appropriate behavior.

References and Suggested Reading

Alberto, P., and A. Troutman. 2009. *Applied behavior analysis for teachers*. 8th ed. Upper Saddle River, NJ: Pearson.

Anderson, D., A. Fisher, M. Marchant, K. Young, and J. Smith. 2006. The cool-card intervention: A positive support strategy for managing anger. *Beyond Behavior* 16 (1): 3–13.

Banks, J., M. Cochran-Smith, L. Moll, A. Richert, K. Zeichner, P. LePage, L. Darling-Hammond, and H. Duffy. 2005. Teaching diverse learners. In P*reparing teachers for a changing world: What teachers should learn and be able to do*, eds. L. Darling-Hammond and J. Bransford. San Francisco: Jossey Bass.

Brendtro, L., M. Brokenleg, and L. Van Bockern. (2002). *Reclaiming youth at risk: Our hope for the future* (rev. ed.). Bloomington, IN: National Educational Services.

Bucalos, A., and A. Lingo. 2005. What kind of "managers" do adolescents really need? Helping middle and secondary teachers manage classrooms effectively. *Beyond Behavior* 14 (2): 9–14.

Cartledge, G., and J. Milburn. 1995. *Teaching social skills to children and youth*. Needham Heights, MA: Allyn and Bacon.

Cartledge, G., A. Singh, and L. Gibson. 2008. Practical behavior-management techniques to close the accessibility gap for students who are culturally and linguistically diverse. *Preventing School Failure*, 52 (3): 29–38.

Chamberlain, S. 2005. Recognizing and responding to cultural differences in the education of culturally and linguistically diverse learners. *Intervention in School and Clinic* 40 (4): 195–211.

Colvin, G. 2004. *Managing the cycle of acting-out behavior in the classroom*. Eugene, OR: Behavior Associates.

Conroy, M., K. Sutherland, A. Snyder, and S. Marsh. 2008. Classwide interventions: Effective instruction makes a difference. *Teaching Exceptional Children*, 40 (6): 24–30.

Crone, D., R. Horner, and L. Hawken. 2004. *Responding to problem behavior in schools: The behavior education program*. New York: Guilford Press.

Crosby, S., K. Jolivette, and D. Patterson. 2006. Using precorrection to manage inappropriate academic and social behaviors. *Beyond Behavior* 16 (1): 14–17.

Crundwell, R., and K. Killu. 2007. Understanding and accommodating students with depression in the classroom. *Teaching Exceptional Children* 40 (1): 48–54.

Curran, M. 2003. Linguistic diversity and classroom management. *Theory into Practice* 42 (4): 334–340.

Duhaney, L. 2003. A practical approach to managing the behaviors of students with ADD. *Intervention in School and Clinic* 38 (5): 267–279.

Elksnin, L., and N. Elksnin. 2006. *Teaching social-emotional skills at school and home.* Denver, CO: Love Publishing.

Emmer, E., C. Evertson, and M. Worsham. 2006. *Classroom management for middle and high school teachers.* 7th ed. Needham Heights, MA: Allyn and Bacon.

Evertson, C., E. Emmer, and M. Worsham. 2006. *Classroom management for elementary teachers.* 7th ed. Needham Heights, MA: Allyn and Bacon.

Fairbanks, S., B. Simonsen, and G. Sugai. 2008. Classwide secondary and tertiary tier practices and systems. *Teaching Exceptional Children* 40 (6): 44–52.

Grossman, H. 2003. *Classroom behavior management for diverse and inclusive schools.* 3rd ed. New York: Rowman & Littlefield.

Hadjioannou, X. 2007. Bringing the background to the foreground: What do classroom environments that support authentic discussions look like? *American Educational Research Journal* 44 (2): 370–399.

Hawken, L., K. Macleod, and L. Rawlings. 2007. Effects of the behavior education program on office discipline referrals of elementary school students. *Journal of Positive Behavior Interventions* 9 (2): 94–101.

Hendley, S. 2007. Use positive behavior support for inclusion in the general education classroom. *Intervention in School and Clinic* 42 (4): 225–228.

Herrell, A., and M. Jordan. 2004. *Fifty strategies for teaching English-language learners.* 2nd ed. Upper Saddle River, NJ: Prentice-Hall.

Joseph, L., and M. Konrad. 2009. Have students self-manage their academic performance. *Intervention in School and Clinic* 44 (4): 246–249.

Kaplan, J. S. 1995. *Beyond behavior modification.* 3rd ed. Austin, TX: Pro-Ed.

Kauffman, J., M. Mostert, S. Trent, and D. Hallahan. 2002. *Managing classroom behavior: A reflective case-based approach.* 3rd ed. Boston: Allyn & Bacon.

Kern, L., and N. Clemens. 2007. Antecedent strategies to promote appropriate classroom behavior. *Psychology in the Schools* 44 (1): 65–75.

Kern, L., and G. Sacks. 2003. *How to deal effectively with inappropriate talking and noisemaking.* Austin, TX: Pro-Ed.

Kern, L., and T. State. 2009. Incorporating choice and preferred activities into classwide instruction. *Beyond Behavior* 18 (2): 3–11.

Law, B., and M. Eckes. 2000. *The more-than-just-surviving handbook: ESL for every classroom teacher.* 2nd ed. Winnipeg, Manitoba, Canada: Portage & Main Press.

Lee, D., P. Belfiore, and S. Budin. 2008. Riding the wave: Creating a momentum of school success. *Teaching Exceptional Children* 40 (3): 65–70.

Lo, Y., and G. Cartledge. 2006. FBA and BIP: Increasing the behavior adjustment of African American boys in schools. *Behavioral Disorders* 31 (1): 147–161.

Martella, R., J. Nelson, and N. Marchand-Martella. 2003. *Managing disruptive behaviors in the schools: A schoolwide, classroom, and individualized social learning approach.* Boston: Allyn and Bacon.

Miller, K., G. Fitzgerald, K. Koury, K. Mitchem, and C. Hollingshead. 2007. KidTools: Self-management, problem-solving, organizational, and planning software for children and teachers. *Intervention in School and Clinic* 43 (1): 12–19.

Minneapolis Public Schools Positive School Climate Team. n.d. Creating a positive school climate for learning: A tool kit for building leaders, teachers, and staff of Minneapolis Public Schools (1st ed.).

http://sss.mpls.k12.mn.us/Positive_School_Climate_Tool_Kit.html.

O'Connor, E., and K. McCartney. 2007. Examining teacher-child relationships and achievement as part of an ecological model of development. *American Educational Research Journal* 44 (2): 340–369.

Rafferty, L. 2007–2008. "They just won't listen to me": A teacher's guide to positive behavior interventions. *Childhood Education*, 84 (2): 102–104.

Rhode, G., W. Jenson, and H. Reavis. 1993. *The tough kid book*. Longmont, CO: Sopris West.

Ryan, J., S. Sanders, A. Katsiyannis, and M. Yell. 2007. Using time-out effectively in the classroom. *Teaching Exceptional Children* 39 (4): 60–67.

Scheuermann, B., and J. Hall. 2008. *Positive behavioral supports for the classroom*. Upper Saddle River, NJ: Pearson/Merrill Prentice Hall.

Scott, T., C. Nelson, and C. Liaupsin. 2001. Effective instruction: The forgotten component in preventing school violence. *Education and Treatment of Children* 24: 309–322.

Simonsen, B., S. Fairbanks, A. Briesch, D. Myers, and G. Sugai. 2008. Evidence-based practices in classroom management: Considerations for research to practice. *Education and Treatment of Children* 31 (3): 351–380.

Sobel, D., and S. Taylor. 2006. Blueprint for the responsive classroom. *Teaching Exceptional Children* 38 (5): 28–35.

Strout, M. 2005. Positive behavioral support at the classroom level: Considerations and strategies. *Beyond Behavior* 14 (2): 3–8.

Sugai, G., R. Horner, and F. Gresham. 2002. Behaviorally effective school environments. In *Interventions for academic and behavior problems II: Preventive and remedial approaches*, eds. M. Shinn, H. Walker, and G. Stoner, 315–350. Bethesda, MD: National Association of School Psychologists.

Utley, C., C. Greenwood, and K. Douglas. 2007. The effects of a social skills strategy on disruptive and problem behaviors in African American students in an urban elementary school: A pilot study. *Multiple Voices* 10 (1&2): 173–190.

Walker, H., E. Ramsey, and F. Gresham. 2004. *Antisocial behavior in school: Evidence-based practices*. 2nd ed. Belmont, CA: Wadsworth/Thomson Learning.

Walker, J., T. Shea, and A. Bauer. 2007. *Behavior management: A practical approach for educators*. 9th ed. Upper Saddle River, NJ: Pearson Education, Inc.

Webb-Johnson, G. 2003. Behaving while black: A hazardous reality for African-American learners? *Beyond Behavior* 12 (2): 3–7.

Weinstein, C., M. Curran, and S. Tomlinson-Clarke. 2003. Culturally responsive classroom management: Awareness into action. *Theory into Practice* 42 (4): 269–276.

Weinstein, C. 2003. *Secondary classroom management: Lessons for research and practice*. 2nd ed. Boston: McGraw-Hill.

West, E., R. Leon-Guerrero, and D. Stevens. 2007. Establishing codes of acceptable schoolwide behavior in a multicultural society. *Beyond Behavior* 16 (2): 32–38.

Zirpoli, T. 2008. *Behavior management: Applications for teachers*. 4th ed. Upper Saddle River, NJ: Pearson/Prentice Hall.

PRECORRECTION

For "Giving Encouraging Feedback"

Name the behavior/skill: "In a minute, you are going to be working with a partner. Remember to give encouraging feedback. This is a way to follow the school rule 'Help each other learn.'"

Review: "Think about what you learned about giving encouraging feedback. When would your partner need encouraging feedback? What is encouraging feedback? Talk about it in table groups, and then I'll call on someone in each group. Now think of one example of what you could say to your partner, and then I'll draw name cards to call on you."

Performance: "Imagine that the person next to you just made a mistake on a math problem. Give him or her encouraging feedback. Now switch." (*Monitor carefully.*)

PRECORRECTION

For "Ignoring Distractions"

Name the behavior/skill: "In a moment, you three are going to work together at the table out in the hall. While you're out there, you'll need to remember how to ignore distractions."

Review: "What are some distractions in the hall?" (*Get one idea from each student.*) "Each of you tell me the three steps to follow for ignoring distractions." (Take a deep breath; Try not to look or listen; Keep working.)

Performance: "Pretend that you are working. When I walk by talking loudly, show me how you'd ignore this distraction." (*Give positive and corrective feedback. Repeat as needed.*)

MINI-LESSON

Teaching the Routine "How to Get Help on In-Class Tasks"

Objective: *Students will correctly follow the routine for getting help (try, ask, wait) when they encounter difficulty on an in-class task.*

Explain:

Show steps of task analysis on poster. Explain and give examples of each step. Ask students to explain/paraphrase each step to partner before going to next one.

How to Get Help on In-Class Tasks

Try If you run into difficulty, look at examples, reread directions, or use resources such as a glossary. Then try again.

Ask If you still need help, ask peers (if allowed) or use signal to teacher (stand book up on desk or write group name on board).

Wait While waiting quietly for help, plan question to ask (not just "I don't get it"), and skip the problem and go on if possible.

Show:

1. Hand out copies of steps and tell students to check off the steps as they see me demonstrate them.

2. Sitting in student desk with math worksheet, "think out loud" the steps ("I'm stuck on this one. Let's see, is there an example like this at the top of the page?" and so on). Call on selected students at random to describe each step that I followed.

3. Demonstrate incorrectly with social studies questions (don't reread directions, call out "I can't do this" in whiny voice). Have students tell partner errors. Call on students at random to correct me.

4. Demonstrate correctly with Ken and Rich (who often have trouble with this). We pretend to be working on a group project. Include the steps of asking peers for help and writing group name on board. Ask class which steps they checked off.

Rehearse:

1. Leave up poster.

2. Give students very challenging worksheets with unfamiliar format and no oral directions.

3. Tell them to use the routine when they need help.

4. Provide positive and corrective feedback to each student on following the steps.

MINI-LESSON

Teaching the Rule "Follow Directions for Answering Questions"

Objective: Students will follow directions for how to answer questions in class.

Explain: (Show transparency.) "The rule is to follow my directions for how to answer questions. This means:

- When I say *raise your hand to answer*, raise your hand quietly, wait until I call on you, then speak.

- When I say *call out ideas* or *call out the answer*, then say ideas/answers out loud as soon as you think of them.

- When I say *everyone together*, then wait for my hand signal and all say the answer at the same time."

Show: (Practice in advance with three students.) "Watch while we show you what following this rule looks like:

- Raise your hand to tell me what 4 plus 4 equals.

- Call out the answer to 3 plus 3 equals . . . 9 plus 6 equals . . . 5 plus 5 equals . . .

- Everyone together, what does 2 plus 2 equal? (*hand signal*) . . ."

Check for understanding: Watch us again. This time, show thumbs up if the three students are following directions for answering, and thumbs down if they are not. (*Show several examples and nonexamples of each. Call on students to explain why they showed thumbs up or down.*)

Rehearse: Now you all are going to practice following my directions for answering while I ask you questions about the reading we did yesterday. Remember to listen carefully for my directions to raise your hand, call out, or for everyone to answer on signal. (*Ask many questions with different directions for answering. Give positive and correct feedback.*)

Critical Management Skills for Communicating with Students

Introduction

Teachers establish a solid foundation for classroom management by connecting with each student, creating a diversity responsive environment, and implementing universal and selected behavioral interventions. Once this foundation is built, teachers are able to focus on the management issues that apply to the lessons and activities they plan throughout the school year.

Teachers must develop certain basic, essential management skills that they employ in each lesson and activity in order to support appropriate behavior, prevent behavior problems, preserve instructional time, and promote learning. In other words, they must develop a positive context for teaching and learning in *each* lesson and activity they teach. While there are many management tools available to teachers, we will present seven critical management skills in detail. Gaining attention, communicating behavior expectations, and acknowledging appropriate behavior are the three critical management skills that are described in this chapter. Four additional critical management skills—monitoring student behavior, arranging the room, planning for logistics, and managing transitions—are described in the next chapter. We have also included suggestions for responding to diversity when using critical management skills and planning for a challenging class.

Responding to Diversity When Using Critical Management Skills

You will need to consider the diversity of your students as you plan for behavior management in a lesson or activity—just as you do when planning

instruction. Perhaps you have students with cognitive, physical, emotional/behavioral, or learning disabilities in your class. Perhaps you have English language learners of various proficiency levels. Perhaps you have students from a variety of cultural (racial, ethnic, socioeconomic) backgrounds. We will suggest strategies for each critical management skill that are meant to meet the varied needs of your students, but we will try to avoid stereotyping and over-generalizing. Remember that behavior interventions are not culture-specific, disability-specific, or otherwise label-specific. In other words, we can't say, "This student is ____; therefore, ____ strategy will work." We can, however, identify interventions that are worth trying. If you are familiar with a variety of management strategies and knowledgeable about diversity and your students, you will be more likely to find ways to support appropriate behavior for all students in your class.

The Challenging Class and Critical Management Skills

A class or group of students is made up of individuals but it also has a character or dynamic of its own. We've all heard teachers say something like, "This is the toughest group I've ever had!" We use the term *challenging class* to refer to a group of students who really keep their teacher on his toes. A challenging class may be more active, more talkative, or more demanding. It may be less compliant, less attentive, less self-controlled, or less skilled. It might be more impulsive, more distractible, more irritable, more competitive, or more argumentative. Perhaps overall it is a group with a great deal of energy that needs to be channeled positively. However it is described, this is a class whose behavior interferes with learning even when your usual universal interventions and critical management skills are used.

If you are a practicum student, intern, or substitute teacher—that is, if it's not your class—it may be best to plan for each class as if it is a challenging class. When students don't have their "real" teacher, behavior problems can increase because students are anxious or need to test to find limits. Also, any class can be a challenging class on early release days, picture day, and so on.

What can you do to be successful with a challenging class? Here are some ideas.

■ Often, providing more structure will help. This might mean tightening up the class rules and routines, or teaching more social skills.

■ It may be that students need to be more thoroughly involved in developing class rules, in problem-solving, and in making choices.

■ Spending additional time building connections with students and fostering a sense of community among students will be time well spent.

■ Finally, a challenging class will require that you strengthen the critical management strategies you use. Try planning for more predictability, consistency, supervision, encouragement, and prompts as you develop your lesson or activity.

Specific suggestions for the challenging class for each of the critical management skills will be provided in this chapter. In addition, several group management games will be described. Making behavior management fun whenever possible, for both the teacher and the students, is helpful in the same way that making instruction fun is important for academic learning and motivation.

An important note: It is also possible that a class develops challenging behaviors because students are reacting to *too* much structure. Be careful that you are not falling into the trap of enacting increasingly restrictive rules ("Stand in line with your hands at your sides at all times, looking straight ahead, and leaving 10 inches between you and the person in front of you.") and increasingly severe punishments ("Losing one recess didn't seem to make you stop what you are doing. Tomorrow you will lose all recesses for the day."). Instead, you may need to back off and give students more choices and responsibilities, involve them in developing class policies and procedures, and so on.

Mrs. Bean and Critical Management Skills

Read about Mrs. Bean and the activity she is planning for her class in the following box. Then, as you read this and the next chapter, think about how Mrs. Bean could use the critical management skills to support appropriate behavior during her planned activity. You may imagine that Mrs. Bean is teaching any grade level.

A Look at Mrs. Bean's Planning

Mrs. Bean is planning an activity that's part of her emphasis on social justice themes. The students have been learning about the importance of taking action when they encounter injustice. Recently, there have been incidents of kids being physically bullied at school and in the community because of differences in what they wear for religious reasons (e.g., head scarves, turbans). The students have chosen to begin acting for social justice by making posters to put up around the school and community that send a message against hate and intolerance of religious diversity. They have already brainstormed specific ideas that they want to communicate on the posters. Today, they will be making the posters, which are intended to be creative and eye-catching, and will be made from a wide variety of materials. Mrs. Bean wants to support her students in completing the posters in the allotted time, using materials and equipment wisely and safely, sharing and taking turns, encouraging each other, cleaning up, and generally channeling their energy, excitement, and passion for social justice into a successful, completed project.

Gaining Attention

The first critical management skill is gaining attention. It is critical to be able to gain students' attention whenever you need it. One time when you'll need it is at the beginning of lessons and activities. You'll also need to regain attention at various other points during your lessons and activities, for example when you need to give additional directions. A great deal of instructional time can be wasted when teachers have to repeat instruction or directions because they didn't have the students' attention. In addition, students may learn that they don't need to listen to the teacher, as everything will be repeated to them. It's important that you plan how to ask for attention and how you want the class to respond.

Signals for Attention

Teachers can ask for attention through various types of signals. Signals can be verbal, visual, sounds, or combinations of the three. Signals can also be interactive or contagious. Examples of verbal signals are "Attention, please," and "Eyes up here." Raising your arm or making mime movements are visual signals. Examples of signaling for attention by using sounds are clapping your hands and playing music. You can also combine types of signals, for example, sound the clicker and then say "Attention, please." Signals can be interactive as well. For example, the teacher chants, "One, two, three, eyes on me," and the students reply, "One, two, eyes on you," or the teacher claps a rhythm and the students clap back. Contagious signals can be effective as well. For example, the teacher can use a visual signal, such as hands on head, that the students are expected to imitate when they see it. It spreads gradually as students notice; in other words, the signal is contagious.

The signal you choose will depend on how difficult you believe it will be to gain your students' attention in a given situation. If students are close to you, quiet, and facing you, it's very easy to gain attention. If students are talking, making noise, moving around, or intensely focused on an activity, it's more difficult to gain their attention. For example, if students are working in labs with partners, it would work better to clap your hands or turn the lights off and on than it would to stand in front of the room with your arms folded or to say "I need your attention" (without shouting).

The signal you choose also depends on how quickly you want attention. You may want something noticeable enough that you can get everyone to pay attention immediately. Or, you may prefer that they finish what they are saying before they turn to you; in that case, use a gradual, contagious signal. If you want them to make a transition (such as going back to their desks or putting their materials away) and then give you their attention, use a signal that incorporates time limits, such as counting backwards or singing a song of a familiar length.

Student Response to Signal

Once you have decided on the signal you will use, you need to decide what you want the students to do in response to your signal. You want them to give you their attention, but what exactly will that look like? Do you want them to stop where they are? Sit down? Look at you? Listen? Should they put down any materials they are using? Stop talking? Freeze? You'll need to specify how you want them to respond.

You'll also need to *teach* the students the signal/response routine at the beginning of the year. (See Chapters 10 and 19 for additional information on teaching classroom routines.) Teach the signals you'll be using as well as how to respond to the signal. Try using a mini-lesson, such as the one in the box on the next page.

Once you have taught the gaining attention routine to your students, at the beginning of each lesson or activity, tell the students which signal you'll use and which response you'll expect. Periodically, you may decide that students need a review or that a new signal/response routine is necessary for a particular lesson/activity.

Using the Gaining Attention Strategy

It's important that you *implement* the signal/response strategy correctly and consistently. Consider the following recommendations:

■ When you give the signal, position yourself so you can see the faces of all your students as they respond and ensure that all of the students are looking at you (Colvin and Lazar 1997).

■ Following the signal, you should remain silent. Make the students responsible—no nagging or giving reminders or warnings.

■ Encourage the students to gently help each other respond to the signal quickly, through nudges, whispered reminders, and so on.

- Don't go on without the class's attention. Insist on attention ("Let's try that again. What should you do when I ring the bell? Right. Do it.")

- Remember to acknowledge students for responding quickly ("You paid attention right away so you could find out what to do next—well done.")

- Of course, be sure *you* are ready to begin as soon as you have their attention.

MINI-LESSON

Teaching a Gaining Attention Strategy

Objective: Class will respond to the signal for attention (bell) within 10 seconds by looking at the teacher with mouths closed and hands still.

Explain:

- When I want your attention, I will ring the bell, like this. What will I do, everyone?

- When I ring this bell, pay attention right away. What do you do when you hear the bell, everyone?

- Paying attention means looking at me with mouths closed and hands still. (*Point to poster.*)

- What does paying attention mean, everyone? (*Point to eye, mouth, hand.*)

Show:

- Watch what I do when I hear the bell. (*Ask helper to ring bell in a moment.*)

  (*Sit next to someone, chat, and play with pencil. When bell rings, correctly pay attention to helper.*)

- Did I pay attention, everyone? What did I do?

Rehearse:

- Now it's your turn to show me how to pay attention when you hear the bell.

- Everyone, turn to your neighbor and talk about your favorite TV programs.

  (*Wait a moment, then ring bell.*) (*Give positive and corrective feedback.*)

- From now on, pay attention quickly (*point to poster*) every time you hear this bell.

Mrs. Bean's Plan for Gaining Attention

Signal to use: Turn lights off/on.

Reasoning: Students will be talking and moving around as they select materials and make posters, so a strong signal will be needed.

Response to signal: freeze; stop talking; listen to directions

Reasoning: They need to stop and listen, but putting materials down or returning to their seats would disrupt their work unnecessarily.

What's another idea for a signal and response?

Being able to gain attention when you need it is critical. You'll need to ask for it, wait for it, and praise or insist on it. Remember Mrs. Bean and the poster-making activity? Above are some of Mrs. Bean's ideas for gaining attention during her activity.

Responding to Diversity When Gaining Attention

Think about the individuals in your class and what might be helpful in gaining attention. For example:

- Using culturally or linguistically significant signals sends an inclusive message. Songs, chants, rhymes, alliterations, and using various languages are possibilities.

- When you have new students in your class who speak little or no English, they'll appreciate consistent, nonverbal, or combined signals for a while.

- Consider hearing or visual impairments as you develop signals for attention. Combined signals (such as a sound and visual signal: knocking on desk and raising your arm) work well in this situation.

- If you have students who are not inclined to respond, involving them in creating signals may increase buy-in. Form teams or select individuals to develop the signal of the day.

- Very active students may respond well to signals that call for an active response, such as Simon Says ("Simon says stand up. Simon says sit down. Fold your hands. Simon says look at me.")

- For students who need a great deal of repetition when learning new information, you can use signals that also provide academic practice. Use content you are teaching that day in an interactive signal. For example, tell the students you will signal for their attention by either saying "vertical axis" or "horizontal axis," and they will respond by saying "y" or "x" and turning to look at you. Choose new vocabulary and synonyms (*gigantic*, *huge*), math facts (6 × 7, 42), or words in two languages (*Monday*, *Lunes*). By using these academic signals, you get "two for one"—a novel way to gain attention and the repetition of new learning.

The Challenging Class and Gaining Attention

If your class struggles with giving you their attention, there are many strategies to try. Precorrect by reviewing and rehearsing the signal and response at the beginning of each lesson or activity. You might consistently choose a strong signal such as ringing a bell or turning off the lights. Use the signal several times early in the lesson and enthusiastically acknowledge a quick response. Use logical positive and negative consequences. Paying attention quickly saves time so the lesson can be completed earlier with free time available; giving your attention slowly wastes time. Insist on quick attention, but also be generous in rewarding it.

Try to make the signal and response fun. Young kids like Knock Knock ("Knock, knock." "Who's there?" "Miss Hoagland." "Miss Hoagland who?" "Miss Hoagland who wants eyes and ears on me."). Your class may enjoy "freeze" as the signal so they can freeze in place. Consider whether you need to make it more adult (use a judge's gavel and "Ladies and gentlemen, may I have your attention, please?"). Older students sometimes appreciate a humorous signal (a toy that makes a mooing sound). Challenge the class to set a goal for a quick response (Do you think I can have the class's attention in

10 seconds?) and reward the class for "beating the clock." Have class teams compete for the fastest response to the signal.

Communicating Behavior Expectations

It is essential to communicate your expectations for behavior to students. This is the second critical management skill. Clarifying expectations acts as a precorrection and prevents behavior problems. Remember that you have already established classroom rules and routines and taught social skills to your students. Now you are going to identify which specific rules, routines, and social skills apply during this particular lesson or activity. Consider the following suggestions for determining and letting students know your behavior expectations.

How to Choose Expectations

Think about your goals for student behavior. Remember that the purpose of rules, routines, and social skills in the classroom is to facilitate student learning and positive interactions.

Then consider what will be happening during this lesson or activity. Decide what behaviors will help the lesson or activity go smoothly, efficiently, and safely, and will allow everyone to learn. Think about the general and specific rules that apply, such as *Show respect by listening to the speaker* or *Do your best by starting work right away*. Determine what previously taught routines students will need to use; for example, routines for getting help, finishing tasks early, and cleanup may be relevant. Decide what social skills students will need to use. Social skills such as sharing, accepting feedback, or disagreeing politely may apply. Once you have identified appropriate behavior expectations, write the expectations into your lesson plan.

How to Communicate Expectations

Next, you will need to communicate the behavior expectations. Do this thoroughly. Don't assume that students understand what you mean by *listening*, *participating*, and so on. Consider the following.

State the behavior expectations. Do this in a firm, direct, polite, and positive way. State *dos* rather than *don't*s ("Raise hands" rather than "No talk-outs") when possible.

Put expectations in writing, and post them. Be sure to use language that is clear and understandable to your students. Posted expectations will act as a reminder for the students during the lesson or activity and will also remind you to be consistent and to acknowledge students for following the expectations.

Explain expectations clearly. Don't simply read them from the poster. You might explain by paraphrasing, elaborating, and using examples and nonexamples.

- "I want everyone to participate. *Participate* means being involved by listening, talking, writing, or doing."

- "In this lesson, *participate* means sharing your ideas when I say 'Tell your partner' or 'Raise your hand.'"

Be specific as you explain expectations. Say, "Listen to ideas from each group member," rather than just "Respect others." Check for understanding to make sure that you have been clear. For example, say, "Carlos always has great ideas. Thumbs up if the group should only listen to Carlos's ideas."

Give more explanation of new expectations. How much explanation is necessary will depend on how familiar the students are with the expectations. The first few times you state the expectation *listen to the speaker,* you may need to explain that *listen* means eyes on the speaker, mouths closed, thinking about what the speaker is saying, and that *speaker* means the person talking, including the teacher or a peer. Also, think about the expected behaviors that are new to the students (e.g., correcting a partner's response during peer tutoring) or more difficult for them (e.g., accepting correction from a peer). Those will need more explanation.

Emphasize those expectations that change. You will need to point out those rules that vary by situation (being in seat during tests versus during projects). Be sure to go over them so that students are clear about which ones apply.

Communicate expectations just before they are needed. You may have different behavior expectations for different parts of the activity or

> ### EXAMPLES OF BEHAVIOR EXPECTATIONS BY METHOD
>
> Behavior Expectations for Teacher Presentations
> - Keep eyes and ears on speaker.
> - Respond in unison.
> - Raise hand to ask questions.
>
> Behavior Expectations for Seatwork
> - Work independently.
> - Stay seated.
> - Raise hand for help.
> - Read a book if finished early.
>
> Behavior Expectations for Partner Work
> - Take turns fairly.
> - Encourage each other.
> - Stay focused on work.

lesson, and for transitions. One set of expectations will apply while you are giving directions and another set when students are practicing with a partner, for example. Communicate these just before they are needed rather than communicating all of them at the beginning of the lesson or activity. For example, communicate your behavior expectations for seatwork when you assign that work, and let students know the expectations for transitioning to small groups right before that change is to be made. You may find it helpful to make yourself a list of typical expectations by instructional method.

Some teachers make multiple posters of behavior expectations—one for each method typically used—and some create multiple sentence strips of expectations. For example, put your expectations related to talking (*raise hands; call out ideas; speak quietly to partner*) on cards that can be added or substituted on one poster (Sprick, Garrison, and Howard 1998).

Follow Through

It's very important to follow through with expectations. Don't state them and then ignore them. Be consistent. For example, if you stated that students must raise their hands, then don't respond

CHAPTER 11   Critical Management Skills for Communicating with Students   **141**

Mrs. Bean's Plan for Behavior Expectations

One expectation for this activity: Use inside voices.

Reasoning: Students need to talk somewhat quietly to maintain a calm atmosphere and avoid disturbing other classes.

How to communicate this expectation: Explain and demonstrate with examples and nonexamples ("Listen as I speak with an inside voice . . .").

Reasoning: Since this expectation is somewhat abstract (an "inside" voice), it needs to be explained thoroughly.

What other behavior expectations should she select, and how could she communicate them?

to callouts. If you don't mind callouts, then don't select *raise hands* as an expectation. Monitor students carefully and acknowledge students for following the stated expectations. Use the words and phrases of your expectations as you praise students and point to the written expectations on the poster. ("Good—everyone is 'participating' by showing a thumbs up or thumbs down.") Remind students of the expectations as needed, again referring to the poster ("Group Two, please remember to *use quiet voices*.").

Communicating behavior expectations is essential. Be sure to develop expectations for all parts of your lessons and activities, and to explain, post, and consistently follow through with them. Now think about Mrs. Bean and the poster-making activity. Look at the box above for Mrs. Bean's ideas for communicating behavior expectations, and add your own.

Responding to Diversity When Communicating Behavior Expectations

It's as important to be a diversity responsive teacher when communicating behavior expectations as when you are teaching academic content. The following strategies will be helpful for many students, including English language learners.

- Use gestures and demonstrate the expected behaviors ("This is what *listening to the speaker* looks and sounds like.") as well as orally explaining behavior expectations. Ask the students to demonstrate the behaviors for you. You may also want to show what *not* to do.

- Add picture clues to the written expectations, such as a picture of an ear for *listening*.

- Be consistent in language and use the same terms as when the rule, routine, or social skill was originally taught.

Students with learning and/or behavior problems may benefit from diversity responsive strategies for communicating behavior expectations. You could:

- teach a mini-lesson in which you explain, show, and rehearse the behavior expectation.

- spend more time clarifying, reviewing, and checking for understanding.

- use behavior expectation posters with brief phrases, simple vocabulary, and a limited number of expectations so they are easy to remember.

- take photographs of a student performing the expectations (e.g., raising hand, mouth closed, eyes on teacher) that she can keep on her desk.

- provide self-management opportunities such as giving students their own small, laminated copy of the behavior expectations with room for them to write + signs when they are following the expectation.

Spending time reflecting on your behavior expectations will help you adjust them when needed. Consider how long you are asking students to stay seated and read or write independently. Many students, including those with attention or hyperactivity issues, will not be successful in following expectations in these situations for long periods. Change the task without changing the content. For example, have students practice math problems on the board, on the computer, and with a partner, as well as writing independently on a worksheet.

Particularly when you are from a different cultural background than your students, think carefully about the behavior expectations you've chosen. Are they necessary? Are they culturally consistent? Consider whether it is really necessary that students sit still and raise their hands before speaking in this lesson. In some cultural groups, exuberant physical and verbal responses are the norm. Perhaps your students are used to asking peers, rather than adults, for help. Could that be reflected in your behavior expectations for this activity? Spend time observing students in a variety of settings and talking to families to learn about cultural differences in these areas.

The Challenging Class and Communicating Behavior Expectations

If your class is having difficulty meeting behavior expectations, think about the particular ones with which they are struggling. Decide whether you need, at least temporarily, to build in scaffolds that support the expected behavior. For example:

- If your students tend to blurt out answers when you ask a question rather than raising hands, then raise your own hand as a prompt, or begin the question with "Raise your hand and tell me . . ."

- If they are eager to talk and have difficulty following expectations to listen quietly, build in more active participation strategies such as *unison responses* and *tell your neighbor*.

- If your class has difficulty cooperating with peers, don't make them share materials; structure group work rather than expecting them to share tasks fairly or take turns on their own; have fewer members per group.

- If your students have a great deal of energy and are eager to move, build in physical movement and responses in your lessons, and alternate active and more sedentary activities.

If the class doesn't seem to take the behavior expectations seriously, be sure that your manner is appropriately assertive (Emmer, Evertson, and Worsham 2006). Speak firmly and confidently. Follow up with stronger positive and negative consequences. You may need to spend more time formally teaching the rules, routines, and social skills that underlie the expectations. Try involving students in developing and self-monitoring behavior expectations.

When it is not your class—that is, if you are a practicum student, student teacher, or substitute teacher—you must clearly establish your expectations for student behavior. Don't assume that because the students understand and follow the usual teacher's rules they will automatically behave the same way with you.

Acknowledging Appropriate Behavior

Acknowledging appropriate behavior, the third critical management skill, means noticing, and letting students know you noticed, when they are doing the right thing. It means positively responding when they use the social skills you taught them, when they follow the class rules and routines, and when they meet behavior expectations. Unfortunately, many of us find it much more natural to notice and respond to inappropriate behavior. We expect and take for granted appropriate behavior, so acknowledging appropriate behavior may take special effort on your part. It's worth that effort, as this critical management skill has a significant impact on student behavior.

When you spend most of your time noticing desirable behavior, you strengthen desirable behavior, decrease the incidence of undesirable behavior, and let students know what behavior you expect. When you acknowledge appropriate behavior, you teach students to notice and appreciate their own behavioral skills. You also create a positive classroom climate for students and yourself. All of us learn better and are happier in places where the emphasis is on what we are doing right and where everyone is being encouraged. Teachers end up going home exhausted and discouraged when they spend the day constantly reprimanding students. Acknowledging the appropriate behavior of a class, a group, or individuals is a very powerful management tool. It's critical to acknowledge appropriate behavior frequently, specifically, sincerely, fairly, and with an emphasis on socially important behaviors.

Acknowledging Frequently

It is essential to pay more *frequent* attention to appropriate behavior than to inappropriate behavior. Sprick, Garrison, and Howard (1998) recommend a ratio of three to one—in other words, acknowledging desirable behavior at least three times as often as paying attention to undesirable behavior. It isn't wrong to pay attention to students when they are behaving inappropriately; at issue is the ratio or balance. The number of times you should acknowledge per time period depends on the student, the group, or the situation. But studies reveal that teachers, both of general and special education, typically just don't praise enough (Lewis et al. 2004). When in doubt, acknowledge more frequently, as long as the acknowledgements are deserved.

Acknowledging Specifically

Acknowledgments are *specific* when they pinpoint the appropriate behavior noticed. Always describe the behavior that you are acknowledging. If you don't, you run the risk of the student not understanding what he did right. "When you finished your work early, you found a book to read" is clear, but "Nice job" or "Thanks for being responsible" are not. Acknowledge what they do, not what they "are." There are various types of specific verbal acknowledgements. We'll describe four of them.

1. *Describe*—Simply describe the behavior noticed. "You shared your materials without arguing." "Everyone listened politely to the guest speaker." "You got started on your work right away today." You are providing informative feedback, and you're telling the student(s) that you are paying attention to effort, success, or improvement.

2. *Describe and label*—You can also describe the behavior *and* label it in relation to rules, routines, and social skills. "You followed the rule of respecting others when you listened to Michelle's opinion without interrupting." "You comforted Elizabeth when her feelings were hurt—that's being a good friend." Use the words of your behavior expectations: "I see that everyone's eyes are on me, that's *paying attention.*" This helps the students connect their behavior to the big picture and emphasizes why the behavior is important.

3. *Describe and praise*—You can choose to describe the behavior *and* praise it. "Wow! Super job sticking to your work when it was tough." "You politely accepted your assigned partner. Excellent. I'm very proud of you." "Fantastic! Everyone

> ### EXAMPLE OF FOUR WAYS TO ACKNOWLEDGE A BEHAVIOR
>
> - **Describe:**
>   "Table Two, each of you found a book to read when you finished your work and didn't disturb others."
> - **Describe and label:**
>   "Table Two, each of you found a book to read. You didn't disturb anyone else. That's following our expectation for *being respectful.*"
> - **Describe and praise:**
>   "Good for you, Table Two. You each found a book to read when finished and didn't disturb others. Well done!"
> - **Describe and prompt self-acknowledgement:**
>   "Table Two, you each found a book to read when finished and didn't disturb others. I bet you feel good about that."

was on time to class today." You're letting the students know that they have pleased you.

4. *Describe and prompt self-acknowledgement*—You can describe the behavior *and* prompt the student to acknowledge herself. "You said how you felt in a calm way, didn't you? You must be proud of yourself." "You strongly disagreed with Bridget but in a very polite way. I bet that wasn't easy; you must be pleased." "You all made the transition in just 1 minute. Do you feel good about that?" You're encouraging the students to behave appropriately for their own reasons, not just to please others. Look at the box above for an example of one behavior acknowledged in four different ways.

Acknowledging Sincerely

Having their appropriate behavior acknowledged shouldn't make students feel manipulated. You need to *sincerely* use words or gestures of encouragement and appreciation. Just as you want to hear those words from family, friends, or employers, students want to hear them from their teachers. Consider these suggestions.

■ · Avoid repetitive words of praise such as constant "good job" comments (Sprick, Garrison, and Howard 1998). Students become immune to them.

■ Students are more likely to believe your sincere descriptions rather than general evaluative comments (Say, "The characters in your story are so unusual; I can't wait to find out what happens to them," rather than "Fabulous writing!").

■ Don't praise the class or individuals for less than their best effort.

■ Don't say things that aren't true, or you will lose your credibility. If a student doesn't read well, don't say, "Wow—you're a great reader!" Instead, say, "You tried sounding that word out. Good reading strategy."

■ Show your sincerity when acknowledging the appropriate behavior of an individual by getting close to the student, looking him in the eyes, and using his name.

■ Always talk *to* the person when you are acknowledging her behavior ("Ruby, you followed directions the first time you were asked."). Don't talk *about* the person ("I really like the way Ruby is following directions."). This kind of comparison praise is often meant as an indirect reprimand of other students (who are not following directions) and is likely to be felt by Ruby as insincere, manipulative, and embarrassing. If you want to use acknowledgements to remind the rest of the class of your expectations, then say, "I'm seeing people with their materials out and ready to learn," or, "Thank you, Jones, for following directions, thank you, JoJo, thank you . . ."

If you don't feel sincere in your acknowledgements, you may need to rethink your expectations for students—perhaps they are too low.

Acknowledging Fairly

Acknowledging appropriate behavior *fairly* means acknowledging all students, but not necessarily the same behavior in all students, and not necessarily with the same frequency.

The focus should be on behaviors that are difficult for individuals. Staying on task for 2 minutes is challenging for some students. Working with less skilled or less popular partners is tough for some students. Perhaps you have students who always follow directions, get their work done, and so on. Do they need acknowledgements? Sure. Perhaps they would benefit from being acknowledged for taking a leadership role, being assertive, acting as a good friend, accepting not getting their way, accepting compliments, or saying they're sorry. Acknowledge those behaviors that individuals need to learn and/or use more frequently or consistently.

Don't get hung up on beliefs that students shouldn't need acknowledgements. The intention is to tide them over until the joys or positive natural consequences of the behavior take over, the behavior becomes a deeply ingrained habit, or the student's own sense of accomplishment is enough to maintain the new or difficult behavior. Don't praise behaviors that are already easy for individuals, except rarely and randomly (to maintain them). Praise effort and improvement. Don't add extrinsic reinforcement for behaviors that are already intrinsically motivated. For example, if a student loves reading, he doesn't need your praise or prize for reading.

Acknowledging Important Behaviors

One more idea to remember is that it's essential to acknowledge *important* behaviors. Sometimes, as teachers, we become too narrowly focused on behaviors that make the school day go smoothly. We need to consider what behaviors are important in life, at work, and in school. Acknowledge independence, cooperation, and kindness to others, not just compliant behaviors like walking in lines or raising hands. Think about the general rules you have established (such as "respect yourself and others") and what behaviors contribute to those goals. Think about the social behaviors that contribute to a diversity responsive environment and a strong class community. Consider the following categories and examples of important behaviors to acknowledge.

Interacting

■ helping classmate

■ accepting partner politely

■ apologizing

Cooperating
- compromising
- contributing ideas
- taking turns

Showing Independence
- rereading directions before asking for help
- taking responsibility rather than blaming others
- resisting peer pressure

Expressing Feelings
- asking for help when frustrated
- calmly accepting *no* for an answer
- using words rather than fists

Working
- starting right away
- ignoring distractions
- sticking to it when difficult

Rule Following
- being on time to class
- responding quickly to signal for attention
- making transition quietly and quickly

Mrs. Bean's Plan for Acknowledging Appropriate Behavior

Behavior to acknowledge: sharing materials fairly

Reasoning: to encourage community-building behaviors and the consideration of others' needs and feelings

How to acknowledge: describing the behavior and labeling it as being *fair* or *kind* ("Rylan, you didn't grab all of the big markers. That's being fair to others and thinking about their needs, too.")

Reasoning: Acknowledging this way will help students identify and take pride in their behavior.

What other behaviors should Mrs. Bean acknowledge, and how should she acknowledge them?

Remembering to acknowledge appropriate behavior is critical. Make sure you are acknowledging important behaviors frequently, specifically, sincerely, and fairly. Think about Mrs. Bean and the poster-making activity. See the box on this page for some of Mrs. Bean's ideas for acknowledging appropriate behavior during her activity.

Responding to Diversity When Acknowledging Appropriate Behavior

Students vary in the types of acknowledgments to which they respond. Sometimes, this is influenced by cultural background.

- You may have students who come from backgrounds where calling attention to oneself or being seen as doing better than others is discouraged, such as certain Native American cultures (Cartledge and Milburn 1996). Those students may prefer to be acknowledged as part of a group rather than individually.

- Acknowledgments such as "I'm so proud of you" that convey warm approval and caring from the teacher work well for some students. Lisa Delpit (2006), for example, writes, "I have discovered that children of color, particularly African American, seem especially sensitive to their relationship between themselves and their teacher. I have concluded that it appears that they not only learn from a teacher but also for a teacher."

- Some students prefer private rather than public acknowledgments. Others may be just the opposite. Be observant of the responses to your acknowledgments and talk to students about their preferences. Avoid over-generalizing and stereotyping.

A student's age may influence the types of acknowledgements that are preferred. Consider the following when planning for older students.

- Older students may prefer quiet, private praise that other students don't hear, or prefer group rather than individual praise ("Your team found a way to include everyone's ideas—that's good collaboration.")

- They may prefer informative feedback without added praise words ("You listened without interrupting when I was speaking.")

- Think about labeling the behavior differently with older students ("You're giving others a chance to think" rather than simply "You remembered to raise your hand") to emphasize the reason the behavior is important.

- Label the behavior as important for success in jobs, college, sports, arts activities, and so on ("You get started on your work right away—your future boss is going to appreciate that." Or, "Good for you for encouraging the others in your group—I bet your coach would be impressed.")

- Make your praise about what's in *their* best interest rather than just about what *you* want, or about rule-following ("You didn't waste any of your time—good decision," rather than "Thank you for not wasting class time," or "You followed the rule of bringing materials to class").

Older students might prefer certain types of acknowledgements; however, always monitor the results of your acknowledgements—do they strengthen appropriate behavior?—to know what works best with an individual.

Verbal acknowledgements can be paired with other types of acknowledgements to be most effective with a variety of students. For example:

- Some students with developmental disabilities may respond well to very frequent and enthusiastic praise combined with big smiles, pats, and hugs.

- Some students may not at first trust or value verbal acknowledgements from adults. Begin by pairing positive feedback and praise with more tangible rewards, and then gradually fade the use of the latter.

- Students who are not always respected or seen as competent by their peers may respond well to being verbally praised in front of the class paired with earning privileges that give them a valued leadership role.

Students may also vary in the ratio of attention for appropriate behavior to attention for inappropriate behavior that works best for them. Mathur, Quinn, and Rutherford (1996) recommend a ratio of five to one for students with emotional or behavioral disorders—that is, attention to appropriate behavior is most effective when given five times for every one time attention is given to inappropriate behavior.

The Challenging Class and Acknowledging Appropriate Behavior

An increase in the frequency of both individual and group acknowledgements can be an effective tool when teaching a challenging class. Be sure to acknowledge appropriate behaviors that replace the inappropriate behaviors the class displays. For example, acknowledge hand raising if the class tends to shout out responses; acknowledge verbal negotiating if the class tends to solve problems through fighting.

If verbal acknowledgments alone aren't strong enough for your group, pair them with rewards for the whole class. This can be done through *group management games* where you combine the critical management skills of acknowledging appropriate behavior and communicating behavior expectations into a game format. This can be helpful by making classroom management fun and motivating for students. Don't use these games all day every day, both for your own sake and to keep the element of novelty for the students.

There are many possible games. Four are described here: The Expectations Game, The Marbles in the Jar Game, The Learning Game, and the Ticket Game. You will be able to adapt these and develop your own by following the general guidelines for using behavior expectations, for acknowledging appropriate behavior, and for using these games.

Group Management Games

The Expectations Game lasts for the duration of one lesson or activity and is used with the whole class or group. The teacher marks, on the behavior expectations poster, when students follow the expectations and when they don't follow the expectations. The box on the next page shows an example of how such a poster might look.

When the class follows the expectations more often than they forget them, they win. The reward

---

EXAMPLE OF A POSTER USED IN THE EXPECTATIONS GAME

Expectation	Followed	Forgot
Eyes and ears on speaker and mouth closed	/	//
Respond in unison when directed	///	
Raise hand and wait to be called on before answering	/	///

---

is typically a privilege that immediately follows the lesson, such as 5 minutes to play Hangman or Simon Says, or to draw and listen to music. As with all of the group games, be sure to select rewards that your students enjoy.

Use the Expectations Game when you want a quick and easy management tool that you can use on the spot. Consider the following applications.

- It's useful when you can foresee problems during a particular lesson or activity, perhaps because of changes in the schedule (an assembly or early release day) or exciting events (the first snow of the year or the day before spring break begins).

- It's useful for practicum students, student teachers, or substitute teachers because it is a short-term game; it starts and ends within an hour or less and is easy to implement. The rewards are simple (e.g., 5 minutes to play Round the World) and don't require elaborate planning or permissions.

- It's useful for helping students recognize behavior that meets and does not meet behavior expectations, since this game incorporates both positive and negative feedback.

The Marbles in the Jar Game can last as long as you choose and is used with the whole class. When the class follows behavior expectations (or otherwise displays appropriate behavior) the teacher drops a marble in a jar. You may also choose to allow individuals to earn marbles for the class; this may be especially meaningful for students who have particular difficulty in behaving appropriately. When the jar is filled to a predetermined level, the class

wins. Lines may be drawn on the jar to represent ¼ full, ½ full, and ¾ full, and interim rewards earned as the marbles reach those lines. A bigger reward is earned when the jar is filled. Select the appropriately sized jar by figuring out how many marbles it will hold, how many opportunities the class will have to earn marbles, and how long it should take the class to earn a reward.

The Marbles Game is very concrete—students can hear the marbles fall into the jar and can see the jar filling. It's also very flexible. Here are some ways to use it.

- You can use it with any expectations, any lesson or activity, any time of day.

- You can combine it with class goal-setting (e.g., the class sets a goal for making certain transitions in less than 1 minute and can earn a marble for doing so.)

- It can be an ongoing game; you can set it up so the class can win shorter-term rewards building to a big reward (e.g., sports day; trip to a restaurant).

The Learning Game lasts for the duration of one unit of study (typically 3 to 10 days) and is used with the whole class or group. On a poster that represents the unit of study (e.g., a poster showing houses around the world for a social studies unit on how climate and natural resources affect shelter, food, and occupations), a grid is drawn (Sobel, Taylor, and Wortman 2006). Decide on the number of squares in the grid based on the length of the unit and opportunities to display expected behaviors. Squares in the grid are filled in when students perform expected behaviors. If a certain percentage of squares is filled in by the end of the unit, students win the chance to participate in a rewarding activity related to the unit of study (e.g., students construct houses, using toothpicks and glue, to match given resources and climate). Remember that this activity will only be used if the class earns it, so don't choose one essential to the unit of study.

The Learning Game is the most elaborate and takes the most setup of the games described here. However, it is worth the trouble for several reasons.

- It integrates behavior management and the academic curriculum, and emphasizes the relationship between learning and behavior.

- You can plan it right along with your academic planning.

- You can have students earn squares for academic contributions as well as for meeting behavior expectations, if you choose.

- Best of all, the rewarding activity provides another learning opportunity for your class.

The Ticket Games can last as long as you choose and are used with individuals or teams of students. When a student follows the expectations, she earns a ticket. You'll need to buy or make tickets, with room for students to write their names on them. The tickets can be generic, or you can make tickets that represent particular behavior expectations (e.g., with a picture of a raised hand). Expected behaviors can be individualized, that is, different students may earn tickets for different behaviors. The tickets can be used in a variety of ways: as tickets to attend events or buy privileges (e.g., 20 tickets for a *no-homework pass*); as chances in drawings/raffles; or as "money" to bid with in auctions.

Ticket Games are helpful in a variety of ways.

- They can be used when students' behavioral skills vary widely and expectations need to be individualized.

- They allow for matching unique student interests with rewards.

- They allow for novelty in delivering rewards. Often, the reward itself is of less value to the students than the anticipation of the raffle drawing or the excitement of the auction itself.

Game Guidelines

There are important guidelines or principles to follow when using all of these games; 10 of these are described below.

1. *These games cannot replace effective instruction and appropriate curriculum.* If the content being taught is not at the correct level of difficulty or if critical teaching skills are not used, then no management game can work for long.

2. *Students must see success (i.e., winning the game) as possible.* You must set high but reasonable, achievable expectations. Don't ask for perfection all at once; instead, focus on improvement or steps in the right direction. For example, if many of the students have difficulty waiting to speak, don't immediately require zero blurt-outs to win the game; instead, require fewer blurt-outs than last time. Choose behaviors that students *can do* but *don't do* consistently. But don't make your expectations too low either, as students will live down to them.

3. *Students must see success as within their control.* You aren't *giving* the points, they are *earning* them. If the students perceive the game as unfair, they won't cooperate.

4. *Feedback must be immediate and accurate.* The checkmarks, marbles, filled-in squares, or tickets are feedback to the students about their behavior, about whether they are meeting the behavior expectations. This feedback has to be both immediate and accurate, just as academic feedback must be. Don't say "I'll give you a point this time, but . . .," just as you wouldn't say, "I'll mark this math problem correct this time, but . . ." If you are having trouble with accuracy and consistency of feedback, it may be because your expectations aren't pinpointed clearly. In short, the best thing to do to support student success is to be objective and honest in how you award points right from the start.

5. *Feedback (both positive and negative) needs to be frequent.* Behaviors won't be learned or strengthened with only occasional feedback. Find a way to remember to make those checkmarks or drop those marbles often. You may want to set a goal for yourself of assigning five points (checkmarks, marbles, squares, tickets) in the first 5 minutes. This will help the students understand exactly what you expect, and they will be more likely to take the game seriously.

6. *Be sure the students can identify what they did to earn or lose points.* When possible, give a verbal acknowledgement ("You all participated by answering in unison, well done!") along with awarding the points, or point to the

written expectation. Tell students that they may not ask for or argue about points *during* the game; handle questions and complaints at another time.

7. *Thoroughly teach the game to the students.* Use critical teaching skills for explaining, giving directions clearly, using visual supports, checking for understanding, and so on. Ask for questions. It's important that the students understand how the game works and how to win so they perceive the results as being fair and earned.

8. *The rewards for winning games must be carefully selected.* Try to emphasize logical consequences. For example, if the class pays close attention during the lesson, the lesson won't take as long, and there will be time available to do something else.

   We'd suggest that you have students win privileges (such as time to draw or to sit where they want) or honors (such as "hard worker" certificates to take home) rather than candy or toys—as long as students find these rewarding.

9. *Don't delay the end of the game or the receipt of the reward too long.* Rewards that take weeks or months to earn are unlikely to be effective in influencing today's behavior. If you want to use a big reward that does take a long time to earn, then build in smaller interim rewards. Rewards also must come as promised. If the class earned 5 minutes to play tic-tac-toe after the Expectations Game, don't say, "Oops, we've run out of time. Sorry." Don't set up the game vaguely either, such as "If you try hard, maybe we'll play Heads Up Seven Up later."

10. *Be sure that peer pressure is positive.* Don't let someone become the scapegoat, and don't let anyone sabotage the game. (If this is a problem, try using a Tickets Game.) Show students how to support each other in meeting the expectations. Decide whether to allow individuals to earn points for the whole class. This can be very helpful when you want to make sure everyone in the class is seen as an important contributor, to encourage inclusion, and to improve someone's reputation, status, or power.

Summary

In this chapter, we have discussed three critical management skills—gaining attention, communicating behavior expectations, and acknowledging appropriate behavior—for teachers to build in to every lesson and activity. In addition, we have provided recommendations that will help teachers increase their diversity responsive management skills and suggestions for the challenging class. Making classroom management planning an integral part of lesson and activity planning will prevent behavior problems and enhance learning. In the next chapter, four more critical management skills will be described.

EXAMPLES OF PRIVILEGES FOR CLASS TO WIN

- time for cooking, knitting, weaving
- making kites, paper airplanes
- listening to music during class
- bead work, clay modeling
- dancing, singing
- suspend a class rule (such as no gum-chewing)
- use computers, phones at break
- eat lunch outside
- extra recess, break, free time
- plan party, dress-up day, skit
- play bingo, do puzzles
- tour bus barn, boiler room, kitchens

References and Suggested Reading

Burnett, P. 2002. Teacher praise and feedback and student perceptions of the classroom environment. *Educational Psychology* 22: 5–16.

Cartledge, G., and J. Milburn. 1996. *Cultural diversity and social skills instruction: Understanding ethnic and gender differences.* Champaign, IL: Research Press.

Cipani, E. 2004. *Classroom management for all teachers: 12 plans for evidence-based practice.* 2nd ed. Upper Saddle River, NJ: Merrill/Prentice Hall.

Colvin, G., and M. Lazar. 1997. *The effective elementary classroom.* Longmont, CO: Sopris West.

Conroy, M., K. Sutherland, A. Snyder, M. Al-Hendawi, and A. Vo. 2009. Creating a positive classroom atmosphere: Teachers' use of effective praise and feedback. *Beyond Behavior* 18 (2): 18–26.

Conroy, M. A., K. S. Sutherland, A. L. Snyder, and S. Marsh. 2008. Classwide interventions: Effective instruction makes a difference. *Teaching Exceptional Children* 40 (6): 24–30.

Darch, C., and E. Kame'enui. 2004. *Instructional classroom management: A proactive approach to behavior management.* 2nd ed. Upper Saddle River, NJ: Pearson Education, Inc.

Delpit, L. 2006. Lessons from teachers. *Journal of Teacher Education* 57 (3): 220–231.

Emmer, E., C. Evertson, and M. Worsham. 2006. *Classroom management for middle and high school teachers.* 7th ed. Needham Heights, MA: Allyn and Bacon.

Evertson, C., E. Emmer, and M. Worsham. 2006. *Classroom management for elementary teachers.* 7th ed. Needham Heights, MA: Allyn and Bacon.

Gable, R., P. Hester, M. Rock, and K. Hughes. 2009. Back to basics: Rules, praise, ignoring, and reprimands revisited. *Intervention in School and Clinic* 44 (4): 195–205.

Grossman, H. 2003. *Classroom behavior management for diverse and inclusive schools.* 3rd ed. New York: Rowman and Littlefield.

Jones, V., and L. Jones. 2009. *Comprehensive classroom management: Creating communities of support and solving problems.* 9th ed. Boston: Allyn and Bacon

Kalis, T., K. Vannest, and R. Parker. 2007. Praise counts: Using self-monitoring to increase effective teaching practices. *Preventing School Failure* 51: 20–27.

Kaplan, J. S. 1995. *Beyond behavior modification.* 3rd ed. Austin, TX: Pro-Ed.

Kauffman, J., M. Conroy, R. Gardner, and D. Oswald. 2008. Cultural sensitivity in the application of behavior principles to education. *Education and Treatment of Children* 31 (2): 239–262.

Kea, C. 1998. Focus on ethnic and minority concerns: Critical teaching behaviors and instructional strategies for working with culturally diverse students. *CCBD Newsletter* (March). Reston, VA: The Council for Exceptional Children.

Kerr, M., and C. Nelson. 2010. *Strategies for addressing behavior problems in the classroom.* 6th ed. Upper Saddle River, NJ: Pearson/Merrill.

Lampi, A., N. Fenty, and C. Beaunae. 2005. Making the three P's easier: praise, proximity, and precorrection. *Beyond Behavior* 15: 8–12.

Lannie, A. and B. McCurdy. 2007. Preventing disruptive behavior in the urban classroom: Effects of the good behavior game on student and teacher behavior. *Education and Treatment of Children* 30: 85–98.

Lewis, T. J., S. I. Hudson, M. Richter, and N. Johnson. 2004. Scientifically supported practices in emotional and behavioral disorders: A proposed approach and brief review of current practices. *Behavioral Disorders* 29 (3): 247–259.

Maag, J. 2004. *Behavior management: from theoretical implications to practical applications.* 2nd ed. Belmont, CA: Wadsworth/Thomson Learning.

Mathur, S., M. Quinn, and R. Rutherford. 1996. *Teacher-mediated behavior management strategies for children with emotional/behavioral disorders.* Reston, VA: Council for Exceptional Children.

Murphy, S., and L. Korinek. 2009. It's in the cards: A classwide management system to promote student success. *Intervention in School and Clinic* 44 (5): 300–306.

Rhode, G., W. Jenson, and H. Reavis. 1993. *The tough kid book.* Longmont, CO: Sopris West.

Simonsen, B., S. Fairbanks, A. Briesch, D. Myers, and G. Sugai. 2008. Evidence-based practices in classroom management: Considerations for research to practice. *Education and Treatment of Children* 31 (3): 351–380.

Sobel, D., S. Taylor, and N. Wortman. 2006. Positive behavior strategies that respond to students' diverse needs and backgrounds. *Beyond Behavior* 15 (2): 20–26.

Sprick, R., M. Garrison, and L. Howard. 1998. *CHAMPs: A proactive and positive approach to class-room management.* Longmont, CO: Sopris West.

Sugai, G., and R. Horner. 2002. The evolution of discipline practices: Schoolwide positive behavior supports. *Child and Family Behavior Therapy* 24 (1): 23–50.

Tucker, C., T. Porter, W. Reinke, K. Herman, P. Ivery, C. Mack, and E. Jackson. (2005). Promoting teacher efficacy for working with culturally diverse students. *Preventing School Failure* 50 (1): 29–34.

Willingham, D. 2005. Ask the cognitive scientist: How praise can motivate—or stifle. *American Educator* 29: 23–27.

CHAPTER 12

Critical Management Skills for Structuring the Learning Environment

Introduction

Critical management skills are applied in all lessons and activities, and are meant to help students behave in ways conducive to learning. Planning for behavior management needs to be an integral part of lesson and activity planning; it's just as important as the decisions made about content and instructional methods. Taking this proactive approach to classroom management will prevent behavior problems and give students the best opportunity to immerse themselves in the interesting, relevant, well-taught lesson or activity you intend to present.

In this chapter, we will continue the discussion of critical management skills begun in the previous chapter. In Chapter 11, we focused on *critical management skills for communicating with students*: gaining attention, communicating behavior expectations, and acknowledging appropriate behavior. In this chapter, we will focus on *critical management skills that structure the learning environment*: monitoring student behavior, arranging the room, planning for logistics, and managing transitions. These four critical management skills will be described in detail, and suggestions for responding to diversity and planning for a challenging class will be included.

Reread the scenario about Mrs. Bean, and the poster-making activity she is planning for her class, in the box on page 136 in Chapter 11. Then, as you read this chapter, think about how Mrs. Bean could use additional critical management skills to support appropriate behavior during her planned activity.

Monitoring Student Behavior

The fourth critical management skill for teachers is monitoring behavior. This is also called *active supervision* (McIntosh et al. 2004) or "withitness" (Kounin 1970). Monitoring lets you know what's going on in all parts of the classroom (or other environment) with all of your students. Monitoring communicates that you're on top of things. It works wonders in preventing and stopping misbehavior, increasing engagement in learning, helping you notice appropriate behavior, and ensuring safety. (See Chapter 7 for information on monitoring student *learning*.)

How to Monitor

You can monitor student behavior by scanning, listening, and moving around. All of these techniques will help you be aware of what's happening throughout the classroom.

Scanning means looking around the room, moving your eyes and head, looking at everyone, and making eye contact. It's easy to make the mistake of just looking at the students right in front of you, or only looking at the students who appear interested.

Listening carefully will also allow you to monitor student behavior. Train your ears to notice changes in sounds in the classroom. These could be gasps or giggles, or a sudden silence. Get a reputation for having eyes in the back of your head.

Moving around the classroom, in addition to scanning and listening, will be a huge help in monitoring student behavior. Walk around the perimeter of the classroom and between desks and tables; stand in various places. Your proximity helps prevent behavior problems and allows you to stop inappropriate behavior without disrupting the lesson. Walking over to stand next to a student while you are teaching will help him attend to the lesson.

Monitoring Situations

How you monitor behavior will depend on what's going on in the classroom. For example, are you presenting? Are the students doing seatwork? Are the students moving around? Each of these circumstances requires different monitoring considerations.

While you are presenting to the class, visually scan the whole group frequently. Avoid having your back to the class for too long, such as when writing on the board. Take care not to be tied to your desk, stool, or projector, but rather present from various spots in the room. When you are reading to the class, stop often to scan, and try walking around as you read. Consider these tips for making monitoring behavior easier during teacher presentations:

- Arrange the room so you can see everyone.

- Arrange the room so you can move around easily.

- Do any needed writing on the board in advance.

- Use an overhead projector or document camera.

While students are working at their desks independently or in groups, moving around to check in with them is especially important. Think about whether to stand behind or in front of individuals as you help them, remembering to position yourself so you can easily and frequently look up to scan the rest of the class. The same is true when you briefly join cooperative learning groups. If you are working with a small group while the rest of the class works independently, be sure to have the small group sit with their backs to the class and facing you so that you are facing the rest of the class and able to monitor behavior.

While students are moving (e.g., during transitions, centers, free time), you need to be moving as well. Supervise transitions and breaks carefully, since behavior problems tend to occur during unstructured time. Stand by the door as students enter or leave the classroom. When students are moving from center to center, scan for bottlenecks or other trouble spots. While monitoring, interact with students so they know you are aware of them. Make eye contact with students, smile at appropriate behavior or frown at inappropriate behavior, and use other nonverbal signals. Interact with students verbally: encourage, remind, redirect, express appreciation, acknowledge appropriate behavior, and connect personally.

Active teacher monitoring is an indispensable management skill. Build it into every lesson and activity. Notice how it is related to other critical management skills: careful room arrangement makes monitoring easier; monitoring is an important part of managing transitions; and monitoring will help you in noticing and acknowledging appropriate behavior. Remember Mrs. Bean and the poster-making activity described in Chapter 11? Below are Mrs. Bean's ideas for monitoring behavior during her activity.

Mrs. Bean's Plan for Monitoring Behavior

How to monitor behavior in this activity: Walk around the classroom as students work on their posters, and check in with each student frequently; position myself to see the rest of the class as I talk with individuals.

Reasoning: My proximity will help prevent misbehavior; scanning the whole class allows me to notice problems before they escalate.

How else could Mrs. Bean monitor behavior?

Responding to Diversity When Monitoring Student Behavior

Be sensitive to cultural differences as you interact with students through signals, gestures, touch, voice, and so on (Seattle Public School District Bilingual Instructional Assistants n.d.). Gesturing with your fingers (as in signaling "Come here") may be considered disrespectful or demeaning by individuals from Somali and Vietnamese cultures, for example. Touching someone on the head is said to be insulting in Oromo (East Africa) and Laotian cultures. When you are unfamiliar with a student's culture, be very observant of negative responses to your actions. Investigate by talking to the student, families, or to others from the same background.

When monitoring, make a special note to check in with students who struggle with starting or completing tasks, have difficulty working with peers, have trouble dealing with frustration, and so on. When you notice student moods or problems early, you can often prevent unfinished work, fights, or meltdowns.

The Challenging Class and Monitoring Student Behavior

Close monitoring is essential with the challenging class. Make a special effort to do your own class preparation in advance so that you are available to monitor student behavior. Be sure to position yourself to supervise transitions. Do more moving around the classroom. Ask yourself whether there are certain methods or activities that are more challenging for students (e.g., independent seatwork, group work, using new materials) and ramp up your monitoring at those times. Good monitoring will help you notice and deal with problems before they escalate or spread. For example, you'll want to notice and intervene when Lilah and Andrew begin arguing over the ownership of a pencil, before it turns into a fight. If you are monitoring carefully, you'll notice when Junior begins building a tower with math manipulatives and can intervene before the idea spreads to others and before the tower crashes to the floor, disrupting the lesson.

Prompt the class to self-monitor and to help each other manage themselves. You might say something like, "Think about where you are and what you're doing. Refocus if needed and carry on," or "Check with your partner or table group. Does anyone need help in getting to work?" Such comments provide important reminders for productive behavior.

Arranging the Room

The fifth critical management skill is using the arrangement of the room to support appropriate behavior. (Evertson, Emmer, and Worsham 2006; Sprick, Garrison, and Howard 1998). The physical arrangement of the classroom can make it easier or more difficult to learn. Focus on what you can

control about the physical environment, rather than what you can't control. There may be nothing you can do about the size of the room or the furniture you've been given, but you probably can change how the room is arranged for a lesson or activity. Using a checklist can help you plan for room arrangement. Each of the items in the checklist will be discussed further.

TEACHER CHECKLIST FOR

Room Arrangement

❑ Am I planning a room arrangement that will allow me to see all students?

❑ Am I planning a room arrangement that will allow students to see (me, each other, board, materials, etc.)?

❑ Am I planning a room arrangement that will minimize distractions for students?

❑ Am I planning a room arrangement that will allow me to move near each student?

❑ Am I planning a room arrangement that will allow students to move without disturbing others?

❑ Am I planning a desk arrangement to match the instructional methods I'll be using?

❑ Am I planning for efficient changes in desk arrangement (if needed)?

❑ Am I planning seating arrangements to match individual needs?

❑ Am I planning seating arrangements to facilitate the inclusion of all students?

Considerations in Room Arrangement

As you think about the room arrangement for a particular lesson or activity, you'll want to consider your perspective, the students' perspective, and the instructional methods you'll be using.

Consider your needs as the teacher and classroom manager as you think about room arrangement.

You'll want to make sure that the room is arranged so that you'll be able to see all of the students. When you are able to see each student, you will notice if they appear to be paying attention, understanding, and participating. You will notice both appropriate and inappropriate behaviors. You'll be able to communicate with each student through eye contact and nonverbal signals (such as a thumbs-up or a head shake). Arrange the room so the students closest to you don't block your view of students farther away. Avoid putting display boards or other equipment in places that impair your ability to see all students.

In addition, you'll want to arrange the room so that you can move around easily. If the room is set up so that you can walk near all students and all parts of the room, you'll be able to prevent or intervene in behavior problems early. You may also need to reach students quickly for safety reasons, such as if a student is having a seizure, is choking, or is about to tip over the projector.

Consider the students' perspective as you plan room arrangement. Set up the room so that the students can see you, each other, the board, the screen, the materials, or whatever else you'll be using. If students can't see, they'll miss learning opportunities, they'll tune out, or they'll find something else to do. Eliminate major distractions when possible; for example, place desks facing away from the door and windows, or close the door and drapes, when loud or interesting events are happening outside the classroom. If students will be moving around, make sure they can do so without bothering others. Think about the location of equipment they need—the pencil sharpener, dictionaries, computers, and so on. Look at the room, as a traffic engineer would, for potential traffic jams, congestion, slowdowns, gridlock, and accidents. Make adjustments that will help students pay attention and avoid problems, and that will help you include everyone and ensure safety.

Consider the instructional methods you'll be using, as this will have an impact on how you arrange desks and tables. If you will be having students sit together on the floor, there will need to be a space for that. If you will be working with small groups one at a time, you'll need an area for that. Examine your basic room design and then plan adjustments for the lesson/activity. For example:

- Arranging desks in pairs that face the front works well for active participation during teacher presentations.

- Putting desks in a circle or U-shape works best for discussions because everyone can see each other as they talk and participation will be more general.

- Separated desks are best for individual work, as students are less likely to distract each other.

- Clusters of desks or tables are best for group work because they facilitate interacting.

Be aware that when the desk arrangement doesn't match the method used (for example, if you have students sitting together in groups but want them to work by themselves), more behavioral self-control is required—perhaps more than the students have.

If you are using several methods in the same lesson or activity, you'll need to select an arrangement that can be easily transformed. For example, if two pairs of desks are clustered near each other and can easily be moved closer or farther apart, then arrangements for individual, partner, or group work are easy to accomplish. Avoid multiple complicated transitions that involve major furniture-moving, as that wastes time and begs for behavior problems.

All arrangements have advantages and disadvantages, and you'll have to balance those. Most important is to decide based on student skills and needs rather than solely on your preference or "style." A careful room arrangement will facilitate your use of other critical management skills, such as monitoring behavior and managing transitions. Think about

---

Mrs. Bean's Plan for Room Arrangement

Issue: Materials need to be accessible to all students.

Plan: Put materials on a table in the center of the room with space for students to walk all the way around the table.

Reasoning: to avoid lines and traffic jams and make it easy for many students to collect materials at once so time isn't wasted and behavior problems (caused by waiting and congestion) are prevented

What other room arrangement issues are there? How could the room be arranged to prevent potential problems?

Mrs. Bean and the poster-making activity. For some of her ideas, look at the box called "Mrs. Bean's Plan for Room Arrangement" on the previous page.

Responding to Diversity When Arranging the Room

When arranging the room for your lesson or activity, think about seating assignments and about individual needs.

- Students who have vision or hearing impairments may need preferential seating. For example, a student with a hearing impairment may need to sit up front to be able to see the teacher's face during teacher presentations but away from an overhead projector with a noisy fan.

- If you have students who use crutches, walkers, or wheelchairs, you'll want to set up the room so they can move around easily, gain access to equipment and materials, and get close to peers when working with a partner or in groups (e.g., wide aisles, specially shaped tables).

- Some students (with or without the label of *attention deficit hyperactivity disorder*) frequently need to stand or move. It may be helpful to put their desks on the sides of the room so they can do this without disturbing or blocking the view of others.

- Students who have difficulty focusing attention will need to be near you during presentations, as will those who frequently need redirection or encouragement.

- Some students may do best if they are seated away from peers during independent work, but don't permanently seat some students away from the rest of the class. That sends a message of exclusion. Create secluded "offices" for quiet work time—not as a punishment, but available for anyone needing an easier place to concentrate.

- English language learners (ELLs) may at times benefit from sitting with those who speak the same first language to allow for "side talk" to aid comprehension (Curran 2003). But you'll want your usual class seating arrangement to promote friendships across linguistic and cultural groups. Be sure ELLs are seated where they can easily see and hear instruction. It's much easier to follow discussions in another language

when you can see the speakers' faces—so having chairs in a circle at those times is helpful. In addition, ELLs (as well as other students) may benefit from having certain parts of the room designated for certain activities, such as group work, silent reading, or playing (Herrell and Jordan 2004), as that acts as a nonverbal communication of behavior expectations.

- Be sensitive about cultural values when you plan who sits by whom (Weinstein, Curran, and Tomlinson-Clarke 2003). Having male and female students seated together, for example, may be problematic for some families for religious or other cultural reasons. Having students who are related to each other sit together may bring up taboos around competition and doing better than a relative. Sometimes, especially for recent immigrants, there are issues among students who are from groups that are traditional enemies in the homeland. As always, consult with families and other cultural experts.

There are many factors in deciding where individuals should sit in the classroom, and teachers are always changing the seating to account for them. The class clown may not do well at the front of the room where he can't resist taking the stage and performing for the audience. There will be students who don't get along and fight if seated together. They should probably be seated apart until they've had the opportunity to learn conflict resolution skills. There will be students who don't have friends and do best near someone sociable and kind; sometimes, these will be students with disabilities newly included in the general education classroom. Students who are highly distractible shouldn't be seated near the class pet or other temptations. Kids who run away shouldn't be seated near the door. Always keep in mind, when you are arranging the room and planning where individuals are seated, that physical inclusion is an important first step toward social and academic inclusion.

The Challenging Class and Arranging the Room

When you have a whole group of students who are very chatty, who have a great deal of physical energy, or who have difficulty focusing, you'll want to take that into consideration as you plan the room arrangement for a lesson or activity. The physical environment can provide structure and support for self-management.

Density of seating is one important variable to consider. Simply moving students farther apart can make a big difference. High-density arrangements, where students have little physical space between them (such as sitting at tables with others or with desks close together), can be very problematic for some classes. It can result in a great deal of chatting, less on-task time, more arguments, and more disruptions. You may be better off providing distance between desks and taking the time to teach students how to move their desks together quickly and quietly for group work rather than having them sit close together all of the time. Preschool and primary teachers who frequently have students sit on the floor for instruction may use marked separate sitting places on the carpet to help students with boundaries and to limit distractions. (Adults sometimes have difficulty paying attention when seated close to friends, too. We're sure many principals have had times when they wished they could separate teachers during faculty meetings.)

Changes in position may also be helpful. A challenging class may benefit from sitting or standing in different places or on different surfaces or furniture in order to be more physically comfortable and attentive, and less fidgety. You may be able to arrange your room to include tables, desks, and chairs of varying sizes. Perhaps you can find room for beanbag chairs, a couch, or rugs. You may be able to free up space so that students can sometimes stand to write on the board or chart paper on the walls. Build these changes into your lessons and activities when appropriate.

When you are planning a lesson or activity, consider the room arrangement options that will support appropriate behavior. Use your creativity in designing a physical environment that provides a positive context for teaching and learning.

Planning for Logistics

A critical aspect of planning the management of lessons and activities is attending to logistics. Logistics is the practical organization, the coordination of details, needed to make a complex event successful. You likely have practice in planning the logistics for trips, maybe even a long backpacking trip, or perhaps for a big party, wedding, or family reunion. In the classroom, planning for logistics in lessons and activities refers to housekeeping tasks such as organizing materials and equipment, planning setup and cleanup, and arranging for assistants when needed. Planning for logistics is the sixth critical management skill.

Importance of Logistical Planning

Your wonderful, creative lessons and activities won't work if you haven't thought about the organization that will make them happen smoothly. Logistical planning can make or break a lesson. The old saying that the devil is in the details applies here. Some activities and lessons are especially complex logistically, such as those that involve a great deal of materials or equipment, or unfamiliar, messy, or potentially dangerous materials and equipment. This is also true for activities and lessons that incorporate centers, those that have multiple parts, or where a great deal of movement and change is required, furniture has to be moved, and additional helpers are needed. But everyday, simple lessons and activities also require logistical planning so that instructional minutes are not lost to forgotten handouts, burntout projector bulbs, a search for a dry erase marker that works, or the slow distribution of materials. Planning for logistics is important for efficiency, safety, protecting learning time, reducing downtime, preventing behavior problems, and ending up with a reasonably tidy room.

Planning for logistics is all about predicting and decision-making; developing lists is essential. Read and analyze your lesson/activity plan carefully and then write in your logistical planning ideas. Alternatively, some teachers begin with a checklist that provides an outline of key components to which they can add the specifics of logistical planning that fit a particular lesson or activity. The box on the next page shows one example of this type of checklist.

Planning for Teacher Equipment and Materials

You need to get yourself ready for the lesson or activity. Make a list of the *equipment* you will need, such as a blackboard or whiteboard, screen, chart paper display stand, television monitor, overhead projector, tape recorder, laptop computer, or FM wireless microphone. Make sure everything is available and ready. Simple things, such as not having enough

TEACHER CHECKLIST FOR

Logistical Planning

Am I planning so that teacher equipment is:

❑ available?   ❑ ready?   ❑ working?

Am I planning for teacher materials to be:

❑ prepared?   ❑ easily available to me?
❑ displayed?

Am I planning so that student equipment is:

❑ available?   ❑ distributed efficiently?
❑ shared effectively?

Am I planning for student materials, such as:

❑ what I need to provide?   ❑ how to
distribute?   ❑ how to communicate what's
needed?

Am I planning for student products, such as:

❑ how to turn in?   ❑ where to store?
❑ how to display?   ❑ how to send home?

Am I planning the specifics of lesson/activity
setup, such as:

❑ what should be set up in advance?
❑ when I can set up?

Am I planning the specifics of lesson/activity
cleanup, such as:

❑ time needed?   ❑ assigned chores?
❑ cleaning materials needed?

Am I planning for assistants, such as:

❑ what help is needed?   ❑ who could
help?   ❑ how I should communicate
tasks/assignments?

room on the board to write or pulling down the
screen and finding that it covers needed information,
can be very frustrating and interfere with your teaching. If you need to borrow equipment, arrange that
ahead of time. Set equipment up in advance, check
that it works, and make sure that you know how to
use it. For example, if you will be using an overhead
projector, you'll need to make sure that the bulb isn't

burned out, that you can turn it on and focus it, and
that you have positioned the projector so that the
image on the screen is large enough and the projector doesn't block students' view of the screen.

List and prepare the *materials* that *you* will be
using, such as your lesson plan outline, computer software, transparencies, pull-down maps, prepared examples, and other visual supports. Be sure your materials
are close at hand and plan how you will display materials (e.g., how and where you will tack up a poster).

Planning for Student Equipment and Materials

Make a list of the equipment and materials that students will need during the lesson/activity. This may
include anything from microscopes to workbooks
to colored pencils. Some of these you may provide,
some may be stored in the classroom, and some may
be student belongings. You'll likely need to plan for
gathering equipment and materials, for distributing
them, for procedures for using them correctly, for
sharing them, and for communicating to students
what materials are needed.

Teacher-Provided Equipment and Materials. You
may need to gather or prepare student equipment or
materials that you are providing just for this lesson/
activity. These could be handouts, books, protrac-
tors, frogs to dissect, calculators, aprons to protect
student clothing, and so on. Sometimes, student
materials are shared among teachers, and you'll
have to arrange in advance to use them. You'll need
to make sure you have enough, and you'll need to
figure out how to distribute them to the students in
an efficient way so learning time isn't wasted. There
are various ways of doing this. Here are some typical options for distributing materials:

■ Teacher puts materials on desks before students
arrive.

■ Students collect materials on the way to their
desks.

■ Teacher passes out materials while giving
directions.

■ Selected students are assigned to be materials-
passers.

■ Student representatives collect materials for
table groups.

Stored Equipment/Materials. Some student materials are stored in the classroom, such as dictionaries, textbooks, math manipulatives, small whiteboards and pens, and supplies such as scissors, glue, rulers, and so on. You'll need to make sure they are easily accessible and decide whether they should be distributed or whether students should go get them when needed. You may need to teach rules and routines for using communal materials. For example, "If you borrow a pencil from the box, return it sharpened at the end of class."

Shared Equipment/Materials. If students will need to share equipment or materials, plan how this will be done. Make sure everyone has fair access to the materials, and avoid situations where students have long waits with nothing to do. Communicate behavior expectations regarding sharing, and make sure students have the cooperative skills needed for sharing and taking turns.

Procedures for Using Equipment/Materials. When students will be using equipment/materials for the first time, or haven't used them for a while, teach them needed procedures. This is especially important for equipment/materials that are fun to play with, are expensive, or could hurt someone. For example, you might teach a mini-lesson on how to use personal whiteboards properly for active participation in a lesson. (See Chapter 6 for an example.) You might need to develop a procedure for using equipment such as microscopes: where to get them, how to set them up, how to use them, and how to put them away.

Student Belongings. Finally, you'll likely need to ask students to use their own belongings—materials that they keep in their desks or packs, such as notebooks, pens, or books. Get in the habit of listing these on the board or screen before they are needed to avoid wasted time as students find them and get them out, and to avoid having to repeat oral directions. Be sure to keep extras available, such as notebook paper.

Products. One last aspect of logistical planning for student materials is to plan for the products students will create during the lesson or activity: how they'll be turned in, stored, displayed, or taken home. This is easy enough for worksheets or papers—perhaps you have a box where papers are turned in, group leaders pick them up and give them to you, or students put them in their notebooks. This is a simple matter of deciding what you want done

and then communicating (saying, writing, showing) that to students. However, some products are large or awkward, are breakable, need to dry, and so on. Some products may be put in cubbyholes or backpacks to be taken home. Some will be stored and displayed later, such as on a bulletin board or suspended from the ceiling. It all takes planning.

Planning for Setup, Cleanup, and Using Assistants

In addition to logistical planning for teacher and student equipment and materials, you may need to do additional planning for the setup and cleanup of the room, as well as for teaching assistants and volunteers.

Setup. For most lessons and activities, there is no elaborate setup of the classroom required. You'll make minor room arrangement changes if needed and have your materials at hand. However, for more logistically complex lessons and activities, careful classroom setup will prevent wasted time and behavior problems. Perhaps you are planning an activity where student groups will rotate through math game centers. Advance setup will result in more time actually playing the games—which means more learning time. Ideally, you will be able to schedule this activity following a break to give you an opportunity to rearrange the room so there is a table and chairs for each center, and clear traffic lanes. You'll need to set up the game materials in each center, post directions, find your timer, and so on.

Cleanup. You may also need to plan for cleanup. Sometimes, this involves putting things back as they were—for example, putting the math games away and rearranging the room. Sometimes it will involve actual cleaning, such as washing paint off the desks, picking up scrap paper, or cleaning up the spilled soil and water after a lesson on planting seeds. Think about what chores will need to be completed, necessary equipment (soap and water, paper towels, extra wastebaskets), and how you'll assign cleanup duties.

Assistants. One last part of planning for logistics involves deciding whether you will need assistants to help with the lesson or activity. These might be teaching assistants, other school staff, parent volunteers, or student helpers. Decide how you will recruit help. Plan exactly what you want the helpers to do (sit by a student who will need extra support,

---

Mrs. Bean's Plan for Logistics

Issue: where to store products (posters)

Plan: clear off back wall, get long punch pins from supply closet, ask parent volunteer to tack up finished posters in two layers as students bring them to her

Reasoning: Tacking posters to the wall will keep them safe and out of the way until we display them in school and community; I need to be available to help class finish up and get ready for lunch, so having an assistant would be helpful.

What other logistical planning does Mrs. Bean need to do?

---

help with distribution or collection of materials, run equipment, circulate and answer questions) and how you will communicate that.

Think about Mrs. Bean and the poster-making activity. Above are some of her ideas for planning logistics.

Responding to Diversity When Planning Logistics

When planning logistics for your lesson or activity, consider individual needs. The following are some examples.

- Think about opportunities for some of your students to practice needed skills or to be involved. Perhaps you have students who would benefit from chances to take positive leadership roles, such as directing the setup or cleanup of the classroom. You might have students (e.g., students with autism spectrum disorders) who need structured opportunities for interactions with others, such as through distributing and collecting materials. Maybe you have students whose social status in the class could be improved by being put in charge of running equipment, and so on. Many students do best when involved and busy—you can arrange for them to help with logistics in various ways.

- You may need to plan for the use of specialized equipment/materials and assistive technology that students with physical and other disabilities use in your classroom. Consider where these are kept, procedures for their use, and other logistical matters.

- Another consideration when planning for student materials is "expected student belongings" and socioeconomic diversity. Some students/families may not be able to afford to buy certain materials. You may be able to arrange for materials to be donated to your class or for "school supplies scholarships" to be available to students. The school may need to provide paper and pencils.

- One issue that sometimes arises around cleanup is cultural differences related to gender roles. In some cultures, cleanup is part of the female domain, and boys are actively discouraged from helping (Seattle Public School District Bilingual Instructional Assistants n.d.).

The Challenging Class and Planning Logistics

Just as with the other critical management skills, providing more structure in the area of logistics will often help the challenging class. For example, if your class struggles with *taking turns using materials and equipment*, you have several options for providing structure and support.

- Structure the lesson/activity so that taking turns is built in ("This half of the class will examine the rocks with magnifying glasses while this half reads. Then, we'll switch.").

- Give the students a procedure to follow ("Each person may use the magnifying glass for 5 minutes. Set the timer when you begin.").

- Precorrect by reminding students of previously taught skills ("Remember what you have learned about fair ways of deciding who goes first, second, and so on, such as using rock–paper–scissors.").

- Acknowledge that taking turns may be an issue, and help students figure out how to do it ("You have 20 minutes for this activity and four students in each group. Decide how many minutes each person may use the magnifying glass and how to keep track of their time.").

Another issue that may arise is *students being distracted by materials or equipment* when they need to be listening to the teacher or peers. Again, you can provide structure to support appropriate student behavior in a number of ways.

- Wait to distribute materials/equipment until they are needed.

- Put equipment/materials on desks while students are in another area of the room to receive directions.

- Teach students a routine for putting materials/equipment in a certain area of the desk and not touching it until told.

A related issue is when students are *not using the materials or equipment in the intended way* (e.g., math manipulatives, whiteboards). Here are examples of ways to solve that problem.

- Provide ample time to play with the materials before the lesson starts in order to decrease novelty.

- Teach how to use materials/equipment correctly (perhaps through a mini-lesson) and praise or otherwise acknowledge appropriate use.

- Make correct materials/equipment use part of behavior expectations and employ a behavior management game (e.g., marbles in jar) to encourage correct use.

In summary, the critical management skill of planning for logistics is an important part of structuring the learning environment. It needs to be part of every lesson or activity plan. Care in planning for logistics will cut down significantly on wasted learning time.

Managing Transitions

The seventh critical management skill is handling transitions. A transition is the process of switching from one thing to another. Transitions include movement from place to place inside or outside the classroom, and changes in task, method, subject, or grouping. Examples of transitions are entering the classroom after lunch, going from the classroom to the library, moving into small groups, switching from math to science, and changing from listening to the teacher's presentation to partner practice to independent work. Think of transitions as bridging the gap between events. Effective transition management incorporates most of the other critical management skills, including room arrangement, communicating behavior expectations, monitoring behavior, planning logistics, and so on. It is included as a separate skill because transitions can be a major source of behavior problems and wasted time if they are unplanned, unstructured, or unsupervised (Mastropieri and Scruggs 2007).

Types of Transitions

Numerous transitions occur before, during, and after lessons and activities. One way to think about transitions is whether they are *routine* or *non-routine* transitions. Routine transitions are those transitions that occur regularly. Non-routine transitions occur only occasionally (or perhaps only once) or are unique in some way. Look at the box on the next page for examples of both types of transitions.

Another way to think about transitions is whether they are major or minor. Minor transitions have less movement and less change both physically and mentally; they are relatively simple and uncomplicated. On the other hand, we consider transitions to be major when the next event:

- is in a different setting (another classroom, library, outdoors)

- requires a different room arrangement or change in seating

- requires big changes in materials or equipment needed

- begins a new lesson or activity

The type of transition has important implications for planning. Obviously, minor transitions require less planning than major transitions. However, even minor transitions can result in lost instructional time

```
EXAMPLES OF TRANSITIONS

Routine Transitions

■ beginning/ending the school day

■ beginning/ending a subject or class period

■ changing classes

■ going to/returning from lunch and recess

■ going to/returning from library, music,
  physical education, art

■ beginning/ending daily tasks (such as
  math warm-up, journal writing, seatwork)

■ beginning/ending daily events (such as free
  time, snack time)

Non-Routine Transitions

■ going to/returning from a special assembly

■ moving from activity to activity during a
  year-end field day

■ gathering materials and setting up a work
  area for an art activity

■ forming groups for a geography project

■ switching centers and partners for science
  experiments
```

and behavior problems when they are unplanned and unstructured. Planning for routine transitions often involves *teaching* them at the beginning of the school year. That will end up saving a great deal of time in the long run.

Teaching Transitions

You will need to decide which transitions to teach to your students. It would be a waste of time to teach non-routine transitions since they will only be used rarely or once. However, establishing and teaching routine transitions will save teacher and class time and allow students to take responsibility for completing transitions independently. (See Chapter 10 for more information on developing and teaching classroom routines.)

Once you have identified the transitions you want to teach, task-analyze them. This means thinking them through and creating a series of steps for students to follow. For example, imagine that you want to develop a routine for the transition from the last lesson/activity to leaving class or school. In this case, you'll decide what you want students to do as they prepare to leave, for example:

1. Copy homework information into calendar.

2. Put needed materials in backpack.

3. Put chair on top of desk.

4. Line up.

After you task-analyze the routine transition, you'll need to decide how to teach it. Often, you'll use a mini-lesson (see Chapter 10), which includes explaining, demonstrating, and providing practice on performing the transition.

If you have taught a transition, then less planning for that transition will be required when you are putting together lessons and activities. Less planning doesn't mean no planning, however. All transitions require some planning and communication with students. Following are suggestions for preparing for and facilitating smooth and efficient transitions of all types.

Advance Preparation for Transitions

Think through the lesson or activity ahead of time, note needed transitions, and analyze how you want those transitions to happen. The teacher needs to prepare himself and also needs to prepare the students.

Preparing yourself for a transition may include the following:

■ planning room arrangement changes and planning for logistics

■ preparing written expectations for transition behavior

■ deciding on directions for major transitions (if they are not routine) and writing them on the board or transparency in advance

■ planning a reminder or precorrection for students on how to perform a routine transition

■ preparing entry tasks, if appropriate, for the beginning of the lesson/activity, especially when that coincides with students entering the classroom. These might be preparation tasks (getting out materials), warm-ups (math fact review), or motivators (solve a riddle). Students are taught to look at the board or screen as they enter to find their task, and are given a time limit.

It is very important that students are aware of transitions to come. They will respond more calmly to change if they have a chance to prepare mentally. Preparing students for a transition may include the following:

- Write the schedule for the day and/or for the lesson/activity on the board or transparency in advance.

- Warn students in advance of transitions by using time alerts. ("In 5 minutes, I'll ask you to leave your small groups and return to your desks for math timings.")

- Build anticipation if students will be leaving an activity they enjoy and may find it difficult to move on. ("Once we have finished the science experiments, we are going on to math, where we are going to play an interesting new game that I think you'll like.")

The transition to the beginning of the next lesson or activity is an important one if you are to begin on time. It is worth your while to make students aware of it in advance.

Just Before the Transition

Immediately before a transition, communicate directions and behavior expectations to the students.

Give clear directions for how to make the transition. (See Chapter 5 for more information on giving directions.) We are not talking about directions for the next task or activity; rather, we mean directions for what to do *during* the transition to prepare for the next event. For example, if students will be moving from one place to another (such as from tables to the carpet), directions would include:

- the order in which to transition (e.g., first this row; one at a time)

- where to go

- what materials to take

If the transition is to partner or group work, directions might include:

- the names of students in each pair or group

- where pairs/groups will meet

- how to arrange chairs/desks

Put directions for major transitions (that have not been taught as a routine) in writing and demonstrate them, as well as stating them verbally. If you have taught the students a routine for the transition or part of it (for example, for moving desks together for small group work or for lining up), remind them of it.

A final point regarding directions—it's always a good idea to put the directions for materials needed, page number to open to, and so on, in writing, whether it is a major or minor transition—it's just plain more efficient. For example, write on the board: "You'll need a red pen, science journal, and science book. Open to p. 45."

Make behavior expectations for transitions clear. Directions tell students what to do during the transition, and behavior expectations tell them *how* to do it. For example, the direction is to move chairs into a circle, and the expectations are to do it quietly and carefully. Behavior expectations for transitions usually focus on talk, movement, and time. Think of expectations as adverbs, such as *carefully*, *quickly*, and *quietly*, that may need further specifying (not running, carrying chair close to floor, in 2 minutes, with inside voices). Don't automatically make "without talking" one of your expectations. Transitions can be a good time for a bit of socializing.

Directions and expectations are often intertwined, especially for minor transitions: "Quickly put your paper away in your take-home folder. When you're ready, stop talking and look at me." Directions and expectations for routine transitions can also be combined, for example:

Lunch Transition

- Collect your ticket or lunch.

- Form line.

- Keep hands and feet to self.

- Walk in the halls without talking.

During the Transition

Clear directions and behavior expectations are meant to provide structure for transitions to prevent behavior problems. Close supervision during transitions is also important. Do the following:

- Carefully monitor behavior by scanning, listening, and moving around.

- Acknowledge students for following the behavior expectations and directions, or redirect them when they are not.

- Have a planned, strong signal to regain attention and begin the next event.

Don't Be Part of the Problem

Your planning has a big impact on the smoothness of transitions. You'll need to have all of your materials and equipment ready. That will help you make your own transition quickly and smoothly so you can support the students in their transition. Plan the schedule carefully so that you allow enough time for activities/lessons and transitions. If you are always rushing the students, transitions will be difficult and stressful for all concerned. Build in breaks and distinguish them from transitions.

Mrs. Bean's Plan for Transitions

Transition: from end of poster-making activity to lunch

Strategies: Provide 15-, 10-, 5-, and 1-minute time alerts for finishing and hanging posters. Write directions and expectations for cleanup and getting ready for lunch on the board in advance: take 5 minutes to quietly and carefully move desks back, pick up scraps of paper and put them in recycling, wash hands, get lunch bag or ticket, form line.

Reasoning: They need strong time-management and procedural support for the major transition from working on their posters to the lunch break.

What other transitions does Mrs. Bean need to plan for? What strategies could she use?

Begin the next activity on time. Don't fall into the habit of giving repeated reminders to hurry students, and don't wait for stragglers if you can avoid it. Provide a reason for making transitions quickly by choosing early arrivers for favored tasks, or by beginning the next activity with an interesting opening, a joke, a riddle, and so on. If much of the class is late, reevaluate the time allowed and/or directly teach the transition routine.

Your goal is to make transitions as smooth, relaxed, and efficient as possible. Provide as much or as little structure as your students need. The ideal outcome of a well-managed transition is beginning the next event on time, with everyone calm, focused, and ready, without anyone feeling rushed or anxious.

Think about Mrs. Bean and the poster-making activity. See the box titled "Mrs. Bean's Plan for Transitions" for some of her ideas.

Responding to Diversity When Managing Transitions

Some students have a difficult time making changes. This might include students with autism spectrum disorders. Try providing a personal copy of the schedule, individual time reminders ("In 3 minutes, . . ."), or a transition buddy.

Gilbert and Gay (1989) describe stage-setting behaviors that some African American students use before beginning tasks, such as gathering materials, looking over the whole assignment, and rechecking directions with teacher and peers. It may be helpful to think of stage-setting as part of the transition and to provide for it when stating expectations and time allowed.

Students who speak little or no English may feel a great deal of anxiety about not knowing what's happening next or why they are leaving the classroom. Help reduce that anxiety by providing a picture schedule that indicates major transitions such as leaving for lunch, library, going home, and so on.

The Challenging Class and Managing Transitions

Transitions can be chaotic if they are not structured carefully. Some groups have particular difficulty with them. If your class struggles with making transitions, consider the following strategies.

- If they enjoy competition, divide the class into teams that compete against each other to see who is quickest to make the transition.

- Teach formal lessons on the most problematic types of transition routines, such as returning to class after recess.

- Communicate the time allowed for each transition.

- Give the students something to do during transitions to keep them focused. Young students may enjoy marching or singing. Older students can be challenged with mental math or riddles to figure out during transitions.

- During difficult transitions (such as from the lunch break to the next lesson) use calming strategies like turning the lights out, playing relaxation tapes or soothing music, or reading a story.

- Develop a file of entry and exit tasks and use them consistently.

Summary

Teachers need to develop critical management skills for structuring the learning environment and for communicating with students. They need to apply them in lessons and activities and to make management planning for lessons/activities as important as instructional planning. Look at Chapter 8 for more ideas for using critical management skills when planning for partner and small-group work. Chapter 20 provides assistance for incorporating critical management skills in all lesson and activity planning, and includes an example of a plan with critical management skills written in.

References and Suggested Reading

Banda, D., E. Grimmett, and S. Hart. 2009. Activity schedules: Helping students with autism spectrum disorders in general education classrooms manage transition issues. *Teaching Exceptional Children* 41 (4): 16–21.

Byrnes, M. 2008. Writing explicit, unambiguous accommodations: A team effort. *Intervention in School and Clinic* 44 (1): 18–24. (For information on room arrangement/preferential seating.)

Cipani, E. 2004. *Classroom management for all teachers: 12 plans for evidence-based practice.* 2nd ed. Upper Saddle River, NJ: Merrill/Prentice Hall.

Conroy, M. A., K. S. Sutherland, A. L. Snyder, and S. Marsh. 2008. Classwide interventions: Effective instruction makes a difference. *Teaching Exceptional Children* 40 (6): 24–30.

Curran, M. 2003. Linguistic diversity and classroom management. *Theory into Practice* 42 (4): 334–340.

Darch, C., and E. Kame'enui. 2004. *Instructional classroom management: A proactive approach to behavior management.* 2nd ed. Upper Saddle River, NJ: Pearson Education, Inc.

DePry, R., and G. Sugai. 2002. The effect of active supervision and pre-correction on minor behavioral incidents in a sixth grade general education classroom. *Journal of Behavioral Education* 11: 255–267.

Emmer, E., C. Evertson, and M. Worsham. 2006. *Classroom management for middle and high school teachers.* 7th ed. Needham Heights, MA: Allyn and Bacon.

Evertson, C., E. Emmer, and M. Worsham. 2006. *Classroom management for elementary teachers.* 7th ed. Needham Heights, MA: Allyn and Bacon.

Gilbert, S. E., and G. Gay. 1989. Improving the success in school of poor black children. In *Culture, style and the educative process*, ed. B. J. Shade, 275–283. Springfield, IL: Charles C. Thomas.

Goodman, G., and C. Williams. 2007. Interventions for increasing the academic engagement of students with autism spectrum disorders in inclusive classrooms. *Teaching Exceptional Children* 39 (6): 53–61.

Grossman, H. 2003. *Classroom behavior management for diverse and inclusive schools.* 3rd ed. New York: Roman and Littlefield.

Herrell, A., and M. Jordan. 2004. *Fifty strategies for teaching English-language learners.* 2nd ed. Upper Saddle River, NJ: Prentice-Hall.

Jones, V., and L. Jones. 2009. *Comprehensive classroom management: Creating communities of support and solving problems.* 9th ed. Boston: Allyn and Bacon.

Kaplan, J. S. 1995. *Beyond behavior modification.* 3rd ed. Austin, TX: Pro-Ed.

Kerr, M., and C. Nelson. 2010. *Strategies for addressing behavior problems in the classroom.* 6th ed. Upper Saddle River, NJ: Pearson/Merrill.

Kounin, J. S. 1970. *Discipline and group management in classrooms.* New York: Holt, Rinehart & Winston.

Law, B., and M. Eckes. 2000. *The more-than-just-surviving handbook: ESL for every classroom teacher.* 2nd ed. Winnipeg, Manitoba, Canada: Portage & Main Press.

Lindberg, J., and A. Swick. 2006. *Common-sense classroom management for elementary school teachers.* Thousand Oaks, CA: Corwin Press.

Mastropieri, M. A., and T. E. Scruggs. 2007. *The inclusive classroom: Strategies for effective instruction.* 3rd. ed. Upper Saddle River, NJ: Pearson.

McIntosh, K., K. Herman, A. Sanford, K. McGraw, and K. Florence. 2004. Teaching transitions: Techniques for promoting success between lessons. *Teaching Exceptional Children* 37 (1): 32–38. (References within article for active supervision.)

Rhode, G., W. Jenson, and H. Reavis. 1993. *The tough kid book.* Longmont, CO: Sopris West.

Seattle Public School District Bilingual Instructional Assistants. (n.d.) *Cultural cues: An inside look at linguistic and cultural differences in Seattle Public Schools,* ed. N. Burke. Unpublished class manual, Bilingual Student Services, Seattle Public Schools, Seattle, WA.

Simonsen, B., S. Fairbanks, A. Briesch, D. Myers, and G. Sugai. 2008. Evidence-based practices in classroom management: Considerations for research to practice. *Education and Treatment of Children* 31 (3): 351–380.

Sprick, R., M. Sprick, and M. Garrison. 1993. *Interventions: Collaborative planning for students at risk.* Longmont, CO: Sopris West.

Sprick, R., M. Garrison, and L. Howard. 1998. *CHAMPs: A proactive and positive approach to classroom management.* Longmont, CO: Sopris West.

Weinstein, C., M. Curran, and S. Tomlinson-Clarke. 2003. Culturally responsive classroom management: Awareness into action. *Theory into Practice* 42 (4): 269–276.

Witt, J., A. VanDerHayden, and D. Gilbertson. 2004. Instruction and classroom management: Prevention and intervention research. In *Handbook of research in emotional and behavioral disorders,* eds. R. B. Rutherford, M. M. Quinn, and S. R. Mathur, 426–445. New York: Guilford.

Writing Your Plan

In the first three parts of this book, you learned about what to teach and how to teach, and about the context for teaching and learning. Now it is time for you to put together the information you have learned and write your plan.

In the first few chapters of this part of the book, you will examine two basic types of plans—lessons and activities—and how to figure out when to write which type of plan. You will also learn that lessons and activities have different purposes. Lessons are generally used to provide instruction to help students meet short-term objectives, whereas activities, often in combination with lessons, help students reach longer-term objectives. Both lessons and activities are very important in the instructional process.

You will also learn about specific types of lesson models and how to decide when to use each. A lesson model is a specific way of instructing. Informal presentation, direct instruction, and structured discovery are the three lesson models presented in this book. Each model is used for a different purpose, and all are effective in helping students learn. Lesson plans for all of these models are relatively easy to learn. By the end of the chapter on each of the models, you will know how to write a new type of plan. Chapter 20 will help you edit the first draft of your plan. This editing step will help ensure that your plan is complete and as responsive to diversity as possible.

This book will conclude with a chapter that will teach you how to use the diversity responsive teaching framework in two ways. First, you will learn how to use it as a brainstorming tool for generating ideas to make lessons and activities diversity responsive. You will also learn to use it as a tool for professional growth that will help you select personal objectives in the area of diversity responsive teaching and analyze the plans you have written.

All of the information you have learned so far in this book will become important as you write your plans. We encourage you to refer back to earlier chapters as you begin writing the specifics of your plan. We want to remind you again that practice will help you become more fluent in writing plans. When you become fluent, writing plans will take less time. Additionally, you may find that you do not need to write as much because many techniques and strategies will become habits and require less thought. (This is the reason that experienced teachers generally do not need to write detailed plans.) We encourage you to use the guides that we have provided as you write. They will act as scaffolds, prompts, or precorrections to support you in planning effective lessons and activities.

Lessons versus Activities

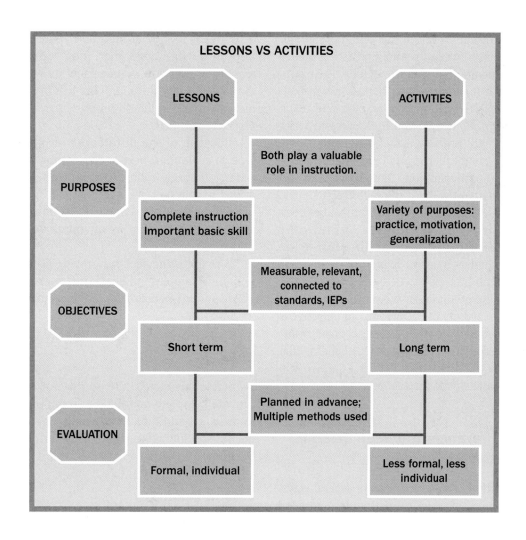

Introduction

It is important to distinguish between lessons and activities, because they have different purposes and different structures. Although teachers use both lessons and activities to help their students learn, *lessons* are used for the teaching of specific knowledge and skills leading to mastery of a short-term objective. *Activities* are used to help students progress toward mastery of a long-term objective. They may introduce and build interest in topics or help students to further process, practice, and generalize knowledge and skills. It is crucial to think carefully about your goals for instruction and to decide when to use lessons and when to use activities.

Lessons and activities each require different planning decisions and tasks. When writing a lesson plan, decide the structure of the teaching so that it lines up with the lesson objective that serves as its foundation. Activity plans need to be congruent also; however, these plans often address the logistics of managing materials, student participation, and interactions rather than actual instruction. When teachers have no clear distinction between activities and lessons, we have noticed a common problem—forgetting to teach!

Recognizing whether you are going to teach an activity or lesson will help you select an appropriate planning format. Think of the lesson or activity plan structure as a form of scaffolding as it provides support in remembering what to include. For example, the format for a direct instruction lesson plan includes a place to write how a teacher will teach the new information, followed by a place to write how students will practice. This ensures that new information is taught thoroughly before students are asked to use the information. The lesson plan format ensures that you will not forget to teach.

It can be difficult to clearly distinguish between lessons and activities, because lessons typically include various activities. Additionally, because lessons vary in length—a lesson might last 30 minutes or 3 days—it can be tricky to determine when a lesson begins and when it ends; therefore, it is hard to know where an activity fits. However, our objective is *not* that teachers will be 100 percent accurate in distinguishing lessons from activities. Our belief is that being aware of the differences between the two will help teachers make good instructional decisions.

Primary Differences between Lessons and Activities

Lessons are different from activities in several ways. As stated earlier, one way to distinguish between the two is to look at their *purposes*. The purpose of a lesson is to provide instruction on important skills or knowledge so that students can individually and independently demonstrate the skill or knowledge. By *individually*, we mean by themselves rather than with a partner or group; by *independently*, we mean without help (i.e., without prompts or corrections from the teacher).

Activities, on the other hand, may have a variety of purposes—introduction of topics, learner motivation, additional experience, elaboration of information, review of information, or additional opportunities for processing, practice, integration, and generalization of skills and knowledge. Notice that lessons provide instruction rather than simply introducing or providing experience with a topic, as an activity might. Notice also that lessons provide complete instruction rather than just review or practice of previously taught skills/knowledge, as activities may do.

Another way to distinguish between lessons and activities is to look at their *objectives*. A lesson has a specific, measurable, short-term objective, and the teacher's intention is that each student will meet that objective by the end of the lesson. Activities are meant to help students progress toward long-term objectives or goals.

Because of the differences in objectives, the type of *evaluation* needed for lessons and activities differs. Teachers follow lessons with formal evaluations of whether each student can independently meet the objective. When evaluations are used following activities, they are often less formal and less individual.

The following sections provide further information and examples to help clarify the key differences between, and elements of, lessons and activities.

Lessons

As previously stated, the purpose of a lesson is to provide complete instruction on important skills or knowledge, and the objective is for each student to meet a specific, measurable, short-term objective by the end of the lesson.

Lesson Example

In this sample lesson, an instructor wants to teach students to spell the plural form of certain nouns ending in *y*, and her intention is that the students can individually and independently do so by the end of the lesson. The objective is that students will write the plural form of 10 listed nouns ending in *y* preceded by a consonant, for example, *berry* to *berries*. The teacher instructs the students by thoroughly explaining the spelling rule, showing multiple examples, providing practice, and giving feedback. Alternatively, the teacher may begin by showing examples and then lead the students to discover the spelling rule or pattern. Following the lesson, the instructor evaluates by giving a test as described in the objective.

This is a lesson because the teacher provides *complete instruction* on an *important basic skill*, spends time *teaching*, and intends to *evaluate* the students to see if they have met the *short-term objective following* the lesson.

Definition of Terms

The italicized terms in the previous paragraph are defined as follows:

- *Complete Instruction* Complete instruction means that teaching needs to happen in order for the students to reach the objective; the students need formal instruction before they can use or apply the knowledge or skill. Sometimes, this will be the very first instruction on the skill/knowledge that the students receive. The topic may be brand-new to them. It's also possible that the students have some familiarity with the topic; they may have had a previous introduction, and the teacher will use strategies in the lesson to connect the new learning to prior knowledge and experience. Sometimes, a lesson is being retaught. The students may have had prior lessons, but the teacher has discovered that there are major misunderstandings, confusions, and errors, and it's clear that the students need more than reminding, more than review and practice. This repeated instruction is thorough instruction, as though this skill or information is being presented for the first time.

- *Important Basic Skill* Important basic skills include academic skills, thinking skills, study skills, social skills, vocational skills, and so on. They are considered basic because they are either important for real-life functioning or they are necessary prerequisites for other important skills. (One could possibly make a case that the skill in the previous spelling lesson example is not important in an age of computers with spell-check capabilities.)

- *Teaching* Teaching can take many forms: it can be highly teacher-directed; it can incorporate peers; and it can emphasize discovery. However, teaching means that the teacher does more than organize and provide activities or give directions, hoping that students learn something. If no teaching is necessary, you do not have a lesson. Instead, you have either an activity or a time-filler.

- *Evaluate* When writing a lesson objective, a standard is established against which a student's learning is evaluated. Teachers also decide the method of evaluating learning at that time. They can use many ways to evaluate—not only written tests. If it is unnecessary to evaluate each student's learning, you are not providing instruction on an important basic skill (in other words, you are not teaching a lesson). If your intention is to provide an "experience," you may have an activity, not a lesson. If your intention is to ask students to demonstrate their knowledge or skill with the help of peers or a teacher, you have an ongoing practice activity, not a completed lesson.

- *Short-term Objective* Lessons are intended to help students reach a measurable, short-term objective. A series of lessons, often combined with activities, leads to the attainment of a long-term objective or goal. *Long* and *short* are not exact terms and cannot be defined precisely. We cannot give exact definitions or numbers, but consider the following example. Mrs. Lopez wants her students to learn to add and subtract fractions with uncommon denominators. She breaks up the long-term objective into several short-term lesson objectives, such as finding least common multiples, converting improper fractions, and so on. She will plan a lesson for each of those short-term objectives. Mrs. Lopez may decide to teach the lesson on least common multiples in 20-minute periods over 3 days. She considers this one lesson because she is not going to formally evaluate until after the third day. She will, however, want to monitor each student's success before going on. The students will not have received all of the necessary instruction to reach the short-term objective until Day 3.

- *Following* The evaluation of the objective following the lesson may occur immediately after the lesson or may occur one day or several days after the lesson. You may need to provide extended practice before evaluating, or you may have found, through monitoring, that you need to reteach before evaluating. However, if you do not intend to evaluate for weeks or months, you may be planning to evaluate whether students meet a long-term objective or goal, not a short-term lesson objective.

Activities

Activities have different intended outcomes than lessons. Activities sometimes look very much like lessons and include some of the same elements. For example, an activity may provide initial information on an important basic skill new to students, but if it is not intended to end with the evaluation of each student's independent performance of that skill, then it is an activity, not a lesson. Activities may lead up to lessons, be part of lessons, follow up lessons, or extend lessons, but they are not lessons. Activities do, however, have a variety of very important purposes.

Activity Purposes and Examples

Although activities are not associated with specific short-term objectives, they are planned with definite intentions. Teachers develop activities as part of their long-term planning and have a clear purpose for activities that help students reach important goals and objectives. Teachers also use activities to help evaluate student needs and progress. Even though activities are not always paired with formal evaluations of individuals, teachers carefully observe their students during activities and examine the products that students create to decide whether additional activities and lessons are needed.

Here are some of the various purposes of activities, along with examples. Notice that activities often have more than one purpose.

1. *Interest-building and motivation for students before beginning a series of lessons*

    Example: Before beginning a series of lessons on magnets, Mrs. Wagner plans an activity.

She gives students different types of magnets and materials, and has them experiment, make predictions, generate questions, and so on. Her purpose with this activity is to create interest and to motivate the students to learn more about magnets, to make sure each student has experience with magnets before beginning the lessons, and to provide practice on critical thinking skills. Mrs. Wagner also uses this activity to assess prior knowledge before deciding where to begin lessons.

2. *To build background information or experience, or to provide an opportunity to recall prior knowledge before a series of lessons* (A lesson typically includes an opening with strategies to motivate students or to help them connect this lesson with prior knowledge. We are differentiating lesson openings from longer, more elaborate activities used before a series of lessons.)

    Example: Mrs. Chenier is planning a major unit of study on environmental protection centered around salmon. She knows that, as Northwesterners, most of her students are very familiar with salmon, and she plans an activity designed to activate that background knowledge and experience. She puts together centers, each with photos, artwork, video clips, or realia related to salmon (e.g., a fishing pole, historical photos of salmon fishing, a video of salmon swimming upstream, Native American carvings of salmon, smoked salmon to taste, photos of orcas and sea lions eating salmon, newspaper clippings about a local salmon festival, and so on). At each center is chart paper on which students are asked to write thoughts, memories, or questions. Mrs. Chenier then uses those writings to lead a discussion and help students set learning goals.

3. *An introduction of skills/knowledge that will be taught thoroughly at a later time*

    Example: Just before the birthday of Dr. Martin Luther King, Jr., Mr. Luczak shows a video and leads a discussion about him. His goal is to provide general information to make sure his students understand the upcoming holiday. He has not written a short-term objective and plans no evaluation. Students will thoroughly study Dr. King's life and contributions later on as part of an American history unit.

4. *A review and practice of knowledge/skills taught previously*

    Example: Mr. Beltre discovers that his students can't divide fractions. They learned how to do so in the past but don't remember how to do it. He doesn't believe that reteaching with a complete lesson is necessary, however. He thinks it will come back to them pretty easily. Instead, he plans an activity in which he shows an example and then, as students start to recall how to do it, asks the students to tell him the steps for dividing fractions—in other words, the students are providing the instruction. He then has them do a number of practice problems and supervises carefully. Finally, he evaluates with a quiz. If they are still struggling, he'll go back and start from scratch with a lesson, rather than an activity.

5. *To teach skills/knowledge that aren't considered important basic skills* (don't require mastery by students, and are not prerequisite to other important skills)

    Example: Mr. Floyd plans an art activity in which he will teach his students to tie-dye. He will include many of the elements of lesson planning—step-by-step instruction, demonstrations, and supervised practice. However, this is considered an activity because tie-dyeing is not an important basic skill (anymore), and because students will each produce a tie-dyed item, but with Mr. Floyd's help. He will not test them later, either by asking them to list the steps in tie-dyeing or by asking them to make a tie-dyed item alone.

6. *Ongoing practice toward long-term objectives or goals*

    Example: Following Ms. VanHenley's math lessons on the multiplication concept and operation, her students can figure out the answers to single-digit multiplication problems using drawings and blocks, but they are not always 100 percent accurate, and they are very slow. Ms. VanHenley plans a series of practice activities—partner flashcard practice and multiplication bingo—to help the students toward the long-term objective of writing answers to multiplication fact problems (0–10) at a rate of 80 digits per minute with no errors. In this case, Ms. VanHenley follows each activity with a timed math fact test to chart individual student progress toward the objective.

7. *Opportunities for students to apply a previously learned skill*

    Example: Students have had earlier lessons on how to write letters. You now plan an application activity in which students write letters to the agricultural extension agent asking for information on rabbit care (there is a pet rabbit in the classroom). You may choose to review earlier lessons at the beginning of the activity, but you are not providing complete instruction on letter-writing.

8. *Opportunities for students to generalize previously learned information*

    Example: Mrs. Begay has previously taught her students to write one-sentence summaries of written material. She is currently teaching her students note-taking skills. She plans an activity in which students will be asked to listen to brief oral presentations and then write one-sentence summaries of them. She will watch carefully to see if the students can generalize their knowledge of summarizing written material to summarizing oral material.

9. *Opportunities for students to integrate knowledge and skills learned from lessons in different subject areas*

    Example: Several teachers co-plan an activity in which students make a garden in the schoolyard. The students will use measuring skills learned in math, information about plant needs for light and water learned in science, and group decision-making skills learned in social skills lessons to select the vegetables to be planted.

10. *Opportunities for students to express their understanding and demonstrate their learning*

    Example: Mrs. Eerkes plans an activity to follow a series of lessons on the Civil War. It will be a simulated debate in Congress on the issue of preserving the union versus states' rights. The students will be divided into two groups and given time to research the issues and to plan their speeches. Mrs. Eerkes has several purposes for this activity: (1) to provide practice in public speaking and cooperative planning and research; (2) to encourage a deeper understanding of the issues involved; and (3) to allow the students to demonstrate their knowledge in an alternative way. She knows that this activity

Figure 13-1	Lesson Plan or Activity Plan?

Ask yourself the following questions:

- Is my purpose to provide instruction on *important* skills or knowledge?
- Do I want my students to reach a *short-term* objective?
- Do I need to be *teaching* rather than simply introducing or providing an experience with a topic?
- Do I need to provide *complete* instruction rather than just review or practice of previously taught skills/knowledge?
- Do I want to evaluate whether students can *individually* and *independently* demonstrate the skill or knowledge?

If your answer to **any** of these questions is **no**, write an *activity plan* (see "Activity Plans" in Chapter 15).	If your answer to **all** of these questions is **yes**, then write a *lesson plan* (see "Lesson Plans" in Chapter 14).
Write preplanning tasks:	Write preplanning tasks:
<ul><li>long-term objective</li><li>activity description</li><li>activity rationale</li><li>prerequisite skills and knowledge; key terms and vocabulary</li></ul> *and* <ul><li>activity beginning</li><li>activity middle</li><li>activity closing</li></ul>	<ul><li>connection analysis</li><li>content analysis</li><li>lesson objective</li><li>objective rationale</li></ul> *and* <ul><li>lesson setup</li><li>lesson opening</li><li>lesson body</li><li>extended practice</li><li>lesson closing</li><li>lesson evaluation</li></ul>

will not allow her to be aware of each student's independent understanding, so she has planned other evaluation methods as well.

Finally, always remember that you need to begin with an objective or objectives and then design the activity to help students move toward those objectives (i.e., use backward planning). When you do this, you will be able to stay focused on what you really want the students to learn. Consider the following example.

Mr. Palm plans an activity for his second-graders about polar bears. He reads a story and then helps the students put together a book that includes drawings and sentences about polar bears. Mr. Palm is providing instruction, in a

sense, because his students do not know many of the polar bear facts discussed in the book. However, he does not really care whether each student memorizes these facts and does not intend to give a test on polar bears. Knowledge of polar bears is not the objective. Polar bears are a vehicle for providing ongoing practice on listening skills, fine motor skills, writing complete sentences, and so on. As he looks at the students' books, he will monitor progress on these skills ("I see that Ralph is still forgetting to put a period at the end of his sentences"), but plans no short-term objective with a formal evaluation. Mr. Palm may have other goals as well—to pique curiosity about animals and nature, or to give the students experience in being authors.

Summary

Lessons have been defined very narrowly and *activities* have been defined very broadly. Lessons have a consistent structure and involve explaining, demonstrating, and monitoring student practice. Activities lack one or more of the attributes of a lesson and have many purposes and structures. Both need to be carefully planned.

Selecting the Appropriate Plan

When teaching students, whether in your own classroom or that of a cooperating teacher during a practicum or student teaching, the two basic types of plans that you will need to write are activity plans and lesson plans. Both require careful thought and become easier and less time-consuming to write with practice. As your understanding of important planning components increases, you will be able to make decisions more automatically with fewer details needed in writing. This is the case with experienced teachers.

When you decide on a topic to teach (or are given a teaching assignment by a cooperating teacher), you need to carefully analyze whether you need to write an activity plan or a lesson plan. Ask yourself the questions in Figure 13.1 on page 176. Figure 13.1 provides a summary of the decisions that will help you determine when to write a lesson plan and when to write an activity plan.

Lesson Planning

Introduction

Putting together a daily lesson is the end result of a complex planning process. This process begins when the teacher determines the overall curriculum to be taught. The curriculum is based on an analysis of student needs, on district or state standards, on generalizations or big ideas from the subject area, and on a student's individual education program (IEP). Once the curriculum for the year or for a particular unit is identified, the teacher divides the content into individual lessons and writes specific lesson objectives, making sure each lesson clearly fits with the goals of the overall curriculum. The teacher then selects a lesson model—direct instruction, informal presentation, structured discovery—that will work best to meet the objective of a specific lesson.

Teachers use lessons to help students attain a specific short-term objective. A lesson typically has a clear beginning and ending, and it will last a few hours at the most. Lessons are followed by an evaluation of each student's learning in relation to the stated objective(s). Series of lessons that lead to the attainment of long-term objectives or goals are often combined, along with activities, into a unit of instruction. Remember that lessons may be developed for individuals or small groups of students as well as for the whole class.

Lessons can be used to teach specific skills and information directly, or to give students the opportunity to discover information on their own or with their peers. The type of content that can be taught through lessons is extremely diverse. Teachers typically use lessons to teach academic content; to develop study skills, social skills, and problem-solving skills; and to promote higher-level thinking. The following objectives help demonstrate the wide

> ### EXAMPLES OF LESSON OBJECTIVES
>
> - When teased in a role-playing situation, students will talk through each of the five problem-solving steps.
>
> - On a list of 25 sentences, students will circle the complete subject in all sentences.
>
> - Given a list of 10 assignments, students will accurately transfer all of them to an assignment calendar.
>
> - Given five 2-step multiplication and division word problems, students will write or draw a description of the problem-solving process they used to find the answer.

variety of skills and knowledge that teachers can address in lessons.

Generic Components of a Lesson Plan

A lesson plan is a written description of how students will progress toward a specific short-term objective. It clearly describes the teacher's statements and actions, which the teacher hopes will result in student learning. All lesson plans include the following eight generic components:

1. preplanning tasks
2. lesson setup
3. lesson opening
4. lesson body
5. extended practice

6. lesson closing

7. evaluation

8. editing tasks

The specific content of the components will vary in different lesson models because each model enables students to progress toward an objective in a different way. The components themselves however, stay the same in every lesson.

The following descriptions of each component include two parts: the purpose of the component and a summary of the type of content that might be included. Our intent is to help you generate ideas, not to list everything that must be included in each component in every lesson plan. It is up to you to select or generate the specifics that are appropriate for the lesson model, the subject matter, and the students you are teaching. As you plan each component, be sure you plan for the diverse needs of your students.

The components are described here in the order in which they would appear in the lesson plan. This is not necessarily the order in which they will be written. When preparing to write a lesson plan, refer to Chapters 16 through 18 for information about the specific model you will be using. Examples of completed plans are included in Chapters 16 through 19.

Component 1: Preplanning Tasks

The purpose of this component is to help you thoroughly think through the content you will teach and the best way to teach it. You will develop a connection analysis, content analysis, objective, and objective rationale, and then choose the lesson model. Each of these preplanning tasks is described below.

-   *Connection Analysis* Think about how this content connects with the larger picture. The lesson planning should begin by identifying the *generalization* or *big idea*, *state standard*, or *IEP goal* that you will address in your lesson.

-   *Content Analysis* The next step is to decide on the specific content you will teach. This is accomplished by completing a thorough content analysis, which helps you think in detail about the lesson content. In turn, this allows you to determine the best way to teach the content.

The term content analysis is a general one. The following are various types of content analyses: a *subject matter outline*, a *task analysis*, a *concept analysis*, a *principle statement*, definitions of *key terms or vocabulary*, and a list of *prerequisite skills and knowledge*.

The type of content analysis done depends on *what* is being taught. When you plan to teach a concept, for example, always include a concept analysis. When the point of the lesson is to teach a skill or procedure, you would always include a task analysis. When teaching information about a topic, a subject matter outline works best. A clearly written principle statement is included when teaching about a cause-and-effect or an if-then relationship. Lessons may have key terms and vocabulary that need to be defined in ways the students will understand. A listing of prerequisite skills and knowledge would also be routinely considered as part of a content analysis. This analysis will help determine whether the content is appropriate for the students and will also help you write the objective. A content analysis is a critical preplanning task. Time spent on analyses will save time later, as the rest of the lesson or activity plan will fall into place more easily (see Chapter 1 for more information on content analyses).

-   *Objective* Select and write a clear, measurable, worthwhile lesson objective. The objective must contain a behavior, the content, the condition, and the criterion so that you can specify in detail what is to be learned and how you'll know if students have learned it (see Chapter 2).

-   *Objective Rationale* Once you have written the objective, you need to actively think about and evaluate its importance and relevance. Reread it and ask yourself the following questions: *Why should my students know about this or how to do this? How will my students benefit from this learning? Does this objective connect to a state standard? Does it relate to an important big idea? Does it lead to an IEP goal?* When you are satisfied with your answers to these questions, you will have an objective rationale. If your answers to these questions help you determine that the objective is not important, write a new one.

Ask yourself the following question: *Does my objective really represent what I want my students to know? For example, do I really care if they can name three types of penguins, or is the purpose actually to practice following directions?* If the purpose is to practice following directions, you would need to write an activity plan, not a lesson plan.

■ *Lesson Model* Now you are ready to determine the best way to teach the objective. This decision can be based on the objective itself, the students, the time available, or the type of content being taught. Lesson models presented in this text are direct instruction (Chapter 16), informal presentation (Chapter 17), and structured discovery (Chapter 18).

Avoid making the mistake of selecting activities and methods and then trying to make up an objective for them. Instead, use backward planning (see Chapter 2).

Component 2: Lesson Setup

The next step of your planning is to develop the lesson setup. The purpose of the setup is to prepare students for the beginning of the lesson. A lesson should not begin until you have the students' attention (that is, they are physically turned toward you, they are listening to you, and so on). Also, you can prevent problems by explaining behavior expectations to students right up front, rather than waiting for problems to occur. Note that you're planning your initial signal and expectations here. Write signals for regaining attention and communicating additional or changed expectations into the plan where needed.

■ *Gaining Attention* Signal to the students to gain their attention; have them look at you and listen to you so the lesson can begin. In some cases, students are ready, so a simple "Let's get started" or "Good morning" is a sufficient signal for attention. In other cases, stronger signals—such as turning the lights off and on or ringing a bell—may be needed to attract their attention. Tell them how to respond to your signal. Wait for attention and then acknowledge it (see Chapter 11).

■ *Communication of Behavior Expectations* It is important to explain the rules, routines, and social skills that apply to the current lesson, that is, how you expect the students to act during the lesson. It is not necessary to review all classroom rules, routines, or social skills—just those most pertinent to the current lesson (e.g., raising hands, getting help, sharing). Write the statement of behavior expectations in language that is positive, appropriate to the age of the students, specific, and clear. Plan to show, as well as say, the expectations to students. Communicate expectations at each transition within the lesson, rather than all at the beginning (see Chapter 11).

In addition to preparing your students for the beginning of the lesson, be sure to prepare yourself as well. Write in any room arrangement changes you want to make and your logistical plans (such as a list of equipment and materials) here as well. See Chapters 11 and 12 for a thorough discussion of planning for all critical management skills.

Component 3: Lesson Opening

The purpose of the lesson opening is to help prepare students for the learning to come. You will typically want to let students know what they can expect to learn, why it is important, and how it builds on what they already know. You will also want to get them excited about learning. To plan the lesson opening, select one or more strategies from each of the following categories:

■ *Motivate and Focus Students* To motivate and focus students, tell or show them the lesson objective, use an attention-getting "set," and tell the purpose, rationale, importance, or application of the lesson objective.

■ *Connect New Learning* To help students see relationships between known information and the new learning, discuss how the learning connects to personal experience and prior knowledge, build background knowledge or context, review earlier lessons or skills, preview upcoming lessons, present an advance organizer, or show a graphic organizer.

An opening generally includes a statement of the objective and the objective purpose. When you state the objective, tell students in their terms what they will know or be able to do at the end of the lesson or activity. The objective purpose lets the students know why the knowledge or skill they are learning is important to them—for example, how it will help them in their daily lives or how it will help them in school. Students respond positively when they understand why they need to learn what you are teaching. Openings can be elaborate or simple, but it is important that all lessons (and activities) have one (see Chapter 4 for more ideas).

Component 4: Lesson Body

The instruction, related directly to the lesson objective, occurs in the lesson body. For this reason, Component 4 is considered the heart of the lesson. The majority of planning time and teaching time is spent on the lesson body. The body is where the content is presented through explanations, examples, demonstrations, or discoveries, and where students begin to process and practice the new skills and knowledge.

Although the specifics of the body vary with the lesson model, the lesson body should always include the following:

1. *Universal Interventions in Instruction and Management* Remember to design your lesson plan to make it more likely that all your students will be successful. Universal interventions should always be included in lessons and activities as they can benefit all students in the class. The following are some examples of universal intervention strategies:

    a. *Universal design for learning and differentiated instruction.* Plan for building in techniques to provide options for students. Think about options in presentations, how to keep students engaged, and how students can express what they know (see Chapter 3 for ideas).

    b. *Responding to diversity.* Build in strategies that address the cultural, linguistic, and skill variation among students in your classroom. Consider the examples you use, opportunities provided to work with peers, practice opportunities, and how to emphasize

vocabulary as examples of responding to diversity. Make sure that the content of your lesson is interesting and meaningful to your students.

c. *Critical teaching skills.* These are instructional "best practices" and are instrumental in helping students learn.

- *Explanations, demonstrations, and directions.* Carefully think through how to present and explain lesson information. Be sure that you have incorporated strategies that will make it easier for all of your students to learn the information you are presenting. Plan to present information in a variety of ways (see Chapter 5 for ideas).

- *Visual supports.* Providing visual supports (pictures, diagrams) can help students better understand and learn the information you present. They are generally very helpful to all students and should be included wherever needed (see Chapter 5 for ideas).

- *Active participation strategies.* Plan frequent opportunities to involve students in the lesson and to rehearse and process the new learning. Use a variety of strategies (see Chapter 6 for ideas).

- *Checks for understanding.* These are strategies designed to help teachers monitor student progress toward an objective early on in the lesson when the teacher is presenting. A teacher's goal is to check individual student learning throughout the lesson, not just eventually when students are working on their own. Consider carefully the strategies you select to help you monitor whether students are understanding the material you present in your lesson. Checks for understanding are those active participation strategies that enable each student to respond at once and that allow you to see each individual student's response (see Chapters 6 and 7 for ideas).

- *Practice strategies.* Provide opportunities for students to practice the newly learned skill or information under the supervision of a teacher. Practice opportunities within the lesson body differ in relation to the model of instruction you use. Remember to include a variety of practice ideas so that students stay motivated and interested (see Chapter 7 for ideas).

   d. *Critical management skills.* These techniques are classroom management "best practices" and are built in to prevent management problems. They include: *gaining attention, communicating behavior expectations, acknowledging appropriate behavior, monitoring student behavior, arranging the room, planning for logistics,* and *managing transitions.* Critical management skills are important at various points in the lesson body (as well as in other lesson components). For example, use these skills when you want to regain student attention, when students work with partners to practice a newly acquired skill, or when students are using manipulatives (see Chapters 11 and 12 for ideas).

2. *Selected Interventions in Instruction and Behavior* These accommodations and modifications are intended to help some students, and they will not be necessary or appropriate for all students in the class. These strategies, when incorporated into lessons and activities, help students be successful in spite of the challenges they may have. For example, they can help students who are challenged in the areas of focusing attention, learning and showing what they know, or following rules (see Chapters 9 and 10 for ideas).

In summary, the lesson body is the section of the lesson where the teaching takes place. Careful planning of how to present information, involve students, monitor learning, and manage behavior is essential.

Component 5: Extended Practice

The purpose of the extended practice component is to plan for developing high levels of fluency, and for providing application opportunities so students can generalize the skill or knowledge. (This is not the same as initial supervised practice included in the body of the lesson which is for establishing high levels of accuracy.) Students will usually need extended practice opportunities prior to evaluation. These opportunities are often provided through activities, seatwork, and homework that help students master, transfer, and retain the information or skill. Monitoring this practice will provide students with important performance feedback and help you determine when students are ready to be evaluated. You will need to make decisions in this component about the following:

- *Practice Opportunities* Describe the plan for providing practice opportunities during and following the lesson. These are in addition to supervised practice. Remember that distributed practice (many short practices) is more effective than massed practice (one long practice). Some students may need a great deal of extended practice, whereas others may need enrichment activities. Be sure that students have an opportunity to practice individually prior to evaluation (see Chapter 7 for ideas).

- *Related Lessons or Activities* It is useful to determine and list the other lessons or activities that will build on this objective, and that will provide opportunities to generalize, integrate, and extend the information.

Component 6: Lesson Closing

The lesson closing helps students tie the material together. It may follow the body of the lesson, or it may follow extended practice. A lesson closing may include a review of the key points of the lesson, opportunities for students to draw conclusions, a preview of future learning, a description of where or when students should use their new skills or knowledge, a time for students to show their work, and a reference to the lesson opening (see Chapter 4 for more ideas). Lesson closings can be elaborate or simple, but you always need to include one.

Component 7: Evaluation

The purpose of the evaluation component is to let you and your students know if learning has occurred and if students have met the lesson objective. It also helps you determine whether it is appropriate to build on the current lesson or whether you need to reteach or change the lesson model, methods, or materials.

The lesson evaluation is actually planned when the lesson objective is written. Look back at the objective to be sure the evaluation matches the objective, and then describe when and where the evaluation will occur. For example, if the objective is to "write a paragraph with a topic sentence," you might plan to have the students write the paragraph the next morning in class. The paragraphs must not be the practice paragraphs they wrote with peer or teacher help. Remember that evaluations need to be of each individual student's independent performance. Do not confuse teaching and testing.

Monitor the students during the body of the lesson and during extended practice to give yourself an idea of when to formally evaluate. It makes no sense to give students a test that you know they will fail. Students may be evaluated again later (on a unit test, for example). They may also be evaluated on an ongoing basis in a variety of contexts. For example, you could evaluate paragraph construction in their journal writing. Learning must always be evaluated following the lesson, regardless of other evaluations planned. This evaluation is essential for deciding whether to move on to a new objective or re-teach the current one (see Chapter 7).

Component 8: Editing Tasks

Editing tasks are addressed in detail in Chapter 20. The three editing tasks are:

Editing Task #1—*Add critical management skills.* Go back through your plan and incorporate critical management skills. In the appropriate spots in your plan, note the following: signals for attention, communication of behavior expectations, planned acknowledgments of appropriate behavior, monitoring of student behavior, room arrangement changes, planning for logistics, and management of transitions (see Chapters 11 and 12). Also add any selected behavioral interventions needed (see Chapter 10).

Editing Task #2—*Double-check for universal and selected instructional interventions.* Make adjustments in any of the following: use of principles of universal design; responses to linguistic, cultural, and skill diversity; strategies to ensure a clear presentation; use of active participation strategies including checks for understanding; and the use of visual supports (see Chapters 3, 4, 5, 6, and 7). Review the selected instructional interventions that you have included. Be sure they are necessary and will meet the needs of the students for whom they were selected (see Chapter 9).

Editing Task #3—*Evaluate congruence.* The final task is to examine your plan for congruence. It is imperative that the various components of a lesson match, that is, that the body of the lesson and the evaluation both match the lesson objective. The same is true of an activity plan (the middle of the activity should match the activity objective). Making your plan congruent helps ensure that students are evaluated on what they were taught and what they practiced (see Chapter 20).

Steps in Writing a Lesson Plan

Writing a lesson plan requires a series of decisions. Even before starting to write the actual lesson plan, you must decide what exactly you will teach and how best to teach it. Experienced teachers are able to do more thinking and less writing when they plan lessons because of their experience. They do, however, often write fairly detailed plans when they prepare to teach new content. This helps them to think through the best way to teach the information they will present. In general, the best way to become fluent in writing lesson plans is to practice. As experience grows, teachers will need to write less because certain aspects of the lessons will become second nature. If you are a beginner include all of the generic components presented in this chapter in every written lesson plan until you gain the necessary experience to reduce your written planning.

The order in which you will write the various components of a lesson plan, however, does not necessarily correspond to the order in which they appear in this chapter or to the order in which you will present them to the students. For example, it makes more sense to write the lesson body before the lesson opening, but you would obviously present the lesson opening to the students before the lesson body. Use the following sequence as a guide for writing your plan.

SEQUENCE FOR WRITING THE
COMPONENTS OF A LESSON PLAN

1. Component 1: Preplanning Tasks
2. Component 4: Lesson Body
3. Component 5: Extended Practice
4. Component 7: Evaluation
5. Component 3: Lesson Opening
6. Component 6: Lesson Closing
7. Component 2: Lesson Setup
8. Component 8: Editing Tasks

It is also important to note that, although Components 2 through 7 are the only ones actually presented to the students, the preplanning tasks component and the editing tasks component are equally as important.

Writing a Useful Plan

When you write a plan for a lesson or an activity, it is important that your finished product not include every word you are going to say. A detailed list of main ideas is much preferred for a couple of reasons. First, when you force yourself to determine what the key ideas are, the essential points of your lesson become very apparent to you and can greatly assist you in presenting information clearly. Secondly, if you are writing plans for others to read, remember that your supervisor, principal, substitute, instructor, or cooperating teacher must be able to follow your main ideas.

Even your complete plan of key ideas will likely be too long to use as a reference as you teach. Make a shorter, outlined version so you can refer to it with a quick glance. This can be done easily with your word processor by saving and printing key sections of your plan. Another idea is to use a set of index cards or a corner of the board to list the main steps that you will follow in presenting your lesson or activity. We encourage you to experiment until you find a tool that works well for you.

TOPIC SENTENCES

- usually (but not always) the first sentenc
- describes main idea
- tells what paragraph is about

How to Write a Reader-Friendly Plan

- Use an outline format whenever possible (major headings, subheadings, bullets, numbers, and indenting).

- Label the transitions from one part of the lesson or activity to another. State directly what is going to happen (for example, "transition to lab stations" or "explain partner rules").

- Use a variety of font sizes and appearances (uppercase and lowercase, bold, and underline).

- Use key words and phrases rather than long narratives.

It is impossible to make a rule that determines how much detail to include in your plan. It is safe to say, however, that any explanation that may be complex or have the potential to be confusing should be put in writing to help ensure it is complete, accurate, and clear. For example, if you are going to teach your students how to write topic sentences, you would not simply write, "Explain topic sentences." This is too brief because the key information you need to emphasize during the lesson is not planned. You would have to rely solely on your memory to ensure that you present the key information your students need to know. It can be very difficult to remember and clearly present all of the key information when you are up in front of a room full of students. You will not want to write every single word you will say to the students either. Something in between is preferable. Look at "Topic Sentences" above, for an example.

Summary

Teachers write lesson plans for topics in all subject areas. Variations in lesson plans result from the specific characteristics of the model of instruction being used in the lesson. Regardless of the lesson model, however, eight important components must be included in all lesson plans. The content within each component will vary.

References and Suggested Reading

Arends, R. I. 2009. *Learning to teach.* 8th ed. New York: McGraw-Hill.

Borich, G. D. 2007. *Effective teaching methods: Research-based practice.* 6th ed. Columbus, OH: Pearson Prentice Hall.

Brown, S. D. 2009. History circles: The doing of teaching history. *History Teacher* 42 (2): 191–203.

Callahan, J. F., L. H. Clark, and R. D. Kellough. 2009. *Teaching in the middle and secondary schools.* 9th ed. Columbus, OH: Allyn & Bacon/Merrill.

Cartwright, P. G., C. A. Cartwright, and M. E. Ward. 1995. *Educating special learners.* 4th ed. Boston: Wadsworth.

Cruickshank, D. R., D. B. Jenkins, and K. K. Metcalf. 2009. *The act of teaching.* 5th ed. Boston: McGraw-Hill.

Gunter, M. A., T. H. Estes, and S. L. Mintz. 2007. *Instruction: A models approach.* 5th ed. Boston: Allyn & Bacon/Pearson.

Irvine, J. J., B. J. Armento, V. E. Causey, J. C. Jones, R. S. Frasher, and M. H. Weinburgh. 2001. *Culturally responsive teaching: Lesson planning for elementary and middle grades.* Boston: McGraw-Hill.

Joyce, B., M. Weil, and E. Calhoun. 2009. *Models of teaching.* 8th ed. Boston: Pearson.

Kellough, R. D., and J. Carjuzaa. 2009. *Teaching in the middle and secondary schools.* 9th ed. Boston: Allyn & Bacon. (See Module 5 in particular.)

Lasley, T. J., T. J. Matczynski, and J. B. Rowley. 2002. *Instructional models: Strategies for teaching in a diverse society.* 2nd ed. Belmont, CA: Wadsworth/Thomson Learning.

Lynch, S.A. 2008. Creating lesson plans for all learners. *Kappa Delta Pi Record* 45 (1): 10–15.

Moore, K. D. 2008. *Effective instructional strategies: From theory to practice.* 2nd ed. Thousand Oaks, CA: Sage Publications.

Orlich, D. C., R. J. Harder, R. C. Callahan, M. S. Trevisan, and A. H. Brown. 2010. *Teaching strategies: A guide to better instruction.* 9th ed. Boston: Houghton Mifflin.

Salsbury, D. E. 2008. A strategy for preservice teachers to integrate cultural elements within planning and instruction: Cultural L.I.V.E.S. *Journal of Social Studies Research* 32 (2): 31–39.

Serdyukov, P., and M. Ryan. 2008. *Writing effective lesson plans: A 5-star approach.* Boston: Pearson.

Smith, M. S. 2008. Thinking through a lesson: Successfully implementing high-level tasks. *Mathematics Teaching in the Middle School* 14 (3): 132–138.

Wiedmaier, C. 2008. Planning for instruction. *National Business Education Yearbook* 46: 37–52.

Wood, J. (in press). *Teaching students in inclusive settings: Adapting and accommodating instruction.* 6th ed. Upper Saddle River, NJ: Pearson.

Yell, M., T. Busch, and D. Rogers. 2007. Planning instruction and monitoring student performance. *Beyond Behavior* 17 (1): 31–38.

Activity Planning

Introduction

Teachers typically use a wide variety of activities during the school day. Some of these activities are necessary routines to organize and manage all of the tasks that need to be done, such as correcting homework or getting ready to go home. Others are meant as fun or relaxing activities to provide a break for students, such as listening to music or singing a song. Certain activities occur daily, such as math timings. Others may happen only occasionally, such as watching a fun video. This chapter is not about how to plan these types of activities, except in those cases where the activity is quite complex, such as morning opening activities.

This chapter is about how to plan for activities that are directly related to the curriculum—activities that introduce, extend, supplement, or enrich lessons. The purpose or rationale for any given activity may not be immediately apparent to an observer, but it is very clear to the teacher.

Purposes of Activities

As discussed in Chapter 13, teachers use activities that relate to the curriculum with various purposes in mind. Activities can often provide the following:

- *Motivation* for students before or during a series of lessons (for example, planning class fundraising activities during a unit on economics)

- *Background information* or enrichment of the students' knowledge and experience before or during a series of lessons (for example, taking a field trip to a salmon hatchery while studying resource conservation)

- *Introduction* of skills/knowledge that will be taught thoroughly at a later time (for example, introducing the addition and subtraction of money amounts before teaching decimals)

- *Review* of knowledge/skills taught previously (for example, a thorough review of place value before introducing addition with regrouping)

- *Ongoing practice* toward long-term objectives (such as playing math games to increase fluency on addition facts or completing art activities that provide practice using fine motor skills or following directions)

- Opportunities for students to *apply* or *generalize* a previously learned skill (for example, having students plan and maintain a daily meal and snack plan that meets good nutrition requirements)

- Opportunities for students to *integrate* a variety of skills learned from lessons in different subject areas (having students practice their writing skills by writing letters to the editor of the local newspaper about pertinent social issues being discussed in social studies, for example)

- *Differentiation of instruction* by dealing with the same content but at different levels (for example, an activity could involve setting up different poetry tasks at various stations and assigning students to stations based on their skills and interests)

It is important to note that various components of a *lesson plan* may have the same purposes as noted for activities; for example, the opening of a lesson may be intended to motivate students. In addition, lessons sometimes incorporate activities to extend the presentation of information. For example, a teacher may have students put together models of the heart during a lesson on the circulatory system. When activities are part of a daily lesson, they should be included within the lesson plan itself. When activities are part of a series of lessons or unit, or when activities are long and complex, it will be helpful to write a separate activity plan.

Teachers typically decide what activities to use while planning units of instruction. Teachers may also plan additional activities based on their assessments of student progress. For example, Mrs. Rabe finds that her students need more practice on the concepts of "above" and "below" than originally planned.

Generic Components of an Activity Plan

An activity plan is a written description of exactly what the teacher will do and say to help students prepare for and complete an activity. The plan may consist of a set of questions to ask the students, a set of explanations that help tie the current activity to other learning, or step-by-step procedures and directions.

All activity plans contain the same generic components, even though the content of each component will vary greatly depending on the type of activity planned. For example, a plan to show and discuss a videotape will look very different from an activity plan for a complex art project. The following explains the purpose of each component and suggests the kinds of decisions that need to be made in each. This is designed to help guide you through the steps for planning your activity. When you are ready to actually write an activity plan, refer to Figure 15.1, "Writing an Activity Plan."

Component 1: Preplanning Tasks

Typically, teachers will develop various activities and lessons to help students progress toward long-term objectives. Keeping this in mind, the preplanning component of the activity plan helps you think through how the current activity connects with important learning outcomes.

The preplanning tasks for an activity include: selecting and writing the long-term objective and identifying connections to standards, broad goals and so forth; writing the activity description and rationale; and analyzing the content for prerequisite skills/knowledge and relevant vocabulary.

One essential part of this component involves developing a thoughtful connection between the objective of the activity and its purpose. This process begins by identifying the *long-term objective* of the activity. This objective is specific and needs to include all four essential components (content, behavior, condition, criterion) so that it is measurable. In addition, be sure you can identify the *generalization* or *big idea*, the *IEP goal*, or the *state standard* to which the objective connects.

Remember that an objective for an activity is different from a lesson objective because students will not necessarily meet the objective by the end of the activity; it could take weeks or longer. An example of an activity objective is that students will write paragraphs that include a topic sentence, three supporting detail sentences, and one closing sentence. Clearly, several lessons and activities would be necessary before students meet this objective. In summary, objectives for activities are considered long-term objectives, whereas lesson objectives are considered short-term objectives.

Another important part of the first component involves selecting an activity that will help students progress toward the long-term objective and then writing an *activity description*. Once you have decided on the objective, brainstorm activities that will bring about this outcome. Be creative. Consider variety, novelty, and student interests. Think about the diversity in your classroom and what kinds of activities would be flexible enough to provide opportunities for all students to be challenged and successful. Select an activity that best fits the objective and the students (or you may choose to plan several alternative activities to differentiate for student needs).

Note that if you are a practicum student or student teacher, your cooperating teacher may already have decided on the topic and the type of activity. For example, he may ask you to plan an art activity that will fit with the unit on Northwest Native Americans or to find a book to read to the students that introduces the theme of friendship. In this case, be sure that you understand the long-term objective.

Once you have selected the activity, write a short description (one or two sentences) that summarizes it. This task will help you distinguish between the desired outcome (objective) and the actual activity. An activity description might appear as follows: "Give students packets of color-coded sentence strips. Each packet includes one topic sentence strip and three supporting detail sentence strips. Working in pairs, students will place supporting detail sentences under each topic sentence strip."

Avoid making the mistake of selecting an activity first and then trying to justify it by making up an objective and rationale. Remember to use backward planning. Choose the objective first and then select an activity to help students achieve the objective.

The final task in thinking about the objective is to construct an *activity rationale*. This is a description of how the current activity will help students progress toward the objective. When you plan the rationale, you may wish to refer to the broad purpose for the activity (for example, to motivate, enrich, practice, integrate, apply, or generalize).

The rationale provides the important connection between the long-term objective and the current activity. It requires carefully thinking through why students need to do the activity. Rationales such as "I thought it would be fun" or "I happen to have this videotape" are definitely questionable. Activities ought to be fun and motivating, of course, but they also need to result in important learning. An activity rationale might look like the following: "This activity is intended to provide ongoing practice in identifying topic and supporting detail sentences. Physically moving the topic and detail sentence strips may make the connections more concrete to the students. In addition, the opportunity to talk through decision-making with a peer partner may increase understanding."

Note that the activity rationale is really a rationale for the current activity rather than for the long-term objective. The rationale for the long-term objective would have been determined when the objective was written.

The other main preplanning task is to think through necessary *prerequisite skills or knowledge*, as well as *key terms and vocabulary*. Carefully consider what information or skills your students need

EXAMPLES OF ACTIVITY OBJECTIVES, DESCRIPTIONS, AND RATIONALES

Example #1

- *Long-term objective*—Students will write answers to addition facts (with sums from 0–20) at the rate of 80 digits per minute with no errors. (State Mathematics Standard: "Add, subtract, multiply, and divide whole numbers")

- *Activity description*—Students will play a bingo game in which math fact questions (for example, 5 + 3 = ?) are called out and students cover the correct answer on their bingo card.

- *Activity rationale*—The game format is intended to increase interest and motivation in gaining accuracy and fluency on math facts.

Example #2

- *Long-term objective*—Students will write five complete sentences that include nouns, adjectives, and verbs, and label these three parts of speech with 100 percent accuracy.

- *Activity description*—I will show a template that explains the structure (parts of speech and syllables) of the cinquain poem, I will show many examples of cinquain poems, and then we'll write a cinquain poem together. Finally, I'll have them write poems of their own where they select the topic and I give assistance as needed. They'll share them with classmates.

- *Activity rationale*—In recent writing lessons, we have been focusing on parts of speech. Due to the structure of the cinquain, this activity will provide my students with additional practice on the specific parts of speech that we have been concentrating on in the past weeks— nouns, adjectives, and –*ing* verbs. This activity also integrates grammar skills and creative writing skills.

to be successful in the current activity. Review, teach, or provide scaffolds or supports as needed. In addition, identify key terms and vocabulary words that need to be defined and taught. Be sure that you define terms using student-friendly language. Also consider the critical management skills that will help the activity go smoothly.

Component 2: Activity Beginning

The purpose of the activity beginning is to prepare students for participating and learning in the new activity. The activity *setup* includes your plan for gaining attention and the communication of behavior expectations. An *opening* is also included in the activity beginning.

You will need to decide on a way to gain the attention of the students at the beginning of the activity, as well as methods of regaining attention during the activity. Let students know how you want them to respond to the signal. Plan your expectations for student behavior during the beginning of the activity and describe how you will communicate them to the students (see Chapter 11).

It's very important that you think about how you will help students understand the purpose of the activity, and how it connects with long-term objectives, with their prior knowledge, and with their personal experience. It may be necessary to build background knowledge for them. You will also want to capture their interest right away and motivate them to participate. Write your plan for the *opening* (see Chapter 4 for more information on openings).

Component 3: Activity Middle

The activity middle is a specific description of what the students and the teacher will do during the activity. Think carefully about what you will be doing, what the students will be doing, and what you will need to communicate to your students. If the students will be listening to or watching something (readings, films, or demonstrations, for example), you will need to plan a set of questions to ask or a series of explanations to make. If the students will be creating something (writing, drawing, or building, for example), you will need to plan a set of directions to give and perhaps plan to show an example of a finished product. If the students are going to be doing something (such as performing

experiments or playing a game), you will need to plan a set of procedures or rules and perhaps plan to demonstrate the process. Activity middles vary according the specific activity to be taught. You may need to develop one or more of the following:

- *A Set of Questions* Plan questions to ask before, during, and after reading a story, playing a musical selection, or taking students on a nature walk. It can be difficult to ask good questions spontaneously. Planning some of the questions in advance will help you ask clear and thought-provoking ones. (See Chapter 4 for more information on planning questions.) Planning will allow you to develop appropriate questions for your English language learners. It will also help you think through the purposes of the questions. For example, when you read a story with your students, you may want to ask questions to emphasize vocabulary words, the meanings of figures of speech, making inferences or predictions, summarizing, or identifying character, setting, and plot.

- *A Series of Statements or Explanations* Prior to a presentation, preview important components. For example, explain that the videotape the class is about to see presents three major factors that contribute to child abuse and that, when the video is over, they need to be prepared to discuss them. Telling students what to watch or listen for will help them focus. Planning these statements in advance will ensure clarity and brevity.

- *A List of Directions* Provide step-by-step directions. For example, list directions for the book covers students will be making for the short stories they have written. Displaying the directions in writing, as well as stating the directions to the students, is very important and will save much repetition. Planning the directions in advance will ensure clarity and completeness.

- *A Sample of a Finished Product* Provide a sample of the item students will be creating. Show a completed book cover or a correctly prepared slide, for example. Seeing a completed product can be very helpful in understanding what to do and what is expected. Be sure to clarify whether students' products need to look exactly like the sample, or whether you are looking for variety and creativity. If the steps in making the product are complex, consider showing samples of the product at various stages of completion.

- *A List of Procedures* Provide a set of procedures for how to get things done. For example, delineate how to experiment with each magnet, how to find partners or form groups, how to share tasks, where to get or how to use materials or equipment, and so on. In addition to stating the procedures, show the written list and demonstrate them.

- *A List of Rules for a Game* Provide a list of guidelines, such as rules for the quiz show game the students will be playing to review social studies information prior to their test. Again, providing a written summary of the rules as well as stating them and demonstrating them is a good idea. Be sure to plan all needed rules to avoid confusion, arguments, and wasted time.

Plan how you will check for understanding after explaining directions, procedures, rules, and so on. For example, you may ask specific questions—"What do you do first? How do you find your partner?"—and call on selected individuals or ask for written or signaled responses. Simply saying, "Does everyone understand?" or "Any questions?" is not effective (see Chapter 7).

While activity middles vary in what is included in them, certain planning elements should always be considered, because they will help meet the diverse needs of the students. One key element is to provide information both verbally and visually, which is an example of a *critical teaching skill* (see Chapter 5). For example, write the rules for a game on a poster as well as saying and modeling them for the students, or demonstrate the preparation of a microscope slide as well as providing a list of procedures. Another key element is to incorporate *active participation* by all students during the activity. For example, when asking questions during a story, have students say their response to a neighbor rather than calling on only one or two volunteers. Some active participation strategies serve as *checks for understanding* so that you can monitor student learning. For example, students can hold up fingers to show how many syllables they hear in a word (see Chapters 6 and 7). A third element is to plan selected interventions or *accommodations* that consider individual strengths and weaknesses. These might include allowing options, such as

(1) having students work individually, with partners, or in small groups; or (2) allowing students to make a presentation rather than writing a report (see Chapters 3 and 9 for many additional ideas).

It's important to remember the following:

- Provide information orally, in writing, through demonstrations, and using other visual supports.

- Incorporate active participation and checks for understanding.

- Plan provisions for individual differences through interventions used universally or selectively.

Finally, plan how you will support appropriate behavior during the activity middle. For example, describe how you will acknowledge appropriate behavior, how you will monitor student behavior, and how you will manage transitions. You may wish to implement a group management game (see Chapter 11).

Component 4: Activity Closing

The activity closing helps students tie it all together. Decide whether it will be important to review key ideas and to preview future lessons or activities. It may be necessary to provide an opportunity for students to draw conclusions, describe their problem-solving processes, or show what they created. You may wish to formally assess progress toward a long-term objective. Activity closings do not necessarily need to be time-consuming and elaborate, but should provide a meaningful ending of some kind (see Chapter 4).

Component 5: Editing Tasks

Editing tasks are addressed in detail in Chapter 20. They are summarized here. The purpose of the editing tasks is to build in critical management skills, to double-check that you included appropriate universal and selected instructional interventions, and to check for congruence. All of these tasks help finalize your plan.

Editing Task #1—*Add critical management skills.* Write in how you plan to gain attention, communicate behavior expectations, acknowledge appropriate behavior, monitor student behavior, arrange the room, handle logistics, and manage transitions (see Chapters 11, 12, and 20). Also add behavior interventions intended for selected students (see Chapter 10).

Editing Task #2—*Double-check for universal and selected instructional interventions.* Be sure that you have included necessary interventions. Think about principles of universal design, clarity of presentation, use of active participation strategies and checks for understanding, and the use of visual supports (see Chapters 3 through 9 and Chapter 20). Selected interventions should address the needs of one or more students.

Editing Task #3—*Evaluate congruence.* Look carefully at congruence. Remember that the various components of activities must match (for example, the activity objective and the activity middle). Congruence ensures an emphasis on the activity objective throughout the plan. In addition, congruence helps students move toward the long-term objective you selected, ensuring that students will be evaluated on what they were taught and what they practiced. Turn to Chapter 20 for directions on how to evaluate congruence.

Steps in Writing an Activity Plan

When you first learn how to write an activity plan, it is important to include all of the generic components in every plan. The order in which you write the components however, will not necessarily correspond to the way in which you would present them to your students. For example, it makes more sense to write the activity middle before the setup, but when the activity is presented to the students, you would obviously present the opening before the middle. Remember that while Components 2 through 4 of your activity plan are the only ones that will actually be presented to students, the preplanning tasks and editing components are of equal importance and should be completed in writing.

Sequence for Writing the Components of an Activity Plan

The following is the suggested sequence for developing the components of an activity plan:

1. Component 1: Preplanning Tasks

2. Component 3: Activity Middle

3. Component 4: Activity Closing

4. Component 2: Activity Beginning

5. Component 5: Editing Tasks

Writing a Useful Plan

Remember that when you write your activity plan, it is important that your final draft serve as a useful resource for you and those who observe you. (See "How to Write a Reader-Friendly Plan" in Chapter 14 for guidance.)

Summary

You will plan many types of activities for your students, and they should all have a clear purpose. Be sure you can state the important long-term objective that the activity will help your students meet. Written activity plans vary greatly because the design of the plan depends on the activity itself. All activity plans however, include the same basic components.

Sample Plans

Look at the framework for diversity responsive teaching (DRT) as you examine the two sample plans ("Tic-Tac-Toe Spelling" and "The Underground Railroad") at the end of this chapter. Ask yourself how the plan incorporates responses to diversity in *what* is taught, *how* it's taught, and the *context* for teaching and learning. We'll give you a start in thinking about how various parts of the plan fit with various components of the framework. We encourage you to look for additional examples of each component and to think about what changes you believe would make this plan even more likely to support all students' success.

Notice that "The Underground Railroad" activity plan is an example of teaching content *about* diversity and of making sure that all *contributors* and *perspectives* are included. Two examples of planning the *how* are: *congruence* in how the key ideas stated in the objectives are developed throughout the plan (questions emphasize key ideas) and the variety of *question* types (high-level and low-level) used. Finally, using *whole-class behavior points* (in a challenging class) is an example of responding to diversity when planning the *context*.

Note that the "Tic-Tac-Toe Spelling" activity will be reviewed in Chapter 20.

Figure 15-1	Writing an Activity Plan

The content of the components in Figure 15.1 describes what typically would be included in each component of an activity plan.

COMPONENT 1: PREPLANNING TASKS

Prepare the following:

- *Long-term objective*—Write the long-term objective for the activity as well as the generalization or big idea, the IEP goal, or the state standard that is being addressed.
- *Activity description*—Prepare a brief summary or description of the activity itself.
- *Activity rationale*—Describe how the current activity helps students progress toward the long-term objective.
- *Prerequisite skills or knowledge and key terms or vocabulary*—Describe those needed for success in the activity.
- *Critical management skills*—Write in those you will use in the activity, such as how you'll arrange the room and handle logistics.

COMPONENT 2: ACTIVITY BEGINNING

Prepare the following:

- *Setup:*
  - *Gaining attention*—Plan to let students know how you will ask for their attention and how they should respond.
  - *Communicating behavior expectations*—Plan how you'll show and tell expected behaviors to students.
- *Opening*—An opening shows students how this activity connects to previous lessons, to personal experiences, or to prior knowledge. It may be used to build background knowledge. The opening also helps to motivate or focus the students.

COMPONENT 3: ACTIVITY MIDDLE

Prepare the following:

- A *description of what* you need to communicate to the students. Depending on the type of activity, you may need one or a combination of the following: a set of questions, a list of statements or explanations, a list of rules, a list of procedures, a sample of a finished product, and a list of directions.
- A *description of how* you will effectively communicate this information to the students (use of critical teaching skills including visual supports, demonstrations, checks for understanding, active participation, and so on).
- A description of the critical management skills you will use to prevent behavior problems (such as acknowledging appropriate behavior, monitoring student behavior, and managing transitions).

(*continued on next page*)

Figure 15-1	Writing an Activity Plan (*continued*)

COMPONENT 4: ACTIVITY CLOSING

- Prepare a description of how you will end the activity. Your closing may involve a class review, students drawing conclusions, teacher previews of future learning, students showing work, or an evaluation procedure (if appropriate).

COMPONENT 5: EDITING TASKS

Remember to use editing tasks to evaluate your plan.

1. Write in critical management skills and selected behavior interventions.
2. Double-check for the use of effective instructional interventions.
3. Evaluate congruence.

TIC-TAC-TOE SPELLING

This is a large-group activity plan.

I. Preplanning Tasks

A. Prerequisite skills or knowledge: How to play Tic-Tac-Toe

B. Key terms or vocabulary: N/A

C. Long-term objective: Given a list of 15 words that contain one to three syllables and end in "–ing," students will write (or spell orally) all words correctly. Students are given lists that match their skill level (one, two, or three syllables, for example). State writing standard: spell age-level words correctly.

D. Activity description: A Tic-Tac-Toe game where partners quiz each other on their spelling words. Correct responses result in placing an X or O on the Tic-Tac-Toe board.

E. Activity rationale: This game is intended to provide students a fun way to practice and memorize their spelling words. This format also provides practice in giving and taking constructive feedback.

F. Materials: poster of game directions, transparency of grids and rules, worksheets with 25 Tic-Tac-Toe grids on each.

II. Activity Beginning

A. Setup

  1. Gaining attention: "Attention, please."

  2. Behavior expectations: "While I'm giving directions, keep eyes on me and raise hands to ask/answer questions unless I say 'everyone' or ask you to call out."

B. Opening

  1. Review: "You have been learning to spell words that end with '–ing'. Call out some examples."

  2. Motivate: "We're going to play Tic-Tac-Toe Spelling today."

  3. Objective and purpose: "Tic-Tac-Toe Spelling will help you memorize correct spelling of words so you can use these words in your writing; you won't need to look up words in a dictionary."

III. Activity Middle

A. Post these written game directions:

  1. Exchange spelling lists with your reading partner.

  2. Partner 1 (*X*) asks Partner 2 (*O*) a word from Partner 2's list.

  3. Partner 2 spells. If correct, Partner 2 places an *O* on a Tic-Tac-Toe square.

  4. If wrong, Partner 1 says "The word _____ is spelled _____. How do you spell _____?"

  5. Partner 1 places a check if correct or a minus if incorrect by the word spelled.

  6. Reverse the roles. Keep playing until time is up.

B. Explain directions for the game using poster and transparency of Tic-Tac-Toe grids and sample word lists.

  ■ Demonstrate with teaching assistant as I explain.

(*continued on next page*)

- Explain that checks and minuses are to keep track of words they know and to make sure all words are asked.
- Check for understanding: After each step, stop and ask a question and request a unison verbal or signal response (e.g., "What would you say if I spelled cat 'K-A-D'?" "What does your partner write if the word isn't spelled correctly?").

C. Check for understanding of all directions: I choose two students to come to the front and model the game procedure as I ask other selected students specific questions such as "Who goes first?" "What does the asker do now?"

D. Distribute Tic-Tac-Toe grids. "Trade spelling lists with your partner."

E. Play the game: Play for 20 minutes. "Complete as many games as possible."

IV. Activity Closing

A. Preview: "Tomorrow, we'll do another practice activity to help you memorize your spelling words."

B. Practice one final time: "Pick one misspelled word from your list (if no words are misspelled, use "challenge words") and spell it correctly in a whisper three times."

THE UNDERGROUND RAILROAD

I. Preplanning Tasks

A. Long-term objectives for activity:

1. Students will explain orally, or in writing, the complex workings of the Underground Railroad (U.R.) to include relevant dates, individuals involved, and numbers of enslaved people rescued, as well as the impact that the U.R. had on slave trade in America.

2. Students will summarize in writing (or in an oral report), contributions made by Harriet Tubman as a key player in the Underground Railroad, including a description of who she was, where she lived, how she became involved, and her contributions to helping free slaves.

B. Activity description: I will read a story about Harriet Tubman and the U.R. My plan is to have students listen for specific information that they will use in a follow-up project. I will help them focus their attention on the information I want them to learn by telling them what to listen for in advance of reading each section. I'll help students process the information they are hearing by using active participation strategies such as table group and partner discussions. I will then follow up with questions designed to check for understanding regarding the key ideas I want my students to learn.

C. Activity rationale: This story will help students move toward the long-term objectives. I typically use the after-lunch story to add breadth to topics being studied in other curricular areas, such as social studies. I selected this particular story because it ties in nicely with our current unit on immigration, in which we look at the reasons that various groups of people came to America and their experiences once they arrived. We have just begun our study of American citizens of African descent and are investigating the issues that led up to the abolition of slavery.

D. Materials: *Traveling on the Underground Railroad* by Steven Everett and key terms and vocabulary words (write on the board before the activity).

II. Activity Beginning

A. Gaining attention: Turn lights on/off (students are returning from recess).

B. Behavior expectations: (1) Stay in seats; (2) Look at me; (3) Listen to the story; and (4) Follow my directions the first time asked. Remember that you are earning points (marbles in the jar) toward a cooking activity.

C. Opening

1. Connecting statements. Say, "We have been studying the reasons why various groups of individuals traveled to America. Yesterday we talked about how the arrival of African Americans was unique. They came here not by choice, but rather by force. Their arrival in America did not represent an escape to 'the land of the free,' but rather the beginning of a life of slavery—property of 'masters' living in the South—being dreadfully mistreated."

2. Focusing statements. Say, "As you know, a significant number of slaves made it to freedom because of the U.R. Today, you will hear more about Harriet Tubman, an African American woman, and how she helped slaves escape on this railroad. You'll also learn about how the U.R. worked. The U.R. was not really a railroad. It was the name used to describe all of the secret places and ways by which slaves traveled to escape from captivity in the South."

(continued on next page)

III. Activity Middle

A. Reminders to myself:

    1. Draw name sticks to help ensure that I select a variety of students to answer questions.

    2. Put marbles in the jar (whole-class behavior points) throughout activity when students are following directions.

B. Review terms: Read definitions and show pictures to emphasize meaning. Say, "There are some very specific vocabulary words that will help you better understand how the U.R. worked. I've written each word and its definition on the board."

    1. Procedure for teaching key terms and vocabulary:

        a. Say each word clearly and have students repeat.

> *AP* = choral read

        b. Use a quick-teach to explain each word; use photographs.

            ■ **Underground railroad:** the name used to describe all of the secret places, routes, and ways by which enslaved people traveled to escape from captivity in the South. *Show photographs of secret places and routes taken by slaves.*

            ■ **Conductor:** guides for the people escaping. *Show photographs.*

            ■ **Station** or **depot:** business or home where escaping people were hidden. *Show photographs* and *emphasize the difference between a station or depot* they may know about (train or bus).

            ■ **Passengers:** the runaway slaves. *Show photographs.*

        c. Leave words on board for students to use as a reference.

        d. Watch for appropriate behavior, acknowledge, and put marbles in jar.

C. Setup for story: Say, "You will need to listen carefully as I read this story to you. You'll hear what it was like to be a slave, how the U.R. got started, and how it worked. You will also hear about Harriet Tubman and why she is to be so admired."

D. Begin reading story. (*Monitor behavior: walk around as I read and check in more often with those students who may have difficulty attending.*)

    1. Section 1: pages 1–6
        a. Before reading, say, "Listen to find out how enslaved people were treated and how they tried to get away."
        b. After reading, ask, "What kind of 'offenses' were the slaves punished for? Why did the slaves want to run away to the North?"
        c. Watch for appropriate behavior and put marbles in jar.

> *AP* = Discuss with table groups, call on individuals (using name sticks).

    2. Section 2: pages 7–12
        a. Before reading, say, "Listen to find out how the U.R. worked and what the various parts of the U.R. were." (*Refer back to key terms and vocabulary words on the board.*)
        b. After reading, ask, "How did the U.R. work? What were the roles of the conductor and of the stations? What was a typical trip on the U.R. like?" Show list of true/false statements about the UR. **CFU:** thumbs up for true.

> *AP* = Raise your hand when you hear one of the words on the board.

3. Section 3: pages 13–20
   a. Before reading, say, "Find out how and when Harriet Tubman first used the U.R."
   b. Acknowledge appropriate behavior and put marbles in jar.
   c. After reading, ask, "What events led to Harriet Tubman's first trip on the U.R.? What was the scariest part of her trip?"
4. Section 4: pages 21–34
   a. Before reading, say, "You will learn how and why Harriet Tubman became involved in helping others use the U.R."
   b. After reading, ask, "Harriet Tubman decided to help others use the U.R. Why? Why did she continue to help for so long even though it was so dangerous?"
   c. Acknowledge appropriate behavior and put marbles in jar.

> *AP/CFU*= Have students discuss with table groups; then call on selected individuals; other students thumbs up or down to agree or disagree.

IV. Activity Ending

A. Have students summarize the key facts about Harriet Tubman that were brought out in the story.

B. Briefly explain connections/similarities between Harriet Tubman and others who will be studied over the next week.

> *AP* = Turn to a partner.
> *CFU* = Call on selected individuals.

C. Preview the follow-up writing assignment about Harriet Tubman and the U.R. They'll need facts to use, so:

> *AP* = tell a partner.

1. Have them construct a concept map with as many facts as possible about U.R. and Harriet Tubman. (They frequently use concept maps as a way to organize facts and information as a review.) Give them 3 minutes to write; then give them 2 minutes to compare with a neighbor. Selected intervention: Have Ellen help Paul fill in his map.

Preface to the Lesson Models

Introduction

A lesson model is an overall teaching approach that teachers use to guide student learning in a specific way toward the attainment of a lesson objective (Arends 2009. In Chapters 16, 17, and 18, we provide information about three important models—direct instruction, informal presentation, and structured discovery. Chapter 19 features examples of how to use direct instruction or structured discovery to teach specialized content: concepts, behavioral skills, and learning and study strategies.

The three models selected for this book were chosen for several reasons. First, they are reasonably easy for teachers to implement, and are very effective when used correctly. Next, certain models of instruction may work better than others for teaching certain types of content. Finally, they represent variety (from direct to less direct) in their approach to teaching, which clearly addresses the fact that not all students learn in the same way.

According to Mercer et al., teachers need to make instructional decisions based on the differential needs of their students. This means that teachers must offer a continuum of teaching methods, including "explicit" and "implicit" instructional approaches, because of the diversity found in classrooms today. They point out that "an allegiance to one method of teaching reduces the range of appropriate instructional choices for teachers and students" (1996, 226). We offer several basic lesson models in this book, with an emphasis on explicit approaches. We also present information on activity planning and suggest using activities for implicit instruction. All of these can add to a teacher's repertoire and provide necessary variety to meet the needs of diverse learners.

Selecting a Model to Use

Students are guided toward a specific lesson objective in different ways, depending on the lesson model used. Some models, such as direct instruction and informal presentation, are often used to teach basic knowledge and skills. Some models, like structured discovery, may be used to promote inductive thinking and problem-solving skills. Because of their varied purposes, a thorough understanding of the characteristics of various lesson models can help teachers determine which particular model will work best for a particular lesson or activity.

A lesson model should always be selected after the lesson objective is written. Decide first where you want students to go (the lesson objective), and *then* decide how to help get them there (the lesson model). Once you have selected the model to use, be sure your written plan reflects the essential elements of the chosen model. For example, if you are writing a direct instruction lesson, the plan should detail how you will explain and demonstrate information, how you will check for understanding, and what types of practice opportunities you will provide, as these are some of the key elements of the direct instruction model. Although all lesson plans contain the same eight components, the content of the components will differ depending on the lesson model you use.

Responding to Skill Diversity When Selecting a Lesson Model

Using a variety of methods and models increases effectiveness and adds variety to your teaching. Because the different methods and models have unique purposes and characteristics, it is important to select themthoughtfully. Carefully consider the content and students you are teaching as you choose methods and models. In addition, variety creates interest for your students and can also make teaching more interesting and fun for you.

Consider these variables when selecting lesson models and methods:

- Evaluate the level of structure that the students need to be successful. Don't assume that all students learn best with, or even prefer, unstructured approaches.

- Recognize that students with learning and behavioral problems often require very explicit instruction. This needs to be followed by focused, active practice with immediate feedback.

- Use the most time-efficient models and methods if the students have fallen behind in the curriculum.

- Evaluate the amount of academic learning time that each student would have in the lesson or activity. For example, having groups of students work together to bake cookies may sound like a good way to practice measurement skills; however, when you look closely, you may see that in an hour-long activity, Joanne spent 30 seconds measuring 1 tablespoon of cinnamon. This isn't much practice!

- Be sure that students have the necessary skills to be successful in the methods you are using. For example, decide whether they have the needed cooperative social skills for small-group projects. These skills may need to be directly taught in advance.

- Small-group instruction may frequently be needed in a classroom of students with diverse achievement levels. Students should be carefully assessed on specific skills to form short-term skill groups. It is important to keep assessing and reforming groups as necessary.

Responding to Cultural Diversity When Planning Lessons

Many cultural variables have implications for the selection of lesson models and the use or structuring of project- or center-based activities. As you plan lessons (and activities), consider the teacher's role,

the pacing of instruction, the amount of talk and movement, the specificity of directions, and other features. When selecting lessons (and activities), consider the following about your students:

- comfort with initiating their own projects, and choosing what or how to learn

- tolerance for structure or lack of structure

- ease with working independently or with peers

- experience with sitting quietly or with maintaining high activity levels

- comfort with the teacher as a co-learner or as an authority

- desire for feedback or direction independent of or dependent on the teacher

- beliefs about asking for help or questioning the teacher

- preference for learning from peers or from adults

Organization of Chapters 16 through 18

We will provide detailed information about direct-instruction, informal-presentation, and structured discovery models in each of these chapters. Each chapter begins with a basic description of a lesson model. Next, we describe typical uses for the model and discuss important elements of each model in "Key Planning Considerations." Finally, Figures 16.1, 17.1, and 18.1 provide summaries of what to include as you write the actual lesson plans. These figures are to be used as guides. Our intent is for you to read carefully *all* of the information provided about each model and use it as a reference when you write your plans. The summaries can serve as reminders of the key information that needs to be included in the written plans. Refer to Chapter 14 for information about generic lesson components.

The content of each component included in each specific model is essential to defining the model. Teachers can add, rearrange, or omit certain component content. However, have a good rationale for doing so. Varying the critical elements of the model too much will result in something other than the model that was chosen.

Note that before you select a specific lesson model to use, you should complete the following preplanning tasks:

- Determine the specific content to be taught in the lesson and analyze that content.
- Write the lesson objective.
- Write the lesson rationale.
- Then, select the model and refer to the appropriate chapter for more information.

Summary

It is important to know a variety of methods and models. Selection will be most effective when you consider your students' needs as well as their interests and strengths. When you provide variety in your presentations and the methods you use, it may automatically create interest for your students. Variety is the spice of life, as the old saying goes!

References and Suggested Reading

Arends, R. I. 2009. *Learning to teach.* 8th ed. Boston: McGraw-Hill.

Gunter, M. A., T.H. Estes, and S.L. Mintz. 2007. Instruction: A models approach. 5th ed. Boston: Pearson.

Joyce, B, M., Weil, and E. Calhoun. 2009. *Models of teaching.* 8th ed. Boston: Pearson.

Mercer, C. D., H. B. Lane, L. Jordan, D. H. Allsopp, and M. R. Eisele. 1996. Empowering teachers and students with instructional choices in inclusive settings. *Remedial and Special Education*, 17 (4): 226–236.

CHAPTER 16

Direct Instruction

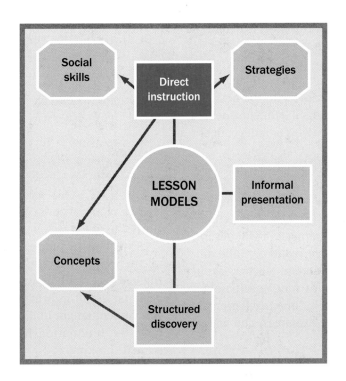

Introduction

Direct instruction is a model of instruction that is often summarized as "I do it; we do it; you do it." That is, the teacher explains and demonstrates the skill, the students do the skill with teacher help, and the students do the skill by themselves. Another phrase that is often used to describe direct instruction is "model–lead–test." It means the teacher shows and tells, leads the students in practicing, and then evaluates the students. Both phrases express that the teacher is carefully guiding the learning of the students and this is precisely the intent of direct instruction. Direct instruction is explicit teaching.

In a direct instruction lesson, events focus on moving students toward a specific short-term objective. Teachers begin by clearly stating the lesson objective and the lesson purpose to the students. They then explain and demonstrate the information or skill to be learned, using many examples. Next, students are given a variety of opportunities to practice the new knowledge or skill while the teacher carefully supervises. The practice may occur first within the large group, then within small groups or with a partner, and finally the practice is done individually. This allows teachers to see how each student is progressing. All components of the instruction are designed carefully to ensure that all students can reach the objective.

Direct instruction lessons are teacher-directed, but this doesn't mean that students are just passive listeners. Rather, they are actively participating throughout the lesson. The teacher uses her creativity to develop engaging ways to present the lesson and to involve students in thinking about, talking about, writing about, and performing the new skill or knowledge.

Teachers provide students with feedback on their performance as they monitor the supervised practice opportunities. This helps ensure that students are accurately practicing the new information or skill. Careful monitoring also allows teachers to determine whether to reteach and when to evaluate.

In the direct instruction approach, teachers present information in small steps so that students can master one step before moving to the next. The direct instruction lesson results in students' demonstrating their new skill or knowledge independently, without help from anyone.

Note that there are two types of direct instruction. One type, often called "Big D. I.," refers to published programs that provide scripted lessons, such as Reading Mastery I and II Fast Cycle (Engelmann and Bruner 1995). In this chapter, we will describe the other type, commonly referred to as "little d. i." In both types of direct instruction, teachers explicitly guide students toward learning specific objectives. However, in "little d. i.," the teacher creates the explanations, directions, examples, and ways to involve students.

Uses of Direct Instruction

Direct instruction lessons play an important role in teaching a wide variety of skills, and knowledge that lends itself to being presented in steps or subskills. Examples of this type of content are procedures (a series of steps), strategies (a specific type of procedure designed to help students learn, study or get organized), principles (relational rules, if/then), and concepts (categories of information). The following box includes some examples of content and topics that can be appropriately taught through direct instruction

---

EXAMPLES OF TOPICS THAT COULD BE TAUGHT USING THE DIRECT INSTRUCTION MODEL

Procedures, including:

- how to serve in volleyball
- how to convert fractions to whole numbers
- how to initiate a conversation

Strategies, including:

- how to read text with comprehension
- how to take multiple-choice tests
- how to proofread assignments

Principles, including:

- If a sentence is a question, then it should end with a question mark.
- If $A(B + C) = D$, then $AB + AC = D$.
- When a CVCe word has a silent e at the end, it makes the previous vowel say its name.

Concepts, including:

- triangle
- socialism
- ecosystem

---

lessons. Notice that direct instruction is often, but not always, used to teach how to do something.

Direct instruction lessons also play an important role in lessons that emphasize higher-level thinking. Higher-level thinking cannot occur without having basic facts and information about which to think. The content taught in direct instruction lessons may form the foundation for lessons that emphasize critical thinking and problem solving. The following are some examples of how higher-level thinking is dependent on knowledge of basic skills and information:

- Mr. Singh wants his students to use the Internet as one resource for the reports they are writing about various countries around the world. He first teaches them computer-access skills through direct instruction.

- Ms. Parker wants her students to design their own science experiments to test certain hypotheses. She first teaches them steps in the scientific method through direct instruction.

Direct instruction lessons also play an important role in the use of certain teaching methods (Arends 2009). For example, if you want to use cooperative learning groups or discussions in your lessons and activities, you will need to directly teach students skills such as reaching consensus, taking turns, active listening, and paraphrasing.

Key Planning Considerations

When writing the body of the direct instruction lesson, carefully consider and plan in detail the explanation, the demonstration, and the supervised practice. The content analysis, which plays an important role in the lesson body, must be planned carefully as well.

Content Analysis

The content analysis of a direct instruction lesson varies according to the content you are teaching. When planning a "how-to" lesson, the content analysis will include a task analysis. When teaching a principle, you will write a clearly stated principle statement. Finally, when teaching a concept through direct instruction, include a concept analysis. Note that the task analysis, principle statement, or concept analysis will be presented and taught as part of the lesson body (see Chapter 1 for more information on content analyses).

Explanation

In the explanation part of the direct instruction lesson body, the teacher tells the information that students need to know to meet the lesson objective. The planning should include both a description of the content to be taught (the *what*) and how the new skill or knowledge will be explained (the *how*). It is important to present all of the information necessary for understanding the new knowledge or skill through elaboration, definitions, specific examples and nonexamples, and so on. (See Chapter 5 for more information on effective explanations.) The explanation section of the lesson body can occur before, during, or after the demonstration part (see the next section).

When the explanation part of the body of the lesson is written, include enough detail to prevent being caught off-guard during the lesson. Do *not* simply write in the plan, "I will explain the steps" or "I'll define each term." It is necessary to plan *how* you will explain—namely, by listing in the plan the key points or ideas you want to convey and the examples you want to include. Write out the definitions of key terms so that they are clear and complete. It is very difficult to spontaneously explain, describe, or define in a clear way. Often, the ideas that seem simplest and most obvious to the teacher are the most difficult to explain.

Typically, the information in this section of the lesson is presented to students both in writing (on a transparency, a whiteboard, a poster, or a handout) and orally. Any explanation that may be complex or have the potential to be confusing to students should be put in writing to help ensure it is complete, accurate, and clear. Also include planning for other visual supports that can add interest and help clarify information. Critical teaching skills such as active participation strategies and checks for understanding are also very important parts of the explanation section, and should be planned carefully. (See Chapters 3–7 for additional information on these topics.)

The content analysis play a very important role in the instruction that occurs during the body of a direct instruction lesson. For instance, a teacher directly shows and explains a task analysis to the students. The same is true of a concept analysis or a principle statement. This is also the time and place when the teacher introduces and teaches key terms if they were not taught in the opening. A well-planned content analysis helps the lesson body take shape.

Remember that it is not appropriate to ask students to provide the initial explanations of the new information, because it is very important that initial explanations are accurate and clear. You can involve students by asking them to review prerequisite knowledge or skills before you provide the explanation. They could also be asked for their ideas and examples after the necessary information has been presented.

Carefully plan how you will check for understanding of the information. Incorporate opportunities for student processing after each step or part of the information, followed by checks for understanding. Remember that calling on one student to paraphrase or give an additional example will not reveal whether all of the students understand. Include strategies that will allow you to check for understanding of *all* students. You might ask the class to identify correct examples by signaling with thumbs up or to write an example on their whiteboards and hold it up for you to see. (See Chapter 7 for more information on how to check for understanding.)

Demonstration

Before, during, or after the explanation, teachers need to demonstrate—show or model—the new knowledge or skill. Demonstrating can mean showing a *product* (for example, "Here is a paragraph that includes a topic sentence and supporting details") or modeling a *process* ("Watch as I make this foul shot," or "Listen as I think out loud while developing my topic sentence"). (See Chapter 5 for more information on demonstrations.) Using a skit or role-play can also effectively demonstrate a new skill. In most cases, the "doing" portion of a demonstration is accompanied by the teacher thinking aloud so students can hear what he is thinking. Use additional visual supports during the demonstration to emphasize key points (e.g., point to steps on the poster as you think aloud). During the demonstration portion of the lesson body, teachers will probably show examples or demonstrate specific steps, but it is essential that they model the whole product or process as well.

Teachers or other experts, rather than learners, should demonstrate the skill or process to provide a correct model for students to follow. This reduces the chance that students will misunderstand and incorrectly practice the new skill. You can ask students to demonstrate later in the body of the lesson (see the next section on supervised practice for further information).

Note that teachers commonly forget to teach before asking students to practice. It is essential that teachers provide complete explanations, multiple examples, and thorough demonstrations. If you find this unnecessary, you are most likely planning a review or practice activity rather than a direct instruction lesson. Another common error that teachers make out of eagerness to promote active participation and involvement is to ask students to do the initial teaching. If students can do the initial teaching, you should be planning an activity rather than a lesson. You can keep students engaged in many ways without neglecting your responsibility to teach clearly and accurately.

Supervised Practice

The supervised practice portion of the lesson body provides an important link between the lesson body and the components that follow. After explaining and demonstrating the lesson information, provide the students with opportunities to practice the new skill or knowledge. At this stage of the lesson, the students practice *all* of the steps or information that was explained and demonstrated. This practice should be provided under your guidance and supervision. Careful observation of student practice can help you judge whether your students understand the information that you presented. Lead, prompt, and give corrective feedback immediately.

The three levels of supervised practice provide varying amounts of scaffolding. They provide a transition from the teacher's directing the action of the lesson to the student's practicing the new knowledge or skill with monitoring by the teacher. The three levels are as follows:

- *Whole-group Supervised Practice* In this type of practice, the teacher takes the lead but involves the class as she does the procedure or strategy, or applies the principle or concept. ("What do I do next, everyone . . .?"). This is a good place to encourage quick-paced active participation and to gradually withdraw prompts. The class takes more and more responsibility for helping the teacher "do" the skill/knowledge.

- *Small-group or Partner Supervised Practice* Peers provide support for each other in these early attempts at performing the new skill. During small-group or partner practice, the teacher monitors carefully while students practice. Students must be given very clear directions about how they are to divide up the work to ensure that all students have the opportunity to practice.

- *Individual Supervised Practice* The final and *essential* level involves asking each student to practice alone while the teacher monitors and corrects ("Work on the next five sentences, and I'll come around and check your work.").

Some key ideas to remember about supervised practice are: (1) always include individual supervised practice; (2) do not move on to supervised practice if checks for understanding show that students are confused; (3) make sure the practice activities provided for supervised practice are congruent with other parts of your lesson; (4) provide supervised practice after each step or part when the content is complex; and (5) remember that supervised practice is not the formal evaluation. (See Chapter 7 for more information on supervised practice.)

Figure 16-1	Writing a Direct Instruction Lesson

When preparing direct instruction lessons, you will typically include the following content within the different components.

COMPONENT 1: PREPLANNING TASKS

The preplanning tasks section is a cover sheet for the rest of the lesson plan. Include the following:

- *Connection analysis*   Identify the generalization or big idea, the IEP goal, and/or the state standard addressed in the plan.
- *Content analysis*   May include a task analysis, a concept analysis, or a principle statement, key terms and vocabulary, and a list of prerequisite skills or knowledge.
- *Objective*   Examples of objectives for a direct instruction lesson could be for students to demonstrate, list, rewrite, give an example, identify, state reasons, perform, label, use a strategy, or compute.
- *Objective rationale*   To help clarify the value of the objective.
- *Critical management skills*   Include those you will use in the lesson, such as how you'll arrange the room and handle logistics.

COMPONENT 2: LESSON SETUP

The lesson setup is the first component of the lesson plan that is actually presented to students. Include the following critical management skills in the lesson setup:

- *Gaining attention*   Let the students know how you will ask for their attention and how they should respond.
- *Communication of behavior expectations*   Plan how you'll show and tell expected behaviors to students

COMPONENT 3: LESSON OPENING

The lesson opening should effectively prepare the students for new learning. Include the following in the lesson opening:

- *Statement of the objective*   Tell students directly what they will be expected to do or know following the lesson. Show students the objective in writing as well.
- *Statement of the objective purpose*   Tell students why the new learning is valuable and useful to them. Give specific examples.
- *Connections*   Relate new learning to prior experience, build background knowledge, and generate interest in the lesson.
- *Active participation strategies*   Involve and focus the students right from the start.
- *Checks for understanding*   Make sure that all of the students understand the objective and purpose of the lesson and have prerequisite skills and knowledge.

(continued on next page)

Figure 16-1	Writing a Direct Instruction Lesson (*continued*)

COMPONENT 4: LESSON BODY

The lesson body looks like a series of repeated steps. First, teachers "show and tell" while checking for understanding; next, conduct supervised practice with feedback; then, provide more "show and tell;" and so on. For less complex lessons, teachers will "show and tell" all steps and then provide supervised practice. Include the following in the lesson body:

- The *explanation* and an accompanying *demonstration*   This teacher "show and tell" is necessary to enable the students to learn the content or perform the skills being taught (or the first step in a sequence). This should include many, varied examples. Don't forget to include *visual supports*.

- *Active participation strategies*   Plan frequent opportunities for student involvement, processing, and rehearsal through oral, written, and signaled responses.

- *Checks for understanding*   These should involve overt responses (that is, they do or say something) from all students so you can determine if students are progressing toward the objective. For example, ask students to identify correct and incorrect examples or produce correct examples.

- *Supervised practice*   You will always include individual supervised practice, but you may choose to first include whole-group, partner, or small-group practice as scaffolding. Remember that this is practice of the whole skill/content and must be congruent with the instruction and evaluation.

- *Universal and selected interventions*   Decide which strategies you will build in or add on to help all students be successful. For example, use an elaborate opening to build background knowledge, individual behavior contracts, large-print worksheet, picture directions, or expanded partner practice.

COMPONENT 5: EXTENDED PRACTICE

Students will need additional practice to develop the fluency necessary for application and generalization of the new skill or knowledge. Seatwork, performance, and homework provide extended practice opportunities, and they should match the individual supervised practice in the body of the lesson. Long-term extended practice is typically provided in the form of activities (see Chapter 15 for more details). Include the following in writing the extended practice:

- List practice opportunities, including in-class activities and assignments as well as homework. Be sure that final practice activities provide students with an opportunity to practice alone. One strategy to consider in this component is differentiation of extended practice opportunities. Some students will need a great deal of extended practice, whereas others will need far less. Emphasize application and generalization.

- A list of lessons and activities, if appropriate, that will build on the objective and additional opportunities for students to generalize, integrate, and extend the information.

COMPONENT 6: LESSON CLOSING

The lesson closing in a direct instruction lesson will occur in one of two places. If extended practice is assigned as in-class work, the teacher may close the lesson after the assignment has been completed. If extended practice is assigned as homework, the lesson closing will occur immediately following the lesson body. Include the following:

- Strategies for closing the lesson, such as (a) a review of key points of the lesson, (b) opportunities for students to show their work, (c) a description of where or when students can use their new skills or

Figure 16-1	*(continued)*

knowledge, and (d) a reference to the lesson opening. Plans that involve students in the closing are especially effective.

COMPONENT 7: EVALUATION

The evaluation component of the direct instruction lesson is planned when the measurable lesson objective is written. Evaluation is designed to determine individual student progress in relation to the lesson objective, which means the student does not receive help from peers or teachers during the evaluation. Careful monitoring of progress during supervised and extended practice activities will help teachers determine when students are ready to be evaluated. When preparing the evaluation, include the following:

- A description of the evaluation. You may want to include a sample in the case of a paper-and-pencil test.

- When and how the evaluation will occur. An example would be to write, "Later in the day, during other activities, I will ask each student to individually and independently draw an example of a right triangle for me. I'll check them off on my class list if they do it correctly."

COMPONENT 8: EDITING TASKS

Remember to use editing tasks to evaluate your plan (see Chapter 20).
1. Write in critical management skills.
2. Double-check for the use of effective universal and selected instructional interventions.
3. Evaluate congruence.

Sample Plans

Look at the framework for diversity responsive teaching (DRT) as you examine the sample plans at the end of this chapter. Ask yourself how the plan incorporates responses to diversity in *what* is taught, *how* it's taught, and the *context* for teaching and learning. We'll give you a start in thinking about how various parts of the plan fit with various components of the framework. We encourage you to look for additional examples of each component and to think about what changes you believe would make this plan even more likely to support all students' success.

Notice that the lesson "How to Summarize a Paragraph" includes *carrier content* about diversity (a story about a friend with a hearing impairment). The lesson plan "How to Write the Components of a Cover Letter" emphasizes *connections* and *importance to students' lives* (getting a summer job). Both of these are responses to diversity when planning *what* to teach.

Both lessons include numerous examples of responding to diversity when planning how to teach. The "How to Summarize a Paragraph" plan includes a variety of strategies in the *opening* (activating background knowledge, stating objective and purpose, and reviewing of prior learning). The plan on "How to Write the Components of a Cover Letter" is a good example of using *universal design for learning* (the teacher explains, shows, and writes the information, and includes response options in the objective).

The lesson "How to Write the Components of a Cover Letter" is an example of a lesson in which the content is personally interesting and relevant to students, which may work to prevent behavior problems. Some *critical management skills* are included in "How to Summarize a Paragraph." All of these are responses to diversity when planning the *context* for teaching and learning.

Note: The sample plans are written in a very detailed form in order that teacher decision-making and planned actions are clear to the reader.

References and Suggested Reading

Arends, R. I. 2009. *Learning to teach.* 8th ed. Boston: McGraw-Hill. (See Chapter 8 in particular.)

Ayers, S. F., L. D. Housner, S. Dietrich, K. Ha Young, M. Pearson, R. Gurvitch, T. Pritchard, and M. Dell'Orso. 2005. An examination of skill learning using direct instruction. *Physical Educator* 62 (3): 136–144.

Borich, G. D. 2007. *Effective teaching methods: Research-based practice.* 6th ed. Columbus, OH: Allyn & Bacon. (See Chapter 7 in particular.)

Carnine, D., J. Silbert, and E. J. Kame'enui. 2004. *Direct instruction reading.* 4th ed. Upper Saddle River, NJ: Merrill.

Coyne, M. D. 2009. Direct instruction of comprehension: Instructional examples from intervention research on listening and reading comprehension. *Reading & Writing Quarterly* 25 (2/3): 221–245.

Eggen, P. D., and D. P. Kauchak. 2006. *Strategies and models for teachers: Teaching content and thinking skills.* 5th ed. Boston: Pearson. (See Chapter 9 in particular.)

Engelmann, S., and E. Bruner. 1995. *Reading mastery 1/11 fast cycle.* Columbus, OH: Macmillan/McGraw-Hill.

Flores, M. M. 2007. The effects of a direct instruction program on the fraction performance of middle school students at-risk for failure in mathematics. *Journal of Instructional Psychology* 34 (2): 84–94.

Guthrie, J. T. 2009. Impacts of comprehensive reading instruction on diverse outcomes of low- and high-achieving readers. *Journal of Learning Disabilities* 42 (3): 195–214.

Joyce, B., M. Weil, and E. Calhoun. 2009. *Models of teaching.* 8th ed. Boston: Pearson. (See Chapter 17 in particular.)

Kamps, D., M. Abbott, C. Greenwood, H. Wills, M. Veerkamp, and J. Kaufman. 2008. Effects of small-group reading instruction and curriculum differences for students most at risk in kindergarten. *Journal of Learning Disabilities* 41 (2): 101–114.

Lasley, T. J., T. J. Matczynski, and J. B. Rowley. 2002. *Instructional models: Strategies for teaching in a diverse society.* 2nd ed. Belmont, CA: Wadsworth/Thomson Learning.

Magliaro, S. G., B. B. Lockee, and J. K. Burton. 2005. Direct instruction revisited: A key model for instructional technology. *Educational Technology Research & Development* 53 (4): 41–55.

Niesyn, M. E. 2009. Strategies for success: Evidence-based instructional practices for students with emotional and behavioral disorders. *Preventing School Failure* 53 (4): 227–233.

O'Brien, J. 2000. Enabling all students to learn in the laboratory of democracy. *Intervention in School and Clinic* 35 (4): 195–205.

Parette, H. 2009. Teaching word recognition to young children who are at risk using Microsoft PowerPoint coupled with direct instruction. *Early Childhood Education Journal* 36 (5): 393–401.

Rosenberg, M. S., L. O'Shea, and D. J. O'Shea. 2006. *Student teacher to master teacher: A practical guide for educating students with special needs.* 4th ed. Columbus, OH: Merrill/Prentice Hall. (See Chapter 6 in particular.)

Rockwell, S. 2008. Working smarter, not harder: Reading the tough to teach. *Kappa Delta Pi Record* 44 (3): 108–113.

Rupley, W. H. 2009. Effective reading instruction for struggling readers: The role of direct/explicit teaching. *Reading and Writing Quarterly* 25 (2/3): 125–138.

Smith, P. L., and T. J. Ragan. 2004. *Instructional design.* 2nd ed. Columbus, OH: Merrill/Prentice Hall.

Taylor, D. B. 2009. Using explicit instruction to promote vocabulary learning for struggling readers. *Reading & Writing Quarterly* 25 (2/3): 205–220.

Timperley, H. S., and J. M. Parr. 2009. What is this lesson about? Instructional processes and student understanding in writing classrooms. *Curriculum Journal* 20 (1): 43–60.

Witzel, B. S., C. D. Mercer, and M. D. Miller. 2003. Teaching algebra to students with learning disabilities: An investigation of an explicit instruction model. *Learning Disabilities Research & Practice* 18 (2): 121–131.

SUMMARIZING WHAT YOU READ

This is a direct instruction lesson for a small reading group.

Component 1. Preplanning Tasks

A. *Connection analysis: State Reading Standard #2*: The student understands the meaning of what is read. *Component 2.1*: comprehend important ideas and details. *Benchmark 1:* demonstrate comprehension of the main idea and supporting details; students summarize ideas in their own words.

B. *Content analysis*

1. *How to summarize a paragraph* (task analysis)
   a. Read the passage.
   b. Tell the "who" or "what."
   c. Tell fact(s) about the who or what.
   d. Tip: Say the summary in as few words as possible.

2. *Prerequisite skills*: writing complete sentences

3. *Key terms or vocabulary: summarize* – to tell about something in a few words.

C. *Objective*: Given a task analysis of how to summarize a paragraph, and two paragraphs of grade-level reading material, students will summarize each paragraph (say the who/what and fact(s) about the who/what) in no more than one or two sentences).

D. *Objective rationale*: Summarizing helps comprehension, and puts material read into manageable form for communicating with others.

E. *Materials: three transparencies* (one for reviewing terms, two that include the task analysis at the top and reading passages on the bottom) and matching handouts; an *evaluation handout* for each student

F. *Room arrangement*: desks in groups of four; make sure all can see the board and screen

Component 2. Lesson Setup

A. *Gain attention*: Play music (tape recorder). "When you hear the music, stop and listen."

B. *Behavior expectations*: eyes on me; participate (point to T-chart: "What does participating look like and sound like?")

Component 3. Lesson Opening

A. *Activate background knowledge*: "Has anyone ever told you about a TV show or a movie they saw? What did they say? Did they tell you every single word that was said and everything that happened? Or, did they tell what happened in a few words?"

> *AP* = tell a partner; then I call on individuals

B. *Statement of objective*: "To tell about something in a few words is easier than saying every single word. Today, you will learn how to summarize or say what you read in a few words."

C. *Pre-teach vocabulary*:

1. *Define summarize*: Point to and read definition of *summarize* on board – to tell about something in a few words. "What is summarize, everyone?"

> *AP* = unison response

(continued on next page)

2. *Examples*: "I could summarize (or tell about in a few words) the story we read last week by saying it was about a girl who sailed around the world, found a monkey and brought it home. While she was sailing around the world, she experienced stormy seas and had an encounter with pirates, but she arrived home safely."

   CFU (check for understanding) = "What's the word that means *tell about in a few words* . . . everyone?"

D. *Restatement of objective; objective purpose*:

1. "Today, you will learn how to summarize paragraphs, rather than whole stories. This means that you will tell about what you read in a paragraph in just a few words."

2. "Summarizing can help you better understand what you read. It also makes it easier to share what you read with others (in a book report, for example)."

Component 4. Lesson Body

A. *Explanation*

- *Show transparency #1 (task analysis and paragraphs).* Say: "Here are the steps to use when you want to summarize a paragraph." (Pass out matching handout to students.)

- Read each step, then ask students to repeat, e.g., "What's step 1, everyone?"

- Say: "Now I'll tell you about each of the steps and show you how they work."

AP = unison response

Note: Explain that some of the paragraphs used in the body of the lesson are about a boy who has a friend who is deaf.

1. *Step 1 – Read the passage.*
   a. *Say:* "When we read a paragraph, we tell ourselves to listen for important information. You will learn to listen for the who/what is talked about in the paragraph and what happened, because that is what you say in a summary. More on that later."
   b. *Do:* Read the paragraph (so the rest of the explanations will make more sense)

2. *Step 2 – Tell the who or what.*
   a. *Say:* The who or what is the person, place, or thing the paragraph is about. For example, in the first paragraph, "Darin" is the who rather than "lips" or "phone" because the paragraph is about Darin. "Lips" and "phone" are details; the paragraph is not about those things. (remind about nouns/pronouns).
   b. *Do:* Point to where the name Darin is circled (the 'who' in paragraph 1). Show more examples of paragraphs where the who or what of the paragraph is circled and explain each example.
   CFU = *Part 1* – Show new paragraph with examples (nouns) and nonexamples (e.g., verbs) circled. Ask questions such as "Is this the who or what that the paragraph is about?" Students use yes/no response cards to respond. *Part 2* – Point to the next paragraph where the who/what is not circled. Say: "Circle the who/what in this paragraph." (Monitor each student's response.)

3. *Step 3 – Tell fact(s) about the who or what.*
   a. *Say:* Could be about what happened, what will happen, or an interesting fact.
   b. *Do:* Point out the facts (circled) about Darin (understands what others say by reading lips, has a phone that flashes when it rings). Show more examples of paragraphs where facts about the who or what are circled and explain each example.

CFU = *Part 1* – Show new paragraph with underlined examples and nonexamples of facts about the "who" or "what." Ask questions such as, "Is this a fact about the 'who' or 'what'?" Students use yes/no response cards to respond. *Part 2* – Point to the next paragraph where the who/what facts are not underlined. Have students underline them. (I check.)

4. *Tip: Say the summary in as few words as possible.*
   a. *Say*: "Rather than restating everything just as it was stated in the paragraph, summarizing means to say the who and what and facts in as few words as possible using any words you choose.
   b. *Do*: Show prepared examples/nonexamples. Explain that the paragraph that tells what was purchased at the grocery store for the class party could be shortened to something like "Jerell and Michelle brought everything that was needed for the party" rather than "Jerell and Michelle went to the store to buy what they needed for the party. They purchased chips and dip, a vegetable tray, six . . ." and so on. I said the summary of the paragraph in a few words. I didn't tell every detail. Explain each example and non-example in a similar fashion.
   CFU = Show a nonexample. Have students rewrite it in a few words. Check each student's work.

Note: Repeat explanation of steps with additional paragraphs if CFUs indicate more instruction is needed.

B. *Demonstration*

1. *Do a think-aloud* of the task analysis (using another paragraph about Darin): "First, I read the passage ready to find who/what and important facts. (Begin reading.) Let's see, is Darin's teacher the 'who'? Yes, he is, because the rest of the paragraph is about him. Now I need to look for facts about Darin's teacher . . . Next, I figure out how to put Darin's teacher and the facts about him together in a few of my own words . . . Let's see, I could say . . ."

2. *End with*, "My summary is: Darin's teacher helps by teaching sign language and how to read lips. He also gives him special equipment like a telephone that flashes so Darin knows when it is ringing."

3. *Repeat the think-aloud* with next paragraph.
   CFU = Say: "Signal with your fingers the number of the step I'm on."

C. *Supervised Practice*
Partner Supervised Practice

1. Pass out new handout. (task analysis and paragraphs)

2. Give oral and written directions on how to share work with partner and on behavior expectations:

"Work with your partner on the next four paragraphs."
   a. "The first person reads and summarizes, while the second person checks. Switch after each paragraph."
   b. "What does the first person do? And then . . .?"
   CFU = "Raise your hand if you agree that the first person should both read and summarize . . . If the second person should give suggestions . . ."
   c. Remind students of the rule about disagreeing politely (behavior expectations).

(*continued on next page*)

3. I monitor and give feedback on summaries and acknowledge polite disagreeing when I hear it.

Individual Supervised Practice

4. "Summarize the next two paragraphs by yourselves. Think how you will use only a few words to summarize. I'll ask each of you to say one of your summaries to me."

5. Monitor and give feedback. Make sure I hear each student summarize at least one paragraph.

Component 5. Lesson Closing

A. Signal for attention with bell.

B. Review: "If your family asks you what you learned today, what will you say . . . everyone?

AP = choral respond

If they ask you why summarizing is important, what will you say? Think about it. . . ."

C. Review steps. "Close your eyes and picture the list of steps." Open your eyes and read them to your partner. (**AP**)

AP = tell your partner

Component 6. Extended Practice

A. Form cooperative learning groups for literature circles.

1. Each member has three paragraphs of written material that come from their chapter books.

2. Members will orally summarize paragraphs to the group.

3. I monitor and provide feedback.

Component 7. Evaluation

Throughout the day, I'll have individual students summarize two paragraphs of appropriate grade-level reading material to me. The paragraphs are about Curtis Pride and Marlee Matlin. This fits in with our unit on famous people with disabilities. I will check students off if they can do it without prompting.

HOW TO WRITE A COVER LETTER

This is a direct instruction lesson for secondary students.

Component 1. Preplanning Tasks

A. *Connection analysis: State Standard, Writing 2.2:* Write for a broad range of purposes including to apply for jobs.

B. *Content analysis*

    1. *Task analysis:* how to write the components of a cover letter
      A. Write the addresses.
      B. Write the opening paragraph.
      C. Write the body.
      D. Write the closing paragraph.

    2. *Prerequisite skills:* writing paragraphs and letters; prior practice with writing about their education and accomplishments; how to write a business letter

    3. *Key terms/vocabulary: cover letter* – a letter that accompanies a résumé; *qualification* – a quality, ability, or accomplishment that makes a person suitable for a particular position

C. *Objective:* Given a personal fact sheet, a job description, and a letter template, students will write or dictate a cover letter that includes two addresses, an opening, a body with at least one paragraph (education, skills, qualifications), and a closing, and provides a convincing argument for being hired.

D. *Objective rationale:* This lesson will help students learn the basics of writing cover letters to send along with résumés, which will in turn help them in their search for a summer job.

E. *Materials: transparencies:* (1) graphic organizer of unit, (2) cover letter/purpose of cover letter, (3) components and samples of cover letters, examples and nonexamples of components, (4) blank cover letter template, posters; *student handout packets:* copies of transparencies, templates, job descriptions, and students' fact sheets from last week's lesson.

F. *Reference:* http://www.wikohow.com/Write-a-Cover-Letter

Component 2. Lesson Setup

A. *Gain attention:* Turn on overhead projector. "When I need your attention, I'll raise my arm and say *listen, please.*"

B. *Behavior expectations:* (on poster) Follow along and participate; raise your hand and wait to be called on before speaking; show respect (listen when others speak).

Component 3. Lesson Opening

A. *Review prior learning*

    1. Say, "This lesson is part of the job search unit. We're learning about job searches because many of you will soon be applying for summer jobs."

    2. Show a graphic organizer of the unit (transparency #1) with "writing cover letter" highlighted.

    3. Remind them of last week's lesson on how to write a résumé. Show an example of a résumé.

B. *Statement of objective; objective purpose*

    1. Say, "Today, we will learn how to write a basic cover letter that would be sent along with a résumé."

(continued on next page)

2. Say, "It's important to know how to do this because a well-written cover letter will increase your chance of getting a job.

C. *Review the term cover letter.*

   Define: (Point to word and definition on the job hunt poster.) "A cover letter is sent with a résumé, not instead of. In it, you try to convince the employer to hire you.

   Elaborate: In it, you introduce yourself, summarize your qualifications, and tell why you would like to work for the company/employer.

Component 4. Lesson Body

A. Explanation and demonstration of product

■ *Show transparency #2* with Part 1: Robby's cover letter (applying for a construction job), and Part 2: "Purpose of a Cover Letter."

■ *Pass out note-taking guide* (letter template). Students will take notes as I present information and assign practice. **AP** (active participation) = note-taking

■ *Point to the poster of the task analysis*: "How to Write the Components of a Cover Letter." Quickly read each step with students. (**AP**)

■ *Explain* each step of writing a cover letter and show examples of each step in a real letter:

Step 1 *Write the Addresses*

Explain the following (while pointing out addresses on Robby's letter):
   a. "The addresses go in the same place as in a business letter—you already know how to write business letters (writer's address—city, state, zip—goes in the upper left-hand corner; company/organization address left margin)."
   AP = students write information on note-taking guide (template).

Step 2 *Write the Opening Paragraph*

Explain the following (while finding specifics in paragraph in Robby's letter):
   a. State what you are seeking (your objective), and match it to their needs (as explained in their ad).
   b. Say something positive or flattering about the business.
      CFU (check for understanding) = *Part 1* – Show new paragraphs and ask students to identify correct and incorrect examples of opening paragraphs by signaling. Call on selected non-volunteers to explain why examples are examples and nonexamples are nonexamples. *Part 2* – Rewrite incorrect example as correct.

Step 3 *Write the Body of the Letter*

Explain the following (while examining Robby's letter):
   a. In one or two paragraphs, describe your qualifications (education, skills, and accomplishments).
   b. Emphasize how you can help the organization. Highlight skills you have that match job needs. Use "buzzwords" such as *collaborate* or *team player*.

> *CFU* = same procedure as in Step #2

Step 4   *Write the Closing Paragraph*

Explain the following (looking at Robby's letter):

    a. State a plan of action (such as they call you or you call them) to arrange a meeting.

    b. Thank them for consideration, note enclosures/attachments, such as a résumé.

> *CFU* = same procedure as in #2

■ See if students can identify all parts of the letter. Have students take out whiteboards. Ask specific questions: Where do you say something flattering about the company? Where do you talk about your accomplishments?"

> *CFU* = write responses and hold up whiteboards

■ Repeat explanation of letter parts with another example if needed (Gail's cover letter).

B. *Demonstration of process*

    1. *Show transparency #4* (blank cover letter template) and posters of a variety of job descriptions and my personal fact sheet. Pass out partially completed template.

    2. *Think aloud each component while filling in template*, using my fact sheet and job description ("Now I write the opening. I need to state the job I'm interested in. . . .")

        AP = Ask class to *call out* what to write next (based on poster of components). They will also copy what I *write* on their partially completed template.

    3. *Ask specific questions about parts of the letter* ("What did I put in my opening?" "Why did I include that?").

        AP & CFU = think–pair–share and then call on selected non-volunteers.

C. *Individual supervised practice*

    1. Hand out the personal fact sheet of an imaginary person.

    2. Pass out a job description (superhero, rock star).

    3. Have students write a cover letter using a template.

    4. I monitor and give feedback to each student.

Component 5. Extended Practice

A. Have students select sample cover letters from my file and label the components.

B. Have students find a sample job description in my file and write a cover letter. (They may use their personal fact sheet and a letter template.)

Component 6. Lesson Closing

A. *Group review of practice*: Have students share successes and trouble spots of writing cover letters. (**AP**)

B. *Preview tomorrow's evaluation*: "Tomorrow, we will write our own, personal cover letters using our own information and a real job description. Please bring in a job description from the newspaper that sounds interesting to you." (Point to assignment written on board and have students enter it on their assignment calendar.)

Component 7. Evaluation

Once the extended practice activities are finished and I have given feedback, students will independently write their own personal cover letter. They will use their personal fact sheet, a job description, and a letter template (as described in the objective).

Informal Presentation

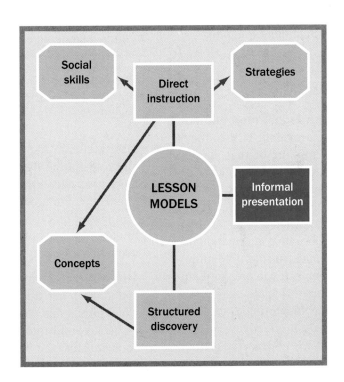

Introduction

The purpose of the informal presentation model is to deliver information to students in a clear and concise manner. Arends (2009) suggests that this teacher-directed model is the most popular one used in schools today. He also suggests that its popularity is no surprise, because it provides a very effective way to help students acquire the array of information they are expected to learn. The main idea of this model is that the teacher first tells the students what they are going to be told, then tells them, and finally tells them what they were told (Moore 2008). Careful planning can make these lessons effective in all subject areas with either large groups or small groups of students who are of varying ages and abilities (Arends 2009).

An effective informal presentation lesson is designed to lead students to a specific objective. The lesson content is delivered in a clear, interesting manner, and the main ideas of the lesson are emphasized through the use of an advance organizer

(Ausubel 1960), graphic organizers, visual supports, and so on. With this model, students are kept actively involved in the lesson and in rehearsing the new information in a variety of ways, such as asking and answering questions, summarizing concepts, discussing key ideas with a partner, or constructing examples. At the end of this type of lesson, students will be able to explain, compare and contrast, define, describe, or apply the new information.

This lesson model provides several advantages. For one, this type of lesson significantly benefits students who have reading or reading comprehension problems, as it can serve as an accommodation for them. They are able to gain necessary information without having to rely solely on written material. This model is also very time-efficient. Instructors can teach large groups as well as small groups of students the same information at the same time.

Uses of Informal Presentation

Teachers generally use the informal presentation model to teach declarative information. That is, they teach knowledge about something or that something is the case, rather than how to do something (Arends 2009; Smith and Ragan 2005). Factual information, principles, and concepts are examples of various types of declarative knowledge.

Teachers can organize declarative information in different ways, depending on the type of information that is to be taught. For example, if you are going to teach a principle, plan a clear principle statement in advance, along with many supporting examples, so that you can communicate it effectively to the students during the lesson. Key ideas regarding factual information are best organized as a subject matter outline for use in an informal presentation lesson. This framework provides the teacher with a mechanism by which to evaluate what information to include and it can help teachers ensure that the content they will present is related and relevant. These methods of organizing content can help the teacher prepare complete explanations to use during the lesson body.

The informal presentation model is appropriately used to present a wide range of topics. In the box that follows, you will find some examples of specific content topics to be used, organized into two of the categories of declarative knowledge.

TOPICS THAT COULD BE TAUGHT USING THE INFORMAL PRESENTATION MODEL

Factual information examples include:

- history of the stock market
- community helpers
- differences between poetry and prose
- the story of Anne Frank
- characteristics of mammals

Principles include ideas such as:

- When the economy is sluggish, interest rates generally go down.
- Drinking alcohol can cause alcoholism.
- Birds migrate when the weather changes.

The following examples illustrate the variety of purposes the informal presentation model can address:

- Mrs. McBride includes content about sexually transmitted diseases (STDs) in a unit she teaches as part of her health class curriculum. She begins the unit with an informal presentation lesson on types of STDs and criteria used to classify them. In this case, Mrs. McBride is using this lesson to *present new information.*

- Mrs. Miller uses an informal presentation lesson to teach her students about various types of cloud formations. This information is to be used as background information for a series of lessons on causes of weather. Mrs. Miller is using an informal presentation lesson to *teach background information* for future lessons.

- Mr. Davis follows a student reading assignment about the causes of the Civil War with an informal presentation lesson. The purpose of the lesson is to *help clarify previously studied information.* He clarifies the information his students gained from the reading assignment.

- Mr. Chin prepares an informal presentation lesson to *conclude a series of lessons* on the civil rights movement. He plans to summarize a number of key points and generalizations for which his students will be held responsible.

- Mrs. Brown uses an informal presentation lesson about volcanoes—complete with a working model—as an introductory lesson to a unit on landforms. The purpose of the lesson is to teach specific content and to *help create interest* in the upcoming unit.

- Ms. Bishop teaches informal presentation lessons on several aspects of computer technology. This content changes far more rapidly than student textbooks are replaced, so the information in her textbooks is often outdated. Ms. Bishop reads extensively to stay current in her field, but the written material she reads is not appropriate for her students. In this case, Ms. Bishop uses informal presentation lessons to *present information not readily available in other sources*, such as textbooks.

Key Planning Considerations

Informal presentation lessons are not difficult to plan if the teacher begins with a thorough understanding of the content to present. When planning the lesson, give special consideration to the following elements.

Content Analysis

The content analysis for an informal presentation lesson will often include a subject matter outline. Whenever the goal is to teach *about* something (rather than to teach *how to* do something) and to teach factual information, a subject matter outline can be an effective way to organize the information to be presented. A well-planned subject matter outline will be used in the lesson body to guide the organization and sequence used to present information.

Careful preparation of the subject-matter outline can be of great benefit. First, it can help ensure that you select content that directly relates to the objective to be accomplished. It can also help ensure that the content is closely related to the big ideas and generalizations that are specific to the content area being studied. It can also help prevent errors in accuracy and ensure that the information to be presented is clear. Finally, the outline simplifies lesson-body planning because it is used to guide the actual presentation that the teacher makes to the students.

Various active participation strategies, visual supports, and presentation techniques will become the main focus of the lesson-body planning rather than organization of the content.

A carefully written subject-matter outline, to be used as a guide for presenting the information, can be an excellent resource for your students as well. You may choose to show the outline to the students during the presentation, or you may give them a copy, or partial copy, to use as a note-taking guide. Another option would be to give them the outline to use as a study guide. They can add more information to it from readings, interviews, videos, Internet sites, or other sources.

There is no set rule about the amount of detail to include in the outline. Provide enough detail to ensure a clear presentation, but not so much detail that the presentation loses focus. Strive to prepare an outline that is detailed, yet brief. Single words and short phrases should serve as cues for information that has been committed to memory. These are preferred to lengthy sentences or narrative (Esler and Sciortino 1991). The outline, which should not be read, should serve as a reminder of what will be said.

When you are going to teach a principle, include a principle statement in the content analysis. Remember that principles are relational rules that prescribe the relationship between two or more concepts. When teaching principles using the informal presentation model, a principle statement serves as the organizer for the presentation itself. It will be explained to the students in detail and shown in writing.

Be sure that you plan in advance how to explain the principle to your students. Begin by writing out the complete principle statement, including the condition and the result or the action that needs to be taken. It can be difficult to correctly or accurately explain the principle spontaneously during the lesson or activity. Next, carefully consider which words are best used as part of your explanation. Finally, be sure that you plan many, varied examples to illustrate the principle. It is important that your students can *apply* the principle to unknown examples (Smith and Ragan 2005).

Content Knowledge

All teachers find themselves in the position of needing to teach lessons on topics they have never taught before. When this happens to you, be prepared to spend some time learning the content before you begin planning how you will teach it. It is difficult, if not impossible, to prepare a complete, accurate presentation outline for use in the lesson if you do not fully understand the subject matter. Your study of the content will help you in choosing interesting and meaningful examples, making relevant comparisons, and connecting information to real-life applications. When using the informal presentation model, thorough content knowledge is absolutely essential. The time you spend learning will be time well-spent, as it will likely result in increased student learning.

Using this model also makes it important to understand how the content fits into the knowledge structure of the discipline from which it comes, because all disciplines have key concepts, generalizations, or "big ideas" that define them as distinct from other disciplines. These concepts form a knowledge structure—perhaps best conceptualized as one enormous subject-matter outline—that provides an organized way to think about and study the information within the discipline, such as categorizing it and showing relationships among categories (Arends 2009). When teaching content from a particular discipline, students learn best if they can see how it fits into the big picture.

Advance Organizer

Use advance organizers to orient students to a new learning task—to focus attention and organize student thinking (Schmidt and Harriman 1998; Arends 2009). The organizer can be a picture, diagram, or statement the teacher makes. For example, use oral introductions to a lesson, written questions presented at the beginning of a chapter in a text, study guides, or graphic organizers as advance organizers (Schmidt and Harriman 1998). Use various visual supports as needed, such as photographs, to help further clarify, explain, or demonstrate the content of the advance organizer.

Advance organizers play an important role in providing students with cognitive scaffolding. First, they help students see how the content they will learn fits into the big picture. Explanations about how the content is organized and how it will be presented further assist students to understand. The preview that the advance organizer provides is a valuable aid to comprehension.

The advance organizer may be seen as the equivalent of the chapter introduction in a textbook. It is generally more abstract than the content of the current lesson (it contains an overriding organizational idea into which the information to come will fit). An example of a verbal advance organizer is, "There are many types of families, but they all have in common the caring for and support of individual members." Designing the organizer can help you plan a presentation that is aligned with this important big idea.

The advance organizer will generally be presented in the lesson opening. The teacher may begin by using one strategy to address prior knowledge, such as a review of previous related lessons, followed by the presentation of an advance organizer. This way, the information to come is linked to prior knowledge. An advance organizer may help students use their prior knowledge, but it should also be designed to relate directly to the information that follows it.

The following are examples of advance organizers:

- Mrs. Thompson explains to her students that opera themes reflect the composer's interpretation of the social climate of the time.

- Mrs. Garcia opens her presentation on the westward movement by stating, "Human migration follows new economic opportunities and/or political upheavals."

- Mr. Jacoby explains the commonalities among sonatas prior to playing recordings by various composers.

- Ms. Tatupu shows a diagram of drugs classified into six types—stimulants, depressants, hallucinogens, inhalants, narcotics, and *Cannabis* products—before providing information about specific drugs.

Checks for Understanding and Active Participation

You need to actively engage students during informal presentations as they should not be passive listeners. Also, carefully monitor their understanding as you present. A variety of techniques can be used to check for understanding when using this model of instruction. These checks should occur throughout the presentation and just prior to moving to extended practice or other activities. Many active participation strategies are appropriate for this purpose. For example, you could ask students to use response cards to signal agreement or disagreement. The important thing to remember is to make sure that students do not leave the presentation with misinformation or misunderstandings.

Information Delivery

Clarity of presentation is a must in this model (See Chapter 5 for many ideas for making your presentations clear.) Also, consider that since the teacher is front-and-center in this model, it is important to make your presentation as interesting and engaging as possible. Here are a few suggestions:

- Plan voice variations, humor, interesting examples and analogies, summaries, and so on to make the presentation smooth and interesting.

- Use cues in the delivery to help students identify key ideas or important points ("Write down this definition in your notes," or "The first three . . . are . . .").

- Stop at certain points during the presentation and give students an opportunity to review their notes and ask questions

- Repeat key points.

- Involve students in repeating key points. For example, use call and response ("One type of drug is a stimulant. What's one type of drug, everyone?")

- Use visual supports to help clarify information (video clips, CD segments, slides, posters, charts, and so on).

The delivery of this lesson is unique because the teacher is "onstage." A good way to prepare for this type of lesson is to practice the delivery before presenting it to the students. You could practice in front of a mirror or teach the lesson to the empty classroom after school. Strive for movement around the room, as well as varied voice inflections, facial expressions, and gestures (R. Keiper, pers. comm., October 2001).

The length of the presentation will depend on the students. Two factors to consider are age and attention span. In a primary classroom, the limit for this type of lesson may be 5 minutes, whereas the teacher's presentation may last 15 minutes in a high-school classroom (Ornstein and Lasley 2004).

Extended Practice

The informal presentation lesson is always followed by extended practice opportunities. The information presented in the lesson body is explored, applied, emphasized, and enriched in the extended practice component of this lesson. Students may study or practice the information in more depth, or they may have an opportunity to synthesize various skills with the knowledge learned in the current lesson. During this portion of the lesson, check individual student progress and decide when the students are ready for evaluation. Carefully select, plan, and monitor extended practice activities. Here are some examples of extended practice tasks:

- Mrs. Wood delivers a presentation on genetic engineering that is followed by small-group discussions of ethical considerations.

- Mrs. Dougan first presents basic information about different types of families around the world. Students then complete various "center" activities where they read, write, draw, and interview peers about their families.

- Mrs. Ross presents information about cell division. Students then go to their lab stations to perform experiments.

- Mr. Nielsen teaches an informal presentation lesson about parts of a research paper. Students then go to the library to begin collecting resources for their own papers.

- Cooperative groups brainstorm scenarios about emergencies prior to Mrs. William's presentation on using 9-1-1.

| **Figure 17-1** | Writing an Informal Presentation Lesson |

The following list describes what is typically included in each component in an informal presentation lesson plan.

COMPONENT 1: PREPLANNING TASKS

The preplanning tasks section is a cover sheet for the rest of the lesson plan. Include the following in this section:

- *Connection analysis*   Identify the generalization or big idea, the IEP goal, and the state standard addressed in the plan.
- *Content analysis*   Include a *subject-matter outline* (which will become the presentation outline) or principle statement, key terms and vocabulary, and necessary prerequisite skills or knowledge.
- *Objective*   In addition to the content objective, a learning strategy objective may be included (such as taking notes from a lecture).
- *Objective rationale*   To help students know why the lesson is valuable.
- *Critical management skills*   Include those you will use in the lesson, such as how you'll arrange the room and handle logistics.

COMPONENT 2: LESSON SETUP

The lesson setup is the first component of the lesson plan that is actually presented to students. Include the following critical management skills in the lesson setup:

- *Gaining attention*   Let the students know how you will ask for their attention and how they should respond.
- *Communicating behavior expectations*   Plan how you'll show and tell expected behaviors to students

COMPONENT 3: LESSON OPENING

A lesson opening should be planned carefully so it will effectively prepare the students for the new learning. An advance organizer is an integral part of the lesson opening in this model. Include the following in preparing a lesson opening:

- *Statement of the objective*   Tell students directly what they will be expected to do or know following the lesson. Show students the objective in writing as well.
- *Statement of the objective purpose*   Tell students why the new learning is valuable and useful to them. Give specific examples.
- *Connections*   Relate new learning to prior experience, build background knowledge, and generate interest in the lesson.
- *Active participation strategies*   Involve and focus the students right from the start.
- *Checks for understanding*   Make sure that all of the students understand the objective and purpose of the lesson, and prerequisite knowledge or skills.
- *Advance organizer*   Design the advance organizer and a plan for presenting it.

Figure 17-1	*(continued)*

COMPONENT 4: LESSON BODY

The lesson body is often a detailed subject-matter outline prepared as a preplanning task, but it could also be organized around a principle statement. Include the following when preparing the lesson body:

- *Subject matter outline*   or other content analysis (such as a principle statement).
- *Interest-builders*   Plan voice variations, humor, interesting examples and analogies, summaries, and so on to make the presentation smooth and interesting.
- *Active participation strategies*   Plan frequent opportunities for student involvement, processing, and rehearsal through oral, written, and signaled responses. Opportunities to discuss content with peers are often useful.
- *Checks for understanding*   Plan relevant and stimulating questions in advance and response strategies that involve everyone. For example, have students signal true/false when asked content questions.
- *Visual supports*   for use throughout the lesson body. You may provide *graphic organizers* such as study guides or presentation outlines (complete or partial).
- *Universal and selected interventions*   Be sure to include interventions that will help all students. Also consider individual student needs and plan necessary accommodations. For example, provide a note-taker or a completed outline for students who have difficulty taking notes.

COMPONENT 5: EXTENDED PRACTICE

The informal presentation lesson always includes relevant extended practice activities, such as following a presentation with a discussion or writing assignment. All extended-practice opportunities must relate directly to the lesson objective and the information presented in the lesson body. Provide individual practice during this component, because students will be evaluated on their individual performance in relation to the lesson objective. You will need to monitor these assignments or activities carefully so you will know when formal evaluation should occur. Include the following when preparing this component:

- A plan for providing extended practice immediately following the presentation or within a day or two. Some extended practice options include reading related materials, watching a video about the topic presented, gathering additional information by doing library research, conducting experiments in the lab, developing questions from the information presented to be used in a team game, and participating in a debate.

COMPONENT 6: LESSON CLOSING

The lesson closing generally follows the lesson body if the extended practice activity is a homework assignment. The closing could also occur after extended practice if practice opportunities are to be completed in class immediately following the lesson body. The closing would then follow the in-class practice. Include the following when preparing the lesson closing:

- Strategies for closing the lesson, such as (a) a reference to the opening (the advance organizer), (b) a review of the key points of the lesson, (c) a preview of future related learning activities, (d) a description of where or when students should use the new knowledge, (e) one last chance to ask questions, (f) having students compare their notes with a partner.

(continued on next page)

| **Figure 17-1** | Writing an Informal Presentation Lesson (*continued*) |

COMPONENT 7: EVALUATION

Teachers may conduct a lesson evaluation immediately after the presentation. More commonly, teachers evaluate after providing extended practice opportunities. By carefully monitoring practice activities, you will be able to tell when students are ready for the lesson evaluation. The evaluation specified in the lesson objective is used to "test" whether individual students have attained the specific objective. When preparing a plan, include:

- A description of the evaluation. You may want to include a sample in the case of a paper-and-pencil test.
- When and how the evaluation will occur, especially if not immediately following the lesson.

COMPONENT 8: EDITING TASKS

Remember to use editing tasks to evaluate your plan.
1. Write in critical management skills.
2. Double-check for the use of effective universal and selected instructional interventions.
3. Evaluate congruence.

Sample Plans

Look at the framework for diversity responsive teaching (DRT) as you examine the sample plans at the end of this chapter. Ask yourself how the plan incorporates responses to diversity in *what* is taught, *how* it's taught, and the *context* for teaching and learning. We'll give you a start in thinking about how various parts of the plan fit with various components of the framework. We encourage you to look for additional examples of each component and to think about what changes you believe would make this plan even more likely to support all students' success.

Responding to diversity when planning *what* to teach is addressed in both lesson plans. First, the Rosa Parks lesson is *about* diversity. It also addresses *skills for a diverse world* as the theme of social justice emerges. In the "Portion Distortion" lesson, students will explore foods that represent their various cultural backgrounds, an example of *completeness* in *what* is taught.

There are examples of planning for diversity in *how* to teach in both lessons. Take a look at the variety of *visual supports* (real food and containers), and scaffolds (partial and complete note-taking guides) used in the "Portion Distortion" lesson. The "Rosa Parks" lesson includes *multiple objectives* (content knowledge and writing), *activating and building background knowledge* (student experience with protest), and the use of *selected interventions* for Bettie (who is deaf) and Stan (who has writing difficulties).

Look at the behavior expectations in the lesson setup for the "Rosa Parks" lesson. Notice that the teacher has clarified how the rule for polite listening applies in this lesson. This rule allows for diverse *perspectives* in showing respect. Examine the extended practice component of the "Portion Distortion" lesson. Notice the transition from the teacher presentation to the activity stations and the movement between activity stations. Has the teacher planned all critical management skills necessary to prevent behavior problems or wasted time? Would you add anything?

References and Suggested Reading

Arends, R. I. 2009. *Learning to teach.* 8th ed. Boston: McGraw-Hill. (See Chapter 7 in particular.)

Ausubel, D. P. 1960. The use of advance organizers in the learning and retention of meaningful verbal material. *Journal of Educational Psychology* 51: 267–272.

Callahan, J. F., L. H. Clark, and R. D. Kellough. 2002. *Teaching in the middle and secondary schools.* 7th ed. Upper Saddle River, NJ: Merrill. (See Part 11, Module 9 in particular.)

Coyne, M. D., E. J. Kame'enui, and D. W. Carnine. 2007. *Effective teaching strategies that accommodate diverse learners.* 3rd ed. Upper Saddle River, NJ: Merrill/Prentice Hall.

Cruickshank, D. R., D. B. Jenkins, and K. K. Metcalf. 2009. *The Act of Teaching.* 5th ed. Boston: McGraw-Hill. (See Chapter 7 in particular.)

Eggen, P. D., and D. P. Kauchak. 2006. *Strategies and models for teachers: Teaching content and thinking skills.* 5th ed. Boston: Allyn and Bacon. (See Chapter 10 in particular.)

Esler, W. K., and P. Sciortino. 1991. *Methods for teaching: An overview of current practices.* 2nd ed. Raleigh, NC: Contemporary Publishing Company.

Freiberg, J. H., and A. Driscoll. 2005. *Universal teaching strategies.* 4th ed. Boston: Allyn & Bacon. (See Chapter 7 in particular.)

Herrell, A., and M. Jordan. 2004. *Fifty strategies for teaching English-language learners.* 2nd ed. Upper Saddle River, NJ: Prentice-Hall. (See Chapter 2 in particular.)

Jacobsen, D. A., P. Eggen, and D. Kauchak. 2009. *Methods for teaching: Promoting student learning in K–12 classrooms.* Boston: Allyn and Bacon. (See Chapter 8 in particular.)

Johnson, L. S. 2008. Relationship of instructional methods to student engagement in two public high schools. *American Secondary Education* 36 (2): 69–87.

Joyce, B., M. Weil, and E. Calhoun. 2009. *Models of teaching.* 8th ed. Boston: Allyn and Bacon. (See Chapter 11 in particular.)

Kame'emui, E. J., D. W. Carnine, R. C. Dixon, D. C. Simmons, and M. D. Coyne. 2002. *Effective teaching strategies that accommodate diverse learners.* 2nd ed. Columbus, OH: Merrill, an imprint of Prentice Hall.

Moore, K. D. 2008. *Effective instructional strategies: From theory to practice.* 2nd ed. Thousand Oaks, CA: Sage Publications. (See Chapter 7 in particular.)

Ornstein, A. C., and T. J. Lasley. 2004. *Strategies for effective teaching.* Boston: McGraw-Hill. (See Chapter 5 in particular.)

Schmidt, M. W., and N. E. Harriman. 1998. *Teaching strategies for inclusive classrooms: Schools, students, strategies, and success.* San Diego, CA: Harcourt Brace College Publishers.

Smith, P. L., and T. J. Ragan. 2005. *Instructional design.* 3rd ed. Hoboken, NJ: Wiley Jossey-Bass Education. (See Chapter 8 in particular.)

Stringfellow, J. L., and S. P. Miller. 2005. Enhancing student performance in secondary classrooms while providing access to general education curriculum using lecture format. *Teaching Exceptional Children Plus* 1-16.

ROSA PARKS AND THE CIVIL RIGHTS MOVEMENT

This is an informal presentation for a large group of students.

Component 1. Preplanning Tasks

A. *Connection analysis*

 1. Primary state standard: *History*: Identify and analyze major issues, movements, people, and events in U.S. history from 1870 to the present with particular emphasis on growth and conflict (for example, industrialization, the civil rights movement, and the information age).

 2. Additional standards:
    a. *Writing standard*: Produce a legible, professional-looking final product.
    b. *Social studies*: Investigate a topic using electronic technology, library resources, and human resources from the community.

 3. *Big idea*: problem/solution/effect (Kame'enui et al. 2002)

B. *Content analysis*: subject-matter outline

C. *Objective*: In a five-paragraph written report, students will explain three or more facts about Rosa Parks (education, birth date, and so on), the events that led to the Montgomery, Alabama, bus strike, and the results of the boycott. (A prepared rubric given to the students will provide more specific detail; for example, include an introduction, conclusion, and so on in the report.)

  ■ They will work toward this objective for several days (the first few days will involve fact-finding, and the second few days will involve report-writing). The students will also practice word-processing skills and Internet search skills.

D. *Objective rationale*: Knowing about Americans who have had a significant impact on events in the United States contributes to overall general knowledge. It is also important for students to see how activists can inspire change without violence.

E. *Logistics (materials and equipment)*: report rubric, advance organizer, presentation outline, newspaper articles and photographs, note-taking guides, document camera, U.S. map.

Component 2. Lesson Setup

A. *Initial signal for attention*: Turn on overhead projector.

B. *Behavioral expectations*: "Remember our rule about polite listening. Sometimes, being polite means not talking at all while someone is presenting, and sometimes, it means responding. During this lesson, polite listening will include calling out a response if you feel strongly about something you hear."

Component 3. Lesson Opening

A. *Review prior learning*

  ■ America prior to the civil rights movement
  ■ segregation
  ■ treatment of African-American people

B. *Preview*

  ■ begin to study the civil rights movement
  ■ how it began
  ■ why it so important
  ■ start by learning about one individual whose bravery made a big difference for African Americans and for America

C. *Activate background knowledge*

- Have any of you taken a stand for something you believe in, at a cost to yourself? (*call on volunteers*)
- I remember when some students left school to attend an antiwar protest . . . think about that during our lesson today.

D. *Objective and purpose; assignment and grading*

- learn about the Montgomery, Alabama, bus boycott – important event in the civil rights movement
- learn about the remarkable woman who inspired the boycott
- Purpose of the lesson is to teach some of our history of race relations and to learn how one person can make a difference.
- What is the purpose of this lesson? Tell your neighbor (**AP**) and then I'll call on someone.
- You will gather information from variety of resources and write a five-paragraph report about Rosa Parks and the boycott.
- Report will be graded, both on the content of the report and the quality of the product. (*Show transparency of rubric.*)

E. *Show advance organizer*: Many important events played a role in changing the relationships between African American and white citizens of the United States.

Component 4. Lesson Body

- Prepare for the presentation.
  - Pass out two variations of the note-taking guide (one blank with only headings and subheadings, and one completed outline as an accommodation for Stan, who writes very slowly and misses key ideas).
  - Say, "During my presentation, listen for and write down the key ideas and facts that I present. You will add to those ideas later when you do some additional research. For now, the goal is to gather some basic information."

    > *AP* (active participation) = students take notes throughout; pause periodically to let them compare notes

  - Make sure I allow time for Bettie to read the transcriber's notes and see photos.
  - Show the subject matter outline. (*Show photographs and newspaper articles on document camera throughout.*)

THE MONTGOMERY, ALABAMA BUS BOYCOTT

I. Events leading to the Montgomery, Alabama bus boycott

A. *Who and when?* Rosa Parks was riding home from work on December 1, 1955 (show photo #1, on bus).

B. *Where?* Cleveland Avenue bus line in Montgomery, Alabama. (Pull down U.S. map.)

C. *What happened?* Rosa Parks refused to give up her seat in the front row of the "colored section" to a white man who could find no seat in the section reserved for whites.

  1. The event defied local ordinances and Alabama state statutes requiring segregation in transportation.

  2. Parks was arrested, jailed, and eventually convicted of violating segregation laws. She was fined $10, plus $4 in court costs (show photo #2, in court).

(*continued on next page*)

3. The black community in Montgomery was outraged.

Ask, "What happened on the bus? When did it happen? How do you think she felt? Has anything like this happened to you?" and so on.

AP = students turn to partners to discuss answers

CFU (check for understanding) = call on selected non-volunteers

II. The Montgomery Alabama bus boycott

A. Protesters formed the Montgomery Improvement Association (MIA) (show photo #3 of MLK).

1. MIA was formed under the leadership of Dr. Martin Luther King, Jr., a minister who recently moved to the city.

2. MIA urged sympathizers not to ride segregated buses and helped them find other transportation.

B. The boycott (show photo #4 of empty buses and people walking), which lasted 381 days, began as a one-day demonstration on December 5, 1955 (show article #1 about the boycott).

Ask, "What organization was formed by protestors? Who gave leadership to the group? How is this protest similar to and different from protests during the American Revolution?"

AP = turn to partners

CFU = call on selected non-volunteers

C. Result of the boycott

1. In November 1956, a federal court ordered the Montgomery buses to be desegregated (newspaper article #2).

2. On December 20, 1956, federal injunctions served on city and bus officials forced them to comply (article #3).

3. On December 21, 1956, Dr. King and Rev. Glen Smiley, a white minister, shared the front seat of a public bus; the boycott was a success (article #4).

Ask, "What were the results of the boycott? Was it successful? Do protesters use boycotts today?"

Say: "Tomorrow, we'll focus on Rosa Parks. Who was this brave woman? What led her to that day on the bus in Montgomery?"

AP = buzz groups

CFU = call on one member to speak for group

Component 5. Extended Practice

Explain today's activity.

1. With your reading partner, generate a list of questions about Rosa Parks and the boycott about which you would like more information.

2. Look for answers in books and on the Internet.

3. Partner #1 records; Partner #2 is On-Task Supervisor. (Pair Gail with Leon.)

Component 6. Lesson Closing

- *Summarize*: The boycott was the first large-scale, organized protest against segregation that used non-violent tactics. Rosa Parks's personal act of defiance helped start something good.

- *Ask for questions* and ask *for comments* about their experience with acting for social justice.

- *Preview*: "Tomorrow, we will see a video and learn more about Rosa Parks, beginning with her early life."

Component 7. Evaluation

- *Checkpoint #1*: Collect and check their notes for accuracy after the videotape tomorrow.

- *Checkpoint #2*: Collect and grade the five-paragraph report.

- *Checkpoint #3*: Students will be asked about information stated in the objective on the unit test.

Source: Parks, Rosa Louise, Microsoft® Encarta® Online Encyclopedia 2001 (http://encarta.msn.com). © 1997–2001 Microsoft Corporation. (Information contributed by Paul Finkelman, B.A., M.A., Ph.D. Professor of Law, University of Akron School of Law. Author of *Slavery and the Founders: Race and Liberty in the Age of Jefferson*. Coeditor of The Macmillan Encyclopedia of World Slavery.)

Note that excellent examples of documents (such as photographs of newspaper articles written during the boycott) are available at the following site: http://www.archives.state.al.us/teacher/rights/rights1.html.

PORTION DISTORTION: AMERICANS' LOVE AFFAIR WITH FOOD

This is an informal presentation lesson for a large group of students.

Component 1. Preplanning Tasks

A. **Connection analysis**: *State Standard Health & Fitness:* Develop and monitor progress on personal nutrition goals based on national dietary guidelines and individual needs.

B. **Content analysis**

1. Subject-matter outline: Portion Distortion and Standard Serving Size (see lesson body).

2. Prerequisite skills: Understands the terms *USDA Food Pyramid, food product label information,* and *serving size.*

3. Key terms and vocabulary: *portion distortion* – misjudging standard portion size, thinking that USDA recommended portion size is larger than it really is, e.g., thinking that the recommended serving size of rice is 1 cup when it is really ½ cup.

C. **Objective**: On an in-class test, students will list examples of standard serving sizes for five foods, each from a different part of the USDA Food Pyramid, and a common object that approximates the standard serving (for example, three ounces of meat is about the size of a deck of cards).

D. **Objective rationale**: Knowing what standard serving sizes look like can help students better judge the amount of calories they are taking in when eating meals or snacks. This can help with weight management.

E. **Materials**: presentation outlines, transparencies, recording sheets, foods (Remember to include a variety of foods familiar to students. Use their meal journals.)

Component 2. Lesson Setup

A. **Gain attention**: "When I say 'attention please,' stop what you're doing and look at me."

B. **Behavioral expectations**: Participate (answer questions, take notes) and be respectful (eyes on speaker, listening).

Component 3. Lesson Opening

A. **Generate interest**

1. Think about weight control for a minute. Which is more important—to watch what you eat or how much you eat? (Seventy-eight percent of Americans believe that what they eat is more important in managing their weight than the amount of food they eat.)

> *AP* (active participation) = ask for a show of hands

2. Both are important: It is possible to gain weight by eating small portions of foods that are high in calories, and also possible to gain weight by eating large portions of foods that are low in calories. For example, a 1 cup serving of pasta may contain the same calories as 4 cups of green beans.

B. **Objective and purpose**:

1. The purpose of this lesson is to help you make better choices when selecting the amounts of food you eat.

2. Today, you will *learn standard serving sizes and how to determine portion sizes for foods you eat* (point to objective written between goal posts on blackboard) so you can adjust your own eating habits. (Too little food can be just as serious a health problem as too much.)

C. **Advance organizer**: People tend to eat the portions they are given or what is on the plate. This tendency can lead to being overweight or obese, and subsequent health problems. Knowledge of serving size can help prevent these problems.

Component 4. Lesson Body

- Delivery reminders.

    1. Move around the room; make eye contact with *all* students.

    2. Use verbal cues such as "First . . . , next . . ." to help students focus on important points.

    3. Stop after each section for a brief summary.

- Pass out note-taking guides.

    1. Provide Jan with an outline that also includes some detail.

    2. Partner John with Ada for the review of notes.

AP = note-taking

- Show subject matter outline (on transparency).

Portion Distortion: Americans' Love Affair With Food

I. The problem with too much food

A. Problems of obesity

B. Heart disease, stroke

C. Diabetes, increased risk of cancer

II. Statistics

A. 55 percent of Americans are clinically overweight

B. 1 in 4 Americans are obese

III. Factors that contribute to obesity (American Institute for Cancer Research)

A. Eating out (poster of fast-food restaurant logos, such as the golden arches)

B. Concept of *portion distortion*

AP = compare notes

- Pause and have students compare notes with a partner here and periodically throughout the presentation.

- Review key points throughout the presentation by asking specific questions, such as, "What problems are caused by being overweight or obese?"
  CFU (check for understanding) = students write answers on whiteboards, hold up; then call on selected non-volunteers.

IV. The food we eat (portion sizes)

A. Standard serving size (show transparency #2)

    1. The *USDA Food Guide Pyramid* shows:
       a. Approximate number of servings to eat per day
       b. Various categories of food
       c. That number of servings (and therefore calories) varies by body size and level of exercise (key idea)

(*continued on next page*)

2. How to find out the *standard serving size:*
   a. Look at containers (show cans of soup, box of scalloped potatoes)
   b. Estimate with fresh foods and fast foods.

B. *Portion distortion*—the American Dietetic Association (show transparency #3)

1. Definition (people are either unaware of or have a distorted idea of the standard serving size)

2. The American Dietetic Association Survey
   a. People were asked to estimate standard serving sizes of eight different foods, including pasta, green salad, beans, and mashed potatoes.
   b. The results revealed that 1 percent answered all questions correctly, 63 percent missed five or more questions, and 31 percent estimated only *one* serving size correctly.

3. Results of portion distortion (larger and larger portions, with more and more people becoming overweight)

■ Ask, "What are standard serving sizes? What is *portion distortion*? How does portion distortion contribute to weight gain?" **CFU** = write on whiteboards, call on selected non-volunteers.

V. How to avoid portion distortion (transparency #4)

1. Measure foods as possible
   a. Read labels.
   b. Count foods (for example, potato chips) or measure (milk).

2. Estimate portions when measuring is not possible.
   a. Explain portion sizes as compared to common objects (for example, 3 ounces of meat is approximately the same size as a deck of cards or a computer mouse, and a serving of cheese is about the size of an adult thumb).
   b. Demonstrate with *real objects.*

■ Ask, "What are two ways to avoid portion distortion?" **CFU** = write on whiteboards.

Component 5. Extended Practice

■ *In-class activity stations.* There are five stations with different foods at each. (The goal is to have students see that "eyeballing" something is often not accurate. Measuring out and learning which common object represents the serving size is better.)
   A. Distribute recording sheets.
   B. Show PowerPoint slide of directions, then explain and demonstrate them.

How Accurate Is Your Guess?

1. Read the standard serving size.

2. Estimate the amount of food that constitutes a standard size by pouring it into bowl (how much cereal is 1 cup, for example).

3. Measure out the portion accurately.

4. Think of a common object of similar size.

5. Record it on a recording sheet.

6. Group 1 begins at Station 1 and so on. (Show transparency of group membership.)

C. *Explain and demonstrate group roles* (written on board) with a student who rehearsed with me in advance.

   1. Member #1 reads and estimates, Member #2 measures, Member #3 thinks of a common object of similar size, and Member #4 records.

   2. The roles switch at each new station (Member #1 becomes #2 and so on).

      Ask specific questions about directions and group roles.

> *CFU* = students signal with fingers the number of the member who does various tasks

D. Show behavior expectations: follow directions, use quiet voices, help each other.

- *Homework assignment*: Identify 10 of your favorite foods—including fast foods—that cannot be easily measured. Determine portions and come up with common objects about the same size.

Component 6. Lesson Closing

- Explain that portion size in the United States is a cultural phenomenon and is not representative of the world.

- Ask: "Why is it important to be aware of portion distortion?

- Assign homework (see Extended Practice).

> *AP* = turn to a partner

Component 7. Evaluation

On the Nutrition Unit Test to be given next week, students will list examples of standard serving sizes for five foods, each from a different part of the USDA Food Pyramid, and a common object that approximates the standard serving.

Structured Discovery

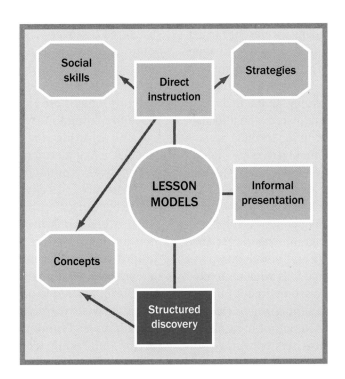

Introduction

The structured discovery model is one in which students "discover" information rather than having a teacher tell it to them. This discovery is planned however; the idea is for students to discover the lesson objective predetermined by the teacher. Students are led to the specific objective in a convergent rather than divergent manner. Structured discovery uses an inductive rather than deductive approach to learning. This model will help round out a repertoire of skills needed to plan lessons.

Structured discovery lessons have a number of similarities to direct instruction lessons. The purpose of both lesson models is for students to reach a specific academic objective. The major difference between them is the route that students take to reach the objective. The lesson body is where the most significant differences between the two models are found. In the structured discovery lesson, the teacher prepares the students for the discovery by presenting examples and perhaps nonexamples for them to explore. In a direct instruction lesson, the teacher is explaining and showing the information that the students need to know to reach the objective. The rest of the lesson body is quite similar in both types of lessons. In structured discovery lessons, the teacher follows the students' discovery by summarizing, reviewing, and providing additional practice with the new learning (supervised practice). These same methods also follow the show and tell component in a direct instruction lesson.

Structured discovery is often confused with the inquiry method or model of instruction. Students "discover" in both models, but the purpose and outcome of the discovery vary significantly. The major goal of structured discovery is for students to learn academic content, whereas the major goal of inquiry is for students to experience and practice the actual process of making a discovery (Arends 2009). For example, students may conduct air pressure experiments in order to discover facts about air pressure. On the other hand, the goal may be for students to practice making accurate scientific observations. In this case, magnetism, or some topic other than air pressure, might have been selected because the topic is solely a vehicle for having students practice observing. In the first example, the teacher would write an objective that focuses on knowledge of air pressure. In the second case, the teacher would write a long-term objective for the skill of making observations. Therefore, inquiry fits our definition of an activity rather than a lesson.

An understanding of the intent of the structured discovery model lays the foundation for using it successfully. The previous paragraphs have described what structured discovery *is* and how it compares to other models. The following tells what structured discovery is *not*. It is *not* a lesson without purpose or focus. It does *not* create a setting where students randomly experiment with materials or information. It also is *not* a time when teachers encourage students to come up with any "creative" idea or conclusion that comes to mind. A teacher would *not* be successful if students had a great deal of fun "discovering," but did not discover the information needed for the next day's lesson. Structured discovery is a model that teachers select when they want to teach content knowledge. The lesson process is an added benefit—a secondary objective—not the major one.

Uses of Structured Discovery

The primary objective in a structured discovery lesson is always an academic one. Teachers may choose to use this model for teaching principles or concepts

---

> ### EXAMPLES OF TOPICS THAT COULD BE TAUGHT USING THE STRUCTURED DISCOVERY MODEL
>
> - definition of a noun
> - rules for punctuation
> - what magnets will pick up
> - when you should call 9-1-1
> - typical locations of cities
> - when to round numbers up or down

in any content area. Some examples are found in the box.

Teachers have several reasons for selecting a structured discovery lesson to teach particular academic content. One reason is increased student motivation. The challenge of "making the discovery" can create an exciting situation for the students and, therefore, may hold their attention more readily. When preparing to teach a topic that students may find uninteresting (for example, a grammar rule), consider using a structured discovery approach. It might provide just the right motivation.

Structured discovery lessons may also be selected because they promote higher-level thinking skills. All students need opportunities to develop their ability to reason and solve problems. Structured discovery lessons are one way to provide this practice. Note that, in addition to the primary short-term academic objective in the lesson plan, you may wish to include a long-term objective that addresses "thinking skills" such as problem-solving, analyzing, asking relevant questions, or drawing conclusions.

A third reason to use a structured discovery lesson is to enhance retention. Students may be more apt to recall what they learned when they have been given the opportunity to figure out something for themselves. The active involvement in the learning can sometime make an impression that will not soon be forgotten.

A structured discovery lesson is a valuable teaching tool, but it is not always appropriate. This type of lesson should obviously never be used when the safety of students is an issue. It would not make sense, for instance, to have students discover how to use a Bunsen burner safely or how to effectively break a fall from a balance beam. Additionally, this type of lesson would not be used when damage to materials or equipment may result. For example, it would be inappropriate for students to discover how to turn off a computer. Issues of safety must always be factored in when selecting topics for structured discovery lessons.

A structured discovery lesson should also not be used when it is likely that students will fail. It would not make much sense, for example, to have students discover how to solve long division problems. It is fairly predictable they would flounder in failure as they repeatedly practiced the wrong way to compute long division problems. It may make sense, however, to have them discover math concepts such as "division." A structured discovery lesson also would not be a good choice when the time involved in making the discovery outweighs the benefit of the discovery itself. It may be possible, for instance, for students to eventually discover how to solve long division problems. However, the time it would take to make such a discovery would most likely decrease the value of making the discovery.

A thorough content analysis can help determine when a structured discovery lesson would be a good choice. Using some good common sense will help here as well.

Key Planning Considerations

Structured discovery lessons require very careful planning to help ensure that students will learn information accurately. These lessons have a good possibility of resulting in student confusion so more planning, rather than less, is the standard. It is especially important to consider the following areas.

Content Analysis

Structured discovery lessons can be used to teach a variety of types of content. Therefore, the content analysis of this lesson will vary. If the objective is for students to discover a concept, write a concept analysis. If students are to discover a principle, include a clearly stated principle statement.

Assessing Prerequisite Skills and Knowledge

Lesson readiness can be determined in two steps. First, it is necessary to analyze the prerequisite skills or knowledge needed to be successful in the current lesson. Secondly, there must be an assessment as to whether the students have the prerequisite skills or knowledge. For example, you plan a structured discovery lesson on adjectives. You know that students must be able to identify nouns to understand adjectives. Therefore, you test your students on noun identification.

Gathering assessment information can be either fairly simple (correcting papers from yesterday's assignment), or more complicated (writing and administering a formal pretest). However, individual student understanding must be assessed regardless.

Writing the Objective

The short-term academic objective written for the structured discovery lesson is no different from an objective written for lessons using other models. The important thing to remember about structured discovery objectives is how they should *not* be written. They should not, for example, say something like, "Students will discover. . ." Objectives for all lessons must state what the students will know or do at the end of the lesson, that is, the outcome. The means to the end is not stated in the objective (see Chapter 2 for more information).

Stating the Objective to Students

Although you will not begin the structured discovery lesson by telling the students the outcome of the learning, because that would spoil the discovery, it is important they understand what they will learn. During the lesson opening, for example, you could tell students they are going to learn about a scientific law or a grammar rule. Save the specifics about the law or rule for later.

Setting Up the Discovery

Teachers usually begin the lesson body component of the structured discovery lesson by presenting examples and nonexamples of the content to be learned. Next, "set up" the discovery by telling students directly what they are to discover (for example, "The underlined words in these sentences are adjectives. Examine the sentences and then see if you can write a definition for adjective.").

Selecting Examples and Nonexamples

Be sure to carefully select examples and nonexamples for these lessons. It is best to start with the clearest, purest examples and nonexamples because of the potential for confusion during the discovery phase. Successive examples can be more abstract or more difficult to discriminate. Present examples and non-examples in the form of individual problems, words or scenarios, pictures, demonstrations, and so on.

Sometimes it is not necessary to include nonexamples. For instance, if you plan a lesson in which students are to discover the relationship between adjectives and nouns, you will not need nonexamples because you are not teaching students to distinguish between an adjective and other parts of speech. A careful content analysis will help you determine whether nonexamples are needed.

Monitoring the Discovery

Once the students have been presented with the necessary examples and nonexamples for making the discovery, their work begins. While students work, the teacher can facilitate the discovery by monitoring carefully and guiding with questions and prompts. It is a good idea to plan in advance how to support the discovery. What will you do, for example, if students seem completely baffled by the initial explanation and examples? Writing down specific questions, statements, or clues will be beneficial, as this will help you prompt students' thinking. You may also want to plan visual cues.

Reviewing the Discovery

One of the tricky parts of a structured discovery lesson is determining whether all of the students have really "discovered." The teacher must take an active role in helping students draw correct conclusions before the end of the discovery part of the lesson. When it appears that the majority of the students have made the desired discovery, the teacher hears from the students about the discovery they made. The teacher can see from this review if the discovery made will help students to be successful in meeting the objective. If not, the teacher will need to correct any misapprehensions. Be sure to use checks for understanding that will allow you to tell if *every* student understands (such as asking students to identify or produce new examples).

Supervised Practice

Next, have students test the discovery. They need to practice the new learning with your guidance. This practice is really a time for students to "test" the accuracy of the discovery they made by trying it out with new examples. It is very important to remember that the part of the lesson where the students "discover" is *not* supervised practice. For example, after the students have discovered principles of air pressure, you would want to provide new problems or demonstrations that would allow them to apply the principles they have learned. This application is the supervised practice portion of the lesson. As students practice, you must monitor to be sure they are using the "discovered" information accurately.

Behavior Expectations

Students often work together with partners or in small groups during the "discovery" portion of the structured discovery lesson. Remember that students may need to be taught or reminded of specific behaviors necessary for working successfully with others. When lessons involve using or sharing materials or equipment, you must address behavioral expectations as well. You may also need to consider students' tolerance for working through feelings of frustration and confusion, as the probability of this happening is greater in this type of lesson.

| Figure 18-1 | Writing a Structured Discovery Lesson |

The following list describes what is typically included in each component in a structured discovery lesson plan.

COMPONENT 1: PREPLANNING TASKS

The preplanning tasks section is a cover sheet for the rest of the lesson plan. Include the following when preparing the preplanning tasks:

- *Connection analysis*   Identify the generalization or big idea, the IEP goal, and the state standard addressed in the plan.
- *Content analysis*   This may be a concept analysis or principle statement, key terms and vocabulary, or necessary prerequisite skills and knowledge.
- *Objective*   Remember that the objective represents the learning outcome, not the learning activities or process. For example, you would not write, "Students will discover. . ." Possible objectives for a structured discovery lesson could be for students to describe, state a principle, identify, define, or give examples.
- *Objective rationale*   To help you clarify the value of the objective.
- *Critical management skills*   Write in those you will use in the lesson, such as how you'll arrange the room and handle logistics.

COMPONENT 2: LESSON SETUP

The lesson setup is the first component of the lesson plan that is actually presented to students. Include the following critical management skills when preparing the lesson setup:

- *Gaining attention*   Let the students know how you will ask for their attention and how they should respond.
- *Communication of behavior expectations*   Plan how you'll show and tell expected behaviors to students.

COMPONENT 3: LESSON OPENING

The lesson opening should effectively prepare the students for the new learning. Include at least the following when writing the lesson opening:

- *Connections*   Relate new learning to prior experience, build background knowledge, and generate interest in the lesson.
- *State the objective*   Tell students, in student-friendly language, what they will learn. Be careful not to give away the discovery, however. Show the objective in writing as well.
- *Objective purpose*   Explain why the new learning is valuable.

COMPONENT 4: LESSON BODY

The lesson body is a detailed, step-by-step description of instruction (that is, what the teacher and the students will be doing). Include the following:

- An explanation of how you will *set up*, *monitor*, and *review* the discovery.
- *Examples and nonexamples*   that will lead students to discover the definition, principle, and so on, that you are teaching. Be sure to repeat, review, and *check for understanding* of the essential learning to ensure that all students have "discovered" the correct information.

(continued on next page)

| **Figure 18-1** | Writing a Structured Discovery Lesson (*continued*) |

- *Supervised practice* with new examples and feedback.
- *Active participation* strategies to keep students engaged.
- Additional *universal interventions* throughout the lesson body, for example, (1) use cues, concrete objects, and leading questions when presenting examples, (2) give explicit directions and demonstrate how students should share tasks in partner or group work, and (3) increase the amount and types of supervised practice.
- *Selected interventions* to meet the needs of some students.

COMPONENT 5: EXTENDED PRACTICE

Extended practice opportunities help students develop levels of accuracy and fluency high enough to ensure they can generalize the skill or knowledge. Some students may need a great deal of extended practice, whereas others may need enrichment activities. Include the following when writing extended practice:

- A plan for providing extended practice immediately following the lesson or soon thereafter.
- A list of lessons or activities that will build on this objective. Any additional opportunities students will have to generalize and extend the information should be included as appropriate.

COMPONENT 6: LESSON CLOSING

The lesson closing may follow the body of the lesson, or it may follow extended practice. Include the following:

- Strategies for closing the lesson, such as (a) a review of key points of the lesson, (b) opportunities for students to draw conclusions, (c) a description of where or when students should use their new skills or knowledge, and (d) a reference to the lesson opening.

COMPONENT 7: EVALUATION

Plan the lesson evaluation when writing the objective so the evaluation matches exactly what is stated in the objective. Remember that evaluation is not necessarily a paper-and-pencil test. Also, remember that its purpose is to determine how individual students are progressing toward the lesson objective, which means the student does not receive help—from peers or the teacher—during the evaluation. Don't forget to test with new examples. Careful monitoring during supervised and extended practice activities will help you decide when evaluation should occur. Include the following:

- A plan for how and when the evaluation will occur
- A description of the evaluation

COMPONENT 8: EDITING TASKS

Remember to use editing tasks to evaluate your plan (see Chapter 20).
1. Write in critical management skills.
2. Double-check for the use of effective universal and selected instructional interventions.
3. Evaluate congruence.

Sample Plans

Look at the framework for diversity responsive teaching (DRT) as you examine the sample plans at the end of this chapter. Ask yourself how the plan incorporates responses to diversity in *what* is taught, *how* it's taught, and the *context* for teaching and learning. We'll give you a start in thinking about how various parts of the plan fit with various components of the framework. We encourage you to look for additional examples of each component and to think about what changes you believe would make this plan even more likely to support all students' success.

The lesson "Punctuating a Series" provides a good opportunity to plan for diversity in *what* is taught. A teacher could easily use information about the local culture or community events as carrier content in the sentences used in this lesson. Can you think of how this could be done with a group of students you know?

The following are examples of planning for diversity in *how* to teach as they appear in both plans. In the "Punctuating a Series" lesson, the teacher has planned numerous *prompts* to support students in making the discovery if they have difficulty. This plan also provides for careful *monitoring* (teacher moves around and listens to students as they work in groups) during their discovery time. The "Magnetic Attraction" lesson shows an example of groups of four students with assigned roles and clearly taught *directions* (written, presented orally, and demonstrated).

The lesson "How to Punctuate A Series" includes a *selected intervention* (behavior contract) for Garth. The teacher uses precorrection, encouragement, and a reminder of the reward he's working toward. Notice the many materials to manage in the "Magnetic Attraction" lesson. What would you do to plan for logistics to prevent behavior problems and wasted time?

References and Suggested Reading

Arends, R. I. 2009. *Learning to teach*. 8th ed. New York: McGraw-Hill. (See Chapter 11 in particular.)

Bilica, K. 2009. Inductive & deductive science thinking: A model for lesson development. *Science Scope* 32 (6): 36–41.

Colburn, A. 2004. Inquiring scientists want to know. *Educational Leadership* 62 (1): 63–66.

Coyne, M. D., E. J. Kame'enui, and D. W. Carnine. 2007. *Effective teaching strategies that accommodate diverse learners*. 3rd ed. Columbus, OH: Merrill.

Cruickshank, D. R., D. B. Jenkins, and K. K. Metcalf. 2009. *The act of teaching*. 5th ed. Boston: McGraw Hill. (See Chapter 8 in particular.)

Guillaume, A. M. 2008. *K–12 classroom teaching: A primer for new professionals*. 3rd ed. Upper Saddle River, NJ: Pearson.

Gunter, M. A., T. H. Estes, and S. L. Mintz. 2007. *Instruction: A models approach*. 5th ed. Boston: Allyn & Bacon/Pearson. (See Chapter 7 in particular.)

Hodge, J. K. 2006. The top ten things I have learned about discovery-based teaching. *Primus* 16 (2): 154–161.

Jacobsen, D. A., P. Eggen, and D. Kauchak. 2009. *Methods for teaching: Promoting student learning in K–12 classrooms*. 7th ed. Boston: Allyn and Bacon/Merrill. (See Chapter 7 in particular.)

Joyce, B., M. Weil, and E. Calhoun. 2009. *Models of teaching*. 7th ed. Boston: Pearson. (See Chapter 3 in particular.)

Kellough, R. D. 2007. *A resource guide for teaching: K–12*. 5th ed. Columbus, OH: Merrill/Prentice Hall.

Orlich, D. C., R. J. Harder, R. C. Callahan, M. S. Trevisan, and A. H. Brown. 2010. *Teaching strategies: A guide to better instruction*. 9th ed. Florence, KY: Wadsworth/Cengage Learning. (See Chapter 9 in particular.)

Pickens, M., and C. J. Eick. 2009. Studying motivational strategies used by two teachers in differently tracked science courses. *Journal of Educational Research* 102 (5): 349–362.

Rosenberg, M. S., L. O'Shea, and D. J. O'Shea. 2006. *Student teacher to master teacher: A practical guide for educating students with special needs*. 4th ed. Columbus, OH: Merrill/Prentice Hall. (See Chapter 6 in particular.)

MAGNETIC ATTRACTION

This is a large- or small-group structured discovery science lesson.

Component 1. Preplanning Tasks

A. *Connection analysis: State Science Standard, Science 2.2*: Think logically, analytically, and creatively.

Benchmark 1: Examine data to verify a conclusion in a simple investigation.

Big idea: the scientific method of forming and testing a hypothesis

B. *Content analysis*

1. *Principle*: Magnets attract objects made of iron or steel.

2. *Prerequisite skill*: how to use a recording sheet.

3. *Key term*: *attract* = pull

C. *Objective*: Students will write, in their own words, the principle that if an object contains steel or iron, it will be attracted by a magnet. (An additional long-term objective is that students will infer a principle from available data.)

D. *Objective rationale*

1. Knowing how magnets work can help students appreciate the various uses of magnets, such as to sort materials (scrap yard), find direction (compass), hold items in place (electric can opener), pick things up (sewing pins).

2. Knowing how to draw conclusions from examining data is a skill that can be applied to many situations. This is an application of the scientific method.

E. *Materials and equipment* (logistics): overhead projector; pins and magnet; 2 transparencies; 5 recording sheets; 20 worksheets; 5 bags of 8 small objects (note that objects have been selected carefully and the only thing the examples have in common is that they are or are not made of steel or iron); 5 magnets; 10 objects (pictured on worksheet); 4 role number cards for each table

F. *Room arrangement*: Students in usual seating (5 table groups of 4 students each)

Component 2. Lesson Setup

A. *Gain attention*: "Let's get started. When I ring the bell, please stop, look, and listen."

B. *Behavior expectations*: "Everyone read the expectations poster together: Sit in seats, eyes on me, listening."

AP = choral reading

Component 3. Lesson Opening

A. *Build and activate background knowledge*

1. Demonstrate magnetic puppets moving on stage.

2. Ask, "How do you think the puppets are moving?" (Puppets have thumbtacks on their feet, and the magnet moving underneath them makes them move).

3. After the answer is discovered, ask, "Have you ever played with a magnet? What were you able to do with it?"

AP = tell a partner

B. *State the objective and purpose*

1. Say, "Today, we are going to discover a rule about which objects magnets can attract (pull). This will help you understand how magnets help us." (Demonstrate key term "attract" by spilling a small box of pins and picking them up with a magnet.)

Component 4. Lesson Body

A. *Set up the discovery*

 1. *Explain and demonstrate* the directions (on transparency #1)

    Discovery goal – discover a rule about which objects magnets attract

    Directions and roles
    a. All draw a role number.
    b. Take objects from bag. (role #4)
    c. Touch the magnet to each object. (role #1)
    d. Sort. Which objects are attracted or pulled by the magnets? Put these in a group. Which objects are not attracted by the magnet? Put these in another group. (role #2)
    e. Record findings on the recording sheet (demonstrate on transparency). (role #3)
    f. All take turns touching objects with magnet to check results.
    g. All discuss results and conclusions and decide on a rule.
    h. Write a rule about what magnets pull. (role #4)

 2. Ask, "What do you do first, everyone . . .? Who records results . . .?" and so on.

> *AP* = unison response

 3. Distribute bags, magnets, and recording sheets (one per group). Point to poster of behavior expectations for group work.

B. Monitor the discovery. Check on each group. If needed, prompt by asking, "What else do they have in common? How are these two different? Are all metals alike?" and so on. Have early finishers write predictions about which other objects magnets would attract or not attract.

C. *Review the discovery.* Ask questions, have table groups discuss (**AP**), then call on non-volunteers from each group.

 1. Ask, "What did you find out about your magnet and objects?"

 2. Ask, "How are the objects in the 'attracted' group alike?" (same color? shape? size? or other characteristic?).

 3. Ask, "What rule did you make about which objects your magnets pulled?"

 4. Write rule on board (if the rule is incorrect, demonstrate by testing it).

 5. "Thumbs up if a magnet would pick up a cotton ball . . . A rubber band . . . A soda can . . . A nail . . ."

> *CFU* (check for understanding) = call on selected non-volunteers to explain responses

D. *Supervised practice (individual)*

 1. Pass out the worksheet.

 2. Explain the directions (shown on transparency #2):
    a. Look at the picture and description of the object.
    b. Write *yes* (would be attracted by magnet) or *no* (would not) next to each.
    c. Write a rationale for each yes/no response (why or why not).

 3. Ask: "What do you do first? Where do you write your rationale?" and so on.

> *CFU* = call on selected non-volunteers

 4. Have students complete worksheets individually. (Point to poster of behavior expectations for individual work.) I monitor, prompt, and provide feedback.

(continued on next page)

5. When finished, collect worksheets.

6. Have students gather around. Using real objects (pictured on the worksheet), select students to test each with a magnet. Ask why they are or are not attracted.

Component 5. Lesson Closing

A. *Review*: "Today, you discovered what magnets attract. What do they attract? What is the rule about what magnets attract?"

B. *Preview*: "Tomorrow, you will learn about the force field surrounding magnets."

> *AP* = tell your neighbor
> *CFU* = call on selected non-volunteers

Component 6. Extended Practice

Explain that they can have more practice in the science center (with new objects).

Component 7. Evaluation

The next day, ask students to write rule/principle statement (see objective) and turn it in.

HOW TO PUNCTUATE A SERIES

This is a structured discovery lesson for a large or small group.

Component 1. Preplanning Tasks

A. *Connection analysis: State writing standard*: The student writes clearly and effectively; applies capitalization and punctuation rules correctly. *IEP goal*: Trish will use correct punctuation (commas, periods, quotation marks) in writing samples.

B. *Content analysis*

    1. *Principle statement or rule*: When a series occurs in a sentence, commas are placed after each item except the last.

    2. *Prerequisite skill*: recognize commas

    3. *Key terms*:
        a. *series* – three or more related items listed consecutively in the same sentence
        b. *punctuate* – using marks or characters to make the meaning clear

C. *Objective*: Given 10 sentences, some of which contain a series, students will place all commas correctly.

D. *Objective rationale*: Knowing basic punctuation marks helps students produce written products that are accurate and clear.

E. *Materials*: two transparencies and two worksheets.

F. *Selected Behavioral Interventions*: Show Garth his behavior chart before class; point out he's close to earning TV time at home. Remind him that he can earn points during seatwork for staying on task and ask him to show me what that looks like.

Component 2. Lesson Setup

A. *Gain attention*: "Let's begin. When I put my hand on my head, do the same, stop talking, and look at me."

B. *Behavior expectations*: "While I'm presenting, keep your eyes on me, and raise hand and wait to be called on if you have a question or comment. Everyone show me what that looks like . . ."

Component 3. Lesson Opening

A. *Review prior learning*: Review already learned punctuation marks: period, question mark, semicolon.

B. *Statement of objective, objective purpose*: "Today, you will learn one of the uses for the comma—to punctuate a series. Knowing this rule helps make your writing clear." (Point to learning target on board.)

C. *Motivate*: "Today you're going to be detectives, figure out the punctuation rule, and then teach it to me."

Component 4. Lesson Body

Reminder to myself: As I monitor seatwork, be sure to mark points on Garth's behavior chart.

A. *Set up the discovery*

    1. Show 10 correctly punctuated sentences – transparency #1. (Note: examples are carefully selected to include sentences with series at the beginning, middle, and end; series of varied

(continued on next page)

lengths; sentences with items that don't meet definition of series, e.g., only two items, or items not consecutive.) Example sentences include:

   a. Tammy, Larry, Johnny, and Sherry are members of my family.
   b. I have friends from Guatemala, Thailand, and Ethiopia.
   c. Important crops like tulips, cucumbers, and berries are picked by farm workers in the Skagit Valley.
   d. Our school has a gym and a lunchroom.
   e. Pizzas made with sausage, peppers, olives, onions, pepperoni, and mushrooms are delicious.
   f. His dad caught salmon and cod in the morning and crab and shrimp in the afternoon.

2. Say, "Look carefully at these sentences and notice when commas are used to punctuate a series. Your job is to make two discoveries. See if you can figure out (1) a definition for a series, and (2) a rule for how to use commas to punctuate a series." (The discovery goals are on transparency #1.)

3. Explain partner work behavior expectations for making the discoveries:
   a. Work with study buddy (review what on-task looks like and sounds like for buddy work).
   b. Roles: One person is the recorder for Task 1, then switch for Task 2; both contribute ideas.

B. *Monitor the discovery*

1. While students work, circulate and listen to their discussions. Ask what they are finding or thinking. (Check in with Alice and Mary frequently.)

2. Prompt, if necessary, by asking questions such as: "Which sentences do not have commas?" "How are they different?" "How many words make up a series?" "What words are related?" "What words make up the series?" "Where is the first comma? Second? Last?"

3. Stop when all or most partner groups seem to have made the discoveries.

C. *Review the discovery*

1. Ask students to tell their discoveries. I write them on the board. We test accuracy of rule and definition on sentences. Correct if needed.
   a. Definition of series
   b. Rule for punctuating a series

> *AP* = students write definition and rule in their language notebooks.

2. Show five sentences without commas, including two sentences that don't need them (transparency #2).
   a. Work through first two sentences and have students talk me through where to put commas. (e.g., Katherine Michael and Robby love track and basketball.)
   b. Ask specific questions such as, "Which words make up the series in this sentence?" "The first comma goes after what word, everyone . . .?"
   c. Slowly read next three sentences aloud and have students raise their hands when a comma is needed.

> *AP* = unison response
> *CFU* = signaled response

D. *Supervised practice (individual)*

1. Pass out worksheet #1 (give Lidia a large print version) which includes 15 sentences, such as:
   a. Some names of famous horses are Trigger Fury Flicka and Blaze.
   b. This class loves to listen to the Beatles and the Rolling Stones at break.

2. Direct students to punctuate the first five sentences.

3. I will move around the room and make sure each student is accurate in placing commas, and will give feedback to everyone.

Component 5. Extended Practice

Seatwork assignment: Assign last 10 sentences on worksheet #1 as more practice, if students are not yet fluent. I'll grade and pass back tomorrow prior to evaluation.

Component 6. Lesson Closing

A. *Final review*: Students explain how to use commas in a series.

B. *Preview tomorrow's lesson*: They will learn another use for commas.

> *AP* = tell a partner

Component 7. Evaluation

A. *Evaluation time*: After supervised practice today or after extended practice.

B. *Evaluation task*: Worksheet #2 with 10 sentences, some of them containing a series of items to be punctuated. (Use sentences about topics that are of high interest.)

CHAPTER 19

Teaching Specialized Content

Introduction

This chapter explains how to teach concepts, behavioral skills, and learning and study strategies. We have included this information in a separate chapter because this content requires somewhat specialized planning. Effective instruction for concepts, behavioral skills, and learning and study strategies is not qualitatively different from teaching other content. It is really more of a difference in instructional emphasis. For example, when planning to teach about concepts, you emphasize using examples and nonexamples; when planning behavioral skill and strategy lessons, you emphasize demonstrating processes and using think-alouds. We have included basic information about each type of content as well as key planning considerations for each.

Teaching Concepts

Regardless of the content area you teach, you will find yourself teaching concepts. Sometimes, concepts are taught within a lesson or activity; other times, they are taught in separate lessons or activities. For example, teachers would most likely teach the concept of "main idea" in a series of lessons and activities. They might teach the concept of "peninsula," on the other hand, within another lesson. Note that the lesson plans that we have included at the end of this chapter are examples of when a concept is taught as a separate lesson.

Concepts Defined

Concepts are categories of knowledge. For example, "island" is a concept. There are many specific examples of islands, such as Lopez, Barbados, and Greenland. They all belong to the "island" category because they have certain attributes in common—that is, they are all land masses completely surrounded by water. Teaching concepts is much more efficient than solely teaching specific examples (Cummings 1990). A geography teacher does not need to teach every island in the world separately, because teaching concepts allows students to generalize. If students understand the concept of "island," they will recognize new places as being islands if they have the necessary traits.

To check your understanding of "concept," consider the following:

EXAMPLES AND NONEXAMPLES OF CONCEPTS	
Examples	**Nonexamples**
President	Harry Truman
Rocking chair	My grandma's black rocker
Impressionist art	Van Gogh's *Starry Night*
Planet	Mars

To determine if something is a concept, see if you can think of more than one example of it. In other words, "lake" is a concept because there are many examples of it—Michigan, Samish, Placid, Geneva,

Victoria, and others. "Mars" is not a concept because there is only one Mars. Other examples of concepts are *friendship, soft rock, fairness, appropriate spectator behavior, on-task, tessellation, mammal,* and *tiny.*

Types of Concepts

Concepts vary according to how concrete or abstract they are, how broad or narrow they are, and the type of definition they have. It is important to think about the type of concept to be taught when deciding how to teach it. Some concepts are very concrete, such as *table* or *flower*. Some are very abstract, such as *truth* or *love*. Many fall in between, like *polygon, family,* or *adverb*. The more concrete a concept is, the easier it is to teach and to learn.

Some concepts are very broad, such as living things. Some are very narrow, such as elephants. Between these two extremes, there are a series of concepts in a hierarchy, as in the following example: *living things, animals, mammals, land mammals, large land mammals, large land mammals living today, elephants.*

When teaching a particular concept, it is important to fit it into a hierarchy of broader and narrower concepts. For example, "We have been learning about geometric shapes. Today, we are going to learn about one type of geometric shape—the triangle. In later lessons, we will learn about different kinds of triangles, such as equilateral triangles."

Typically, instructors should not teach a very narrow concept, such as "elephant," through a formal concept lesson (unless, perhaps, the students are training to be wildlife biologists). Of the many, many concepts, it is necessary to select those that are most important and useful for the students to learn.

Concepts also vary according to how they are defined. For example, "table" is defined in terms of one set of attributes—that is, a table has a flat surface and at least one leg. This is called a *conjunctive concept*. Other concepts—called *disjunctive*—are defined in terms of alternative sets of attributes. For example, a citizen is a *native* or *naturalized* member of a nation (Martorella 1994, 161). A strike in baseball is a *swing and a miss*, a *pitch in the strike zone*, or a *foul ball* (Arends 2004, 329). A third type of concept—*relational*—is defined in terms of a comparison, such as the concept of "big." A mouse is big in comparison with an ant, but it is not big compared to a dog. The concept "big" has no meaning except in relation to something else.

As you analyze a concept and select examples or nonexamples in preparation for teaching, it is important to recognize whether you are teaching a conjunctive, disjunctive, or relational concept.

Effective Models for Teaching Concepts

When concepts are taught as a separate lesson or activity, they may be taught using the direct instruction model or the structured discovery model. The direct instruction model uses a deductive approach, whereas the structured discovery model uses an inductive approach. Each model requires different steps initially. However, the last two steps are the same in both models.

Direct Instruction Model

The following steps illustrate how concepts are taught using the direct instruction model:

- Teacher (T) names and defines the concept.
- T states the critical and noncritical attributes of the concept while showing examples and nonexamples of the concept.
- T provides new examples and nonexamples and asks students to discriminate between them.
- T asks students to explain their answers—that is, to refer to critical attributes present or absent.

Structured Discovery Model

The following steps illustrate how instructors teach concepts using the structured discovery model:

- Teacher (T) names (usually) the concept.
- T shows examples and nonexamples.
- T asks students to examine the examples and nonexamples and to identify critical and non-critical attributes.
- T asks students to define the concept or explain the concept rule.
- T provides new examples and nonexamples and asks students to discriminate between them.
- T asks students to explain their answers—that is, to refer to critical attributes present or absent.

Teaching concepts using the direct instruction model provides less opportunity for confusion or misconceptions and is more time-efficient. This model is useful when students have little prior knowledge of the concept.

Teaching concepts using the structured discovery model may provide an approach that is more interesting or motivating to students, and that provides practice in inductive thinking skills. This model is useful in helping students refine their understanding of familiar concepts.

Students typically have some prior knowledge and experience of a concept before it is taught. It is helpful to assess and to build on each student's knowledge. Also, it is important to ascertain whether the student has formed inaccurate concepts because of limited experience, such as thinking that all people who speak Spanish are from Mexico, all fruits are edible, or all islands have people living on them.

Both direct instruction and structured discovery models are effective for teaching concepts. Each model has advantages. First, determine the concept to teach, and write the objective. Then, weigh the advantages of both models. Select the one that best meets the needs of the students.

Key Planning Considerations

Concept Analysis

A careful concept analysis is essential for effective concept teaching. A concept analysis includes a definition, critical and noncritical attributes, and examples and nonexamples of the concept. Chapter 1 includes an example of a concept analysis. Another example is found in the box in the next column.

Developing a definition at an appropriate level for the students is important. Dictionary definitions are not always the best to use. A better source may be the glossary of content-area textbooks. The language and complexity of the definition must be suitable for the students. For example, the definition of "mammal" or "square" would be stated differently for first-grade students than for tenth-grade students.

When analyzing a concept, list the critical and noncritical attributes that will be most helpful in distinguishing that concept from similar ones. Critical attributes are essential characteristics of a concept. For example, "four sides" is a critical attribute of a square. However, when defining a concept, any

---

EXAMPLE OF A CONCEPT ANALYSIS

Concept: "complete sentence"
Definition: a word or group of words that express a complete thought
Critical Attributes: includes a subject and a verb, begins with a capital letter and includes an end mark (period, question mark, or exclamation point), and is a complete thought
Noncritical Attributes: number of words; topic of sentence
Examples: The building fell down. / He is a very fast runner! / Is Superman an imaginary character?
Nonexamples: The baby panda. / Ran all the way to the store! / her hair is red

---

one critical attribute is necessary but not sufficient to defining the concept. A square must have four sides, but the sides must also be of equal length. Noncritical attributes of a concept are those that are not necessary. Whether the length of those equal sides is 3 miles or 3 inches is unimportant. Size is a noncritical attribute of a square. A square is a square whether it is big or small.

Carefully select examples and nonexamples to bring out all of the critical and noncritical attributes of the concept. It is important to begin with the "best" examples, or the examples that are the clearest and least ambiguous. Gradually introduce examples and nonexamples that are more difficult to differentiate. For example, do not begin with a platypus as an example of a mammal, or with a rhombus as a nonexample of a square (Howell and Nolet 2000).

When you plan how you will teach the concept, there are various factors to consider. You will need to plan many examples and nonexamples, because you must use different sets for the initial presentation, the practice, and the evaluation. This ensures that students have not merely memorized the examples and that they understand the concept and its attributes. Also, when presenting examples and nonexamples, use cues such as underlining, colors, and arrows to emphasize critical attributes and then gradually fade the cues. These visual supports are especially helpful in the diverse classroom. Planning many examples and non-examples and the use of cues helps strengthen student understanding.

Objective

Think carefully about what your students need to learn in order to understand and use the concept you are teaching. Possible objectives for concept lessons include (1) defining the concept, (2) listing critical attributes of the concept, (3) recognizing examples and nonexamples of the concept, (4) stating why something is an example or nonexample, (5) producing examples, (6) stating similarities and differences between related concepts, (7) using the concept in a novel way, or (8) producing a graphic organizer of the concept. Each of these possible objectives requires careful planning in order for students to successfully reach it.

Opening

When opening concept lessons, it is very important to assess what students already know about the concept and to find out if students have any misconceptions about the concept. It may be useful to brainstorm or conduct "think-to-writes" (writing down everything you know about reptiles in 2 minutes, for example). These strategies will also help students connect the new learning with prior knowledge. When possible, help students make connections to personal experience. For example, if you are going to teach the concept "democracy," ask about the students' experiences in electing the class president. It is also best to use some type of organizer that shows the relationship of the concept you are teaching to broader and narrower concepts, or to related concepts, such as *islands* and *peninsulas*. Remember that you would not state a specific objective that includes the definition of the concept at the beginning of a discovery lesson.

Closing

There are many ways in which a concept lesson can be closed. Here are some options:

- reviewing the concept definition, critical attributes, and best examples

- discussing related concepts or previewing future lessons on related concepts

- reviewing the purpose of learning the concept

- describing how students can use their knowledge of the concept in the future

- asking students to show their graphic organizers or new examples

- asking students to expand or correct their "think-to-writes"

To summarize, concepts are categories of information found in all content areas. When they are taught as a separate lesson/activity, both direct instruction and structured discovery lesson models can be effective. A carefully designed concept analysis will help students develop a clear understanding of the concept they are studying, and make it more likely they will reach the objective.

Teaching Behavioral Skills

What are behavioral skills? Behavioral skills are the skills needed for success in school that go beyond academic and learning skills. They are needed to follow rules and routines and to meet behavior expectations, and include important social skills needed to interact with others and to deal with feelings. The term *social skills*, in turn, encompasses many categories and examples. It includes very broad cognitive–behavioral skills, such as interpersonal problem solving, anger management, and empathy. Social skills also include narrow, specific interpersonal skills such as accepting compliments or greeting others. Sometimes, a social skills curriculum is adopted that includes lifelong skills needed not only at school but in the community, at work, in the family, and so on.

The list of examples on the next page is meant to indicate the enormous range of behavioral skills needed to be successful in school and beyond.

Why teach behavioral skills? Children come to school with a wide variety of experiences and opportunities. Some students come to school with experience sitting quietly, using materials, listening to instruction, and working independently. Others will need to be taught to do so. Some students come to school skilled at making friends, getting along with adults, expressing feelings, and understanding the feelings of others. Others need help in learning to work or play with others, to resolve conflicts, or to

---

EXAMPLES OF BEHAVIORAL SKILLS

- listening
- waiting for help
- disagreeing politely
- starting conversations
- accepting *no*
- staying out of fights
- keeping hands to self
- paying attention
- playing games
- asking permission
- setting goals
- answering in unison
- monitoring time

- following directions
- taking turns
- giving help
- joining activities
- negotiating
- lining up
- sticking to your work
- working independently
- offering help
- telling the truth
- sitting in seat
- raising hand
- challenging ideas

- asking for help
- controlling impulses
- sharing tasks
- responding to teasing
- responding to an accusation
- accepting consequences
- speaking quietly
- walking in the halls
- dealing with embarrassment
- expressing concern for others
- bringing materials to class
- moving desks in place
- standing up for others

---

manage feelings. A few students may already be rejected by others, are dangerously aggressive or withdrawn, and are in desperate need of help in developing social skills. Because social competence is essential for success in school and in life, many schools are beginning to take a proactive, universal approach by making social skills instruction a regular part of the curriculum, as well as providing more intense, selected instruction for those individuals who need it.

Regardless of background, all students will need to be taught your classroom expectations, rules, routines, and the social skills specific to the methods you use. In Chapter 10, we explained that there are a variety of ways to teach behavioral skills and we focused there on using precorrection and mini-lessons. In this chapter, we will describe how to use full lessons to teach behavioral skills.

Choosing the Lesson Model to Use

Teaching behavioral skills is similar to teaching other principles, procedures, or how-to lessons. You begin with a principle statement or task analysis of the skill and then teach the components or steps using *direct instruction*. As in all direct instruction lessons, you will include an explanation and examples for each part or step. You will demonstrate the use of

the behavioral skill, and you will ask the students to practice the skill by performing it. You will evaluate whether each student has met the lesson objective by having the student perform the skill individually and independently.

Note that when teaching behavioral skills, it is critical to attend to generalization. For this reason, it is very important to follow initial direct instruction lessons with planned activities. (See Chapter 15 for information on activity planning.) This gives students the opportunity to apply the skill in a variety of contexts. For example, following an initial lesson on *dealing with losing*, a game activity could provide an opportunity to apply that skill.

Key Planning Considerations

Content Analysis

The content analysis for a behavioral skill lesson typically includes a principle statement or a task analysis. For example, you may be planning to teach students when to tell on someone and write the principle statement as, "If someone is doing something dangerous to him/herself or to others, then tell an adult."

Many behavioral skills take the form of procedures to follow. Task-analyze by listing the steps for using the behavioral skill, including the steps that involve stopping to think and making decisions. For example, here is a task analysis for a behavioral skill:

Accepting No *for an Answer*

1. Stop and take a deep breath.

2. Look at the person.

3. Say *okay*.

4. Do not argue.

Published social skills programs are good sources of task analyses. Witt et al. (1999) task-analyze classroom routines. Be sure to adjust whatever task analysis you choose to meet the needs of your students.

Explanation

In the explanation component of behavioral skill lessons, you will tell students the information or knowledge needed to follow the rule, perform the routine, or use the social skill. Refer to the principle statement or task analysis, and be sure that it:

- is written and has a title.

- is brief, simple, and easy to understand and remember.

- is posted and includes pictures if possible.

Explain the behavioral skill thoroughly. (See Chapter 5 for a complete discussion of giving effective explanations.) Include the following critical teaching skills.

1. Explain each step through paraphrases, descriptions, elaborations, and so on. ("If an adult tells you *no*, say *okay* or *all right* in a polite voice. That means your voice is calm and quiet, and not sarcastic.")

2. As part of the explanation, give examples and nonexamples of each step. ("Listen as I say *okay* in a polite voice. . . . Now listen as I say it in a rude voice.")

3. Check for understanding of each step. ("Thumbs up if my voice is polite. . . . Now let me hear each of you say *okay* in a polite voice.")

4. Use active participation strategies, such as involving students in repeating and reviewing the steps through call and response. Students need to memorize the steps in order to actually use them; repetition will help. ("The first step is to stop and take a deep breath. What is the first step, everyone?")

Demonstration

In behavioral skill lessons, demonstration means the teacher (or other expert) will act out or model the behavioral skill in a scenario that is meaningful to the students. For example, demonstrate the skill of "accepting *no*" in a scenario in which a teacher refuses to allow a student to sit by a friend in math class. Demonstrate the skill of *finding something to do when you finish your work early* in a scenario common to your students and classroom, for example, finishing the assigned math problems before math period is over.

It is important to demonstrate *before* you present information about the behavioral skill as well as *after*. Seeing the skill modeled first will help the students understand your explanations and provide a common background experience. The initial modeling will give you something concrete to tie your explanations to and let you use examples familiar to the class. Modeling again after presenting information will allow students to see the steps of the behavioral skill in action and together.

GUIDELINES FOR DEMONSTRATING (MODELING)

Each step or component of the behavioral skill needs to be modeled clearly and correctly, so be sure you and your assistants rehearse in advance. Goldstein and McGinnis (1997) and Sheridan (1995) provide the following guidelines:

- As you act and talk, point to the steps or components written on a poster.

- Be sure to "think aloud" as you are acting. For example, say "Hmm. Let's see. I need to take a deep breath before I say anything."

- Stay in character. Don't say, "Next I would take a deep breath." Instead, do it—take a deep breath.

- Model with a co-actor when appropriate. For example, another person is needed to take the role of the adult saying *no* when you model "accepting *no*."

- Keep it simple. Model one skill at a time, each step in sequence, without a great deal of extra detail.

- Check for understanding by assigning students to watch for different steps and asking them to describe how the step was demonstrated, following the modeling.

- You may choose to show a nonexample as well for clarity.

- Be sure you model the skill working, that is, having a positive outcome: "Thanks for accepting *no* so calmly. You may sit by Ichiro later during lunch."

Generalization will be encouraged if you select scenarios relevant to your students and model a variety of scenarios showing different applications, such as accepting *no* at home and at school, from peers and adults, and for major and minor requests.

Supervised Practice

Following the explanation and demonstrations, the students must practice the behavioral skill by performing it and receiving feedback. Performing the skill means acting it—not just discussing it or writing about it. This may take the form of authentic practice, role-playing, or both.

Authentic Practice In this type of supervised practice, students practice the skill in a real, rather than imagined, situation. You will schedule an event that will provide a real opportunity for every student to use the skill as you guide, monitor, and give feedback. For example, in a lesson for teaching the skill *what to do when you finish your work early*, the supervised authentic practice could be for you to give them a short task and more than enough time to complete it. As they finish early, you guide them in using the skill that you have just explained and demonstrated. You may need to provide several practice opportunities so that every student receives feedback. Authentic practice isn't always possible or desirable. For example, you wouldn't purposely set up a real situation for students to practice responding to teasing or dealing with embarrassment.

EXAMPLES OF AUTHENTIC PRACTICE FOR BEHAVIORAL SKILLS

- *Saying "please" and "thank you"*—Practice is snack time, where the snacks are out of the children's reach and they must request them.

- *Sharing*—Practice is an art activity where you don't provide enough materials for every student.

- *Accepting assigned partner politely*— Practice is an assignment where each student is assigned a partner to work with whom they would not ordinarily choose.

- *Reaching consensus*—Practice is planning a class party where the students must agree on the food, music, and activities.

Role-Playing In this type of supervised practice, students practice the behavioral skill in an imagined scenario. You may begin by having the students brainstorm situations or scenarios when they will need to use the skill; then, select the first student to take the lead and choose other students for supporting roles. For example, students could role-play *apologizing* in a scenario where they bump into someone or break someone's toy. They can role-play *responding to peer pressure* in a scenario where they are pressured to skip school or use alcohol.

GUIDELINES FOR SUPERVISED PRACTICE (USING ROLE-PLAYING)

Each student should have multiple opportunities to play the lead role and to receive feedback. Each student demonstrates asking permission and accepts *no* as an answer, for example. This may mean scheduling the supervised practice over several days. Goldstein and McGinnis (1997) and Sheridan (1995) provide the following guidelines:

- Some students may need scaffolding. They may need to discuss how they will demonstrate each step, or have the opportunity to rehearse with peers first. You may provide support by pointing to the steps on a poster, prompting as they role-play, or providing a script.

■ If a student makes an error during the role-play, stop her right away, correct the error, and have her redo the role-play. You can correct the error through prompting, modeling, or directly telling the student the correct step.

■ Assign other students steps to observe and on which to give feedback (active participation).

■ Promote generalization by having students provide ideas for scenarios, and by observing them in a variety of settings for scenario ideas. This ensures that the practice scenarios are relevant to the students' lives. When possible, go to the actual settings to practice, such as going to the playground to practice joining games.

■ To prepare students for the real world, include scenarios where the skill does not work, such as when the teasing does not stop, they do not get to join the game, or they do not receive permission. Teach alternatives.

■ Provide for cultural diversity by role-playing options and varying scenarios. For example, some students when *dealing with teasing* will be more comfortable with passive responses such as ignoring the teasing or getting help. Others will be more comfortable with more assertive responses such as telling the person to stop or making a joke.

Extended Practice

This component is key in promoting generalization. It is essential to provide a great deal of additional practice in real-world applications. Extended practice often takes two forms: follow-up practice at school and homework.

At School The teacher can plan extended practice for students to use the skill over the next few days following the body of the lesson. Depending on the skill, this practice may occur during free time, partner or small-group work, class discussions, centers, recess, lunch, or planned activities in the form of games or projects. Use a complete precorrection or simply tell the students ahead of time to use the skill ("Remember to practice taking turns while using the computers for your projects."). Coach and prompt the students during the practice situation, and debrief following. Also watch for those unplanned teachable moments.

Homework Students may be given homework assignments to use a behavioral skill. Provide a form with a place for the students to list the steps in the skill or write the principle statement, to describe where, when, and with whom they used the skill, and to describe the results. The form can also include a place for students to self-evaluate their use of the skill, and a place for others (e.g., teachers, parents, coaches, day-care providers, or peers) to initial that they saw the student use the skill. Homework can incorporate goal-setting or be written in the form of a behavior contract. The purpose is to have the student practice using the skill in a variety of situations.

To summarize, behavioral skills are important for success in school as well as in all other parts of a student's life. These skills can be taught directly through explanation, modeling, and performance practice. Promoting generalization through well-planned extended practice is very important.

Best practices for teaching behavioral skills such as teaching in the context of real-life scenarios, demonstrating (modeling) the skill, and using role-playing with peers are very helpful for *English language learners*. Pre-teaching vocabulary, incorporating language patterns, and using visual supports will also be beneficial.

Teaching Learning and Study Strategies

It is fairly common today to find strategy instruction as part of the regular classroom curriculum. This is not really surprising when one considers the increasing student diversity found in schools today.

What are strategies? Strategies are special kinds of procedures. You will recall that procedural knowledge refers to knowing *how to* do something. Strategies then, are techniques designed to help students understand *how to* be more effective learners.

Why teach learning and study strategies? Knowing the expectations for students described in the state standards helps teachers plan what they will teach. Simply knowing the expectations, however, is not very helpful in planning for students who have difficulty learning, remembering, and using information. Students who have effective strategies for learning and studying definitely have an increased chance of performing well on tasks necessary for school success. The learner with missing or ineffective strategies is often at risk for school failure. This is really what strategy instruction is all about: helping students learn and study in more efficient ways so they can be more successful in school.

What are different types of strategies? Learning strategies (sometimes called *cognitive strategies*) and study strategies (sometimes called *study skills*) are the two basic strategy types. These types of strategies differ in their focus. A *learning strategy* facilitates the use of higher-level thinking behaviors, such as decision-making, self-motivation, and self-monitoring (Deshler, Ellis, and Lenz 1996). For example, using a strategy for finding the main idea requires students to make decisions about what they are reading by asking themselves questions such as, "Does this idea encompass all of the important details in this paragraph?" Therefore, a strategy to find the main idea is an example of a learning strategy.

A *study strategy*, on the other hand, is more similar to a standard procedure, as described in Chapter 1. The students work through an ordered series of steps that requires limited use of higher-level thinking skills such as decision-making or self-monitoring. For example, a proofreading strategy in which students complete steps such as "Check to see that each sentence begins with a capital letter" would be considered a study strategy. The strategy steps can be completed without the use of higher-level thinking skills. Deciding whether a letter is uppercase or lowercase is pretty cut-and-dried. Learning strategies achieve cognitive goals (Arends 2004), whereas study strategies achieve procedural goals, and both are important.

Selecting Strategies to Teach

All kinds of strategies can be taught to help students study and learn. Thinking about their purposes can help teachers select appropriate ones. Some strategies are designed to help students gather information from texts and presentations (for example, strategies that teach students how to take notes from a lecture or read for comprehension). Other strategies help students retain information for later use (for example, learning how to use mnemonic strategies or construct concept maps). Still other strategies help students show what they know (learning how to proofread assignments or take multiple-choice

tests, for example). One additional group of strategies helps students develop personal organizational habits (learning how to maintain an assignment calendar or complete assignments, for example).

You can decide which strategies to teach your students by carefully analyzing the trouble spots they encounter when trying to perform school tasks. Information about specific strategies is readily available in journals and texts. (See the resources listed at the end of this chapter for more information.)

Choosing the Lesson Model to Use

Direct instruction is an effective model to use for teaching strategies. Due to the teacher-directed focus of this model, the path to successful implementation of the strategy is fairly straightforward and easy to follow. Begin the strategy lesson by clearly establishing the value of the strategy and what the students will be expected to know and do. Follow this with the presentation of the strategy steps (developed through a task analysis). Next, explain and demonstrate each step. Finally, give feedback as the students practice. These key components of direct instruction provide an effective lesson design for the purpose of teaching strategies.

Key Planning Considerations

Content Analysis

Use a task analysis to organize the content of a strategy. Because strategies are usually written as a series of steps or subskills, the task analysis is already written for you. In addition, the strategy steps almost always include a built-in remembering technique (usually a first-letter mnemonic device), which is very helpful for students when trying to recall the steps. For example, the letters in the RCRC memorization strategy stand for *read, cover, recite*, and *check* (Archer and Gleason 1990). Each letter represents a step of the task analysis needed to complete the strategy. Note that the task analysis and remembering technique will be used during the presentation of information and demonstration portions of the lesson body.

Opening

The opening of a strategy lesson is a good time to establish the importance of the strategy and the effect its use can have. You could begin by using a technique designed to motivate students, such as asking a question that describes a problem caused by not using the strategy. You might ask, "How many of you have ever lost points on a writing assignment because it was not complete?" Another important part of the opening is to tell the students the objective ("Today, you will learn a technique for checking your written work before you turn it in so that you can be sure that it is complete."). Complete the opening by stating the objective purpose using a specific example, such as saying, "Using this strategy can help ensure that you receive full credit for your work and can help improve your grade."

Explanation

During the explanation section of the lesson body, it is important to explain, tell about, and describe the strategy steps to the students. There are numerous ways to do this effectively. Thorough descriptions and detailed elaborations of strategy steps, clear connections to what students already know, and providing numerous examples can be especially effective when teaching strategies. (See Chapter 5 for other ideas). This is most effective when you show the task analysis (use a transparency or a poster) to the students and then explain it and give examples of each step. Strategies often have a mnemonic device built in to help students remember the strategy steps. Pointing out and referring to the mnemonic device in the strategy throughout the lesson helps students remember the key steps or subskills.

At some point, students need to memorize the steps of the strategy so they can be more automatic in using the steps. However, you will need to decide in advance of your lesson whether memorization will be part of the initial lesson. If you do not plan for your students to memorize the steps at this point, be sure to provide a visual support of the strategy (a poster of steps, for example) during all phases of your lesson. If you do want your students to memorize the steps, plan ample practice opportunities so students can learn them.

Demonstration

It is also very important to demonstrate or model the use of the strategy after or during the explanation portion of the lesson. Using the think-aloud technique is very effective, as it allows students to see the steps being used and hear the thinking that is necessary to complete the steps. For example, in the COPS (C = *capitalization*; O = *overall appearance*; P = *punctuation*; S = *spelled*) error-monitoring strategy (Schumaker et al. 1981), the teacher would say, "Let's see, 'C' stands for *capitalization*. Have I capitalized the first word in every sentence? Yes. I capitalized 'The' in the first sentence," and so on.

Be sure that your actions and thoughts during this component of the lesson are obvious (exaggerate if needed) and that students can easily see and recognize what you are doing. Depending on the complexity of the strategy, you may need to model it numerous times before students are ready to try it. In some cases, you may wish to model a number of times over several days.

Extended Practice

The extended practice portion of the strategy lesson is meant to provide opportunities that help students become fluent in their strategy use and to facilitate generalization. These opportunities are often organized as in-class practices, although carefully structured homework assignments can be effective also. Consider the following as you plan extended practice opportunities:

- Use in-class practice activities if your goal is to provide frequent, varied practice opportunities so that using the strategy will become a habit. As you work through various content areas, point out when it would be appropriate to use the strategy, and then have students practice it. Over time, your role in this area can decrease.

- Plan carefully organized homework assignments for students to effectively practice the learned strategies at home. For example, include a strategy check-off sheet with a homework practice assignment. A parent or sibling could check off the steps as the student completes them.

- Generalization of strategy use requires special attention. Even though a student may know how to use a strategy, this does not guarantee that the student *will* use the strategy in various settings. You can increase the likelihood that students will generalize strategy use if you provide practice sessions in a variety of settings, with varied materials, and with prompts to use the strategy.

For example, if you have taught a reading comprehension strategy, plan for students to practice the strategy with science, social studies, and other subject matter. In all cases, use interesting materials for practice sessions to help increase a student's interest in using the strategy.

To summarize, strategy instruction provides students with a valuable tool to use in school. Using effective strategies can increase the possibility that students will experience success with school tasks. When strategies become habits, students become more independent, effective learners.

Sample Plans

Look at the framework for diversity responsive teaching (DRT) as you examine the sample plans at the end of this chapter. Ask yourself how the plan incorporates responses to diversity in *what* is taught, *how* it's taught, and the *context* for teaching and learning. We'll give you a start in thinking about how various parts of the plan fit with various components of the framework. We encourage you to look for additional examples of each component and to think about what changes you believe would make this plan even more likely to support all students' involvement and success.

Notice that the behavioral skill lesson "Standing Up for Someone" teaches content that helps prepare students with skills *for a diverse world*. In addition, teachers can use this lesson to create a diversity responsive *social environment* in their classrooms. The lesson "Designing Mnemonic Devices" gives an easy opportunity to respond to diversity in *what* is taught. The content of the lists to be memorized could be based on student interests, for example. Can you think of other ways to use the lists—perhaps to teach *about* diversity?

The "Polygon" lessons illustrate how the same concept can be taught in two different ways. Both lessons include a clear, detailed concept analysis. The "Standing Up for Someone" lesson includes a number of interesting universal instructional interventions. The extended practice activities are used for the purpose of generalization. Notice that they come after the evaluation for that reason. In addition, the supervised practice extends over 2 days. This allows each student to role-play more than once.

The behavioral skill lesson is an example of a universal behavioral intervention. Notice that it is part of a series of lessons meant to prevent bullying. Can you think of other universal behavioral interventions for preventing bullying? For example, what classroom rules might you establish? Notice that partner practice is incorporated in the "Polygon" concept lessons. If you had a student with serious difficulties paying attention and completing work, how could you use peer support as a selected (antecedent) intervention for him?

Note: The sample plans are written in a very detailed form in order that teacher decision-making and planned actions are clear to the reader.

References and Suggested Reading for Concepts

Arends, R. I. 2004. Learning to teach. 6th ed. San Francisco: McGraw-Hill. (See Chapter 9 in particular.)

Boulward, B. J., and M. L. Crow. 2008. Using the concept attainment strategy to enhance reading comprehension. *Reading Teacher* 61 (6).

Cummings, C. 1990. *Teaching makes a difference.* 2nd ed. Edmonds, WA: Teaching, Inc. (See Chapter 11 in particular.)

Eggen, P. D., and D. P. Kauchak. 2006. *Strategies and models for teachers: Teaching content and thinking skills.* 5th ed. Boston: Allyn and Bacon.

Gunter, M. A., T. H. Estes, and S. L. Mintz. 2007. *Instruction: A models approach.* 5th ed. Upper Saddle River, NJ: Allyn & Bacon. (See Chapters 5 and 6 in particular.)

Howell, K. W., and V. Nolet. 2000. *Curriculum-based evaluation:teaching and decision making.* 3rd ed. Belmont, CA: Wadsworth/Thomson Learning.

Martorella, P. H. 1994. Concept learning and higher-level thinking. In *Classroom teaching skills,* 5th ed. J. M. Cooper, 153–188. Lexington, MA: D.C. Heath.

Moore, K. D. 2008. *Effective instructional strategies: From theory to practice.* 2nd ed. Thousand Oaks, CA: Sage Publications.

Sabornie, E., and L. deBettencourt. 2009. *Teaching students with mild and high-incidence disabilities at the secondary level.* 3rd ed. Upper Saddle River, NJ: Prentice Hall/Pearson.

Smith, P. L., and T. J. Ragan. 2005. *Instructional design.* 3rd ed. New York: Wiley & Sons. (See Chapter 9 in particular.)

References and Suggested Reading for Behavioral Skills

Allsopp, D., K. Santos, and R. Linn. 2000. Collaborating to teach prosocial skills. *Intervention in School and Clinic* 35 (3): 141–146.

Dunlap, G., P. Strain, L. Fox, J. Carta, M. Conroy, B. Smith, L. Kern, M. Hemmeter, M. Timm, A. McCart, W. Sailor, U. Markey, D. Markey, S. Lardieri, and C. Sowey. 2006. Prevention and intervention with young children's challenging behavior: Perspectives regarding current knowledge. *Behavioral Disorders* 32 (1): 29–45.

Elksnin, L., and N. Elksnin. 1998. Teaching social skills to students with learning and behavior problems. *Intervention in School and Clinic* 33 (3): 131–140.

Goldstein, A., and E. McGinnis. 1997. *Skillstreaming the adolescent: New strategies and perspectives for teaching prosocial skills.* Rev. ed. Champaign, IL: Research Press.

Gresham, F. 2002. Teaching social skills to high-risk children and youth: Preventive and remedial approaches. In *Interventions for academic and behavior problems II: Preventive and remedial approaches*, eds. M. Shinn, H. Walker, and G. Stoner, 403–432. Bethesda, MD: National Association of School Psychologists.

Gresham, F., M. Bao Van, and C. Cook. 2006. Social skills training for teaching replacement behaviors: Remediating acquisition deficits in at-risk students. *Behavioral Disorders* 31 (4): 363–377.

Kerr, M., and C. Nelson. 2010. *Strategies for addressing behavior problems in the classroom.* 6th ed. Upper Saddle River, NJ: Pearson/Merrill.

Kolb, S., and A. Griffith. 2009. "I'll repeat myself, again?!" Empowering students through assertive communication strategies. *Teaching Exceptional Children* 41 (3): 32–36.

Lane, K., J. Wehby, and C. Cooley. 2006. Teacher expectations of students' classroom behavior across the grade span: Which social skills are necessary for success? *Exceptional Children* 72 (2): 153–167.

McIntosh, K., and L. MacKay. 2008. Enhancing generalization of social skills: Making social skills curricula effective after the lesson. *Beyond Behavior* 18 (1): 18–25.

Moss, P. 2007. Not true! Gender doesn't limit you! *Teaching Tolerance* 32: 50–54.

Patterson, D., K. Jolivette, and S. Crosby. 2006. Social skills training for students who demonstrate poor self-control. *Beyond Behavior* 15 (3): 23–27.

Robinson, T. 2007. Cognitive behavioral interventions: Strategies to help students make wise behavioral choices. *Beyond Behavior* 17 (1): 7–13.

Sargent, L. 1998. *Social skills for school and community.* Reston, VA: Council for Exceptional Children.

Schoenfeld, N., R. Rutherford, R. Gable, and M. Rock. 2008. ENGAGE: A blueprint for incorporating social skills training into daily academic instruction. *Preventing School Failure* 52 (3): 17–28.

Seattle Committee for Children. 1992. *Second step: A violence prevention curriculum.* Seattle: Seattle Committee for Children.

Sheridan, S. 1995. *The tough kid social skills book.* Longmont, CO: Sopris West.

Smith, S., and D. Gilles. 2003. Using key instructional elements to systematically promote social skill generalization for students with challenging behavior. *Intervention in School and Clinic* 39 (1): 30–37.

Sugai, G., and T. Lewis. 1996. Preferred and promising practices for social skills instruction. *Focus on Exceptional Children* 29 (4): 1–16.

Walker, H., E. Ramsey, and F. Gresham. 2004. *Antisocial behavior in school: Evidence-based practices.* 2nd ed. Belmont, CA: Wadsworth/Thomson Learning.

Witt, J., L. LaFleur, G. Naquin, and D. Gilbertson. 1999. *Teaching effective classroom routines.* Longmont, CO: Sopris West.

References and Suggested Reading for Strategies

Archer, A., and M. Gleason. 1990. *Skills for school success.* North Billerica, MA: Curriculum Associates.

Ashton, T. 1999. Spell checking: Making writing meaningful in the inclusive classroom. *Teaching Exceptional Children* 32 (2): 24–27. (This title provides a strategy for the effective use of a spell-checker.)

Bass, M. L., and D. G. Woo. 2008. Comprehension windows strategy: A comprehension strategy and prop for reading and writing informational text. *The Reading Teacher* 6 (17): 571–575.

Boyle, J. R. 2001. Enhancing the note-taking skills of students with mild disabilities. *Intervention in School and Clinic* 36 (4): 221–224.

Boyle, J. R., and M. Weishaar. 2001. The effects of strategic note-taking on the recall and comprehension of lecture information for high school students with learning disabilities. *Learning Disabilities Research and Practice* 16 (3): 133–141.

Bui, Y. N. 2006. The effects of a strategic writing program for students with and without learning disabilities in inclusive fifth-grade classes. *Learning Disabilities Research & Practice* 21 (4): 244–260.

Bryant, D. P., N. Ugel, S. Thompson, and A. Hamff. 1999. Instructional strategies for content-area reading instruction. *Intervention in School and Clinic* 34 (5): 293–302. (This title provides strategies for word identification, vocabulary, and comprehension skills.)

Casteel, C. P., B. A. Isom, and K. F. Jordan. 2000. Creating confident and competent readers: Transactional strategies instruction. *Intervention in School and Clinic* 36 (2): 67–74.

Cegelka, P. T., and W. H. Berdine. 1995. *Effective instruction for students with learning difficulties.* Boston: Allyn and Bacon.

Cohen, L. G., and L. J. Spenciner. 2009. Teaching students with mild and moderate disabilities. 2nd ed. Columbus, OH: Merrill. (See Chapter 11.)

Conley, M. W. 2008. Cognitive strategy instruction for adolescents. What we know about the promise, what we don't know about the potential. *Harvard Educational Review* 78 (1): 84–106.

Cubukcu, F. 2008. Enhancing vocabulary development and reading comprehension through metacognitive strategies. *Issues in Educational Research* 18 (1): 1–11.

Czarnecki, E., D. Rosko, and E. Fine. 1998. How to call up note-taking skills. *Teaching Exceptional Children* 30 (6): 14–19.

DeLaPaz, S. 2001. STOP and DARE: A persuasive writing strategy. *Intervention in School and Clinic* 36 (4): 234–243. (This title provides a strategy for writing persuasive essays.)

Deshler, D., E. S. Ellis, and B. K. Lenz. 1996. *Teaching adolescents with learning disabilities: Strategies and methods.* 2nd ed. Denver, CO: Love Publishing. (See Chapters 3–9 for strategies in reading, writing, test-taking, note-taking, math, and social skills.)

Dewitz, P. 2009. Comprehension strategy instruction in core reading programs. *Reading Research Quarterly* 44 (2):102–126.

Ellis, E. S., D. D. Deshler, B. K. Lenz, J. B. Schumaker, and F. L. Clark. 1991. An instructional model for teaching learning strategies. *Focus on Exceptional Children* 23: 1–24.

Englert, C. S. 2009. Connecting the dots in a research program to develop, implement, and evaluate strategic literacy interventions for struggling readers and writers. *Learning Disabilities Research & Practice* 24 (2): 104–120.

Fontana, J., T. Scruggs, and M. Mastropieri. 2007. Mnemonic strategy instruction in inclusive secondary social studies classes. *Remedial and Special Education* 28 (6): 345–355.

Friend, M., and W. D. Bursuck. 2009. *Including students with special needs: A practical guide for classroom teachers.* 5th ed. Upper Saddle River, NJ: Pearson. (See Chapter 10 in particular.)

Gorlewski, J. 2009. Shouldn't they already know how to read? Comprehension strategies in high school English. *English Journal* 98 (4): 127–132.

Gleason, M. M., G. Colvin, and A. L. Archer. 1991. Interventions for improving study skills. In *Interventions for achievement and behavior problems,* eds. G. Stoner, M. R. Shinn, and H. M. Walker, 137–160. Silver Spring, MD: National Association of School Psychologists.

Guzel-Ozmen, R. Modified cognitive strategy instruction. *Intervention in School and Clinic* 44 (4): 216–222.

Joseph, N. 2006. Strategies for success: Teaching metacognitive skills to adolescent learners. *The New England Reading Association Journal* 42 (1): 33–39.

Kester, P., and C. Donna. 2009. But I teach math! The journey of middle school mathematics teachers and literacy coaches learning to integrate literacy strategies into the math instruction. *Education* 129 (3): 467–472.

Kinniburgh, L. H., and E. L. Shaw. 2009. Using question-answer relationships to build reading comprehension in science. *Science Activities* 45 (4): 19–28.

Landi, M. 2001. Helping students with learning disabilities make sense of word problems. *Intervention in School and Clinic* 37 (1): 13–18. (This article provides a strategy for solving math word problems.)

Lebzelter, S., and E. Nowacek. 1999. Reading strategies for secondary students with mild disabilities. *Intervention in School and Clinic* 34 (4): 212–219. (This article provides decoding, vocabulary, and comprehension strategies.)

Lewis, R. B., and D. H. Doorlag. 2009. *Teaching special students in general education classrooms.* 8th ed. Upper Saddle River, NJ: Pearson/Merrill Prentice Hall.

Lovitt, T. C. 1995. *Tactics for teaching.* 2nd ed. Columbus, OH: Merrill/Prentice-Hall.

Lovitt, T. C. 2000. *Preventing school failure: Tactics for teaching adolescents.* 2nd ed. Austin, TX: Pro-Ed. (See Chapter 3 on study skills, in particular.)

Lovitt, T. C. 2007. *Promoting school success.* 3rd ed. Austin, TX: Pro-Ed. (See Chapter 7 on study skills.)

Mastropieri, M. A., and T. E. Scruggs. 1998. Enhancing school success with mnemonic strategies. *Intervention in School and Clinic* 33 (4): 201–207.

Mastropieri, M. A., and T. E. Scruggs. 2007. *The inclusive classroom: Strategies for effective instruction.* 3rd ed. Upper Saddle River, NJ: Pearson. (See Chapter 11 on teaching study skills.)

Meltzer, L. J., B. N. Roditi, D. P. Haynes, K. R. Biddle, M. Paster, and S. E. Taber. 1996. *Strategies for success: Classroom teaching techniques for students with learning problems.* Austin, TX: Pro-Ed. (See Chapters 3–6 on strategies for spelling, reading comprehension, written language, and math.)

Mercer, C. D., and A. R. Mercer. 2005. *Teaching students with learning problems.* 7th ed. Upper Saddle River, NJ: Pearson. (See Chapter 13 in particular.)

Naughton, V.M. Picture it. *The Reading Teacher* 62 (1): 65–68.

Olson, J. L., and J. M. Platt. 2003. *Teaching children and adolescents with special needs.* 4th ed. Columbus, OH: Merrill/Prentice Hall. (See Chapters 6 and 9 in particular.)

Polloway, E. A., and J. R. Patton. 2008. *Strategies for teaching learners with special needs.* 8th ed. Columbus, OH: Merrill/Prentice-Hall. (See Chapter 12 on study skills.)

Protheroe, N., and S. Clarke. Learning strategies as a key to student success. *Principal* 88 (2): 33–37.

Reithaug, D. 1998. *Orchestrating academic success by adapting and modifying programs.* West Vancouver, BC: Stirling Head Enterprises. (This title provides strategies for reading, writing, spelling, and math.)

Rogevich, M. E. 2008. Effects on science summarization of a reading comprehension intervention for adolescents with behavior and attention disorders. *Exceptional Children* 74 (2): 135–154.

Rozalski, M. 2007. Practice, practice, practice: How to improve students' study skills. *Beyond Behavior* 17 (1): 17–23.

Ryder, R. J. 1991. The directed questioning activity for subject matter text. *Journal of Reading* 34 (8): 606–612.

Schumaker, J. B., D. D. Deshler, S. Nolan, F. L. Clark, G. R. Alley, and M. M. Warner. 1981. *Error monitoring: A learning strategy for improving academic performance of LD adolescents* (Research Report No. 32). Lawrence, KS: University of Kansas Institute on Learning Disabilities.

Scott, V., and L. Compton. 2007. A new TRICK for the trade: A strategy for keeping an agenda book for secondary students. *Intervention in School and Clinic* 42 (5): 280–284.

Sporer, N. 2008. Improving students' reading comprehension skills: Effects of strategy instruction and reciprocal teaching. *Learning and Instruction* 19 (3): 272–286.

Strichart, S. S., and C. T. Mangrum II. 2010. *Study skills for learning disabled and struggling students – Grades 6-12*. Upper Saddle River, NJ: Merrill.

Terrill, M., T. Scruggs, and M. Mastropieri. 2004. SAT vocabulary instruction for high school students with learning disabilities. *Intervention in School and Clinic* 39 (5): 288–294.

Tracy, B. 2009. Teaching young students strategies for planning and drafting stories: The impact of self-regulated strategy development. *Journal of Educational Research* 102 (5): 323–331.

Tracy, B., R. Reid and S. Graham. 2009. Teaching young students strategies for planning and drafting stories: The impact of self-regulated strategy development. *Journal of Educational Research* 102 (5): 323–332.

Vaughn, S, C. S. Bos, and J. S. Schumm. 2008. *Teaching students who are exceptional, diverse, and at-risk in the general education classroom.* 4th ed. Boston: Allyn and Bacon. (See Chapter 17 in particular.)

Vaughn, S., and J. K. Klinger. 1999. Teaching reading comprehension through collaborative strategic reading. *Intervention in School and Clinic* 34 (5): 284–292.

Williams, J. P. 2009. Embedding reading comprehension training in content-area instruction. *Journal of Educational Psychology* 101 (1): 1–20.

Wood, D., and A. Frank. 2000. Using memory enhancing strategies to learn multiplication facts. *Teaching Exceptional Children* 32 (5): 78–82.

POLYGON: A DIRECT INSTRUCTION CONCEPT LESSON

This is for a large group of students.

Component 1. Preplanning Tasks

A. *Connection analysis: State Standard, Mathematics 1.3*: Understand and apply concepts and procedures from geometric sense. *Benchmark 2*: Use multiple attributes to describe geometric shapes.

B. *Content analysis*

1. *Concept analysis*
   a. Concept name: *polygon*
   b. Definition: A polygon is a two-dimensional, closed figure of three or more sides made by joining line segments, where each line segment intersects with exactly two others at its endpoints.
   c. Critical attributes: two-dimensional, closed figure with three or more sides, made of joined line segments, each line segment intersects with exactly two others at its endpoints
   d. Noncritical attributes: size, shape, color, patterns inside or out
   e. Examples: Triangle (three sides), quadrilateral (four sides), pentagon (five sides), or hexagon (six sides). Both regular and irregular polygons need to be included in examples.

   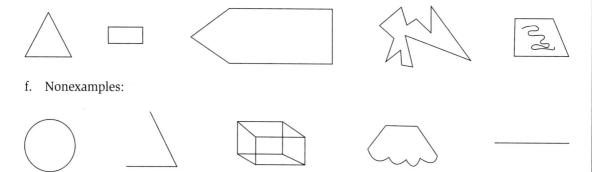

   f. Nonexamples:

2. *Prerequisite skills or knowledge*: Know how to identify when the endpoints of line segments intersect.
3. *Key terms and vocabulary*: line segment, endpoint, intersect

C. *Objective*: Given 12 geometric figures on a worksheet, student will circle (or point to) the 7 polygons.

D. *Objective rationale*: Polygons are basic geometrical shapes and recognizing them is a prerequisite skill for other geometrical concepts, such as regular and irregular polygons.

E. *Logistics* (materials and equipment): overhead projector, three transparencies, math workbooks, worksheet for evaluation.

F. *Room arrangement*: no change needed to usual arrangement; make sure everyone's partner is present.

Component 2. Lesson Setup

A. *Gain attention*: Play musical chords. "When you hear the music, give me your attention right away."

B. *Behavior expectations*: Raise hands to contribute, listen to explanations and comments of teacher and peers, and keep eyes on the speaker.

Component 3. Lesson Opening

A. *Review prior geometry lessons*

1. Discuss the various shapes ("What are they?") in the current geometry unit.

B. *State objective and objective purpose*

1. Say, "Today, you are going to learn how to identify our new shape, polygons. You will learn a definition and the characteristics that make a polygon."

2. "This lesson will help prepare you for future lessons, such as learning about various types of polygons."

3. "Builders all over the world use polygons as they create various structures (show photos). Artists sometimes use polygons as well (show photos of abstract paintings). You'll likely use polygons in your life and work, too."

Component 4. Lesson Body

A. *Explanation*

1. Show transparency #1 (concept analysis with polygon definition, list of critical and noncritical attributes, and examples and nonexamples of polygons).

2. Read the definitions with students. Discuss critical and noncritical attributes, pointing out attributes in the examples, and then pointing out noncritical attributes.

3. Show new examples/non-examples on a transparency. Point to various examples/non-examples of attributes and ask students which is which.

> *AP* (active participation) = choral reading

> *CFU* (check for understanding) = students signal with yes/no response cards

B. *Demonstration*

1. Show transparency #2 (with a list of questions to ask to help decide if shapes are polygons, and more examples and nonexamples).

2. Think aloud with the first two examples to show how to use questions to analyze shapes (a poster of questions will remain on the whiteboard tray).
   a. Is it two-dimensional?
   b. Is it made of line segments?
   c. Is it a closed shape?
   d. Does each line segment intersect with exactly two others at its endpoints?
   e. Are there at least three sides?
   f. If the answer to all of these questions is *yes*, the shape is a polygon.

3. Repeat questions with the next four examples and nonexamples. Ask the students if they agree with conclusions (have some incorrect ones).

> *CFU* = thumbs up/down

C. *Supervised practice* (Have students take out their *yes* and *no* response cards.)

1. *Partner practice*
   a. Show transparency #3 (list of questions and new examples and nonexamples).
   b. Have students determine whether each shape is a polygon (first five shapes). Prompt the use of the five questions.

(continued on next page)

2. *Individual practice*
   a. Point to each of the last five shapes and have students signal. (Have Leah help Molly with reading the questions if needed.)

Component 5. Extended Practice

A. *Provide a seatwork assignment.* Have students circle the polygons on math workbook page 55, which shows 25 shapes with 15 polygons.

Component 6. Lesson Closing

A. *Final review of information learned*

1. Say, "Today, we learned . . ."

2. Quickly review the concept analysis (transparency #1).

> *AP* = students call out each essential attribute as I review it.

Component 7. Evaluation

A. *Provide a worksheet* of 12 geometric figures, 7 of which are polygons.

1. Say, "Your ticket to lunch is to find the polygons on the worksheet. Circle each one as you find it."

2. Ask, "How do you show which are polygons?" **AP/CFU** = tell a partner, call on selected non-volunteers.

3. Students complete worksheets individually and independently. (Parent volunteer will evaluate Stephan. He will point to the polygons.)

POLYGON: A STRUCTURED DISCOVERY CONCEPT LESSON

This is for a large group of students.

Component 1. Preplanning Tasks

A. *Connection analysis*: *State Standard, Mathematics 1.3:* Understand and apply concepts and procedures from geometric sense. *Benchmark 2:* Use multiple attributes to describe geometric shapes.

B. *Content analysis*

1. *Concept analysis*
   a. Concept name: *polygon*
   b. Definition: A polygon is a two-dimensional, closed figure of three or more sides made by joining line segments, where each line segment intersects with exactly two others at its endpoints
   c. Critical attributes: two-dimensional, closed figure, with three or more sides, made of joined line segments, each line segment intersects with exactly two others at its endpoints
   d. Noncritical attributes: size, shape, color, patterns inside or out
   e. Examples: Triangle (three sides), quadrilateral (four sides), pentagon (five sides), or hexagon (six sides). Both regular and irregular polygons need to be included in examples.

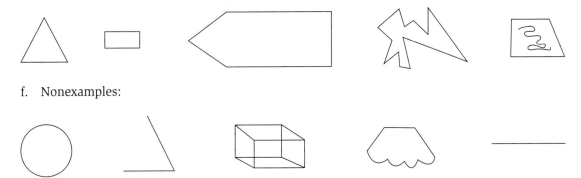

   f. Nonexamples:

2. *Prerequisite skills or knowledge*: Know how to identify when the endpoints of line segments intersect.
3. *Key terms and vocabulary*: line segment, endpoint, intersect

C. *Objective*: Given 12 geometric figures on a worksheet, student will circle (or point to) the 7 polygons.

D. *Objective rationale*: Polygons are basic geometrical shapes and recognizing them is a prerequisite skill for other geometrical concepts, such as regular and irregular polygons.

E. *Logistics* (materials and equipment): overhead projector, four transparencies, math workbooks, worksheet for evaluation.

F. *Room arrangement*: no change needed to usual arrangement; make sure everyone's partner is present.

Component 2. Lesson Setup

A. *Gain attention*: Play musical chords. "When you hear the music, give me your attention right away."

B. *Behavior expectations*: Raise hands to contribute, listen to the explanations and comments of the teacher and peers, and keep eyes on the speaker.

(continued on next page)

Component 3. Lesson Opening

A. *Review prior geometry lessons*

   1. Discuss the various shapes ("What are they?") in the current geometry unit.

> *AP* = brainstorm

B. *State objective and objective purpose*

   1. Say, "Today, you are going to learn how to identify our new shape, polygons. You will learn a definition and the characteristics that make a polygon."

   2. "This lesson will help prepare you for future lessons, such as learning about various types of polygons."

Component 4. Lesson Body

A. *Set up the discovery*

   1. Show transparency #1 (examples and nonexamples of polygons).

   2. Say, "Some of these shapes are polygons. Watch me as I circle them" (*circle them*).

   3. Say, "You have 5 minutes to see if you can figure out how all of the circled shapes are the same."

B. *Monitor the discovery*

   1. Walk around and prompt as needed, such as, "Are all of the shapes the same color?" "Are the shapes closed?" and so on. Ask questions about both critical and noncritical attributes.

C. *Review the discovery*

   1. Construct a concept analysis together on transparency #2.
      a. Ask, "In what ways are the circled shapes the same?" (*write critical attributes*).
      b. Ask, "Can you think of a way to write a definition for a polygon?" (*write definition*). Say, "If this is a complete definition, thumbs up. If not, thumbs down.

   2. Read definition and critical attributes.
      a. Repeat the procedure with each critical attribute, having students give thumbs up or down.

> *CFU* = (check for understanding)
> = thumbs up/ down

   3. Show transparency #3 (list of questions to ask to help decide if the shape is a polygon and examples and nonexamples of polygons). Explain how to use questions to analyze shapes.
      a. Is it two-dimensional?
      b. Is it made of line segments?
      c. Is it a closed shape?
      d. Does each line segment intersect with exactly two others at its endpoints?
      e. Are there at least three sides?
      f. If the answer to all of these questions is *yes*, it is a polygon.

D. *Supervised practice*: Have students take out their *yes* or *no* response cards.

   1. *Partner practice*
      a. Show transparency #4 (list of questions and new examples and nonexamples).
      b. Have students determine whether each shape is a polygon (first five shapes). Prompt the use of the five questions.

   2. *Individual supervised practice*
      a. Point to each of the last five shapes and have students signal. (Have Leah help Molly with reading the questions if needed.)

Component 5. Extended Practice

A. *Provide a seatwork assignment.* Have students circle the polygons, on math workbook page 55, which shows 25 shapes with 15 polygons.

Component 6. Lesson Closing

A. *Final review of information learned*

> 1. Say, "Today we learned . . ."
>
> 2. Quickly review the concept analysis put together as a class (transparency #2).

> *AP* = Student call out each critical attribute as I review it.

B. *Application*

> 1. "Builders all over the world use polygons as they create various structures (show photos). Artists sometimes use polygons as well (show photos of abstract paintings). You'll likely use polygons in your life and work, too."

Component 7. Evaluation

A. *Provide a worksheet* of 12 geometric figures, 7 of which are polygons.

> 1. Say, "Your ticket to lunch is to find the polygons on the worksheet. Circle each one as you find it."
>
> 2. Ask, "How do you show which are polygons?"
>
> 3. Students complete worksheets individually and independently. (Parent volunteer will evaluate Stephan. He will point to the polygons.)

> *AP/CFU* = tell a partner, call on selected non-volunteers.

BEHAVIORAL SKILL LESSON: STANDING UP FOR SOMEONE

This is a direct instruction lesson for a small group.

Component 1. Preplanning Tasks

A. *Connection analysis*: This lesson is part of an anti-bullying and "acting for social justice" program. *Related state standard in civics:* Understand individual rights and their accompanying responsibilities, explain why democracy requires citizens to exercise their own rights and to respect the rights of others.

B. *Content (task) analysis* for "standing up for someone" (steps adapted from Goldstein and McGinnis 1997):

1. Decide if the person is not being treated right by others.
2. Decide if the person wants you to stand up for him or her.
3. Decide how to stand up for the person.
4. Do it.

C. Key term/vocabulary: *bystander*

D. *Lesson objective*: In a given role-play, students will correctly think aloud and demonstrate each step in standing up for someone.

E. *Objective rationale*: Standing up for someone who is being treated unfairly or unkindly is an important part of friendship and community-building and helps prevent bullying at school. It also has a larger application as part of acting for social justice.

F. *Logistics*: materials = graphic organizer; poster with steps (tape these on board); small whiteboards; homework forms; backup and evaluation scenarios

G. *Room arrangement*: Make space in front for skit/role-plays; shift chairs so all face the front.

Component 2. Lesson Setup

A. *Gain attention*: "Let's get started. When I say 'attention please' during the lesson, stop in place, look at me, and listen."

B. *Behavior expectations*: "Look at the behavior expectations written on the board. To be successful in this lesson, you'll need to listen when others are speaking and contribute ideas. Who remembers what 'contribute' means?"

Component 3. Lesson Opening

A. Show graphic organizer of components of the anti-bullying program. "You've learned a lot about types of bullying, bullies, and victims. Today we'll learn about what bystanders can do. A bystander is someone who watches but isn't part of what's happening and is neither the bully nor the victim. What is a bystander?" **CFU** (check for understanding) = write definition on scratch paper.

B. With parent helpers, do a skit in which someone (Chuck) is not being treated right (called a "retard" and excluded from a game), and a bystander does not know how to help. (Watch for and afterward acknowledge 'listening.')

C. Ask students for examples of when they have needed this skill in their lives. (Acknowledge for 'contributing ideas.')

D. Remind them that it's not just about bullying. Review earlier discussions of wrong ways to treat other people: disrespectfully, unfairly, unequally, unkindly.

E. Point to the objective and rationale (both written on board). "You're going to learn how to 'stand up for someone.' What will you learn, everyone?" **AP** (active participation) = unison response.

Component 4. Lesson Body

A. *Demonstration*

1. "We're going to do that skit again—this time with a bystander (me) who does know how to help."

2. "When I point to my head, it means I'm thinking out loud."

3. "Watch and listen carefully as I 'stand up for someone'—as I stand up for Chuck."

B. *Explanation*
Show and explain steps written on a big poster. **AP** = choral read; think–pair–share (TPS). (Acknowledge for 'listening to others' and 'contributing ideas.')

1. Step 1 = *Someone treated wrong?* In this step, you'll decide if the person is not being treated right by others. Ask yourself, *Is this person (friend, classmate, stranger) not being treated right (disrespectfully, unfairly, unequally, unkindly) by others (child, adult, group)?* **TPS** = How was Chuck treated? Why is it important to help people you don't know or aren't friends with? **CFU** = read examples and nonexamples of someone treated wrong and have them identify by signaling with thumbs up/down.

2. Step 2 = *Wants my help?* In this step, you'll decide if the person wants you to stand up for him or her. Ask yourself, *Does this person want my help? How can I find out?* (Ask directly, read body language, or think how you would feel.) **TPS** = Did Chuck want help? How do you know? **CFU** = read examples/nonexamples of someone wanting help; thumbs up/down. If the person doesn't want help, stop here.

3. Step 3 = *How can I help?* In this step, you'll decide how to stand up for the person. Ask yourself, *What shall I do to help?* (Remember the rules: Do not get hurt and do not make it worse.) Consider the options of (1) telling the other person to stop; (2) explaining why it is unfair; (3) saying something nice to the person not being treated right or walking away with him; and (4) getting help (always use the last two in dangerous situations). **TPS** = How did I help Chuck? What else could I have done? **CFU** = read scenarios; students signal with fingers the number of the best way to help; call on various students to say why.

4. Step 4 = *Do it.* In this step, you'll go ahead and help. Remember to: Use "I" statements in a calm voice if you choose to say something, and don't be unkind back. **CFU** = say examples/nonexamples of calm and appropriate responses; thumbs up/down.

C. *Demonstration*

1. **AP** = select students to watch for each step (change for each scenario)

2. With parent volunteers, model three scenarios showing different ways of helping (demonstrate a student at recess being taunted and pushed around by older kids; the class laughing when a student struggles during oral reading; and a student being unfairly accused by teacher of starting a fight). Model one scenario where person is not being treated wrong (a big brother not letting little kid play in the street). Model one where person doesn't want help (someone being teased about his name).

(Position myself to monitor behavior)

3. **CFU** = after each modeling, call on selected students to describe how each step was used.

(continued on next page)

D. *Supervised (performance) practice*

1. Have the group brainstorm other scenarios that they have seen (be sure to get at least one from each student). (Acknowledge for 'contributing ideas.')

2. Select Edgar to role-play first, allowing him to choose the scenario. (Parent volunteers will play other parts.) Leave the poster up for role-players to refer to.

3. Ask questions of Edgar to set the scene, such as, "Where is this happening?"

4. Assign steps to watch for to other students.

5. Stop, correct, and redo if errors.

6. After role-play, ask for feedback from peers and adults. "Give feedback politely by referring to the behavior, not the person."

7. Continue until each student has done a role-play. (Select Jareese to go second.)

Component 5. Lesson Closing

A. "Close your eyes. Picture a hallway in our school. Someone is being bullied and you're a bystander. What will you do? Everyone together, say the steps . . ."

B. "We will talk about this skill again as we study civil rights issues in social studies class."

Component 6. Continuation

A. The next day, model a scenario of a student having his lunch taken and being made fun of for being "foreign," while pointing to each step on poster (review).

B. Then each student will role-play another scenario (continued supervised practice).

Component 7. Evaluation

A. The following day, pull students aside, one at a time, to role-play the skill using a new scenario that I provide.

B. Use parent volunteers to play the other parts.

Component 8. Extended Practice for Generalization

A. Provide homework. "Write the steps on a homework form, noting each time you use the skill this week and how well you do."

B. Have parents initial that they read the homework form.

C. Conduct a follow-up activity, having students videorecord themselves role-playing a scenario they create, and then having the class critique.

D. I will explain the skill to the recess supervisor and she will give good-citizen awards to those who use the skill this month. I will do the same in the classroom.

E. Hold a review session in 2 weeks.

STRATEGY LESSON: DESIGNING MNEMONIC DEVICES

This is a direct instruction lesson for a large group.

Component 1. Preplanning Tasks

A. *Connection analysis*: This strategy helps students progress successfully toward many state standards, as many require that students have mastered large quantities of information. *IEP objective*: Molly will use memorization strategies as appropriate when preparing for content tests.

B. *Content (task) analysis*: See lesson body for Designing Mnemonic Devices (steps adapted from Archer and Gleason 1990).

C. *Prerequisites*: Know the RCRC strategy (Archer and Gleason 1990).

D. *Key terms/vocabulary*: *strategy* – a plan or method; *mnemonic devices* – tricks for memorizing

E. *Objective and rationale*

1. Given three lists of related items, students will design a word or sentence mnemonic device for each that makes sense.

2. This will help students organize information to be memorized in preparation for tests and increase scores on tests.

F. *Logistics* (materials and equipment: overhead projector, transparencies with the last test results, task analysis, lists of related information, and an evaluation worksheet

Component 2. Lesson Setup

A. *Gain attention*: Ring bell. "When you hear the bell, give me your attention. Show me what that looks like."

B. *Behavior expectations*: Students will look and listen, answer questions, raise hands, and wait to be called on.

Component 3. Lesson Opening

A. *Motivator*: Present a list of 10 facts (transparency #1) and follow with quiz. Then, present another list, tell them a first-letter mnemonic, and follow with another quiz. Compare scores.

> *AP* (active participation) = write

B. *Objective and purpose*: "You will be happy to know that today you are going to learn how to create your own memory tricks. They will help you memorize information better and in less time."

C. *Review RCRC* by having students call out the words in unison.

> *AP* = call-outs

Component 4. Lesson Body

A. *Explanation and demonstration*

1. *Quick-teach the words mnemonic device (key term) and strategy (vocabulary word).*
   a. Point out where the words are written on the board.
   b. Explain each word (one at a time) by providing definitions, giving synonyms and showing.
   c. After showing and explaining a word, ask questions such as "What is a plan or method called, everyone?" Students answer "strategy."

(continued on next page)

2. *Explain the steps of the task analysis (below)*
   a. Talk through transparency #2, which shows the task analysis, *and* point out poster of task analysis. For example, "One strategy that you can use is called the word strategy. This is when. . ." and so forth.
   b. Provide an enlarged version on a handout for Leah.

   D*esigning mnemonic devices (task analysis)*
   I. Using the word strategy:
       i.   Underline the first letter of each item to be memorized (list of words, task parts, steps, and so on). For example: Superior, Huron, Erie, Michigan, Ontario.
       ii. Determine whether a word can be made from the first letters (reorder the letters if necessary): *HOMES*. If the word strategy works, go to (iii). If not, go to (iv).
       iii. Memorize the word and item that goes with each letter of the word using RCRC.
   II. Using the sentence strategy:
       iv. Reorder the first letters of the words and create a sentence (*fruit, meat, vegetable* = the phrase, *very funny man*).
       v.   Memorize the sentence and item that goes with each word in the sentence using RCRC.

   > *AP* = think–pair–share; *CFU* = call on selected non-volunteers

3. *Ask for definitions, paraphrases of steps, and purpose of strategies*

4. *Do a think-aloud of the steps* using the following lists of subject matter, which include both word and sentence strategy (five food groups: fruits, vegetables, meat, dairy, fats/oils/sweets; parts of an insect: head, thorax, abdomen).
   a. Pass out whiteboards.
   b. Have students work steps along with me.
   c. Emphasize that there is more than one answer.

   > *AP* = they write what I write

5. **CFU** = provide new content (types of rocks: sedimentary, igneous, metamorphic).
   a. Students will work each step on whiteboards ("Do step one, show me," and so on).
   b. If more instruction is needed, use these examples: famous warriors of the nineteenth century, primary colors, exports from California.

B. *Supervised practice*: Monitor and give feedback.

1. *Partner practice*
   a. Give partners two more examples and a checklist of strategy steps.
   b. Have Partner 1 do the first example, while Partner 2 checks it off, and then reverse the roles. (Put roles in writing on poster.)
   c. Use the following examples of football game winners: Burlington, Anacortes, Sehome, Snohomish; parts of a plant: roots, stem, leaves, and sometimes flowers.
   d. Partner Darin with Kristin to help with reading.

2. *Individual supervised practice*
   a. Have individuals work two more examples (parts of a volcano: parasitic cone, base, summit, crater, and magma reserve; colors of the rainbow).

Component 5. Lesson Closing

- *Review*: Go back to transparency #1 of test items. Have partners create mnemonic devices for missed groups of facts. Share with class.

AP = think–pair–share

Component 6. Extended Practice

- Do *in-class practice activities*:
  During the next 2 days, we will look for examples of information in various content areas. Students will need to memorize these and develop a mnemonic device for each one, such as the states in the Pacific Northwest region or examples of foods that are low in fat.

Component 7. Evaluation

- *Worksheet* with three lists of related pieces of information. Students will develop a mnemonic device for each one.

CHAPTER 20

Editing Your Plan

Introduction

Once you have written the first draft of your plan, you need to edit it. This is as important for writing lesson and activity plans as it is for any other writing task. There are three main editing tasks for analyzing your plan for completeness and effectiveness. The first editing task is to determine how to incorporate critical management skills and to write them into the plan. The second editing task is to double-check your plan to make sure that you have used appropriate universal and selected instructional interventions given the content and your students. The third editing task is to examine for congruence so that you can make sure that the various parts of your plan match. These editing tasks will help you increase the chances that your lesson or activity will be successful for all.

This chapter can be used in a couple of ways. You can use it as a guide for analyzing your plan to make sure that it is as complete and as carefully thought-through as possible. You cannot predict everything that might happen during your lesson or activity, but careful thought can help you predict and prevent many management problems and confusion with content. This chapter (and the following chapter) will also serve as a summary of many of the key ideas in this book, a way for you to review what you have learned.

Following are the three main editing tasks. Each task explanation includes a variety of questions to ask yourself that will provide guidance as you edit your plan. The first two editing tasks also include example plans.

Editing Task #1: Editing for Critical Management Skills

The first editing task is to add in the *critical management skills* that will help your lesson or activity run smoothly. At this point, your plan is pretty much complete in terms of what you'll teach and how you'll teach it. Now it is time to focus on the context for teaching and learning, specifically by adding in strategies for preventing and solving behavior problems. How much written planning you do depends on you (whether you use critical management skills automatically as you teach) and depends on your students (whether you have a challenging class). Each of the following critical management skills comes with a set of questions that you can ask yourself to help you select appropriate strategies. Look back at Chapters 11 and 12 for a complete description of seven critical management skills.

- Plan how to *gain attention* during this lesson/activity.
  1. Choose an appropriate signal for attention. To choose the signal, think about what the students will be doing just before the lesson or activity starts, how interested they are likely to be, and what they will be doing during various parts of the lesson/activity. Ask yourself the following:
     - Do I need a strong signal to gain attention at the beginning?
     - Will students be working with peers, moving around the room, or engaging in

something new and exciting during this lesson/activity? If so, what signal will be best seen or heard?

2. Also decide how you want students to respond to the signal for attention. Plan how you will explain the signal and response and write this into the "setup" component of your plan. Ask yourself the following:

   ■ When I signal, do I want them to look and listen? Stop talking? Put down materials? Stop where they are?

   ■ Do they need to practice responding to the signal?

   ■ Will any individuals need extra support in responding to the signal quickly? How can I provide this?

■ Plan *behavior expectations* for this lesson or activity.

1. Decide what behavior expectations apply in this lesson or activity, and write them in your plan (and on the board or a poster). Look at the various parts of the lesson/activity and analyze the rules, routines, and behavioral or social skills required. Ask yourself the following:

   ■ Do I need to communicate expectations for making transitions, getting help, what to do when finished, talking, movement, and so on?

   ■ Do I need to remind students to use social or behavior skills such as active listening, sharing materials, following directions independently, disagreeing politely, accepting assigned partner, and so on?

2. Plan how and when you will communicate behavior expectations, and write this into the plan where needed. Ask yourself the following:

   ■ Will initial expectations need to change as the lesson or activity progresses, for example, change "raising hands" to "calling out" to "speak quietly to your partner"?

   ■ Should I briefly state the expectations? Explain them thoroughly? Demonstrate them? Check for understanding?

   ■ Do students need to practice following them?

■ Will any individuals need extra support in following these behavior expectations? How and when will I supply that?

■ Plan how and when you will *acknowledge appropriate behavior*. Write reminders into your plan. Ask yourself the following:

   ■ What behaviors will be a challenge to this group?

   ■ What behaviors will be a challenge to individuals?

   ■ What behaviors are essential to the success of this lesson or activity?

   ■ Which students need more acknowledgment than others?

   ■ Have I considered whether students prefer public or private and group or individual acknowledgments?

   ■ Have I planned to use a variety of acknowledgments?

   ■ How strong will the acknowledgments need to be?

■ Think about how and when you should *monitor* student behavior during this lesson or activity. Write reminders into the plan. Ask yourself the following:

   ■ When should I scan the class and move around the room? How will I remind myself to do so?

   ■ Where should I stand at various points in my lesson/activity?

   ■ Will I need to be careful how I position myself when working with individuals or small groups so I can monitor the whole class?

   ■ Will I need to write anything on the board, on transparencies, or on slides in advance so that I will not have my back to my students while I am teaching?

   ■ Who will need extra encouragement or prompting (for example, for getting started, sticking with a long task)?

   ■ Does the activity or lesson include transitions that I need to carefully monitor?

   ■ How can I connect with each student during this lesson or activity?

- Plan the *room arrangement* that will work best for this lesson or activity, and write it in your plan. Stand in the classroom and visualize your lesson or activity happening. Think carefully about what you and your students will be doing during the various parts of your plan. Remember that the room arrangement needs to match the methods you plan to use and the students' skills and self-control. Ask yourself the following questions:

  - Will I be able to see everyone? Move around easily? Get to each student quickly?

  - What desk arrangement will match the methods I'll be using?

  - What will students need to be able to see?

  - Will students need to be able to concentrate without distractions?

  - Will students need to work closely with other students?

  - Do students need a writing surface, or could they sit on the floor?

  - Will students need to move around? Where?

  - Will any individuals need special seating assignments for this lesson/activity?

  - Will I need to make changes in furniture arrangement during the lesson or activity? If so, how and when will I make those changes?

- Write in ideas for planning for *logistics*. Ask yourself the following:

  - What materials need to be gathered or duplicated?

  - Should I list student materials needed on the board?

  - What equipment needs to be set up or borrowed and checked?

  - How will materials be distributed or picked up?

  - Do I need to do any special setup for the lesson/activity?

  - What is the plan for cleanup, including the time needed?

  - Will I have assistants helping with this lesson or activity? If so, what should each do? How and when will I communicate this?

- Think about how to manage *transitions*. Write reminders into the plan. Ask yourself the following:

  - What kinds of directions for transitions are needed? Detailed? Brief?

  - How will I communicate directions for transitions?

  - How will I communicate behavior expectations for transitions?

  - Will written schedules and/or time alerts ("3 minutes left") be needed to help students prepare for transitions?

  - Could I plan something fun at the beginning of the next activity to encourage a quick transition?

  - Would some of my students benefit from picture schedules or transition buddies?

- Additional things to think about include the following:

  - Have I done everything I can to teach effectively and to make content interesting, clear, personally and culturally relevant, complete, and so on for all students?

  - Have I used curricular and instructional modifications and accommodations that will help all students be academically successful and thus prevent behavior problems due to frustration, lack of challenge, and so on?

  - Will any students need selected behavioral interventions to be successful in this lesson or activity?

Application of Editing Task #1

On the following page is an example of a plan (from Chapter 15) with critical management skills written in. It begins, however, with a description of a teacher's thoughts about management issues in this particular activity. You would not write these thoughts into a plan, but we include them so you see the reasoning that underlies the decisions the teacher makes and understand the notes he writes in the plan.

Editing Task #1 involves planning for the use of critical management skills and writing them into the plan. Taking a proactive approach to behavior

TIC-TAC-TOE SPELLING ACTIVITY PLAN

Teacher thoughts:

- My students love to play Tic-Tac-Toe, so the transition to this activity will be quick and it'll be easy to gain their attention at the beginning of the activity. It won't be so easy later to regain their attention when they are playing. I'll use a familiar strong signal (clicker) and response (freeze).

- Desks are already in pairs facing front, and that will work both for giving directions and for playing the game.

- They know the "sit with reading partner routine," so a simple statement will be enough to direct them to the right desks.

- I'll need two sets of behavior expectations: one for when I'm giving directions and one for when they're playing the game. I'll put one set on each side of a poster so I only have to turn it around to change the expectations.

- Several students struggle with getting started, even when they really enjoy an activity. I have them sitting in the front of the room near me.

- A variety of behavioral and social skills are needed in this activity:

  - *Taking turns* – Many of my students struggle with this, so I'll structure it through partner role descriptions.

  - *Giving and receiving feedback* – I've recently taught a social skills lesson on this and will use a precorrection just before the game starts, put "give polite feedback" on the behavior expectations poster, and acknowledge polite feedback often.

  - *Winning and losing / good sportsmanship* – WD really struggles with that. I'll precorrect privately with him before the activity starts by having him tell me and show me what good winners and losers do. Later, I'll acknowledge him through our private signal because he doesn't like his friends to notice him being praised.

Component 1. Preplanning Tasks

A. *Prerequisite skills or knowledge*: How to play Tic-Tac-Toe

B. *Key terms or vocabulary*: N/A

C. *Long-term objective*: Given a list of 15 words that contain one to three syllables and end in "–ing," students will write (or spell orally) all words correctly. Students are given lists that match their skill level (one, two, or three syllables, for example). State writing standard: spell age-level words correctly.

D. *Activity description*: A Tic-Tac-Toe game where partners quiz each other on their spelling words. Correct responses result in placing an X or O on the Tic-Tac-Toe board.

E. *Activity rationale*: This game is intended to provide a fun way for students to practice and memorize their spelling words. This format also provides practice in giving and taking constructive feedback.

F. **Logistics**: – poster of game directions, transparency of grids and words, worksheets with 25 Tic-Tac-Toe grids on each; set up overhead projector/screen; write list of student materials needed on board (pencils, spelling list); ask teaching assistant to help me demonstrate, monitor, and acknowledge polite feedback

G. **Room arrangement**: desks in pairs facing front.

Component 2. Activity Beginning

(**Transition**: As students enter the room, point to materials list on board; remind them to sit in the desks they use for reading partner activities and that we'll be playing Tic-Tac-Toe.)

A. *Setup*

  1. **Gain attention**: "Attention, please. During the game, I'll ask for your attention by clicking the clicker. You'll freeze. Let's try it."

  2. **Behavior expectations**: Point to poster. "While I'm giving directions, keep eyes on me and raise hands to ask/answer questions unless I say 'everyone' or ask you to call out. Where should your eyes be, everyone? Show me what to do if you have a question."

B. *Opening*

  1. *Review*: "You have been learning to spell words that end with '–ing'. Call out some examples."

  2. *Motivate*: "We're going to play Tic-Tac-Toe Spelling today."

  3. *Objective and purpose*: "Tic-Tac-Toe Spelling will help you memorize correct spelling of words so you can use these words in your writing; you won't need to look up words in a dictionary."

    (Watch for and **acknowledge** 'eyes on me.')

Component 3. Activity Middle

A. *Post these written game directions*:

  1. Exchange spelling lists with your reading partner.

  2. Partner 1 (*X*) asks Partner 2 (*O*) a word from Partner 2's list.

  3. Partner 2 spells. If correct, Partner 2 places an *O* on a Tic-Tac-Toe square.

  4. If wrong, Partner 1 says "The word ___ is spelled ___. How do you spell ___?"

  5. Partner 1 places a check if correct or a minus if incorrect by the word spelled.

  6. Reverse the roles. Keep playing until time is up.

B. *Explain directions for the game using poster and transparency of Tic-Tac-Toe grids and sample word lists.*

  (**Logistics**: Make sure I have these with me and that the projector works this time!)

  ■ Demonstrate with teaching assistant as I explain.

  (**Acknowledge** eyes on me.)

  ■ Explain that checks and minuses are to keep track of words they know and to make sure all words are asked.

  ■ Check for understanding: After each step, stop and ask a question and request a unison verbal or signaled response ("What would you say if I spelled *cat* 'K-A-D'?" "What does your partner write if the word isn't spelled correctly?" and so on.)

  (**Acknowledge** participating.)

C. *Check for understanding* of all directions: I choose two students to come to the front and model the game procedure as I ask other selected students specific questions, such as, "Who goes first? What does the asker do now?"

  (**Monitor behavior**: move around room.)

(*continued on next page*)

D. *Distribute Tic-Tac-Toe grids.*

(**Logistics**: Use this week's paper-passers.) "Trade spelling lists with your partner."

(**Expectations**) Turn poster around. "Stay with your partner and use quiet voices. (precorrect) Remember to give each other feedback politely. Who remembers what *politely* looks like and sounds like? If your partner spells the word correctly, say *you're right* or *good spelling*. If incorrect, who remembers what to do? Let's try it. I'll spell and you give me feedback. *Dog* is spelled B-I-G . . ."

E. *Play the game*: Play for 20 minutes. Complete as many games as possible.

(**Acknowledge** the three in front if they start quickly; otherwise, prompt them. **Monitor** all pairs often. **Acknowledge** for following directions (especially MB and FL), taking turns, giving/receiving feedback politely, and good sportsmanship (signal WD).)

(**Transition**: Alert them when 5 minutes are left, then 1 minute.)

Component 4. Activity Closing

(**Gain attention**: clicker. **Acknowledge** for quick response. **Acknowledge** group if they improved in giving polite feedback.)

A. *Preview*: "Tomorrow, we'll do another practice activity to help you memorize your spelling words."

B. *Practice* one final time: "Pick one misspelled word from your list (if no words are misspelled, use "challenge words") and spell it correctly in a whisper three times."

(**Logistics**: Ask this week's cleanup crew to collect and recycle grid worksheets. I collect their marked spelling lists.)

(**Transition**: Tell students to quietly and quickly return to their usual desks and do the *get ready for lunch* routine.)

---

management and building positive behavior support strategies into your lessons and activities is an important part of planning.

Editing Task #2: Editing for Instructional Interventions

(See Chapters 3–9.) We assume that you used the guides provided in the various lesson and activity plan chapters when you were writing your initial plan. So, the editing task for *instructional interventions* is really just a double-check. This reread of your plan gives you a chance to make any final revisions that you feel are necessary. The following are questions to ask yourself as you double-check your plan for the use of effective instructional interventions:

Focusing Attention (See Chapter 4.) Ask yourself the following:

- Is the content or structure of this lesson or activity automatically interesting to my students? Do I need a snappy opening to grab

their attention? Is the relevance of the learning obvious? Have I planned specific examples of why this content is important to know?

- Have I written questions to ask my students? Count them. How many are convergent? Divergent? High-level? Low-level? Given the content and objective, does this seem about right?

- How new or complex is the knowledge or skill? Is another review during the closing a good idea? Do my students need some prompts on when to use this content?

Presenting Information (See Chapter 5.) Ask yourself the following questions:

- Have I organized the lesson content in a way that helps my students to understand? Do I need a task analysis? A principle statement? A subject matter outline? A concept analysis?

- Have I planned to incorporate universal design for learning by saying, writing, and showing the knowledge or skill?

- Have I carefully considered which components of effective explanations should be included, e.g., descriptions, comparisons, paraphrases?
- Have I included appropriate demonstrations such as modeling, or showing products and/or processes?
- Is the new information complex or complicated? Do I need to break it down into smaller portions for presenting?
- Have I planned how I will give directions for related tasks and assignments?
- Do I have a variety of visual supports? Do my visuals support understanding of the content I am teaching? Are they easy to see and appealing to look at?
- Is the vocabulary I use appropriate for the students? Do I need to teach key terms and/or vocabulary?

Promoting Active Participation (See Chapter 6.) Ask yourself the following:

- Is the content new or complex? Have I used enough rehearsal strategies and processing strategies?
- Is it a long lesson? Will I be talking a great deal? Have I used enough strategies to keep students engaged?
- Have I incorporated active participation strategies during all appropriate components of the lesson or activity?
- Have I used a variety of active participation strategies to meet the different individual needs of my students (for example, not just written responses, because some struggle with writing)?
- Have I selected strategies that involve every student or just one student at a time?

Planning Practice and Monitoring Progress (See Chapter 7.) Ask yourself the following:

- Is the information complicated? If so, am I giving students a chance to practice after each step or two?
- Have I planned opportunities for students to practice with varying degrees of scaffolding, for example, supervised practice or extended practice?
- Do students have an opportunity to practice individually before they are evaluated?

- Have I provided opportunities for students to receive feedback on their performance at various spots during the lesson?
- Have I planned checks for understanding early and often? Am I checking the understanding of all students or just a few?
- In the evaluation section of my plan, am I asking my students to perform the same skill they were taught? Is my evaluation realistic? Is my evaluation relevant? Does my evaluation match my objective?

Planning Partner and Small-Group Work (See Chapter 8.) Ask yourself the following:

- Do my students know how to work together, for example, how to cooperate, to share, to listen, to encourage, or to challenge each other? If not, can I teach or review the specific skills they need for this lesson/activity?
- What size groups will work best in this situation?
- How will I decide who is in what group (random selection, reading partners, by skills)?
- How will students share tasks? Shall I assign specific roles?

Selected Interventions (See Chapter 9.) Ask yourself the following:

- Do I need any additional universal interventions?
- Are all of my students likely to be successful? Have I considered my students with special needs, my English language learners, cultural variation?
- Are the selected interventions that I have included necessary? Will they meet the needs of the students for whom they were selected? Should any of the selected interventions be built in for everyone rather than added on for some?

Application of Editing Task #2

Remember that Editing Task #2 is a double-check of the use of universal and selected instructional interventions. In the box on the next page, you will read a description of Ms. Moore's third-grade class. Following the box is a multiplication lesson plan she wrote for her students. Included in it are

A Look at Ms. Moore's Planning

Ms. Moore has written a large-group direct instruction multiplication lesson plan for her third-graders. As she wrote her plan, she considered the following. First, one of her students has difficulty writing—it isn't that he can't write, it is that his handwriting is large and awkward. Next, two of her students are not yet accurate on their multiplication facts. Finally, her class as a whole has trouble sitting and concentrating for long periods of time. One student, Alyssa, finds it especially difficult to stay focused. When Ms. Moore wrote her plan in the first place, she tried to take into account this information. Now it is time for her to go back and double-check her plan to see if her students' needs are addressed as-is or if she needs to revise any part of her plan.

As you read through the plan, see if you notice additional adjustments that could be made to Ms. Moore's plan in terms of universal and selected instructional interventions.

some of the thoughts that she had as she edited her plan for instructional interventions. Although you would not write these thoughts into your plan, we provide them to show you how one teacher applied Editing Task #2 as she double-checked her lesson for effectiveness.

In summary, Editing Task #2 is a double-check for the use of universal and selected instructional interventions. It is meant to be a quick check, not a time-consuming task. Sometimes, just spending a few minutes looking at the plan you have written will help you catch errors that could have adverse effects on student success. It is well worth the few minutes it takes.

MULTIPLICATION (3-DIGIT BY 1-DIGIT WITH REGROUPING) LESSON PLAN

Component 1. Preplanning Tasks

A. *Connection analysis*: State Standard: *Mathematics 1.1*: Understand and apply concepts and procedures from number sense. *Benchmark 1*: Computation: add, subtract, multiply, and divide whole numbers.

B. *Content (task) analysis*: How to Multiply 3-Digit by 1-Digit Numbers with Regrouping in the Ones and Tens Columns

1. Multiply the ones: bottom ones by top ones.
2. Write down the ones; "carry" the tens.
3. Multiply diagonally: bottom ones by top tens, add the "carried" tens.
4. Write down the tens; "carry" the hundreds.
5. Multiply diagonally: bottom ones by top hundreds, add the "carried" hundreds.
6. Write down the hundreds and thousands.

[*I think my task analysis needs this much detail. My students really benefit from very explicit and detailed procedures; it helps prevent confusion. I'm going to leave it as-is.*]

Note: Write the steps (with an example) on a poster so students can refer to them throughout the lesson.

[*Having the steps on a poster for all to see makes it possible for students to focus on how to do each step rather than focus on trying to memorize the steps. On second thought, I think it might be better for Alyssa to have the steps on a card on her desk; it can help her focus.*]

C. *Prerequisite skills*: 1-digit by 2-digit multiplication with regrouping, 1-digit by 3-digit multiplication without regrouping, multiplication facts, place value

D. *Key terms/vocabulary*: to "carry" = regrouping, adding the first digit in a number to the next column

E. *Objective*: Given 10 problems on a worksheet (3-digit by 1-digit with regrouping in the ones and tens columns), students will write the answers with no more than one error.

[*Even though students must write answers to the problems, I don't think this will be a problem for Robby. On second thought, the worksheet doesn't have enough space between problems for ease of writing—I'll need to change this. This will help Robby as well as other students.*]

F. *Objective rationale*: This lesson helps prepare students for real-life situations involving this type of problem (for example, store purchases), and provides practice on multiplication operations.

G. *Materials*: *Worksheets* (redo the evaluation worksheet with more spacing); *transparencies*: (a) task analysis (task analysis card for Alyssa), (b) 25 problems, (c) dice game rules/partner roles; *dice game*: four 5–10 cubes for each partner group, individual whiteboards (in desks)

Component 2. Lesson Setup

A. *Signal for attention*: "Let's begin."

B. *Behavior expectations*:

1. Look at me while I talk.
2. Raise your hand, wait to be called on before speaking.
3. Respect others (hands to self, listen when someone else is talking).

> *CFU (check for understanding)* = ask questions such as, "Show me what you would do if I was talking and you wanted to make a comment."

(continued on next page)

Component 3. Lesson Opening

[The students were all successful in yesterday's lesson (a prerequisite to this one), and because they are motivated by success, I think the opening is fine as-is—no need to be elaborate.]

A. *Review prior learning*: Say, "We've been working on multiplication skills, and yesterday, you learned to multiply a 1-digit number by a 2-digit number with regrouping. Let's review together."

$$\begin{array}{r} 65 \\ \times\, 5 \\ \hline \end{array}$$

1. "What is the first step? Everyone . . ." (5×5)

2. "Then what? Everyone . . ." (Carry the 2)

3. Repeat steps and prompts for the following problems:

$$\begin{array}{r} 45 \\ \times\, 8 \\ \hline \end{array} \qquad \begin{array}{r} 67 \\ \times\, 4 \\ \hline \end{array} \qquad \begin{array}{r} 18 \\ \times\, 9 \\ \hline \end{array}$$

> *AP* (active participation) = choral responses

[On second thought, I'm going to have students use their whiteboards at this point, in addition to choral responses. That way, I will have a better idea that all of my students are ready for this lesson. The whiteboards will allow me to check the understanding of individuals.]

B. *Statement of objective; objective purpose*:

1. *Say*, "Now that we have *reviewed,* we are *ready to start* today's lesson. We will be working with the same type of problem, but instead of multiplying 1 digit by 2 digits, we will multiply 1 digit by 3 digits."

2. *Say*, "*This skill is important—for a variety of reasons* (store purchases, more complicated multiplication, and division problems). For example, let's say that you are shopping for pens that cost $3.98 each. You want to purchase 3 of them for using at school. The objective today will help you know how to figure out how much they will cost altogether."

[On second thought, because this type of math isn't really inherently fun and exciting for my students, I think I will use some of their names in the examples I use here, for example, Kelly went to the hardware store to buy three squirt guns. Each squirt gun costs $5.38. How much will all three squirt guns cost? This could increase interest.]

Component 4. Lesson Body

A. *Explanation* ("tell" the task analysis)

1. *Show transparency #1* (shows task analysis and an example problem done in steps).

2. *Explain steps and problem.* Point out how similar this is to what they've been studying, just adding one more step.

[On second thought, I'm going to make the poster very fancy as a way to interest students. I'll fashion it after a cartoon.]

B. *Demonstration* ("show" the task analysis)

1. *Show* transparency #2 (contains 25 problems to use as needed throughout rest of lesson).

2. *Say*, "I'll work a few problems. You watch and listen to how I work them."

3. *Think aloud* each step as I work the problem, for example:

$$\begin{array}{r} 73 \\ \times\, 5 \\ \hline \end{array}$$

   a. "Multiply the ones" (5 × 3) "What's 5 times 3, everyone . . .?"
   b. "Write down ones" (5), "carry the tens" (1).
   c. "Multiply diagonally—ones times the tens"; "What's 5 times 7, everyone . . .?"

   > AP = choral responses to facts

[The choral response will help students stay with me during my demonstration. I think that is all that is needed here. I'll be checking their understanding later on.]

   4. *Repeat think-aloud* with additional problems; for example, "Let's read the first problem together, everyone . . . Multiply 9 times 2, what's that, everyone . . . ?"

   > AP = choral responses to facts

172	229	875	226
× 9	× 8	× 5	× 7

   5. *Check understanding* of steps. Have students take out individual whiteboards.
      a. *Show* next problem. Have students copy problem.
      b. *Ask specific questions* to review steps, for example, "Do the first step. What should you do next?"

   > AP = write on whiteboards

[This type of CFU will give me a good way to make sure that everyone understands the various steps of working these problems.]

[I think my use of active participation is good—lots of opportunities for all students to respond. This will help with concentration.]

   > CFU = ask students to hold up their whiteboards after each step.

C. *Supervised practice*

   1. *Whole group-supervised practice*: Say, "Let's work a few problems together. Please copy and work the first problem." (Have students hold up their whiteboard after they have completed the first problem, then the second one and so forth.)

      a. *Work* three to five problems with the whole group:

129	782	348
× 6	× 9	× 5

      b. Have students put whiteboards away.

[I'm wondering if I really need to include this whole-group supervised practice part. On the one hand, I don't want students to tire of working problems, but on the other hand, this is their first chance to work all steps of the problems at once with feedback. I think that instead of having them work problems on their whiteboards, I'll work the problems and have them say answers to a partner and then call out answers. I know they will find that approach more engaging.]

   2. *Partner supervised practice*: "Four Cube Multiplication Game"
      a. Show transparency of game rules and number cubes.
      b. Explain each step.
         Game Rules:
         1) Each partner gets 4 cubes.
         2) Partners each roll their 4 cubes at the same time. (If a 1 or 10 is rolled, roll that cube again.)
         3) Each of you use the numbers you roll to make your own 3-digit by 1-digit multiplication problem, e.g., if you rolled: 5, 7, 9, and 6, you could make these problems and more:

795	976	657
× 6	× 5	× 9

(continued on next page)

4) Write and solve the problem on your paper.
5) Trade papers and check each others' work.
6) The partner with the greatest product wins one point (and marks it on game board).
7) Keep playing until one player has 10 points.

[On second thought, instead of just telling directions for the game, I'll demonstrate actually playing it. I'm going to select a student who I think may have some trouble getting the idea of the game, and that student will play the game with me as a way to demonstrate to all.]

> *CFU* = ask specific questions about game rules (e.g., "What happens if someone rolls a 1?") and call on selected non-volunteers to answer

    c. *Form partner groups* (they choose their own partner) and pass out materials. Give signal to start. I walk around and monitor.

[On second thought, I'm going to have them work with their reading partners. Since they are used to working with their reading partners, I won't need to be concerned about them working together cooperatively.]

  3. *Individual supervised practice:*
    a. Show the next five problems:

$$354 \times 5 \qquad 643 \times 9 \qquad 834 \times 5 \qquad 795 \times 2 \qquad 252 \times 9$$

    b. Explain that students are to write out complete problems and work them on whiteboards.

> *CFU* = say, "Point to where you work the problems."

    c. As students work, I monitor and give feedback. After checking everyone, have a few students work problem on overhead and have all students check their own problems.

[I think this monitoring plan will work, but I'll want to make sure that I check in with Alyssa right at the start to help her get focused. Have Robby and Gail use their multiplication table charts and check in with them a bit more often than others to check multiplication fact accuracy.]

Component 5. Extended Practice

■ *Assign homework if needed – explain and write assignment on board.* Assign "evens" on page 86, #1–#20 (3-digit by 1-digit multiplication problems with regrouping in the ones and tens column) as homework to be completed before evaluation, if supervised practice results indicate that my students are accurate with this skill, but not fluent (they work slowly). Otherwise, the evaluation will come after the supervised practice.
[On second thought, I really need to check for understanding of the homework directions. I'll have students write down the assignment on their assignment calendar, and then I'll go around and check each student's calendar.]

Component 6. Lesson Closing

■ *Review*

  1. Show the transparency of the task analysis. Quickly say each step.
  2. Work one final problem, thinking out loud while working the steps.

> *AP* = students repeat

[On second thought, I think I need to add in another example to show the value of this skill—generalize the skill to real life. I also want to include Alyssa's name in the example to help her focus. For example, "Suppose that Alyssa wants to buy beads so that each of her birthday party guests can make a necklace. Each necklace takes 125 beads. How many beads will she need to buy so that each of her 8 guests can make a necklace?"]

Component 7. Evaluation

A *worksheet* of 10 problems will be completed at the end of the period (or the following day if extended practice is needed), independently and individually.

Editing Task #3: Evaluate Congruence

Evaluating lesson or activity congruence is the final editing task. As you worked through your initial planning, you undoubtedly thought about the connection between the various plan components. Therefore, this editing task is really just another double-check to ensure that the various pieces match. Here's an easy way to determine congruence.

A Strategy for How to Determine Congruence

1. *Reread or paraphrase the objective.*

2. *Look at the opening and closing of the lesson or activity, and ask*:

   - Am I telling students about the objective (opening)?

   - Am I referring back to the objective (closing)?

3. *Look at the main part of the lesson or activity, and ask yourself the following questions*:

   - Am I explaining (or reviewing) the skill or information described in the objective?

   - Am I demonstrating the skill or information described in the objective?

   - Am I having students practice the skill or information stated in the objective?

4. *Look at the evaluation section of the plan, and ask yourself this question*:

   - Am I testing (or will I test) students on the very same skill/knowledge I explained, demonstrated, and had them practice?

If your answer to all questions is "yes," then your plan is congruent. If you answered "no" to even one question, revise before completing your final plan.

The following is an example of a lesson in which *none* of the components match:

Objective: Students will write sentences that include adjectives.

Teaching: The teacher shows and tells how to identify adjectives in a sentence.

Practice: Students are asked to list adjectives that describe a given object.

Evaluation: Students write the definition of *adjective*.

Application of Editing Task #3

Making your plan congruent helps ensure that students are evaluated on what they were taught and what they practiced. Go back to the lesson plan used for Editing Task #2 and evaluate it for congruence. List the objective, the teaching, the practice, and the evaluation. Do they all match?

Summary

The editing tasks component of your lesson and activity planning is a critical one. Here you have an opportunity to write in strategies that impact classroom management and to double-check your use of instructional interventions and congruence in your plan. Remember that you cannot foresee everything that is going to happen in your lesson or activity, but you may be surprised how much you can predict when you carefully analyze your plan prior to teaching.

Using the Framework for Diversity Responsive Teaching

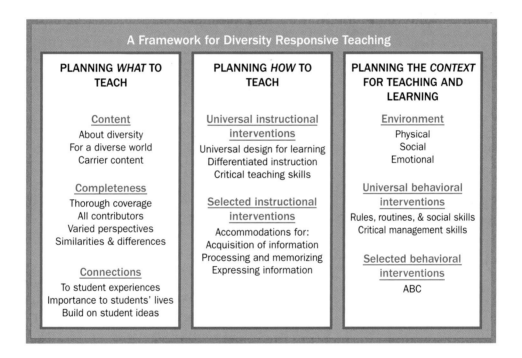

A Framework for Diversity Responsive Teaching

PLANNING *WHAT* TO TEACH	PLANNING *HOW* TO TEACH	PLANNING THE *CONTEXT* FOR TEACHING AND LEARNING
Content About diversity For a diverse world Carrier content	Universal instructional interventions Universal design for learning Differentiated instruction Critical teaching skills	Environment Physical Social Emotional
Completeness Thorough coverage All contributors Varied perspectives Similarities & differences	Selected instructional interventions Accommodations for: Acquisition of information Processing and memorizing Expressing information	Universal behavioral interventions Rules, routines, & social skills Critical management skills
Connections To student experiences Importance to students' lives Build on student ideas		Selected behavioral interventions ABC

Introduction

We began our book with the diversity responsive teaching framework, goals for diversity responsive teachers, and an example of diversity responsive teaching (see the Introduction of this book.) The following chapters provided specific information about responding to diversity in what you teach, how you teach, and in planning the context for teaching and learning. We are going to end our book by returning to that framework and those goals with two additional examples. We will show how two teachers use the framework to take a careful look at the "what," "how," and "context" when planning an activity and a lesson. We recognize that it would not be possible, or necessarily even desirable, to respond to diversity in all three of these areas in every lesson and activity that you teach. We do suggest, however, that teachers can respond to all three areas in many lessons and activities once they get into the habit of thinking about them as they plan. Using the framework can help develop that habit of mind.

In this chapter, we will describe two different ways to use the framework. One way to use the framework is as a support in brainstorming diversity responsive ideas for lessons and activities before writing plans. The other way is to use it as a tool when you want to reflect on your skills as a diversity responsive teacher by examining a lesson or activity plan you've already written.

Using the Framework for Brainstorming

The framework can be useful in helping you generate ideas for diversity responsive strategies to include in lessons, activities, or units of instruction. In this case, you'll use it when you are ready to design learning experiences after consulting state standards and big ideas, and developing measurable objectives.

The procedure to follow in using the framework this way is simply what works best for you. Use it to help you brainstorm as many ideas as possible for diversity responsive teaching in a particular lesson or activity. Then, when you are ready to write your plan, you'll have lots of ideas from which to choose. We suggest that you think about the objective(s), your students, and the three aspects of diversity responsive teaching (what, how, and context) when you begin brainstorming. Keep in mind that your goal is to ensure that all of your students are successful, involved, and challenged by the lesson or activity.

Following is an example of a teacher (Mrs. Choo) using the framework to generate ideas for incorporating diversity responsive teaching into an activity she is planning for her students. She predicted a problem—that her students wouldn't be interested in what she was going to teach them over the next few weeks—and wanted to use the framework to try to solve or prevent that problem through this activity. She uses the framework because she believes that diversity responsive teaching strategies work to engage students and to support their success in learning.

Notice as you read this example how Mrs. Choo's thinking reflects the goals of a diversity responsive teacher. We think you'll find that she clearly knows her students as individuals, appreciates their similarities and differences, connects with families and the community, strives to teach so that all her students are challenged and successful, and attempts to prepare them for diversity in the world.

A Look at Mrs. Choo's Planning

Mrs. Choo will be teaching a poetry unit. It's part of the curriculum for this grade level. She has developed measurable objectives based on state standards and big ideas and has written a series of lesson and activity plans. However, she is concerned because her students think they don't like poetry. They groaned when she told them they'd be starting the poetry unit next week. From their comments, they seem to think that poetry has nothing to do with them, that it's boring, and that it's beyond their understanding and skill.

Mrs. Choo decides to plan an elaborate activity to introduce the unit of instruction about poetry. She believes that it will be time well-spent if it results in her students' being interested and excited about poetry. She wants an activity that involves and challenges *all* of her students and convinces them that they can be successful in the poetry unit because they already know something about poetry. She decides to use the diversity responsive teaching framework to help generate ideas for this activity.

In the next three sections, you will read about Mrs. Choo's brainstorming. As you read, think about other ways she could be diversity responsive in her planning for what she teaches, how she teaches, and the context for teaching and learning.

Planning **What** *to Teach*

Mrs. Choo began by looking at the "Planning *What* to Teach" component of the framework: content, completeness, and connections.

Content and Completeness She had already carefully considered these areas when writing the unit. For example, she will be teaching about poets from a variety of backgrounds, and this will include poets from some of the same cultural backgrounds as her students. Her students have a strong interest in social justice and fairness, and she developed a lesson on the poetry of protest.

Connections Mrs. Choo thought her students would need to feel a direct and immediate connection with poetry to get "hooked." She tried to think what personal experience with poetry her students might have and how she could activate this background knowledge. She came up with jump rope chants. Students in her school are jump rope fanatics; both boys and girls jump rope and they are extremely competitive. She decided the first activity could involve the students collecting jump rope chants. She would have them write down the ones they know and hear in the schoolyard. She would also have the students interview their parents and grandparents about the jump rope chants they remember; extended families and a strong oral tradition are very important in the community. Mrs. Choo thought this would be another important connection for the students, because one of the big ideas in this unit is that poetry has many purposes and roots. Jump rope chants would be a great example of this.

Planning *How* to *Teach*

Mrs. Choo next looked at the "Planning *How* to Teach" part of the framework: universal and selected instructional interventions.

Universal Instructional Interventions Mrs. Choo thought about how she could use universal design and differentiated instruction in the activity to make sure all her students are successful and challenged. One aspect of universal design is building in options for student responses—that is, how they express their learning. She thought that she wanted all students to collect jump rope chants, to organize them in some way, and to examine their similarities and differences. But students could choose to create books of chants, do an oral presentation, or create a multimedia presentation.

Another aspect of universal design is providing for multiple means of student engagement by offering different supports or scaffolds to challenge individuals appropriately. Mrs. Choo thought that having students work in teams could be one way to provide support. She could form teams of students with different strengths (in writing, in using technology, in interpersonal skills for interviewing, and so on). She thought more about the writing aspect of this activity because many of her students struggle with writing. Mrs. Choo decided that providing tape recorders and interview scripts would reduce some of the writing demands.

Selected Instructional Interventions Mrs. Choo next considered students who have other challenges. Ivan, a student with severe cognitive and physical disabilities, spends some time in her classroom each day and will need major modifications. He has an IEP objective for using assistive technology devices, including various on/off switches. The class will be using quite a few devices with switches, like tape recorders, video cameras, and computers for this project, so Ivan will have many opportunities to work on his own objective. That made her think of another student who can be very difficult to motivate but loves gadgets and would love to have a chance to use the new digital video camera that Mrs. Choo got through a grant. A third student is very gifted academically, and Mrs. Choo has wanted to find more ways to challenge her. This student could benefit from opportunities to take a leadership role. Perhaps she could lead a team that takes on a more elaborate project. Mrs. Choo realized she will need to carefully plan these selected interventions, but this gives her some ideas to start with.

Planning the Context *for Teaching and Learning*

Mrs. Choo now consulted the "Context for Teaching and Learning" part of the framework: environment, universal behavioral interventions, and selected behavioral interventions.

Environment She began by thinking about how this activity could contribute to creating a diversity responsive *physical* environment. She thought she might have the students display photographs and quotations from the interviews on the walls of the classroom. This would certainly be welcoming to families. She next thought about the *social* environment. She had been looking for more ways to include Ivan socially (her student with severe cognitive and physical disabilities). Putting him on a team with students who are potential friends and allies will help. Also, his mother and grandmother are very fun and great with children. The team would definitely enjoy interviewing them, and that would give Ivan an important role. Mrs. Choo next looked at the *emotional* environment component. She thought about the varied family structures of her students. It might be a good idea to emphasize interviewing elders in the community rather than just using the words *parents* and *grandparents*. As a matter of fact, it would benefit everyone if the interviews went beyond family members. Some cultural groups in the community aren't represented in the class, and this could be a way for the students to connect with those groups. In addition, one student recently moved in with a foster family. He's in touch with family members in another part of the state and perhaps could interview them over the phone, as well as interviewing his foster family. That could be emphasized as a strength and an advantage to his team.

Universal Behavioral Interventions The class could probably benefit from a behavioral skill lesson focusing on requesting and conducting interviews in a polite way. She could connect that with earlier lessons on polite forms such as saying *please* and *thank you*, starting conversations, and asking for help.

Selected Behavioral Interventions One of her students uses a self-management system for completing assignments on time. Once his team has planned their project, she could work with him on setting goals for completing his part on time.

YOUR TURN

You've read about Mrs. Choo's idea for an activity to introduce her poetry unit.

- Do you think this activity will work to interest her students in poetry? Will it be time well-spent? Can you think of a different way to introduce the poetry unit?

- Is her idea likely to involve and challenge all of her students and convince them that they can be successful in the poetry unit? What additional diversity responsive teaching and management strategies could she include in her poetry activity?

Summary

Mrs. Choo has used the framework to brainstorm many ideas for an activity. When she starts writing the activity plan, she will probably change or throw out some ideas and add still others. She'll need to

get much more specific, of course. When she is done writing and editing the plan, she may decide to use the diversity responsive framework one more time to self-reflect.

Using the Framework as a Tool for Self-Reflection

The second way to use this framework is as a tool for self-reflection about your growth as a diversity responsive teacher. Responding effectively to diversity takes reflective thought, as well as time and practice, and is a process rather than an outcome. Use the framework periodically to analyze a lesson or activity that you have planned. By doing this, you can check up on your use of diversity responsive strategies in general or those particularly useful in addressing

---

A Look at Mr. Perez's Planning

Mr. Perez works hard to make his lessons responsive to the diversity in his classroom, and the one included here is no exception. He selected the topic of the lesson itself (teaching the rule "include everyone") because he wants to make his classroom a place where students feel welcome. Then, as he developed his plan, he carefully included what he thought were appropriate universal and selected interventions considering the needs of his students. After he wrote his plan, he used editing tasks to make adjustments that he felt were appropriate to provide support for all of his students. He now believes that his plan is ready to teach.

Mr. Perez decided to use the framework for analyzing this particular lesson because he thinks it is fairly representative of the type of lesson he teaches. He plans to assess his overall use of diversity responsive teaching strategies, but he really wants to focus on what he has planned for Olga, his new student. He's not sure that he has provided enough support for her.

As you read through Mr. Perez's plan, look for examples of strategies that reflect best practices in responding to diversity.

specific types of diversity or need. Analysis of your plan will give you information for reflection.

You can work your way through a specific lesson or activity plan using the framework in at least two ways. First, you could work through it component by component, stopping after each component to evaluate your response to diversity in *what* and *how* you taught, and the *context*. Another way would be to look over the whole plan and then evaluate the *what,* the *how,* and the *context,* as well as your response to each. Use whichever way (or a combination of both) is the easiest for you to gather the information you need for self-reflection. The important thing is that you are taking necessary steps to positively impact your skills as a diversity responsive teacher.

The example on the previous page "A Look at Mr. Perez's Planning" shows a teacher using reflection in an attempt to refine his teaching so that all students are challenged and successful. This is a major goal for the diversity responsive teacher. Once you have read the example, stop and read Mr. Perez's lesson plan which begins on page 300. This plan is the one he uses to assess his current use of diversity responsive teaching strategies. After you have read the lesson plan, come back to this spot and read about Mr. Perez's students (below). Once you know his students, you will be able to better determine the potential effectiveness of the strategies he has included in his plan.

Mr. Perez's Students

Now you will meet Mr. Perez's students. This will help you better understand Mr. Perez's analysis of his use of diversity responsive teaching (DRT) strategies and ideas. Mr. Perez has a fairly typical mix of students, and he really enjoys all of them. His students display a range of skill levels; for example, some of his students are reading below their grade level, while three read above grade level. As a whole group, they are active yet focused, but have difficulty sitting for long periods of time. Four of his students are English language learners. Both of his Spanish speakers (Carlos and Rosa), and one of his Russian students (Mikhail) are fairly fluent in English, but his new student, another Russian speaker (Olga), speaks very little English. One student (Julia) spends part of the day in a special program for gifted learners and has definite strengths in creative writing, language, and drama. Two of Mr. Perez's students, Jimmy and Jake, receive special education services because

of disabilities. Jimmy has significant skill deficits in language, reading and writing due to a learning disability. Jake displays many acting-out behaviors (name-calling, noncompliance with following directions, for example) and consequently has had some difficulty establishing relationships with the other students. The class is made up of 23 students: 12 boys and 11 girls. The students who speak Spanish come from families who make their living by following the farm harvest and working throughout several states. This means they are in Mr. Perez's room for just the next few months. The occupations of the parents of his other students vary from professional (for example, teacher) to retail sales positions.

The following is Mr. Perez's analysis of his lesson plan using the framework as his guide. He considered his response to diversity in *what* he taught, *how* he taught it, and the *context* for teaching and learning that he created. As you read through Mr. Perez's thoughts, see what additional ideas you have.

Planning **What** *to* **Teach**

Mr. Perez began by looking carefully at the first component of the framework and thinking about the content he selected, the specifics of the content to be taught, and what connections he had made to his students' lives. He really didn't think that the issue of completeness applied to this lesson, but he saw that he did address the areas of content and connections. Here are some examples.

- Mr. Perez chose to teach the "Including Everyone" rule because it is a behavioral skill that his students need both in the classroom and in society at large (for a diverse world). He wants all of his students to be accepting and tolerant of all people. He also thought about the students in his class who have difficulty establishing relationships with others. For example, his students from migrant families will only be in school for a short amount of time, and he recognizes that it is hard, especially for the shy one (Rosa), to develop friendships in this context. His student with social challenges (Jake) displays behaviors that have led to some isolation. He thought this lesson could be of extra help for these students.

- He included a number of strategies to try to connect this lesson to the experiences and interests of his students. He used photos of his students and selected real-life scenarios that he saw

Lesson Plan

Topic: Teaching the Rule "Include Everyone"

Component 1. Preplanning Tasks

A. *Connection analysis*: This is part of a series of lessons and activities for creating an inclusive social environment in the classroom.

B. *Task analysis*:
How to follow the rule "Include everyone" in activities at school

1. If you see someone alone, invite him or her to join you or your group.

2. If someone asks to join you or your group, say *yes* in a welcoming way.

3. When you are given a partner or group/team member, accept him or her politely.

C. *Lesson objective*: Students will apply the rule to include everyone in activities at school by inviting others to join them, saying *yes* to someone who asks to join, and accepting assigned partners/members politely, in three out of three role-plays.

D. *Rationale*: It is important that students learn to work and play with everyone at school to create an inclusive and safe environment, and because these are important skills for living in a diverse society.

E. *Key terms/vocabulary*:

- *include*: make someone feel invited, welcomed, and accepted
- *join*: become part of an activity or group
- *invite*: ask someone to do something with you
- *welcoming*: acting glad that someone is joining you
- *accept*: taking someone as partner or group/team member
- *politely*: with good manners in words and body language

Note: Teach these words to English language learners (ELLs) the day before and create a word bank to post on the wall.

Component 2. Lesson Setup

A. *Transition*: (1) Point to diagram of desk partners and seating assignments (on screen) when students arrive in class. (2) Check with Jake to make sure he has his self-monitoring chart ready to use. (3) Set vibrating timer to use as a reminder to "Check Jake" which means to acknowledge him for appropriate behavior and/or to notice if he is marking his chart.

B. *Gain attention*: Knock on desk. "When I knock on the desk [do it], it means I want your attention. Stop talking [cover my mouth] and look at me [point to my eyes]."

C. *Behavioral expectations*: "Be a polite audience. That means sit quietly and listen carefully without talking so that everyone can see and hear the skit." Note: Repeat "sit," "quiet," and "listen" with modeling and gestures.

> CFU (check for understanding) = "Pretend the skit is going on right now. Show me what you will do to be a polite audience."

Component 3. Lesson Opening

A. *Preview*: "Remember yesterday when we talked about creating a happy and safe class? A place where feelings don't get hurt? A good place to be? Today we're going to have some sixth-graders

show us what a class looks like when it is *not* happy, *not* safe, *not* a good place for everyone."
Note: Write these three phrases on the board. Use gestures to emphasize "*not*."

B. *Begin skit*: Sixth-graders do a skit of nonexamples of the rule *including everyone*: Carlos is not in-vited to make paper airplanes with other boys; girls refuse Sally when she asks to sit with them during art; kids make rude comments and facial expressions when assigned partners. (Acknowledge for being a polite audience. Check Jake.)

C. *Statement of objective and purpose*: "We don't want to have a class like the sixth-graders showed us—where some kids feel sad and lonely or mad and embarrassed—so we're going to have a rule that says 'Include everyone.' Today, you're going to learn how and when to follow that rule at school."

Component 4. Lesson Body

A. Demonstrations and explanation

[Behavior expectations: "Participate and follow directions for unison responses, thumbs up, and other signals."]

1. *Say/write rule* (Include everyone) *on board.*
   a. "What's the rule?"
   b. "Let's think about those two words." (Point to and say *include*.)
      i. Call five students up to the front. (Include the two least proficient ELLs.) They hold hands in a circle. Then break hands to include teacher. Say that they included me. Repeat.
      ii. "What does the word *include* make you think of? What are some examples?"
      iii. "What about the word *everyone*? Who does that mean?"
   c. Summarize: "*Include everyone* means welcome and accept all kids at school." Point to the rule.

> AP (active participation) = unison response (Acknowledge participating, Check Jake.)

> AP = brainstorm (If needed, prompt for *invite, welcome,* and *accept* and point to word bank.)

> AP = choral read

2. *Show task analysis*:

   How to follow the rule "Include everyone" in activities at school:
   a. If you see someone alone, invite him or her to join you.
   b. If someone asks to join you, say *yes*.
   c. When you're given a partner, accept him or her politely.

3. *Demonstrate* (with assistants):

   "Watch while we show you what it looks like to follow the rule three ways."
   a. Model inviting someone to join my group at lunch.
   b. Model saying *yes* when someone asks to help us make a bulletin board.
   c. Model politely accepting an assigned field trip buddy. (Check Jake.)

4. *Explain*
   a. "We are going to talk about three ways to *include everyone*. These are (show with fingers) (1) when you see someone alone, (2) when someone asks to join you, and (3) when you are given partners."
   b. Uncover three posters, one at a time. (Each has a photograph of class members acting out one of the three aspects of the rule and shows pattern sentences of the words they use.)

(*continued on next page*)

    c. Point to poster #1. Read title: "If you see someone alone, invite him or her to join you."

    d. Discuss the picture: Two kids are working on their spelling words and they see a girl who is alone; she has no one to work with. How might she feel? They follow the rule by inviting her to work on spelling with them. How does everyone feel now?

    e. Read the pattern sentence under the photo: "Come and *work* with us." (Insert the *work* word card in sentence.) She says, "Okay. Thanks." What else could they say? "Come and *sit* with us." (Change word card in pattern sentence.)

    f. **CFU** = show/describe other photos that are examples and nonexamples; "Signal by clapping when the rule is followed."

    g. Follow the same process with the other two posters.

AP = unison reading (Acknowledge for responding. Check Jake.)

AP = unison reading

5. Demonstrate (with assistants):

"Watch and give us a thumbs up (CFU) if we are following the rule." (Think aloud and use pattern sentences, e.g., "Come and *play* with us.")

    a. Model inviting someone to join us in jump roping.

    b. Model saying *yes* when someone asks to sit by me on bus.

    c. Model politely accepting an assigned team member for pickle ball.

6. **CFU** = Remind them of Carlos in the first scene of the skit (playing with paper airplanes). Ask, "What could the boys have said to Carlos to include him? Write it on your scratch paper or whisper it to me." Monitor. Call on several to share. Repeat for other scenes. (Check Jake.)

B. Supervised practice (individual practice with a partner)

1. *Give directions for practice* (say and point to written directions on board). "You'll be taking turns being the inviters, askers, accepters, and so on. Follow these steps:

    (1) Turn to your desk partner. Decide who is A and who is B.
    (2) Collect six scenario cards.
    (3) Partner A reads Scenario 1, and both act.
    (4) Decide if both agree rule was followed. Redo if necessary.
    (5) Switch. Partner B reads Scenario 2.
    (6) Continue with Scenario 3, and so on."

2. *Demonstrate following directions* (with assistants).

    a. Use example scenario cards: "Partner A is playing kickball with other kids at recess and sees Partner B alone;" "Partner B and classmates are working on their science reports and see that Partner A is alone." (Reading level of scenarios vary per desk partner group.) (Check Jake.)

    b. **CFU** = signal with fingers when we are following step #1, #2, and so on.

3. *Explain behavior expectations*: Say, "Stay on task; give each other polite feedback as you've learned. Raise your hand when finished."

4. *Monitor practice* (with assistants): Ask questions; give feedback; be sure to listen to each student. (Acknowledge for following directions, giving polite feedback. Check Jake.)

Component 5. Lesson Closing

A. *Summarize*: "You have learned three ways to include everyone so the class is a happy and safe place to be. I will leave these posters up to remind you."

B. *Prompt generalization*: Hand out cards. "Write or draw one way you plan to follow the rule today at recess. Tape it to your desk." (**AP**)

Component 6. Extended Practice

A. Assign partners/groups several times tomorrow and prompt polite acceptance.

B. Precorrect before recess and lunch for the rest of the week.

C. Reward "including" with good citizen certificates.

Component 7. Evaluation

Pull each student aside over next few days and give scenarios to role-play. I will look for students to apply the rule correctly in each role-play without any prompting from me.

happen in his own class and in other settings since the beginning of the school year. These scenarios are directly connected to his students' own experiences, and they will help students see how important it is to learn the skill. These connections to real life can help make content meaningful to students.

- The skit during the opening also provides common experience and background knowledge so students have something with which to connect the new learning. It should grab their attention and be memorable and motivating, especially when acted by older students. Because of the context, Mr. Perez determined a skit would be easier to follow than just describing situations or reading scenarios.

Planning How *to Teach*

Mr. Perez moves on and consults the next component of the framework. This component causes him to carefully think through his use of universal and selected instructional interventions. Here are some specific examples of *universal interventions* that he has included.

- Various strategies in this lesson reflected general approaches to universal interventions, such as universal design and differentiated instruction. In numerous places throughout the plan for example, Mr. Perez planned to say, write, and show the information he was teaching, such as when he explained the rule. He also emphasized the lesson information in a variety of ways, such as through the skit, a variety of visual supports, partner practice, modeling,

and so forth. He incorporated scaffolds (such as pattern sentences) so that all students could be successful. In addition, he allowed students to show their understanding by writing, saying, or drawing.

- Mr. Perez's plan included numerous critical teaching skills. For example, he gave clear explanations orally, in writing, and by demonstrating. He used checks for understanding throughout his lesson that allowed him to monitor the learning of every student (for example, when he had students hold up the number of fingers that represented the step number). He also incorporated numerous types of opportunities to respond—that is, for active participation (choral responses, turning to partners, and so on)—because that would help keep all of his students engaged. Mr. Perez carefully monitored students at each step of the way as they worked toward the objective. When students worked in partners, he moved around the classroom to make sure that each partner group was practicing correctly.

- Mr. Perez recruited assistants to help with the lesson so that all students could receive more support during checks for understanding and supervised practice. He rehearsed the modeling scenarios with his assistants in advance so that he was able to present a clear and correct demonstration of the rule being followed.

- He included numerous opportunities for choral responses and choral reading, because that provides comfortable rehearsal of information for his students who are learning English and actively engages all students.

Mr. Perez originally included an intervention that he intended to use selectively. When he completed editing tasks however, he thought again about his students, and he decided that the strategy he selected would actually benefit many students. He built in the following as a *universal intervention* rather than adding it on.

- He used actions to help clarify word meaning, thereby benefitting all the students, including ELLs. For example, acting out the term *include* would be better for everyone rather than simply saying a dictionary definition, especially for such an abstract term.

After thinking about universal design, differentiated instruction, and critical teaching skills, Mr. Perez knew that several of his students would need additional support. He included the following *selected interventions* for those students.

- He planned to pre-teach vocabulary to his ELLs. He thought about pre-teaching the words to all students but decided that it was not necessary or appropriate to do so.

- When Mr. Perez wrote up the scenarios, he simplified the vocabulary in those to be used by Jimmy and his ELLs. This accomplished two things. First, Jimmy could work independently with his reading; and second, the students learning English could practice their reading in a comfortable way. Julia helped write the scenarios that she and her partner used. Julia's strength in writing, and her flair for the dramatic, made for some interesting scenarios. It wouldn't have been appropriate to simplify the vocabulary for everyone.

Planning the Context *for Teaching and Learning*

The final component of the framework helped Mr. Perez examine his setup of the classroom environment as well as his use of universal and selected behavioral interventions. The following are examples of *universal interventions*:

- Mr. Perez took great care to pair desk partners so that everyone would feel supported. For the

ELLs, he assigned desk partners who are good language models and who will help, but not do it all. He partnered Olga with Mikhail, who is a more fluent speaker. Mr. Perez then considered the compatibility of all the desk partner groupings. For instance, he matched Jimmy with Michael, who is friendly, supportive, and a great role model.

- Mr. Perez wrote into his plan reminders to acknowledge appropriate behavior. He knows this strategy is very effective in supporting students who are following behavior expectations. It also serves as a reminder to those students who may have difficulty.

- He used simplified language for giving behavior expectations. He explained some words, such as *sit, quiet,* and *listen,* with modeling and gestures. This especially helps Jimmy and the students who are learning English, but it is a good reminder for many of the students.

After reviewing all of the strategies to use with the whole class, Mr. Perez decided that Jake could benefit from an additional support, and added this *selected intervention*:

- Jake is learning how to manage his own behavior through self-monitoring. Mr. Perez thought that this particular lesson could be one where Jake had some difficulty with compliance, so he gave Jake a self-monitoring chart to tape on his desk so that he can track his compliance with directions. Mr. Perez also made sure that he provided him with the support that he needed by increasing the amount of attention he gave to Jake for following directions.

Mr. Perez wrote a lesson plan and then used the diversity responsive teaching framework to analyze that plan. He did this in order to identify his current use of diversity responsive teaching strategies in what is taught, how it's taught, and the context for teaching and learning. Next he will use this information to reflect on his strengths and weaknesses as a diversity responsive teacher and plan for the further development of his skills. Read the box called "Mr. Perez's Reflection."

Mr. Perez's Reflection

- Preteaching vocabulary and the use of gestures, pictures, and so forth are helpful for his English language learners who speak some English, but he isn't sure they are enough for Olga. He has been told she is in the early production stage. As he thinks through this lesson, it occurs to him that he really isn't sure that she is progressing as fast as she could in learning English. He notes that he needs to gather more information about additional strategies that might benefit her. Perhaps he can talk with the teacher who works with ELLs and get more ideas and resource materials.

- He feels good about his use of universal instructional and behavioral interventions. He's particularly pleased with his use of active participation strategies and checks for understanding.

- The behavior system that he set up for Jake doesn't work as well as he'd like. He needs to set aside some time to really study the system to see if he can figure out why it isn't all that effective. He likes the idea of self-monitoring but it just isn't working as well as he had hoped. Mr. Perez decides to talk to other teachers at the next grade-level meeting and get their ideas. He also decides to look at his collection of journals for articles on using self-management with students.

These are some of the ideas that Mr. Perez had as he reflected on the information he had gathered. Can you identify other areas of strength in this lesson as well as targets for change?

Summary

Mr. Perez used the diversity responsive teaching framework as a way to gather information for self-reflection about his growth as a diversity responsive teacher. This is not something that he does after every lesson, but he does it regularly. He considers the needs of his students, the goals of the diversity responsive teacher, and all elements reflected in the diversity framework. This exercise provides him with important food for thought.

Final Thoughts

Teachers need to be aware of the diversity in their classrooms and respond to it effectively if all students are to be successful in school. We recognize that this can seem like a daunting task at first, and many teachers may feel that they do not know where or how to begin. We have found that this feeling is not an unusual one among teachers. We hope that our framework has helped break down this task into manageable parts that will help you in your pursuit of creating a diversity responsive classroom. Remember that responding to diversity is a process that evolves over time, not something that happens overnight.

We think that one important factor in the professional growth process of diversity responsive teaching is the development of habits. It is probably unrealistic to think that you can respond to all diversity all of the time. It *is* realistic, though, to respond to much diversity much of the time. The framework we have presented to you and all of the information that fits into it gives you many places to begin developing the habit of being responsive to diversity. Our challenge to you is to select an idea that you haven't tried before: try it, see how it works, then try something else, and so on. We wish you the best!

Index